THE ANTIQUARY'S BOOKS

GENERAL EDITOR: J. CHARLES COX, LL.D., F.S.A.

REMAINS OF THE PREHISTORIC AGE IN ENGLAND

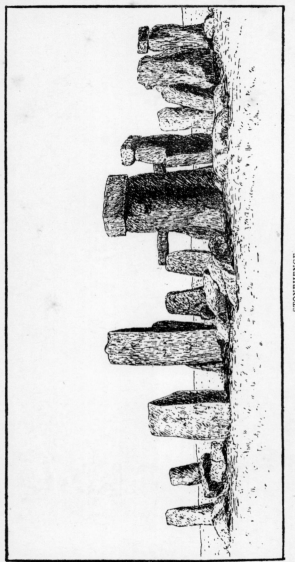

STONEHENGE

REMAINS OF THE PREHISTORIC AGE IN ENGLAND

BY

BERTRAM C. A. WINDLE, Sc.D., F.R.S., F.S.A.

PROFESSOR OF ANATOMY AND ANTHROPOLOGY
IN THE UNIVERSITY OF BIRMINGHAM

ILLUSTRATED BY EDITH MARY WINDLE

METHUEN & CO.
36 ESSEX STREET W.C.
LONDON
1904

TO

THE ILLUSTRATOR OF THIS VOLUME

IT IS DEDICATED

WITH MUCH AFFECTION

BY HER HUSBAND

CONTENTS

CHAPTER VII

CHAPTER VIII

CHAPTER IX

CHAPTER X

CHAPTER XI

CHAPTER XII

LIST OF ILLUSTRATIONS

The figures taken from *Archæologia* and *Proc. Soc. Antiqs.* are reproduced by kind permission of the Council.

[W.] from author's collection.

[U.B.] from Museum of University of Birmingham.

PREFACE

THE object of this book is to give an account of the material relics of the Prehistoric period still to be seen in this country, and to that object the writer has endeavoured to adhere as closely as possible. To lay before his readers facts rather than theories has been the end always kept in view, and this not merely because space is limited and materials are many. There has been a vast amount of theory-spinning in connection with the early epochs of which this book treats, theory-spinning, in part not merely permissible but even necessary, but in part wholly superfluous. To judge from the accounts of Palæolithic Man which occur in some books on Prehistoric Archæology, it might be supposed that the writers had enjoyed the privileges possessed by Mr. Peter Ibbetson and the Duchess of Towers, and had dreamed themselves backwards so as to have actually seen and studied the men of whom they write—so closely are the habits, the appearance, and even the speech of our very remote ancestors described and descanted upon. To the scholar such discourses are of little moment. He is able to sift out the valuable portions of such books, when they possess any, from the valueless. But to the general reader it is otherwise. He is not to be supposed to be capable of knowing which statements are facts and which surmises. To dispense with theorising, as hinted above, in such a subject as this would be impossible, even if it were desirable; nor has the attempt been made. But so far as is possible theory has been set aside for facts, and at least the reader has been warned when he is treading upon doubtful ground.

It is the intention of the series, of which this book forms a part, that the antiquities described should be those of England, and here again, as far as may be, the plan indicated has been acted upon. But it would be impossible to write an adequate account of prehistoric objects confined entirely to this island, still more to the southern part of it only. It has been necessary to allude to other parts of the world, and notably to France, for without the French discoveries, a clear and consecutive account of the various epochs of the Prehistoric period would be impracticable. As far as possible, however, the objects described have been taken from English sources, and the lists at the ends of the chapters have been confined entirely to objects found in the counties of England.

Perhaps it may be permissible and even advisable to say a word at this point about these lists. They are strictly "Trial-Lists," and though very great pains have been taken to make them accurate and complete, no one can be better aware than their author that, from the nature of things, they must necessarily suffer from sins of commission and omission. In the body of the book the author has tried as far as possible to describe objects which he has himself seen and studied, but it is obviously impossible for any one person to have seen and checked all the places mentioned in the lists. The lists have been compiled from the Ordnance Map, from Murray's and other County Handbooks, from Proceedings of various societies, and from other sources. After much consideration, and acting on the advice of competent authorities, it has been decided that the lists shall appear, and it is hoped that they may be at least useful as a basis for a more perfect compilation in the future.

The author must not forget to acknowledge the help

which he has received in compiling these lists from his brother local secretaries of the Society of Antiquaries. Some of these gentlemen apparently did not receive any of the several letters addressed to them, since no reply could be obtained from them, but by the large majority most kindly help was at once and willingly given. The author can only hope that he may be able some day to repay in kind the assistance for which he is most truly grateful. In addition to these local experts, various lists have been looked through by Canon Greenwell, Mr. Gowland, Mr. I. Chalkley Gould, to whom the author's thanks are due and are here expressed. He has also to thank his friends, Professor Haddon, F.R.S., Mr. Henry Balfour, Baron A. von Hügel, Dr. Blackmore, Mr. St. John Hope, Mr. Gowland, and the Rev. R. A. Gatty, for advice of various kinds. And he must express his acknowledgments to those societies and individuals who have allowed the reproduction of drawings from their proceedings of works.

The author desired, as far as possible, to have a new set of illustrations and not to repeat the figures which have done duty so frequently in other books on the subject. That all the figures should be absolutely new was impossible, but a large number are, and all have been drawn or redrawn by the author's wife. To enumerate the sources from which information has been obtained for the purposes of this book would be an impossible task here, and it is hoped that it has been rendered unnecessary by the copious references to the literature which have been given throughout.

B. C. A. W.

Maids Cross, Solihull

NOTE

AN asterisk prefixed to any name in the lists indicates that the place is one of special importance.

REMAINS OF THE PREHISTORIC AGE IN ENGLAND

CHAPTER I

INTRODUCTORY—DIVISIONS OF THE PREHISTORIC PERIOD

THOUGH the intention of this book is rather to describe the various classes of objects connected with the Prehistoric era, than to give a continuous description of that period, it is clear that some prefatory account of the epochs into which the time with which we are dealing has been divided, and of the objects characteristic of each, must be submitted to the reader before the special task of the book is attacked. And this account again will itself require to be prefaced by some notice of the geological history of the later periods of the world's history in which the presence of man may either be proved, or, though at present unproved, may be looked for as possible. In considering the problems presented by inquiries into prehistoric archæology, one must never forget that many of them, and especially those connected with the earlier periods, are almost exclusively geological in their nature, and can only be solved on geological lines. Hence in deciding such a question as that, for example, of the nature and date of eoliths, there are two distinct matters for discussion. First as to the artificial

B

or natural character of the objects, which is a point to be decided by a prehistoric archæologist, experienced in comparing flints worked by man with others whose fractures and facets are the product of purely natural forces.   But after this is determined, there is a second matter for discussion—the age of the gravels in which the implements are found ; and this is, of course, a purely geological problem, and must be solved by a geologist, or, at least, on geological principles.

Geological time is divided into Palæozoic, Mesozoic, and Cainozoic periods, the first-named being the most ancient.   With this great period, and with the Mesozoic which succeeded it, we have no concern in this book, nor need their subdivisions here be mentioned.   At the Cainozoic period we must look a little more closely.   It is subdivided into Tertiary and Quaternary eras, and each of these has further subdivisions, which may be set out as follows:—

Tertiary (commencing with the oldest beds) :
> **Eocene.**
> **Oligocene.**
> **Miocene** (unrepresented in Britain).
> **Pliocene.**

Quaternary :
> **Pleistocene.**   Terrestrial, Alluvial, Estuarine, Marine, and Glacial Beds of Palæolithic Age.
> **Recent.**   Terrestrial, Alluvial, Estuarine, and Marine Beds of Neolithic, Bronze, Iron, and Historic Ages.

Over the consideration of the two older divisions of the Tertiary period we need not linger, for, so far, no suggestion that man existed during their continuance has been made.   The earliest objects which have been attributed to him have been found in miocene deposits, and without, for the moment, considering whether these objects are really what they have been claimed to be, we will take up the geological story at this point. The Miocene period appears to have been one of a somewhat tropical character, since the nearest representatives of many of its most characteristic plants are to be found in India and in Australia. During the Pliocene period these conditions gradually altered, the flora, from which the characteristic palms of the previous age have disappeared, indicating a more temperate climate. To this succeeded, in the Pleistocene age, alternating periods of Arctic cold and of more genial weather, to which the name of the Glacial epoch has been assigned. During the Arctic parts of this period Britain, then, and in the preceding epoch, connected with the rest of the continent of Europe by dry land, was covered in large part with huge glaciers, whose traces, in the shape of erratic blocks, moraines, and other evidences of ice-action, are still to be seen in many parts of the island. But the course of events, so far as the subject-matter of this book is affected by geological considerations, may be set down in tabular form, as summarised from Woodward's *Geology of England and Wales*. As before, the table commences with the older period, and gradually conducts us to the present.

PLIOCENE :
At the end of this period, when the Cromer Forest and Norwich Crag Series were laid down, there were indications of approaching cold.

PLEISTOCENE :
The history of this the earlier division of the Quaternary period has been subdivided by geologists into the following periods :—
(a) Elevation of the land with severe glacial conditions. The earliest boulder clays deposited.
(b) Submergence of considerable areas and deposition of marine sands and gravels, such as the shelly sands and gravels of Moel Tryfan, Macclesfield, Blackpool, etc.

(c) Elevation of land, accompanied by intense glacial conditions, with great ice-sheets formed by confluent glaciers, extending over large tracts of country.

(d) Britain continental, with climate changing from intense cold to temperate and genial.   Arctic and southern mammalia, mammoth, rhinoceros, hyæna, etc., visit Britain, according as climatal conditions become suited to their needs.   Plateau gravels (in part) and raised beaches (in part) formed.   Mammaliferous gravels. *Palæolithic implements.*

(e) Severe glacial conditions, with glaciers and coast-ice, affecting more particularly Scotland, Wales, and the northern districts of England.

(f) Retreat of the ice, and periods of small local glaciers on the higher mountain regions, when Britain was probably isolated, and land of less extent than now.

RECENT :

(g) Britain again becomes continental.   Summer and winter temperatures more excessive than now.   Age of great forests.   Incoming of recent fauna.   Raised beaches (in part), river gravels, and some cave deposits belong to this period.

(h) Depression bringing about final insulation of Britain. Climate humid.   Decay of forests and growth of peat-mosses.   Modern beaches and marine deposits (Burtle beds, etc.), blown sand, etc., submerged forests.

(i) The present.

(During the whole of the recent period *Neolithic and other evidences of Man's presence* are discoverable.)

In addition to the notes in the table above as to the mammals of the different periods, a few further observations must be made, and for this reason. The age of implements made by man has often to be determined, indeed in many cases can only be determined, by a consideration of the objects with which they have been discovered. Amongst these the most important are the teeth and bones of extinct mammals. If, for example, undoubted implements can be shown to have been found in undisturbed strata with the teeth and other relics of a given species of elephant, then, if we know the relative date of the elephant in question, we can assign a period for the implements found with its remains. During the epoch which the table covers there was, as will be noticed, an earlier period during which large mammals, now extinct, formed an important part of the fauna. To this succeeded a later period when, the larger mammals having died out, the fauna was characterised by animals similar to, indeed for the most part identical with, those of the present day. In France the earlier part of the first period was specially characterised by the mammoth, the later by the reindeer. To be a little more specific, the following list of the more important mammals may be added :—

In the latest **Pliocene** period the remains of three species of elephant are to be met with, namely—

> *Elephas meridionalis.*
> ,, *antiquus.*
> ,, *primigenius* var. (rare).

With these existed a hippopotamus (*H. amphibius*), a rhinoceros (*R. etruscus*), and horse, deer, hyæna (*H. crocuta,* var. *spelaeus*), and the glutton.

In the **Pleistocene** period two elephants are found, viz.—

> *Elephas antiquus*, the straight-tusked or early elephant.
> ,, *primigenius*, the mammoth.

It will be noticed that *E. meridionalis*, met with in the earlier period, has now disappeared from the fauna. In addition to the elephants were two species of rhinoceros—

> *Rhinoceros tichorhinus*, the woolly.
> ,, *leptorhinus*, the small-nosed.

And there were also the cave-lion and cave-bear, the sabre-toothed lion (*Machairodus latidens*), the leopard, lynx, glutton, and cave-hyæna. All these are now extinct, at least in this country, but of the following, also met with in the period under consideration, all have been met with in **recent** deposits, and some exist at the present day amongst our native fauna. The horse, urus (*Bos primigenius*), roe-deer, red-deer and reindeer, the Irish elk, wild boar, brown bear, fox, wolf, wild cat, otter, badger, etc.

With these prefatory remarks of a geological character, we may now pass to the consideration of the important question—When did Man first make his appearance? It is a question which cannot be answered with any certainty at present, since there is much difference of opinion on the point amongst scientific men. It is not wonderful that such should be the case when it is considered that the decision rests upon the nature of certain very rude stone implements. Are these the work of man, or are they shaped by natural forces? Such is the question which has to be answered when dealing with the point now under consideration. Nor is the determination an easy matter from the very nature of things. The stone implement in its first inception was doubtless nothing more than a conveniently shaped natural stone. The Semangs, a tribe of the Malay Peninsula, use no other stone implements than these to the present day, and find them when supplemented by fragments of shell, of wood, or of bamboo, sufficient for their simple needs. To identify stone implements of the Prehistoric period belonging to this category is almost, if not absolutely, impossible. And the first touches applied to such implements, in order to render them a little handier to grasp or more efficacious as weapons or tools, must necessarily have been slight, and with difficulty distinguishable from the operations of nature.　But, with all allowances of this kind, it must be admitted that the verdict of the scientific world is, so far, decidedly opposed to the acceptance as genuine works of the hand of man of the flints discovered by the Abbé Bourgeois at Thenay (Loire-et-Cher) in miocene beds, or by M. Ribeira in strata of the same period at Otta in Spain.　For the present, then, we must seek a later period for the advent of man.

To many observers the first undeniable implements are those known as eoliths, to which full consideration will be given in a later chapter.　It is true that some eminent authorities still refuse to concede that these objects are anything else but the product of nature ; but there is a considerable weight of opinion on the side of those who accept these flints as genuine arte-facts.　But when this point is cleared up, the whole question is not settled. Granted that they are the work of man's hands, there is still some difference of opinion as to the age of the gravels in which they have been found, some authorities assigning them to the Pliocene, others to the Pleistocene period.　Here, again, the balance of opinion inclines to the earlier date, but until the matter has been finally adjudicated upon, no certain argument as to the existence of man in the Pliocene period can be drawn from these implements.　An important step in the settlement of the matter has recently been made, for Dr. Blackmore has himself found eoliths at Dewlish in Dorset, associated in undisturbed beds with the remains of *Elephas meridionalis*. Now this particular elephant, as was noted above, belongs to the Pliocene period, and had disappeared before Pleistocene times.　If, therefore, there is no doubt, and it must be confessed that little seems to be possible, as to the natural collocation of these objects, the question of the pliocene date of eoliths must be regarded as settled.

Still it must be admitted that much doubt still exists as to the date of the advent of man. No person, at any rate, would hesitate to go as far as Lord Avebury has gone in the summing-up of the subject which he gives,[1] though some would claim that the earlier period there alluded to is not merely probable, but actually proved. "Whether," writes the author just mentioned, "man existed in Britain before the Glacial period, or during the inter-Glacial periods of a more genial climate, there is still some difference of opinion, though it seems probable; but there can be no doubt that he was here soon after the final disappearance of glacial conditions, and coexisted with the mammoth, the woolly-haired rhinoceros, the hippopotamus, the musk-sheep, the gigantic Irish elk, the great bear, and the cave-lion." Let us leave the question of eoliths for the time, and grant, for the sake of argument, that they are to be accepted. Starting with them, the periods of Prehistoric time, with certain characteristics of each, may be shown, in tabular form, the table being, in almost every particular, identical with one drawn up by Fischer, on the basis of the observations of Piette[2] (see opposite page).

It will now be necessary somewhat to develop the information contained in this table, and first of all it should be made quite clear that when the Palæolithic, or Neolithic, or Bronze *periods* are spoken of, all that is implied is that certain phases, or stages, characterised by these names have been passed through, apparently by

---

[1] *Scenery of England*, p. 82.

[2] *L'Anthropologie*, vol. vii. p. 633. Piette's even more recent classification may be found in *Zentralbl. f. Anthrop. Ethn. u. Urgeschichte*, 1901, p. 65. It is perhaps well to point out that there are many classifications and divisions of the Prehistoric period, and will probably be many more, each marking a fresh stage in our knowledge. That which is given above will serve to indicate the main chain of events, however much it may require subsequent emendation in details.

ERA.	PERIOD.	EPOCH.		
ANTHROPOID.				
ANCIENT. Large mammals now extinct.	WARM. Elephas antiquus. Rhinoceros Merckii.	*Passage.* Homo—Elephas antiquus—E. meridionalis—E. primigenius. Probably Pliocene. Eoliths.		EOLITHIC.
		Chellean. E. antiquus predominant. Implements mostly oval, with a cutting edge at the point. Body thick after the shape of an almond or peach stone.		
	GLACIAL. Elephas primigenius. Rhinoceros tichorhinus. Ursus spelæus.	*Mousterian.* E. primigenius. Rh. tichorhinus. Ursus spelæus.	Transition. E. primigenius and E. antiquus	PALÆOLITHIC.
			Mousterian properly so-called. Points and scrapers.	
		Papalian, or equidian, or ivory.	Rounded sculptures.	HIPPIC.
			Bas-reliefs.	
			Champ-levé & simple gravings.	
MODERN. Existing fauna.	TRANSITION.	*Cervidian.* Present fauna with reindeer in S. of France.	*Reindeer.* Simple gravings. Harpoons of reindeer horn. Needles.	GLYPTIC.
			Red Deer. Simple gravings. Needles. Harpoons of reindeer and stag's horns.	
		Asylian. C. elaphus. Coloured Pebbles. Reindeer emigrating north.		NEOLITHIC.
		Shells. Strong vegetation.		
	PRESENT.	*Polished stone celts.*		
		Bronze, with overlap of polished stone.		
		Early Iron, with overlap of bronze.		

many, perhaps by most, of the races of the world. Comparatively few of the types of implements made during the stone period afford us conclusive evidence as to the period in it to which they belong. Moreover, stone implements continued to be manufactured long after bronze was known, indeed, for certain purposes stone is still utilised in all countries for the manufacture of implements. The objects characteristic of the different periods are only the dominant features, at given moments, in a continual stream of progress. And the course of this stream has neither been identical nor synchronous in different countries, not even in the countries of what we now know as Europe. To take an extreme example: many, if not most, of the primitive races, when discovered for the first time by white men, have been found to be still employing stone implements and ignorant of the use of metal. Thus they are dwellers in a Stone Age, a phase of development from which their discoverers had long emerged. And so in earlier times it must not be supposed that the whole of Europe emerged at the same time from the Stone Age and entered that of metal. The discovery of bronze, or the earlier discovery of copper, once made, spread, probably slowly, from one, or perhaps—for there is no reason to suppose that the discovery may not have been independently arrived at in various places—from several points, into regions previously unacquainted with the use of metals. Hence we shall be expressing the point more clearly if we say that, so far as we know, all races have gone through a stage of civilisation during which the use of metal was unknown. This we call the Stone Age, and it is customary to divide it into two main portions or periods—Palæolithic and Neolithic. The implements of the earlier period are found either in the old gravels of rivers—the river-drift implements—or in caverns. Of the two the river-drift have been generally supposed to be the earlier in date, but this is a point which cannot be considered to be finally settled. The neolithic implements present many types unknown in the earlier period, though there are others which are common to both. They are, however, surface implements, and are not found in river-drifts. They may, of course, be found in caves, just as much more modern objects may, but when this is the case, as will be seen from the description shortly to be given of Kent's Hole and other caves, the palæolithic are separated from the neolithic implements, and lie in different strata. It must not be supposed that during the Stone Age implements were made of nothing but stone. No doubt, throughout all the history of the human race, man has made implements of wood and other substances. But stone is, of all these materials, the least perishable, hence the fact that we have so many more relics of this class than of any other. But the caverns of the Palæolithic period, and particularly the relics of the later parts of this epoch, often called in France the Magdalenian epoch, show us that man had become an expert in fashioning implements of bone and in adorning them with ornamentation. This is the Glyptic period of the table on page 9. It has been commonly assumed that in Britain at least, and indeed in Europe, there was a great and unbridged gap between the older and the newer ages of stone. That there must have been a continuity somewhere was, of course, conceded, but it was claimed that in this part of the world there was no evidence of any such link, and that the neolithic civilisation was of a kind wholly different, and not even derived from the palæolithic civilisation of the same district. Recent discoveries in France seem, however, to show conclusively that the continuity between the two ages is distinctly traceable in that country. It will be well to devote a little consideration to this matter, since the facts to be related have come under notice in quite recent years, and have as yet scarcely made their way into English text-books. The most important researches are those which have been carried out by M. Piette in a cave or grotto known as Mas d'Azil, on the left bank of the river Arise, in Ariége.

The layers found in this place, taken in historical order, are as follows :—

(i.) Gravel and mud with charcoal, traces of hearths and bones.

(ii.) Black archæological layer. Flints of magdalenian type. Bone implements, including needles and harpoons. Belongs to the last part of the Cervidian epoch.

(iii.) A layer of sand indicating an inundation or inundations.

(iv.) Black archæological layer, belonging to the last part of the reindeer epoch. Bone harpoons and engravings. Flint implements of magdalenian type. With these are found small round scrapers (see Fig. 30) and fine knife-shaped implements, the precursors of those of a later time.

(v.) A further layer of sand resembling (iii.) and due to a similar cause.

(vi.) Red layer owing its colour to masses of peroxide of iron. Reindeer remains absent, but many stags' horns. Harpoons made from them. Pierced stags' teeth. Magdalenian implements of flint and other implements like those in the fourth layer. Small pebbles, polished at one end, which may have been employed as chisels or cutting instruments.

(vii.) Bed containing many shells of *Helix nemoralis*. Perforated harpoons of stag's horn. Flint implements like those of the last layer and other varieties. This layer corresponds to the kitchen-middens of other parts of the world.

(viii.) Black muddy layer containing obvious neolithic implements and fragments of pottery, and at its more superficial layers masses of verdigris, showing the Bronze Age to have been in existence.

Here there seems to be a clear transition from one period to the other, but it must be admitted that to some this is not evident. Boyd Dawkins,[1] for example, considers that "there is no proof of transition in this sequence, but of mixture." When, however, the subject of bone implements comes to be dealt with, the facts to be brought forward in connection with the subject of harpoons will add further testimony to the fact that here may be seen the transition era between the different periods of the Stone Age. Piette[2] teaches that the period of transition which succeeded the Glacial epoch commenced when the modern fauna began to replace the ancient, which was on its way to extinction, *i.e.*, after what he calls the Equidian epoch. This period of transition he divides into three phases. (i.) The Cervidian, during which the reindeer continued to occupy the land and the old industries of the earlier periods were still in vogue ; (ii.) the Asylian (named from the grotto described above). The reindeer had disappeared, and the art of graving and sculpture had been forgotten. Man now took to colouring the curious pebbles, to be described in a later chapter. (iii.) The shell period (*coquilliére*), a time of rich vegetation. Amongst the relics of this time large numbers of snail-shells are found. This period has also been called Campignian, from Campigny, a place where somewhat similar, but less striking, results have been obtained by d'Ault du Mesnil and others. By Laville[3] the term "*couches infra-néolithiques*" has been applied to the beds belonging to this period of transition, which he has studied in the district of the Seine. Here he has found (i.) a Chelleo-Mousterian (early Palæolithic) layer, which some might describe as purely Chellean ; (ii.) A Mousterio-Magdalenian layer. In neither of these has any fragment of

[1] *Man*, 1903, p. 59.   [2] *L'Anthropologie*, vii. 388.
[3] *Bull. et Mém. de la Soc. d'Anthropologie de Paris*, ser. v. t. ii. p. 206.

pottery been found, but in the latter was discovered an axe-head of almost neolithic form. The next two layers (iii. and iv.) are those which he calls infra-neolithic, since they lie between i. and ii., which all would admit to be palæolithic, and two further layers (v. and vi.) which are equally undoubtedly neolithic. Further observations, less conclusive in their nature, have been made by Boule[1] in connection with objects found in and on the shores of Lake Karar in Algeria. Such being some of the evidence for the existence of a Mesolithic period in France, one may ask, Is there anything of a similar nature in this island? Several attempts have been made to bridge over the supposed gap here, but so far, it must be admitted, without complete success. The late General Pitt-Rivers[2] in his account of his excavations at Cissbury raised the question as to whether the objects there discovered might be looked upon as a transition between the palæolithic and neolithic types. But these implements may quite well be merely celts in the middle stage of manufacture (see p. 69), in fact, this is the general opinion as to their nature. Brown[3] considers that he has been able to establish the continuity of the various periods as a result of his observations at East Dean and elsewhere. He classifies stone implements as follows : (i.) *Eoliths.* — Roughly hewn pebbles and nodules and naturally broken stones showing work, with thick ochreous patina found on the plateaux of the chalk and other districts in beds unconnected with the present valley drainage. (ii.) *Palæoliths.* —Implements from the higher river-drift of the present valleys, and such as from their forms are of the same age, but are found in the oldest breccia deposit of some limestone caverns. These implements are made from nodules,

---

[1] *L'Anthropologie*, t. xi. p. 1.

[2] *Archæologia*, xlii.

[3] *Journal of the Anthropological Institute*, xxii. p. 66.

and, as may be gathered from their form, were generally used in the hand, without haft. (iii.) *Mesolithic.*—Implements which from their form, and in many cases from the character of the deposit in which they are found, appear to be of an intermediate age, between the Palæolithic and Neolithic periods. The implements are of flat pear-shape, or of more decided axe-form. There is no implement with unworked butt. The implements are made from flakes struck off nodules taken directly from the chalk. (iv.) *Neolithic.*—Implements of polished stone or delicately flaked. A further description of mesolithic implements is given by Worthington Smith, to whose pages[1] the reader in search of additional information may be referred. In Ireland, Knowles[2] claims identity between certain neolithic implements found in White Park Bay, County Antrim, and the palæolithic types of France. His idea is that they may have been fabricated by tribes travelling northwards in the wake of the reindeer, which was deserting the southern parts of Europe, and that these tribes continued to make palæolithic implements whilst little by little becoming influenced by neolithic civilisation. "I am convinced," he writes, "that a good contingent of those tribes who used the Mousterian and Solutrian" (both palæolithic) "types of implements came to the British area, and that the best examples of their art and skill are to be found among the flint implements of the North of Ireland." In Scotland discoveries have been made at the MacArthur Cave near Oban, which seem to point to a period of transition being traceable there. In this cave on the bed-rock was a layer of gravel. Above this was a shell-bed with flint scrapers, and many bone implements. Amongst these were flattened harpoons, double-barbed, and some perforated like those of Mas

---

[1] *Man, the Primæval Savage*, p. 299.
[2] *Proc. Royal Soc. of Antiquaries of Ireland*, vii. p. 1.

d'Azil and Reilhac (Lot). This was probably a layer of transition type. Specimens from this cave are in the National Museum of Antiquities in Edinburgh, and no one examining them can doubt the identity of the type of the harpoons with those mentioned. Fig. 46 might well have been drawn from one of the Scotch examples. Above it was another layer of gravel, surmounted by an upper shell-bed of the kitchen-midden type, above which again was humus.

Similar finds have been made at a rock-shelter at Druimvargie, near Oban, and at Oronsay.[1] To sum up. Many are convinced that the period of transition has been demonstrated, at least in France ; others still remain unconvinced. Most persons would hesitate to claim that it had been shown to exist in these islands, though there is at least some evidence for it ; and one may hope and even expect that before long this will become more convincing in the light of future discoveries. Considerable space has been given to this point because it is one of great controversial interest at the present moment. Much less space will be required to finish the remaining points of a preliminary nature. No one doubts that the knowledge of bronze, probably, in some parts of the world, preceded by a period when pure copper was used, became diffused amongst the same peoples as those who made the neolithic implements. Here there is no trace of a hiatus ; indeed, on the contrary, there is abundant evidence of a very extensive overlap, for some of the most highly finished

[1] Further papers on this subject, which cannot be dealt with here, are Boyd-Dawkins, *Journal of Anthropological Institute*, xxiii. 242, who does not think that the progress of discovery has yet bridged over the abyss separating the Palæolithic age of the Pleistocene period from the Neolithic age of the Prehistoric period in any part of the world ; Woldrich, *L'Anthropologie*, l. 488, "Caves of Cracovia ; James, *Journal of Anthropological Institute*, i. 50. Cf. also *ib.* p. 321 ; Laville, C. R., *Cong. Internat. d'Anth. et d'Arch.*, 1903, 201 ; Capitan, *ib.* p. 206.

implements of stone, the perforated and polished axe-heads, and perhaps also the finer arrow-heads, were made, and perhaps only made, at a time when bronze was being forged. Bronze arrow-heads are almost unknown in this country, their place having apparently been taken by cheaper substitutes in stone. Similarly the bronze gradually faded into the early iron period, both metals being used side by side at the same time, as indeed, for their diverse purposes, they are at the present day. The theories as to the discovery of bronze and other matters of a general character untouched upon in this chapter will be dealt with in later parts of the book.

c

CHAPTER II

STONE IMPLEMENTS—METHOD OF MANUFACTURE

DURING a large part of the Stone Age, and the entire of the Bronze and of the Iron, implements were made of other materials than that from which each period receives its name. But as the materials which give their names to the several eras were those which dominated the manufactures of each, it will be well to deal with them before passing to the consideration of any of the other objects associated with the Prehistoric period. Moreover, there is another reason, namely, that the dating —the relative dating, of course—of such things as earthworks and tumuli depends upon a knowledge of the stone, bronze, or iron objects which have been found in them. In fact, the question of stone implements is one which underlies all the problems of early archæology, and a knowledge of it is essential to all who would study and understand the early history of our race, and, indeed, it may be said, the history of all races in their primitive condition. There is one other piece of knowledge which is of almost equal value, and that is, a knowledge of the age of different kinds of pottery, and for estimating the period of the larger relics of the later Prehistoric period, such as earthworks, this knowledge is invaluable. But pottery was not invented until after the end of the older stone period in Europe; at least, if it was there are no fragments which have come down to us. Hence for the earlier portions of the history of man we are dependent upon a knowledge of stone implements. The present chapter will be devoted to the consideration of certain questions connected with the manufacture of stone implements, the varieties of which will be dealt with in the next.

How are Stone Implements to be recognised as the work of Man?

In the case of many forms there can be no reasonable doubt as to the nature of the implement. For example, no one would argue that a grindstone or a mill-stone, both of them stone implements of the present time, or a stone mortar, made by a North American Indian at a distant date, were objects fashioned merely by nature's art. Nor could such finely worked tools as the Scandinavian dagger shown in Fig. 1, or the Egyptian knife (Fig. 2), be mistaken for anything else but what they are—the work of highly skilled artists in the handling of stone. Nor, finally, would anyone suppose that the different kinds of arrow-heads, some of which are shown in Figs. 32, 33, 34, were natural forms. It is true that sagittiform chips are common enough in some parts of the country. There are quantities of them, for example, in the gravels of the Warwickshire Avon, into which they have been washed from the glacial drift of the eastern side of the county, and some of these have from time to time been put forward as true arrow-heads. But the trained eye could never be deceived by the resemblance—it is only a slight resemblance—between these and

FIG. 1
FLINT DAGGER
Danish (⅔)

the genuine works of man's hands. In all the cases cited above, and in many others of which mention will be made in later pages, no person whose attention had ever been drawn to the subject could for a moment feel any doubt as to the artificial character of the object. But it is not so in every instance. In fact, it is only in comparatively recent years that any of these flint implements have been noticed, and the ultimate recognition of the earlier forms has only been accomplished after a length of time and a somewhat heated controversy. As far as is known, the earliest example discovered and recorded is an exceedingly interesting specimen of the palæolithic type, which is now to be seen in the British Museum (Case 105, Prehistoric Department), which was described in the Sloane Catalogue as "A British weapon found, with elephant's tooth, opposite to Black Mary's, near Grayes Inn Lane." This specimen appears to have been discovered at the end of the seventeenth century, and was preserved—one may say by accident—down to a period when its nature and significance were appreciated.

FIG. 2
FLINT KNIFE
Egyptian (½)

In Dugdale's *History of Warwickshire*, and in Frere's account of his discoveries at Hoxne (1797), stone implements are recognised as having been the weapons of a people unacquainted with the use of metals. But it was not until

Boucher de Perthes made his classical discoveries at Abbeville that the attention of scientific men was really drawn to the subject and search made for similar objects in other places. In Fig. 3 an example of one of the flints found at Abbeville in 1861 is represented, and it is perhaps not astonishing that when the discovery was first made public there were many who refused assent to the conclusions of the discoverer. In time, as we know, opposition was worn down, and no one now doubts that these and many thousands of similar implements which have been found elsewhere are genuine products of man's industry. History seems to be repeating itself in the case of the so-called eoliths. These objects, which have only come under discussion within recent years, are still regarded as natural forms by some authorities of the greatest eminence, though year by year more and more persons

FIG. 3. PALÆOLITH
Abbeville (¾)

are becoming convinced that the claims put forward in favour of their artificial character are just. As regards flakes and other objects which cannot be given any definite name as implements, there are several points to be noticed. Taking, first of all, those made of flint, it may be pointed out that every fragment of flint in a non-flint district, unless it has been brought there as gravel or in some other accidental manner at a later date, was probably brought there by Neolithic Man, and will generally show signs of having been worked by him. For example, all over the Cotswolds, which are oolitic in geological character, flint flakes of various sizes as well as arrow-heads and other implements are to be found. All of these are neolithic in nature, and in such a country the eye of the observer can hardly fail to be caught by the sight of fragments of flint in freshly-ploughed fields and elsewhere, because of the absence of this stone from the natural formations of the district.   In districts where flint occurs naturally, as a part of the chalk or as part of the drift, and in river gravels, as it does in some districts of Warwickshire, it is less easy to distinguish the artificial from the natural fragments, and in all cases some definite rules must be known in order that an artificially-worked flint may be distinguished from a natural form.   Now (i.) in detaching a flake from a lump of flint by means of a blow, the operator will require a tolerably flat surface on which to strike if his action is to be effective, and the striking stone is not to slip upon that which is struck without detaching a flake from it.   Hence at the end of the flake where the blow has been given there will be seen a small portion of the original flat surface which received the impact.   (ii.) In the next place, when a flake is detached, by means of a blow, from a piece of flint, especially if resting on the hand or on some elastic pad, the plane of fracture between the two is not flat, but at the end nearest the place where the blow was struck there will be seen on the surface of the flake a rounded elevation known as the " bulb of percussion." To this will naturally correspond a depression on the surface of the block from which the flake has been detached. This bulb is due to the elastic nature of the flint, and its method of production is fully described by Sir John Evans.[1]   He

---

[1] *Ancient Stone Implements*, p. 273.

says, "If a blow from a spherical-ended hammer be delivered at right angles on a large flat surface of flint, the
part struck is only a minute portion of the surface, which
may be represented by a circle of very small diameter.
If flint were malleable, instead of being slightly elastic, a
dent would be produced at the spot; but being elastic,
this small circle is driven slightly inward into the body of
the flint, and the result is that a circular fissure is produced between that part of the flint which is condensed
for the moment by the blow, and that part which is left
untouched. As each particle in the small circle on which
the hammer impinges may be considered to rest on more
than one particle, it is evident that a circular fissure, as it
descends into the body of the flint, will have a tendency
to enlarge in diameter, so that the piece of flint it includes
will be of conical form, the small circle struck by the
hammer forming the slightly truncated apex. . . . If the
blow be administered near the edge, instead of in the
middle of the surface of the block, a somewhat similar
effect will be produced, but the cone in that case will be
imperfect, as a splinter of flint will be struck off, the
fissure probably running along the line of least resist-
ance." The bulb of percussion may almost be looked
upon as a hall-mark of human work. Almost but not
quite, for it is obvious that it may be produced by any
kind of suitable blow, and such a blow might conceivably
be given by a piece of stone falling from a height, for
example, from the face of a cliff, upon a flat piece of flint
lying on the sand below. But (iii.) if the flake shows on
the opposite side to that which bears the bulb marks of
the detachment of other flakes, in the shape of ribs indicating the lines of separation, then its artificial character
may be said to have been established. In districts where
flint does not occur and where some other hard kind of
stone, *e.g.* quartzite, has been employed for the manu-

facture of implements, the recognition of artificial flakes is much more difficult and may be impossible. Here there is no bulb of percussion to help, and the flakes may be the result of frost or other natural agencies and not of man's handiwork. But in the case of flint flakes the flat top, the bulb on one side and the ribs on the other, should be looked for. The characteristics of more definite implements will be dealt with in later chapters.

How were the Flints procured?

It is probable that in many cases mere surface flints were picked up and worked as far as possible, but there is abundant evidence that prehistoric man had discovered, what the Brandon flint-knapper still knows, that flints from the depths of the earth can be more satisfactorily manipulated than those from the surface, and that those of a particular layer may be better than others found above or below them. In fact, at Brandon itself there are extensive traces of ancient quarrying for flints at the place known as Grime's Graves. These quarries were investigated by Canon Greenwell,[1] who found that there were more than 250 pits, representing the shafts of quarries. That which he examined was 28 feet in diameter at its mouth, and 39 feet in depth. The first 13 feet of the shaft was through sand, below which the chalk was reached. The shaft then passed through a layer of flints, whose quality did not satisfy the excavators, until it reached another stratum, known nowadays as the "floor-stone," and used for the manufacture of gun-flints. In order to follow up this layer, galleries, 3 feet 6 inches in height, were made in the chalk, picks formed from the antlers of the red-deer being used for this purpose. The marks of these implements, as also of the cuts made by the edge of an axe of basalt, were clearly seen in the galleries, in

[1] *Journ. Ethnol. Soc.*, N.S., ii. p. 419.

which were also found rude cups of chalk, which had apparently served the miners as lamps during their operations. Similar quarries were discovered by Pitt-Rivers at Cissbury, and others have been found at Spiennes, in Belgium, in France, Egypt (Seton-Karr), and in other places.

How can we know the uses of the implements?

It must be admitted that in a certain number of cases we have to guess at the use which was made of a given implement, but in a surprisingly greater number there is no reason at all for doubt. This is largely due to the fact that the implements of the early man of this continent closely resemble the tools now, or lately, made and used by savage races. Thus the arrow-heads of stone made during the Neolithic and Bronze periods are the fellows of stone arrow-heads made in other parts of the world, and leave no doubt as to what they were intended for. A similar statement might be made about stone axes, particularly those of a polished type, and, with perhaps some reservations, as to the implements which we speak of as scrapers and knives. Again, it has to be remembered that in many cases a given implement was not used for one purpose alone. It would be difficult to mention the various uses to which a sailor or a boy applies his pocketknife; and, similarly, some at least of the stone implements must have been contrived to play a double part, or even several parts. Thus, for example, it is not difficult to see that the palæolithic implement represented in Fig. 4 may have been a weapon, a knife for skinning animals, an ordinary scraper by which the skin when removed was cleaned, and a concave scraper by which meat was removed from the bones, or sticks rounded and smoothed.

How can we tell their periods?

Some indication as to the manner in which information of this character is arrived at has been given in the previous chapter, and more will be given in those which are to follow. But a few points may here be dwelt upon. And first it should be mentioned that the locus is far more important

FIG. 4. PALÆOLITH
Caversham (⅓)

than the shape or form in determining the relative date of an implement. To make this matter clearer, let us consider one or two cases. Near Torquay there is a celebrated cavern known as Kent's Hole or Cavern, which was first brought into notice, early in the last century, by the Rev. R. McEnery, a Catholic priest, and was afterwards fully explored under the direction of the late Mr. Pengelly, whose name will always be associated with the discoveries made therein. Put as briefly as possible, the following layers were discovered in this cave, the order given being that of their discovery, *i.e.,* the most recent are first mentioned :—

(i.) Blocks of limestone from a few pounds to one hundred tons, which had fallen from the roof.

(ii.) The Black Mould. Composed almost entirely of decayed vegetable matter, and from three inches to one foot in depth. This layer contained Roman and pre-Roman pottery, bronze implements, and others of stone and bronze.

(iii.) A floor of stalagmite from three inches to five feet in thickness.

(iv.) The Black Band. Found in only one part of the cave. This consisted of charred wood and was four inches in depth.

(v.) The Cave Earth. A light red loam.
In (iii.), (iv.), and (v.) were found bones of the mammoth, rhinoceros, cave-lion, and cave-bear, flint flakes, and nuclei, and bone implements.

(vi.) A second stalagmitic floor, twelve feet thick in places, containing bones of the cave-bear.

(vii.) The Breccia, a dark-red sandy deposit, free from limestone, containing bones of the cave-bear, and rude flint and chert implements.

Now supposing, as was the case here, that there has been no disturbance of these objects, but that they occupy the position in which they were first placed, then there can be no doubt that the implements in the Breccia are older than those above the second stalagmitic floor, and these again than those in the Black Mould. Where there is undisturbed stratification there is satisfactory evidence of difference of age, and when we find a certain type characteristic of low strata in various places we may begin, but cautiously, to associate with the same period other implements of similar character not found in relation of strata but by themselves. But we must be quite clear that we have to do with undisturbed strata, and must also bear in mind that extraordinary disturbances have taken place even in caverns as the result of floods. McKenny Hughes has given a vivid description of a flood on Ingleborough which he himself witnessed, and of the results which it produced in the caves and their floors. " Underground passages," he says, "high above the present water-channels, were swept clean by the body of water forced through them under enormous pressure. Caves that had been sealed up for years with barriers of stalagmite, which one would have thought might have defied the rush of any flood, were burst open. Most of this débris— all, in fact, that was moved by the first rush of water—was carried down the valley. Some remained about the mouth and some in embayed corners in the caves. Here we saw fragments of stalagmitic floors, mixed up with débris washed in from the swallow-holes above. Some might have seen here evidence that, after the cave had been formed and occupied and gently filled with earth and coated and partitioned by stalactite and stalagmite, there came an age of flood—perhaps of submergence—when the old deposits were re-sorted, the old floors broken up, and that the cave then entered upon another phase of its history. How different the facts ! It was all over in three hours." Another caution must be offered in connection with the facility with which small objects are able to work their way down through heat-cracks in the earth, through mice-holes and other burrows, and through the pipes left by the decay of roots. In all cases of juxtaposition of strange objects these points should be borne in mind, and, if possible, a search made, to see if the contiguity of the objects can be accounted for in any of these ways.

To take another case. Let us suppose that bronze and

stone implements are found together in an undisturbed tumulus : is this any evidence that they were made at the same time ? Not the least, for the stone implement may have been a treasured heirloom laid with some specially respected or beloved dead one, or it may have been placed there from superstitious motives, on account of its antiquity. Such a collocation only tells us that the tumulus was not earlier than the bronze period. It is on other evidence that we have to rely for the statement that stone implements continued to be made during the bronze period. For example : if we find with bronze or copper remains not merely flint implements but also cores and chips and all the evidences of manufacture, then we may reasonably conclude that the two forms of manufacture were proceeding at the same time. Or, again, we reason that stone arrow-heads were used and made during the bronze period from the facts that they are constantly associated with interments of that character, and that bronze arrow-heads are objects almost unknown. The reason for this is not far to seek ; the arrow-head was a thing very likely to be lost, and it was much cheaper to lose one of stone than one of the far more valuable metal.

A further indication as to period is the character of the implement. Compare the eoliths in Fig. 10 with the Scandinavian dagger in Fig. 1. The probability is that the dagger is much later than the other object, the probability, that is, from the shape alone. But from this point of view we have no real indication, for the two might quite well have been made at the same time, one by a tyro, the other by a skilled artist ; one for a temporary use, with the idea that it would be immediately thrown away, and need have no particular labour wasted over it, the other with the intention of becoming the treasured possession of some connoisseur of the period. Hence undisturbed position in strata, or in connection with the remains of animals

extinct after a definite geological period, are good indications of date. Indications from position require to be
checked by a careful examination of the strata with a
view to ascertaining whether they have been disturbed or
not, and indications from shape, except in certain directions, which will be mentioned in later chapters, must be
dealt with in a cautious manner.

Of what kinds of stone are the implements made?

Of a very great variety, must be the answer to this
question. For choice, in this country, flint, as being a
hard stone, yet one easily worked and capable of being
fashioned into many useful implements. It is clear that it
was carried from places where it naturally occurred to other
districts, either in a worked or unworked condition. Hence
it may actually have been an article of commerce at a very
early period. Where flint was unattainable some other
hard stone was employed, for example, quartzite. A
palæolithic implement of this substance was found in the
gravels of the Rea, near Birmingham, by the late Mr.
Landon, and other implements of the same kind have
been found in the caves at Creswell Crags. Of smaller
implements of the same kind in the collection of Mr. Moore
of Tutnal may be mentioned an arrow-head, which is very
neatly made from a split pebble of quartzite, one of the
myriads of this kind found in the western drift all round
Birmingham. In parts of England where that substance
is found, chert is employed for the manufacture of implements, and large worked fragments (see Fig. 5) have been
found in quantities in the Broom gravel pit (Dorset), as
well as other implements of flint.

Serpentine, greenstone, diorite, chalcedony, and jasper,
are amongst the kinds of stone utilised in different parts
of the world, and to these, amongst many other varieties
of rock, may be added that very beautiful substance, jade.

No implements of this nature have, I believe, been found in Britain, but many have been discovered on the Continent.   Dr. Munro[1] estimates that in all Europe

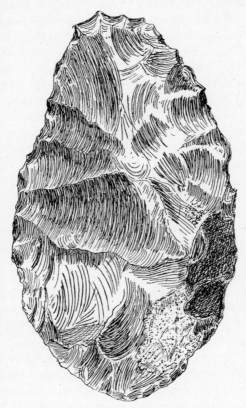

FIG. 5.   PALÆOLITH, CHERT
Broom (⅔)

500 to 600 worked objects in nephrite, 300 to 400 in jadeite, and about 200 in chloromelanite have been discovered.   In the station of Murach, on Lake Constance alone, nearly

[1] *Lake Dwellings of Europe.*

500 implements have been found with 154 chips and sawn fragments, whilst the stations on this lake have altogether supplied more than 1,000 jade implements. Implements of this substance have also been found in Moravia and Hungary.[1] There has been a considerable discussion as to the source of the jade, since it was supposed that this mineral did not occur in Europe. Rudler,[2] having investigated the matter, admits that the known occurrences of nephrite and jadeite in Europe are as yet very limited. He points out, however, that discoveries of these minerals have occasionally been made in Europe and America, thus proving that the substances are not so limited geographically as was formerly supposed. He thinks it probable that, if searched for, they will be found among the metamorphic rocks of Europe, and concludes that the balance of evidence is in favour of the view that jade is indigenous in the countries where the implements have been found. A further discussion of the question, particularly as it relates to America, will be found in Wilson's work on *Prehistoric Art*.[3] Of course, as has already been hinted, materials have at an early period been brought from one part of the Continent to another. I have myself a knife-shaped implement apparently of the beeswax flint of Pressigny, in France, which was found in a Swiss Lake Village.

Before leaving this part of the subject it may be noted, in confirmation of the statement already made, that primitive man adapts the materials at hand to his necessities, that various other substances have been used instead of stone in different parts of the world for purposes for which stone has been used elsewhere. Thus the inhabitants of the New Hebrides make axe-heads of the hinge-part of the shell of

---

[1] *L'Anthropologie*, i. 104.
[2] *Journal of Anthropological Society*, ser. i. xx. 332.
[3] Published by the Smithsonian Institution, p. 455.

tridacna, a huge bivalve, which resemble closely the stone celts of the polished stone period in Ireland and elsewhere. The natives of Australia make admirable arrow-heads out of glass bottles, and also out of the insulators of telegraph wires. Indeed, it is said that they are so fond of the latter, and have caused so much inconvenience by annexing them, that it has been found wise to leave a number of fragments of broken bottles at the bottom of the telegraph poles, in order to provide the material which would otherwise be sought at its summit. Specimens of arrow-heads made from both of these materials may be seen in the Pitt-Rivers Museum at Oxford, and with them the simple tools by which they were worked. Fig. 6 shows an arrow-head of glass and the implements with which it was made, and Fig. 7 the hands of the Australian in the act of making it. These points are mentioned to illustrate the statement that prehistoric man, in all probability, had other implements than those of stone, some of which, being of a more perishable nature, have not survived until the present day. This would not apply to such things as shells, but to objects of wood, and perhaps of some other materials.

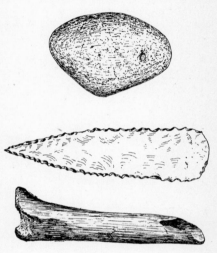

FIG. 6

GLASS ARROW-HEAD AND IMPLEMENTS USED
IN ITS MANUFACTURE
BY NATIVE AUSTRALIANS

D

How were the Stones worked?

This is a large question, and those desirous of fuller information than can be given here may be referred to the early chapters of Sir John Evans' work on *Ancient Stone Implements*. Some statement of the various processes of which we have knowledge must, however, be made, and we may commence with some observations by Holmes,[1]

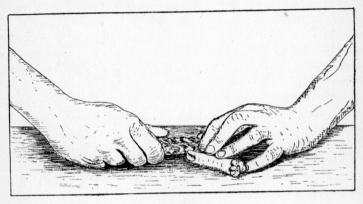

FIG. 7

METHOD OF MANUFACTURE OF GLASS ARROW-HEAD
BY NATIVE AUSTRALIAN

who has made a special study of the subject. "The shaping processes," he writes, "by means of which stone was made to assume artificial forms adapted to human needs, are varied and ingenious, and their mastery is of the greatest importance to all primitive peoples. These processes are distinguished by such terms as breaking, flaking, cutting, drilling, scraping, pecking, grinding, and polishing. All are purely mechanical; none are chemical, save a possible use of fire to induce changes

[1] "Stone Implements of the Potomac. Chesapeake Tidewater Province." *Fifteenth Annual Report of the American Bureau of Ethnology.*

in the rock in some parts of the quarry work. A wide range of operations is represented, and these may be conveniently arranged in four groups : (i.) *fracturing*, represented by the terms breaking, flaking, and chipping ; (ii.) *incising*, including cutting, picking, and scraping ; (iii.) *battering*, including such acts as bruising, pecking, and hammering ; (iv.) *abrading*, as in rubbing, drilling, boring, sawing, and polishing. These acts are employed according to the nature of the stone or the results desired ; as, for example, fracture is employed where the stone to be shaped is brittle like flint, jasper, or quartz ; incision is employed where the stone is relatively soft, such as soap-stone, serpentine, and the like ; battering is applied to tough materials, capable of resisting the shocks of per-cussion, like granitic rocks and many of the eruptives. Nearly all varieties are capable of being shaped by grind-ing and rubbing." Certain of these processes, especially in relation to British implements, must now be considered a little more closely. *Chipping* is the process of removing fragments from a piece of flint by blows given with another stone. It is obvious that the operation may have one of two ends in view. The object may be to dress a stone weapon, that is, to shape the central mass of the selected piece of stone into an implement, the flakes knocked off being worthless, or at least of secondary importance. By such processes were produced the palæolithic implements, and, generally speaking, the class of implements known as celts. Or, on the other hand, the object may have been to detach flakes from the central mass, which flakes would afterwards, either as they were detached, or after secondary working, be utilisable as implements. Here the central mass, or "core," is the worthless, or com-paratively worthless, portion of the original stone. Fig. 8 from Holmes' paper illustrates the first process in the operation of shaping a pebble. The process in connection with a piece of flint would not be quite the same, and has already been indicated in connection with the bulb of percussion. It is obvious that instead of striking the stone to be shaped with another, the same result may in some cases have been attained by striking the stone to be shaped against another lump of stone. Or again, where it was desired to remove very small flakes, a punch of some kind may have been employed between the stone to be shaped and the hammer.

Flaking is a process which is allied to chipping, but the term is perhaps better confined to the finer work, which may have been executed by pressure or by nipping off fragments of the stone to be worked. The Scandinavian implement (Fig. 1), or the Egyptian (Fig. 2), must first have been roughed out of masses of flint by the method of chipping. Then when the desired shape had been arrived at, the further elaboration was obtained by a more delicate process. At least, this seems probable, for, as a matter of fact, we do not know how this extremely beautiful "ripple-flaking" was produced.

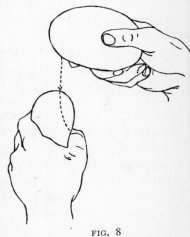

FIG. 8

FLINT FLAKING BY PERCUSSION
Holmes

A few instances of how flaking by pressure has been executed by primitive races will show how the same process may have been carried out in prehistoric times. The Esquimaux flake their arrows by means of an instrument with a handle of fossil ivory and a tongue or blade made of a slip from the horn of a reindeer and inserted in it. The piece of chert from which the arrow-head is to be made is placed on a block of wood in which a spoon-shaped cavity is cut. Then the flaker is pressed gently along the edge of the stone, alternately on either side and in a vertical direction. By this means fragments are removed until the desired shape of the head is attained. Fig. 9 from Holmes' paper will explain the process of removing splinters by pressure in a less elaborate manner than that just described. It is possible that some of the implements afterwards to be mentioned under the name of "fabricators" may have been used for purposes of pressure-flaking, though in more recent times an instrument more elastic in its character seems to have been employed. Such tools may quite well have been utilised also by prehistoric man.

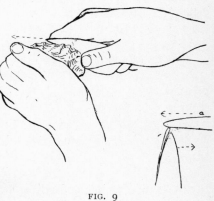

FIG. 9

FLINT FLAKING BY PRESSURE
Holmes

Pressure properly applied is able to detach quite large flakes from a central core of hard stone like obsidian. The beautiful flakes of this substance, said to have been used for sacrificial purposes in Mexico, seem to have been thus produced. Sir John Evans quotes a description of this operation from Torquemada, which may here be reproduced. "One of these Indian workmen sits down upon the ground and takes a piece of this black stone, about eight inches long, or rather more, and as thick as one's leg, or rather less, and cylindrical; they have a stick as large as the shaft of a lance, and three cubits or more in length; and at the end of it they fasten firmly another piece of wood eight inches long, to give more weight to this part; then, pressing their naked feet together, they hold the stone as with a pair of pincers or the vice of a carpenter's bench. They take the stick (which is cut off smooth at the end) with both hands, and set it well home against the edge of the front of the stone, which is also cut smooth in that part; and then they press it against their breast, and with the force of the pressure there flies off a knife, with its point and edge on each side, as neatly as if one were to make them of a turnip with a sharp knife, or of iron in the fire." Finally the glass and earthenware arrows made by the native Australians are worked with a pebble, and the fine tooling is effected by nipping off bits from the edge with the aid of a notch in the broken shank-bone of a sheep. This process is illustrated in Fig. 7, which is taken from a drawing in the Pitt-Rivers Museum, made on the spot from observation of the workman at his task. It may be added that many experiments have been made in recent times on methods of flaking and otherwise working flint by Sir John Evans and others, and will be found described in his book. Flint Jack's forgeries, generally rather rude in character, are tolerably well known, whilst the more artistic efforts of a modern Brandon workman may be seen in various museums, and the work of the present curator of the Pitt-Rivers Museum, could he have had the use of his present tools, would have won him a high place amongst prehistoric artificers.

Grinding and *polishing* were effected upon fixed, and not rotatory, stones, and the rubbing was done lengthwise, as the striation shows. *Sawing* seems to have been rarely practised in this country, but has been used in the case of Swiss and other axe-heads, perhaps with a flint flake. Possibly sand and water may also have been used in the operation. Or strips of wood or bone may have been used with sand. *Boring*, Sir John Evans thinks, was carried out in various ways : (i.) By chiselling, or picking with a sharp stone. (ii.) By grinding with a solid grinder, probably of wood. (iii.) By grinding with a tubular grinder, probably of ox-horn. (iv.) By drilling with a stone drill. (v.) By drilling with a metallic drill. With regard to the use of these processes at different periods, Dr. Blackmore says : " Eoliths are hacked, palæoliths are chipped, and neoliths are flaked. Hacking, chipping, and flaking are the characteristics of the three stone periods." And Sir John Evans sums up his account of the different processes by saying :—

" (1) In the Palæolithic, River-gravel, or Drift period implements were fashioned by chipping only, and not ground or polished. The material used in Europe was, moreover, as far as at present known, mainly flint, chert, or quartzite.

" (2) In the Reindeer or Cavern period of Central France, though grinding was almost, if not quite, unused, except in finishing bone instruments, yet greater skill in flaking flint and in working up flakes into serviceable tools was exhibited. In some places, as at Laugerie-Haute, surface chipping is found on the flint arrow-heads, and cup-shaped recesses have been worked in other hard stones than flint, though no other stones have been used for cutting purposes.

" (3) In the Neolithic, or Surface Stone period of Western Europe, other materials besides flint were largely used for the manufacture of hatchets ; grinding at the edge and on the surface was generally practised, and the art of flaking flint by pressure from the edge was probably known. The stone axes, at least in Britain, were rarely perforated.

" (4) In the Bronze period such stone implements, with the exception of mere flakes and scrapers, as remained in use were, as a rule, highly finished, many of the axes being perforated and of graceful form, and some of the flint arrow-heads evincing the highest degree of manual skill."

CHAPTER III

STONE IMPLEMENTS—EOLITHS—PALÆOLITHS

I N the opinion of some, though, it must be admitted, not of all, competent to pronounce an opinion upon stone implements, the oldest objects of this character are those known as eoliths. These objects, having been originally found on the chalk plateau of Kent, are sometimes also called plateau implements, but the name which has been set at the head of this chapter is that which they usually receive, and that which will be adhered to in this book. In the case at the Blackmore Museum containing the fine series of these objects they are defined as " stones having evidence of use and often shaped by use ; all showing human intelligence in the selection of suitable size and form." This definition, framed so as to include even the rudest forms, must now be somewhat developed. In the first place, then, as mentioned in the last chapter, eoliths are hacked, not chipped, still less flaked. That is, the splinters and fragments which were removed from the stones were removed by men who were not familiar with the peculiar property possessed by flints of fracturing in thin flakes if the proper direction be given and the right amount of force applied to the blow. The trimming given to the implements is very slight. It has generally been made on the edges of rude natural flints taken from an old flint drift. The secondary fragments removed for purposes of trimming have been taken off perpendicularly to the plane surfaces of the stone, and have the appearance of having been hacked off, perhaps by means of the small hammer-stones found with other varieties of eoliths. These last-mentioned forms may be taken as a type of

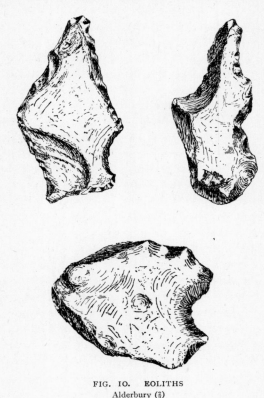

FIG. 10.   EOLITHS
Alderbury (⅔)

the simpler kind of eolith, which was really a natural stone used for certain purposes and showing signs of having so been used. Of these Sir J. Prestwich[1] has written : " Besides the implements of definite patterns,

[1] *Journal of Anthrop. Inst.*, xxi. 246.

there is a large, probably the larger, number which, though not the result of chance, show no special design. Amongst these are the natural flints which have been selected for use as the hammer or trimming stones, the result being that the flint has become chipped at the ends or round the sides undesignedly, but still in a manner that could not have resulted from natural wear. In a similar way, some are roughened at the end like the large pebbles or balls used at a later Neolithic period, exhibiting patches of rough abraded surface, the result of repeated blows." Again, these stones are almost invariably stained a deep warm, brown colour, in this respect resembling the flints of the drift in which they are found. This colour spreads over the worked as well as the unworked parts, though it may be lighter in shade on the former than on the latter. Signs of considerable wear are not wanting in the rounding and blunting of the working edges, a result, evidently, of much rolling and knocking about.

Considering their extreme rudeness, it is perhaps not surprising that considerable doubt and even much scepticism has been shown as to their being genuine works of the hands of man. This point must now be considered. In the first place it will be admitted by all that one would expect the earliest tools used by man to be either natural objects or a very slight advance upon such objects. This is not a description which could be applied to the implements of palæolithic type. Mr. Bell[1] well says : " The palæolithic implement is, on the face of it, a very advanced and artistic production. Neither in shape nor in workmanship does it show any indications of a prentice hand, and far from being the firstborn of human tools, must represent the last stage in a long series of artistic development." But though this is true enough, it does not

[1] *Journal of Anthrop. Inst.,* xxiii. 266.

follow that in the eoliths we have these early rude implements. Their recognition depends mainly on the fact
that they present a definite series of simple but well-
defined types. If one found here and there a stone shaped
as eoliths are shaped, it might be difficult to claim for it
that it was the work of man's hands, but when large
numbers are discovered, belonging, as will shortly be
shown, to one or another of several simple but very
clearly marked types, it becomes more difficult to enter-
tain any hesitation as to their real nature. But a long
series must be examined, such a series as is exhibited
at the Natural History Museum, South Kensington, or,
better still, such a series as is to be seen in the Blackmore
Museum. Having examined these, the hill at Alderbury,
close by, should be ascended, and the implements sought
out *in situ*.

When a series such as that just mentioned is examined
it becomes clear that two special objects seem to have been
in the mind of the manufacturers. In many cases the idea
has been to work in the side of the implement a semi-
circular notch, looking, as one describer has put it, like a
piece bitten out of a slice of cake (see Fig. 10). The result
attained is similar to that achieved by the makers of the
"hollow" or concave scraper of the Neolithic time. The
appearance of the notch in all implements of this type is
wonderfully similar, a fact which alone renders it improbable that it could have been otherwise formed than
by the hands of man. Moreover, the same notch may be
found worked in similar manner in other materials than
flint, *e.g.* greensand. The same notch may also be found
in palæolithic implements (see Fig. 4), where it seems to
have fulfilled some purpose secondary to the main purpose
of the implement, just as a button-hook, for example, may
be added to a pocket-knife, the main object of which is to
provide its owner with an implement of a cutting nature.

A hollow, notched implement of the kind mentioned was evidently, whatever may have been its purpose, for as to this we can only make guesses, a very useful tool in the estimation of primitive man. In the eolithic type we seem to possess the earliest form yet known. It was handed down in the palæolithic implement, when man had learnt to do better things than merely hack stone. And finally it developed into the concave scrapers of the neolithic form, of which, perhaps, the most remarkable are the exceedingly thin and delicate examples found in Ireland. In other cases the idea of the artificer has been to work the implement for a point, a boring-tool being perhaps in his mind (see Fig. 10). Sometimes the point has been the sole object, but more often motives of economy in time seem to have led to its combination with the hollow—again the old story of the pocket-knife. These notches were sometimes arranged (as in Fig. 10) on either side of a long pointed implement, or on the broad side of a piece of flint, with a comparatively small point between them, the whole outline then resembling that of a Cupid's bow or ⌣⌣. The former of these is the double-edged scraper, the latter, the bow-scraper of the South Kensington classification. Besides these, the most common forms, there are other types of eoliths, such as hammer-stones and punches, bruised at the place where they have been used for pecking fragments off other pieces of flint. There is also a beak-shaped scraper or pick, and other forms included in the collection at South Kensington are broad flakes with trimmed edges, pointed implements of the spear-head form, and ovoid Abbeville types. As already mentioned, there is still a doubt as to the geological position of these implements, for unfortunately, so far, except in the case of the Dewlish find (see page 7), no fossils, shells, bones, or teeth have been discovered in the gravels containing them. By many, perhaps by most geologists, the gravels

have been assigned to the Pliocene age, but Professor
Hull, in a discussion following a paper by Mr. Bullen
on the subject, refused to place them later than the mid-
Pleistocene period.   But the collocation at Dewlish with
Elephas meridionalis seems to leave little doubt of the age
of at least those particular examples.[1]

Palæoliths.—As to the genuineness of objects of this
class no person entertains any doubt, so that words need
not be wasted in proving that they are of human manufacture.   They fall into two categories, not from their
shape so much as from the places in which they are
found, namely, River-drift and Cave implements.   As
there seems some probability, though the question is
by no means settled, that the former may be the older,
it will be well to commence with them.   As their name
implies, they are found in gravels deposited by rivers,
and by rivers too, forming parts of the present drainage
system of the country, though often at a very much
higher level than the existing stream.   The distance of
the higher gravels from the stream by which they were
originally deposited is some measure of the time which
has elapsed since the gravels were laid down and the
implements washed into them.   That the implements
have been in the gravels from the time of their original
deposition is shown by the fact that they and the unworked flints amongst which they are discovered are
stained in a similar manner.   Moreover, the surfaces of

[1] The following may be consulted on the subject of eoliths : Prestwich,
Controverted Questions of Geology, 1895 ; *ib. Journ. of Anthrop. Soc.*, xxi.
246 ; Harrison, *ib. ib.* 263 ; Jones, R., *ib.* ser. ii., i. 53 ; *ib. Natural Science,*
v. 32 ; Bullen, *Victoria Inst. Trans.,* June 18, 1900 ; *ib. Geol. Mag.,* Dec. iv.
vol. x. no. 465 (with full bibliography) ; Darbishire Mem. and Proc. Manchester Lit. and Phil. Soc. 1901–2 ; Kennard, *Natural Science,* 1898, 34. For
the discovery of similar implements near Pretoria, South Africa, see Leith,
Journ. of Anthrop. Soc., s. ii., i. 258.

the flint tools have often been greatly worn, all the sharpness having been taken off the chipped portions by rolling in water with other stones, gravel, sand, and other materials. This is particularly the case with what Worthington Smith calls the most ancient implements (see Fig. 11). A caveat must be put in, however, as to regarding these abraded implements as the oldest, for a more ancient implement may have a fresher look, if by chance it has been subjected to less rolling about than its younger brother. But allowing, as is highly probable, that these are the oldest implements, what is their character? They fall into two classes, classes to which, by the way, most palæolithic implements belong, the pick-shaped and the ovate. The former class consists of implements with

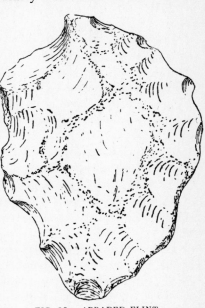

FIG. 11. ABRADED FLINT
(W. G. SMITH'S "OLDEST TYPE")
Farnham (⅓)

a broad, heavy, usually unworked butt or base, more or less comfortably held in the hand, for it seems that these implements were not hafted, but used as we now see them. From this butt the tool tapers to a more or less elegantly shaped point. In Fig. 12 there is an example of a very beautifully shaped implement of this kind from the Broom pit. It is of the pick-variety, but is so sharply trimmed that it was probably intended to act also, if not primarily, as a knife. The implements of the most ancient type resemble this in general outline, but are clumsier and, of course, much more abraded than this example. The ovate or rude oval form, of which an example of the abraded type is shown in Fig. 11, is trimmed all round to an edge, and has no untrimmed butt, nor is it provided with a special pointed extremity. These oldest implements, says Mr. Smith, "are known at once by their great amount of abrasion, their grey-brown, deep brown-ochreous, or chocolate colour, and their rude make." They had, he thinks, already attained enormous antiquity at the time when tools of lesser age were made and deposited in the same river gravels in which these older ones are now found. Speaking of a much abraded, dull, and deeply ochreous implement found near Canterbury, he says that there are chips upon it made at the time when the implementiferous gravels of Canterbury were laid down, which chipped parts are lustrous and non-ochreous. He also believes that the eoliths of Ightham are no older than this class of implement, so that perhaps they may have been constructed at the same time. But at present we can do little but surmise about the earliest tools, since there remain so many problems unsolved in connection with them. The other implements from the River-drift, those, that is, of a later period perhaps, and certainly of less abraded character and non-ochreous patination, may be divided into the following groups, though the order in which they are placed does not in any way indicate any sequence or relation of age.

(i.) Flakes, which may or may not show some traces of chipping at the edges. These may be (a) external, i.e., the first chips struck off a block of flint, showing, therefore, the crust on one side; (b) ridged, of triangular section, extremely rare; (c) flat, commoner than the last; this variety presents generally shorter, thicker, and broader examples than the later or surface period;

(*d*) polygonal, the commonest variety. Flakes of all kinds seem to have been used for cutting and scraping purposes. Some flakes have been provided with a serrated edge, reminding one of the flint-saws of the later age, and probably intended for a similar purpose.[1]

(ii.) Scrapers. Implements in which the end or the side has been trimmed to a bevelled edge, generally semicircular when the work is at the end of the implement. These tools, which are amongst the commonest in the neolithic series, are rare in the River-drift, though they are met with amongst the objects found in the caves.

(iii.) The pointed or pear-shaped picks, of which mention has already been made (see Figs. 12 and 13).

(iv.) Ovate or sharp-rimmed implements. These are found of all sizes, from comparatively small implements to the large flat objects of the Broom type (see Fig. 5). It is a curious point about these that if they are held up so

FIG. 12.   PALÆOLITH, FLINT
Broom (⅔)

[1] *Man*, 1903, 156.

E

that the edge can be examined it will be found to present a sinuous outline instead of a straight one. This sinuosity is so arranged as to give the outline the form of a long s, but reversed, thus ⟨, not ⟨. The fact is that in the

FIG. 13. PALÆOLITH
St. Acheul (⅔)

process of manufacture the stone has been so shaped as to resemble somewhat the twisted paddle of a screw-propeller. It was at one time thought that there was some purpose in this peculiar conformation, but it seems probable that it was simply the result of the method adopted of chipping the stone, and had no other significance. In the case of some palæoliths recently discovered at Ipswich,[1] it is stated that a fine oval implement shows signs of having been worked for hafting, as also does a smaller chisel-shaped form. This is unusual, for, so far, the evidence seems to point to the tools of this period having been used in the hand and without hafts.

Although the implements now under discussion are called River-drift, and are found in river gravels, it is quite clear that they have been washed down into their present positions, and did not originate there. There seem to have been regular manufactories of these implements, and one of them has been most carefully investigated and described by Mr. Worthington Smith.[2] The palæo-

[1] *Nature,* May 22, 1902.   [2] *Man, the Primæval Savage.*

lithic workshop in question was situated at Caddington, near Dunstable. It lay by the side of a pool or lake on a chalk hill, covered with brick-earth, and its level was from four to thirteen feet below the modern surface, *i.e.*, that amount of soil had been deposited since the period when some tribe of early inhabitants of this country sat down by the pool to make weapons and tools for themselves out of flint. Chalk-with-flints, red clay-with-flints, and boulder-clay were in their neighbourhood on higher ground, which has now been worn away and has disappeared.

At certain spots in the neighbourhood of this pool and others flints were manufactured into implements. "It is at these spots," says Mr. Smith, "that the sharp thin flakes occur in hundreds, together with implements finished and unfinished. It is curious that perhaps only some four or five yards off, and on the same old land surface, not a single worked stone or flake can be found." The old land surface is naturally represented by a line in a section of the brick clay, in the midst of which it is placed, and it appears that this particular band has long been known and avoided by the men engaged in getting the clay, not merely because the stones injure the bricks if included in them, but quite as much because they dread the thin keen-edged artificially struck flakes, which suddenly cut their fingers down to the bone. Here we have to do with the product as it was turned out, and as keen and sharp as the day it was made, not worn and rolled by the action of water. By dint of unwearied patience and great labour Mr. Smith was able to prove to a demonstration that the spot which he was examining was the genuine manufactory, for he was able to piece together the fragments which had been chipped off by the original workmen and restore the block either wholly or entirely to its first state. An example of this is shown in Fig. 14, which Mr. Smith has kindly permitted me to reproduce. The figure on the right shows the finished implement, that on the left the pieces which were removed in its construction. In this figure, then, we get the appearance of the block before its artificer had begun to work upon it. In one of his attempts

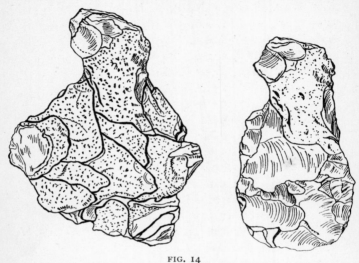

FIG. 14

IMPLEMENT FREE FROM FLAKES (RIGHT) AND WITH FLAKES REATTACHED, THE HEAVY LINES SHOWING THE REATTACHED FRAGMENTS (W. G. SMITH)
Caddington (⅔)

at piecing together Mr. Smith constructed what one might perhaps call a shell of flint with a central cavity, the materials of which he had not discovered. Into this cavity liquid plaster-of-Paris was poured. The cast thus obtained presented all the features of a core, and represented the missing mass of flint perhaps transported from Caddington to some other part of the country. Another interesting example of a palæolithic workshop floor has been found near Ealing, and extends over an area of about forty feet square.[1]

[1] *Proc. Soc. Antiquaries,* s. ii., xi. 211.

Cave Implements.—The cave is such a natural habitation, ready-made for the occupation of man, that it is in no way surprising that we should find so many relics of the past races of this and other countries in them. Sometimes these grottoes are true caverns or recesses in limestone produced by a river outside or by the action of subterranean streams, in which cases long winding galleries may have been formed, an intricate system of chambers being the result. Or it may be that the natural agencies of water and frost have wasted away the lower and perhaps softer strata of a cliff, leaving those above to overhang the ground. Such rock-shelters, as they have been called, in order to distinguish them from the cave proper, could obviously be with ease converted into a place of habitation for man, and, as a matter of fact, were so utilised, as in the case of Bruniquel in France. Although the term cave-implements is now being applied to objects belonging to the older stone period, it must not be supposed that the caves were only places of habitation at that time. On the contrary, as has already been shown in the cases of Kent's Cavern and the grotto of Mas d'Azil, successive layers of objects have been found showing that successive generations, if not races, have made a home within their walls. At times it is possible that these races may have been separated from one another by long intervals. We can lay little stress upon the rapidity of the deposition of stalagmite, as affording a geological or archæological clock, since conditions of various kinds may accelerate or retard the process. At Kent's Cavern one " Robert Hedges of Ireland " inscribed his name with the date 1688. The carving, when first discovered by Mr. McEnery in 1825, was " glazed over and partly effaced." At the present time there is about $\frac{1}{20}$th of an inch of stalagmite over it. At this rate of progress it would take about 4,000 years to form an inch, and in parts of the cavern the stalagmite floor, one of two floors, is twelve feet thick. On the other hand, Professor McKenny Hughes says that "when the great storm of 1872 broke up the floors at the mouth of Ingleborough Cavern I saw modern ginger-beer bottles which had been buried a foot deep in the stalagmite." But at the most rapid rate of progress one must allow that a very long period must have been covered by the time necessary for the construction of the floors of Kent's Cavern. In other cases the occupation may well have been more continuous, as at Mas d'Azil, where the continuity seems to have been mainly broken by occasional inundations of the neighbouring river, inundations which may have driven from their abode its inhabitants but for a comparatively short time, perhaps even only a few days.

The walls of some European caves have been decorated in Palæolithic times with illustrations of the animals of the period. One of the most celebrated of these is the cave of La Mouthe in the Dordogne, France,[1] where hearths of different periods, Palæolithic and Neolithic, have been discovered. Here are seven designs or panels representing (1) the bison, *Bos priscus,* with a much exaggerated hump ; (2) ox ; (3) reindeer ; (4) wild goat ; (5) mammoth ; (6 and 7) horses. In this cavern was also found a lamp of red sandstone, on which was a well-executed head of a goat. The annexed drawing (Fig. 15) of the mammoth is an example from the walls of the cave of Combarelles,[2] where there are no less than 109 figures representing other kinds of animals. Other caves with pictures on the walls are those of Pair-non-Pair (Bordeaux), Chabot (Ardoche), Font-de-Gaume, Les Eyzies (Dordogne), and Altamira (Spain). No objects

[1] *L'Anthropologie,* viii. 592 ; ix. 596 ; xii. 670. *Bull. et Mém. Soc. d'Anthrop. de Paris,* ser. v. t. iv. 191.

[2] *Bull. et Mém. Soc d'Anthrop. de Paris,* ser. v. t. iii. 527.

of this kind have as yet been found in any cavern in these islands. The caves having been inhabited by so many generations of people, if not by different peoples, it will be understood that a great variety of objects has been discovered within them, belonging to the Palæolithic, Neolithic, and later periods, in fact, in the case of the

FIG. 15. MAMMOTH
Wall of grotto of Combarelles (⅛)

Victoria Cave at Settle, down to the time when the native Britons fled before the face of the invading Saxon hordes. The sequence of objects in the caves being much more complete in France than in this country, it will be better to deal with it first, and then give a few notes respecting our own caves and their contents. According to the classification of M. de Mortillet, somewhat modified in that given on p. 9, the **Chellean** period comes first. This is not a period, however, belonging to the cave-series, but to that of the river-drift. It is sometimes called the Acheulean period from the place St. Acheul. Leaving this aside the first cave-period is that of Le Moustier, the **Mousterian** era. The cavern from which this period takes its name is situated on the right bank of the Vézere, and about ninety feet above its present level. The climate during this period was cold and damp, and the mammoth, the woolly rhinoceros, the cave-bear, and the musk-sheep or ox, were the characteristic animals of the fauna. The implements are worked on one side only into choppers or side-scrapers. On the opposite side to the cutting-edge part of the crust is retained for the purpose of ensuring a firm grip. Pointed implements wrought into shapes something like spear-heads are also found. Instruments of bone are almost entirely wanting.

The **Solutrean** period owes its name to the rock-shelter at Solutré (Saone-et-Loire), a settlement on a plateau at the base of a limestone escarpment, by which it was to some extent sheltered. Laugerie Haute, by some considered to afford more typical examples of the work of the period which certainly underlie a deposit of Madelainean date, and Cro-Magnon, celebrated for the skeletons there discovered in 1868, are other settlements belonging to this period. The climate seems to have been mild and dry. The horse existed in large herds, hence the term equidian sometimes given to this period, though not co-terminous with it ; the reindeer and the mammoth were also amongst the fauna, but the rhinoceros had disappeared. The characteristic implements are lozenge and leaf-shaped heads, delicately chipped, and closely resembling arrow-heads, which perhaps may be their real nature, also lance-heads or daggers chipped on both surfaces. The working in stone reveals a great advance upon that of the preceding period. There is also a great improvement in the construction of objects of bone and horn, but this will be dealt with separately when the objects made of these materials are considered by themselves. A bridge between this period and the next seems to be afforded by the cave of Les Eyzies, in the Dordogne, where Madelainean harpoons made of reindeer horn outnumber the implements of stone.

The **Madelainean** period itself receives its name from the cave of La Madelaine, in the Dordogne. The climate during this period was cold and dry, and there was a great development of the northern fauna, particularly the reindeer, after which animal the era has sometimes been called. It forms the earlier part of the Cervidian epoch of Piette's table. The mammoth became extinct

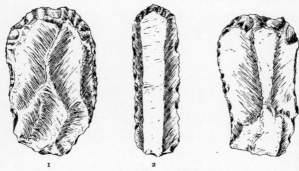

FIG. 16. SCRAPERS, LONG
1. Avebury. 2. French. 3. Icklingham

during this time. It may be looked upon as the great epoch of work in horn and bone. These will be fully dealt with in a later chapter. As far as stone implements are concerned, the examples do not show as high a pitch of skill or workmanship as those of the Solutrean time. Perhaps this may have been because the facility with which the softer materials of horn and bone were worked tempted man to decline the more arduous task of shaping stone to the lance-heads and other forms of the earlier date. That it was an earlier date there can be no doubt, for, as mentioned above, Solutrean objects underlie those of the Madelainean time at Laugerie Haute. The rock-shelters at Laugerie Basse and Bruniquel also belong to this period. The stone implements include flakes and long scrapers (see Fig. 16², for the type), pebbles with depressions in them of a mortar-like character, hammer-stones and in some cases flint saws. Side-scrapers are rare and leaf-shaped blades are entirely absent. From the later Madelainean period in which the antlers of red deer to some extent replaced the horns of the reindeer as material for the manufacture of harpoons and other implements we arrive at the **Asylian** epoch, called after the grotto of Mas d'Azil, which is regarded by many as a true transition era between Palæolithic and Neolithic times. As this grotto has already been dealt with in the first chapter, it will not be necessary to touch further on the subject here.

Of English caves the most celebrated is Kent's Cavern, to which sufficient allusion has already been made. Others in Devonshire are at Brixham and Newbury. The Cresswell caves (Robin Hood, Church-Hole, and Pin-Hole) in Derbyshire are also of great interest. Under a layer of stalagmite up to a foot in thickness is an upper bed containing quartzite implements of a somewhat similar character to that discovered at Saltley in the gravels of the river Rea. Flint and ironstone tools have also been found, with implements of bone of various kinds, and an incised head of a horse with a hog-mane, the only work of art of the madelainean type found in England. In this layer are bones of the woolly rhinoceros, reindeer, lion, hyæna, hippopotamus, etc. The lowest bed, which is three feet thick, and consists of red sand and clay, contained implements of Acheulian type associated here, as elsewhere, with bones of the reindeer, woolly rhinoceros, mammoth, hyæna, and horse.[1]

[1] For fuller information on the subject of caves, Boyd-Dawkins' *Cave-Hunting* should be consulted, also the following : *Report of the Committee of the Royal and Geological Societies on Brixham Cave ; L'Anthropologie,* xii., p. 130, list of French caves ; Keane, *Ethnology,* p. 78.

In Europe traces of palæolithic man have been found outside England, in France, Spain, Portugal, Belgium, Germany, Austria, and Italy. His relics have not been discovered in those countries which did not become habitable until after the retreat of the glaciers, thus no traces have been discovered in Scandinavia, nor in the Alpine districts, nor in the greater part of North Germany. Outside Europe remains belonging to this class have been found in the quaternary strata of North Africa (Algiers and Egypt), in India (Deccan), and, according to some, in Western North America, though there is still some doubt as to the age to which these last implements really belong. In South Africa (Swaziland) implements have been found in river-gravels, very much of the same kind as those discovered at Broom, and probably palæolithic.[1] A list of river-drift implement localities in England, arranged according to counties, is given at the end of this chapter. In Evans' book most of the same places will be found arranged according to the river systems to which they belong. In the Prehistoric Room at the British Museum there is a large map of England, on which the localities both of cave and river-drift implements are marked by pins, a most instructive demonstration of the subject which should be carefully examined. Attention should also be called to the truly admirable *Guide to the Antiquities of the Stone Age in the Department of British and Mediæval Antiquities in the British Museum*, published by the Trustees. The learner who takes this book in his hand and studies the cases containing the specimens which it describes will have little difficulty in gaining a good idea of the objects belonging to this and the later stone periods.

[1] R. Jones, *Journ. of Anthrop. Soc.*, N.S., i. p. 48.

LIST OF CAVES IN ENGLAND AND WALES

DEVONSHIRE.—Brixham, Windmill Hill Cavern.
   Happaway Cavern.
   Newbury, Tor Bryan Cave (also neolithic objects, see
      Proc. Soc. Antiq., s. ii., viii. 249).
   Plymouth, Cattedown Cave.
   Torquay, Kent's Hole (*Trans. Devon. Assoc.*, ii. 469;
      iii. 191 ; iv. 467).

MONMOUTH.—King Arthur's Cave, near Whitchurch, Ross.

SOMERSET. — Cheddar (neolithic and late Celtic objects in
      Gough's Cavern).
   Wookey Hole, near Wells.   Palæolithic.

DERBYSHIRE.—Cresswell Crags.

YORKSHIRE.—Settle, Victoria Cave (palæolithic and late Celtic
      objects).
   Skipton, Lotherdale Cave.   Palæolithic.

WALES.—Cae-Gwyn, Vale of Clwyd (*Quart. Journ. Geol. Soc.*,
      1888, 112).
   Cefn, near S. Asaph.
   Coygan, S. Caermarthenshire.
   Ffynnon Beuno.
   Long Hole, Gower.
   Moyles Mouth, Oyle Cave, Pembroke.
   Pont Newydd.

LIST OF LOCALITIES WHERE RIVER-DRIFT IMPLEMENTS HAVE BEEN FOUND

BEDFORDSHIRE—

Biddenham, near Bedford.
Biggleswade.
Bossington, near Leighton Buzzard.
*Caddington (W. Smith, *Man the Primæval Savage*).
Cardington.
Dallow Farm, near Luton.
Harrowden.
Henlow.
Honey Hill.
Houghton Regis, near Dunstable.
Kempston.
Leagrave Marsh, near Luton.

BUCKINGHAMSHIRE.—Great Missenden.

BERKSHIRE—

Grovelands, near Reading.
Pig's Green.
Ruscombe, near Twyford.
Sonning.
Wallingford.
Wokingham.

CAMBRIDGESHIRE—

Barnwell.
Cambridge.
Chatteris.
Chesterton.
Kennett.
Swaffham Fen.

DEVONSHIRE—

*Broom, near Axminster.
Colyton.
Kentisbere, near Collumpton.

DORSETSHIRE—

Dewlish.
Hawkchurch.
Wimborne Minster.

ESSEX—

Abberton, near Colchester.
Ardleigh, near Colchester.
Barking, St. Swithin's Farm.
Barking, Wallend.
Dovercourt, near Harwich.
Felstead, North End Place.

ESSEX (*contd.*)—

Farmstead, Lake's Farm, Cramshall Lane.
LexdenPark,nearColchester.
Leyton, Grove Green Lane.
Quendon.
St. Osyth's, near Colchester.
Shoeburyness.

Stanway, near Lexden.
Stratford.
Walton-on-the-Naze.
West Bergholt (several of these discovered by H. G. Laver, Esq., and communicated to me).

HAMPSHIRE—

Barton.
Bournemouth.   [ampton.
Hillhead, 9 N.E. of South-

Lee on the Solent.
Southampton Common.

ISLE OF WIGHT—

Bembridge.
Foreland.

Sea View.

HERTFORDSHIRE—

Abbot's Langley.
Ayot St. Peter.
Barton Green.
Bayford.
Bedmond.
Bengeo.
Bishop's Stortford.
Fisher's Green, Stevenage.
Hamstead End, near Cheshunt.
Harpenden.
Hemel Hempstead, near.
Hertford.

Hitchin.
Ickleford, near Hitchin.
Ippollitts.
Kenworth, Mount Pleasant.
Knebworth.
North Mimms, south of Hatfield.
Stocking Pelham.
Ware.
Watford.
Welwyn.
Wheathampstead.

HUNTINGDONSHIRE—

Abbot's Ripton.
Elton, near Oundle.

Hartford, near Huntingdon.
Little Orton, near Peterborough.

KENT—

Aylesford.
Bishopstone.
Canterbury, near.
Chatham.
Chatham, Otterham Quay.
Chilham.
Crayford Station.
Currie Farm.
Erith.
Folkestone.
Gillingham, near Chatham.
Gravesend.
Greenhythe.
Green Street Green.
Herne Bay.
Horton Kirby.
Ightham.
Knock Hall Lane.

Limpsfield.
Lullingstone.
Marden.
Northfleet.
Ospringe, near Faversham.
Reculver.
Reculver, Wear Farm.
St. Mary Hoo.
Stoke.
Studwell.
Swale Cliff.
Swanscombe (*Man*, 1903, 155).
Teynham Station, near.
Thannington.
Tweedale.
Wickham, near Bromley.

LINCOLNSHIRE.—Lincoln, near.

MIDDLESEX—

Acton, various places near here.
Dawley, West Drayton.
Ealing Dean.
Enfield, Bush Hill Park.
Enfield, Forty Hill.
Gunnersbury.
Hackney Downs, near Shacklewell.
Hanwell.
Highbury New Park, near Stoke Newington.
London. (Implements have been found in the City, Gray's Inn Lane, Clerkenwell, London Fields, Dalston, Kingsland, Homerton, Hackney, Lower Clapton, Stamford Hill, Mildmay Park, South Hornsey, Abney Park Cemetery; see Smith, "Primeval Savage" and *Nature*, xxvii. 270.)
Lower Edmonton, Rowan Tree Farm, and other localities near.
Mill Hill, near Acton.

NORFOLK—
Feltwell, Shrub Hill.
South Wootton.
Thetford, Red Hill.
Weeting.
West Runton, near Cromer.
Whitehill.

OXFORD—
Bagley Wood, near Iffley.
Broadwell.
Caversham.
Hinksey, in Thames.
Ipsden.
Marston Ferry.
Wolvercote.

SUFFOLK—
*Brandon gravel-hill.
Bury St. Edmunds.
Eriswell.
Fornham All Saints.
Higham, Ballast Pit, G.E.R. near Bury St. Edmunds.
*Hoxne.
Icklingham.
Ipswich (*Jl. Anth. Inst.*, 1903, 41).
Maid's Cross, Lakenheath.
Melford Junction.
*Mildenhall.
Santon Downham.
Sicklesmere.
Stutton.
Sudbury.
Westley.
West Stow.

SURREY—
Battersea and many other localities on Thames, for which see Evans, p. 588.
Farley Heath.
Farnham.
Frimley.
Peasemarsh, near Guildford.
Peperharow.
Wracklesham.

SUSSEX—
Brighton.
Friston and Crow Link Gap, near Eastbourne.

WARWICKSHIRE.—Saltley.

WILTSHIRE—
Ashford in the Water.
Bemerton, near Salisbury.
Breamore.
Britford.
Downton.
Fisherton.
Knowle Farm, near Savernake.
Lake.
Milford Hill.
Pewsey.
South Newton.

CHAPTER IV

STONE IMPLEMENTS—NEOLITHIC TYPES—OVERLAP WITH METAL

AS in other portions of the Prehistoric period, so in connection with the period with which this chapter is concerned, it is impossible to assign any date, in an ordinary chronological manner, for the commencement of the Neolithic period in this country or elsewhere. Most probably there is no such date, for the reason that there was no sharp distinction between this period and that which preceded it. It is clear that the introduction of metal is a definite milestone on the road of civilisation, but the acquisition of a new and improved method of working stone can scarcely be regarded in the same light. The polishing of stone was a distinct advance, but the majority of the implements of the Neolithic period are not polished. Hence, as already pointed out, it is not always possible with safety to decide, apart from its place of discovery, whether a given implement is palæolithic or neolithic, that is, a certain range of implements, for, of course, there are many as to which no reasonable doubt can arise. Scandinavia is a country which so far has afforded no evidence of palæolithic implements, so that here the problem is somewhat narrowed down. As to the date of the appearance of man—in the neolithic stage of culture—in this part of the world, we have some evidence, dim and doubtful, it is true, but perhaps a shade less so than in most other cases. Denmark, as its peat-mosses show, has had four distinct periods of vegetation during the time that the country has been occupied by man. From the commencement of history down to the present day the beech has been the chief tree in its forests. Before the beech the pedunculated oak flourished. This was preceded by the sessile oak, which had in its turn succeeded the Scotch fir. It has been urged that a period of not less than 2,500 years must be allowed for the rise, progress, and decline of each of these successive vegetations. Here we enter the region of surmise, for there is no convincing evidence for the figure above-mentioned. Still we obtain some idea of the number of years which must have elapsed since men, skilled in the skill of the neolithic stone-worker, first made their way into the Danish peninsula. Along the shores of its coast are found great heaps of shells, chiefly of the oyster, the refuse of the meals of an early race of inhabitants. These mounds or kitchen-middens (Kjokkenmöddings) contain flint implements of a rude character, and also fragments of pottery. It has been claimed for them that they are relics of the earliest times of the Neolithic period, and if so, they may be compared with the shell-layer of the grotto of Mas d'Azil. But there is another view, that the heaps were the refuse of a people, in a very backward stage of civilisation, it is true, but not necessarily of very early date. This view seems to gain some support from the fact that some of the rude implements met with amongst the rest of the débris actually appear to have been made from polished objects. This, at least, is clear, that the implements are of a much humbler type than the more finished works characteristic of a part of the Neolithic period, and particularly in the same part of the world. The kitchen-middens belong to a stage of civilisation still existent in Tierra del Fuego, and have been found in England (Hastings, Ventnor, Tenby, on the Wash, and in Devon and Cornwall); Scotland (Oban, Moray Firth, Loch Spynie); Ireland (Cork Harbour, White Park Bay, County Antrim). They have also been met with in France, Portugal, Sardinia, Florida, Japan, Chili, Massachusetts, and Georgia. Everywhere they represent a stage of civilisation of a low type, where shell-fish formed the chief food-material and where little trouble was expended on shaping the flint implements, which are not much altered from the flakes originally detached from the central core. Kitchen-middens, then, afford no safe test of age. They "cover the whole field from Palæolithic to modern times, some being very old, others still in progress, so that each has to be taken on its merits."[1] As to size, Petroff[2] writes: "The time required for the formation of a so-called layer of kitchen refuse found under the sites of Aleutian or Innuit (Eskimo) dwellings, I am inclined to think less than indicated by Mr. Dall's calculations. Anybody who has watched a healthy Innuit family in the process of making a meal on the luscious echinus or sea-urchin, would naturally imagine that in the course of a month they might pile up a great quantity of spinous débris. Both hands are kept busy conveying the sea-fruit to the capacious mouth; with a skilful combined action of teeth and tongue the shell is cracked, the rich contents extracted, and the former falls rattling to the ground in a continuous shower of fragments until the meal is concluded. A family of three or four adults, and perhaps an equal number of children, will leave behind them a shell monument of their voracity a foot or eighteen inches in height after a single meal. . . . The heaps of refuse created under such circumstances during a single season were truly astonishing in size. They will surely mislead the

---

[1] Keane, *Ethnology*, p. 77.

[2] *American Naturalist*, July, 1882, teste Keane.

ingenious calculator of the antiquities of shell heaps a thousand years hence."

Even if we allow that the flints of the kitchen-middens are the earliest objects which can fairly be assigned to the Neolithic or surface period, we cannot any further continue a consecutive classification, for the very reason that the objects which we have to classify are surface objects and not found in strata like some of those associated with the Palæolithic age. It is perhaps only at the two ends that we can attempt anything like a relative chronological arrangement. The kitchen-midden implements may be the earliest, and these are at one end. Other implements seem to have been made solely, or perhaps mostly, after a knowledge of bronze had diffused itself, and that is the other end. For the rest, the only method of classification is by types, and to a consideration of these the rest of this chapter will be devoted.

Celts.—Those who desire to study the very curious etymology of this word must be referred to the pages of Sir John Evans' work ; for us here it will be sufficient to say that the term connotes an axe-head, whether of stone or bronze; and this being the most important and characteristic implement of both periods will, in each case, first receive attention. In the case of the stone implement there is a remarkable similarity of type in, one may fairly say, all parts of the world, for the stone axe-heads of America, Fiji, New Zealand, and Ireland, are many of them of almost identical pattern, and are clearly fashioned everywhere in response to a common demand. In the manufacture of these implements in this country there were evidently three stages. In the first a block of flint or other hard stone was so chipped as to approximate to the shape at which it was finally intended to arrive, blocked-out, so to speak. Suppose the workman to have been dissatisfied with his product, or weary of labour. The partly-finished tool is thrown away and never completed. When picked up by some latter-day archæologist such an object may be mistaken for a very rude implement or even for one of palæolithic type, for there is a considerable resemblance between the two types. Yet it may be an implement of quite a late date, archæologically speaking, but an implement which has never got beyond the blocking-out stage. In the second stage finer work is applied to the object under manufacture. Smaller pieces are removed from it by careful flaking, perhaps by pressure, until it begins to assume the shape and characteristics of the neolithic celt.

In Fig. 17 will be seen an example, from Cissbury, which has arrived at this stage. Probably it was a final stage in many cases, perhaps always during the earlier part of the Neolithic time. A man pressed for time, in a part of the country where food was hard to get and the strain of life severe, may well have contented himself with an instrument of this type, even though he may have been aware that by taking more time and expending more labour he could have put a handsome polish upon his tool, and perhaps made it a more useful weapon. At any rate, it seems highly probable that a good many of these rough (*i.e.* unpolished) neolithic celts were never intended to be polished, but are the finished object, not a mere stage in the manufacture. In the third stage we have two distinct divisions—the

FIG. 17. ROUGH STONE CELT
Cissbury (⅔)

celts polished only at the cutting edge, and the celts which are polished all over. The first class show a desire for utility alone, the second for beauty as well as for utility. An implement carefully sharpened at the edge and for some little distance behind is no doubt a better cutting tool and a more deadly weapon than one which is rough and blunt. But one cannot see that the polishing of the remainder of the tool, and particularly of that part of it which is to be hidden in the haft, is of any advantage, and if this way of looking at the question is the right one, then one must assign the additional and un-necessary polishing to the love of art, the æsthetic sense, which awakens in man when the excessive pressure of the struggle with nature has been to some small extent dimin-ished. The finished product in the shape of a neolithic celt is an axe-shaped implement, polished all over. As regards the finishing of the edges, there are two distinct forms. There is a type met with in Denmark, for example, with squared edges, and there is another type met with, for example, in Ireland, with rounded edges (see Figs. 18 and 19). Both these types are met with in England, and possibly it may turn out that they are typical of two different races. Besides the ordinary form of celt with which I have been dealing hitherto, there are one or two other types of which some mention must be made. The bored celt or stone hammer (see Fig. 83) seems to have been a very late implement, perhaps unknown until after the introduction of bronze. The utility of an implement into which a handle was inserted, as opposed to one which was inserted into a handle, may have been suggested to primitive man by some naturally perforated piece of stone. Judging by what we know of present-day primitive races, it does not seem to have been an idea easily arrived at, or perhaps one ought to say an idea which much com-mends itself to the savage mind. In the Pitt-Rivers

Museum at Oxford there is an ordinary iron axe-head with the aperture for the reception of the helve carefully hammered up. This axe-head was traded off to the inhabitants of New Guinea. The man into whose possession

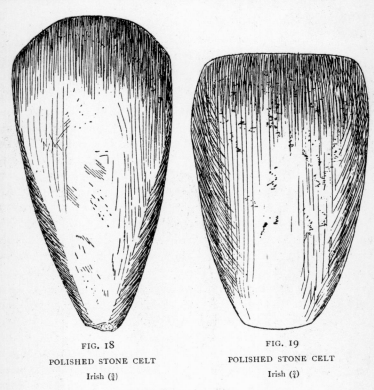

FIG. 18
POLISHED STONE CELT
Irish (¾)

FIG. 19
POLISHED STONE CELT
Irish (¾)

it came evidently thought that the hole in the head was some unaccountable bit of foolishness, for he first carefully hammered it up with the aid of a couple of stones, and then proceeded to fit his new weapon into a wooden haft, just as he had been accustomed to do with his old stone implement. Another very distinct type of celt is the chisel-shaped (Fig. 20), of which are found the three forms or stages belonging to the ordinary celt, the rough-chipped type, the type chipped at the cutting edge (Fig. 21 [1]), and the type polished all over (Fig. 21 [2]). It is useless to attempt to speculate as to the use of these implements, but they exist and form a distinct class. Another implement merging into the rough celt has been called a grubbing-tool, and is very likely, perhaps

FIG. 20. ROUGH CHISEL-
SHAPED CELT
Dewlish (¾)

2

FIG. 21
CHISEL-SHAPED CELTS
1. Rough, Newhaven,
Sussex. 2. Polished, Ex-
ceat, Sussex (¾)

1

amongst other purposes, to have served that end. One of these implements is shown in Fig. 22, and evidently might have been used to kill an animal or to injure a man, quite as well as to grub up some edible root. One cannot too carefully bear in mind that it is not always possible to imagine to ourselves the exact object for which a certain implement was made, and that many implements must have been intended to have been put to a variety of uses. Take the implement shown in Fig. 22. No one can handle it without feeling that it really is a most useful tool for

FIG. 22

FLINT INSTRUMENT—LARGE SCRAPER OR SMALL GRUBBING-TOOL

Tower Field, Suffolk (⅓)

a variety of purposes. The natural shape of the flint has been made use of to provide a boss which will prevent the hand from slipping, and the cutting edge has been carefully flaked. It is almost as hard to place an implement of this kind in any particular category as it is to say what it might have been intended for. The fact is that it is a kind of general utility implement, and like many others which we find, a real testimony to the ingenuity of the man who made it, an instrument available for digging, for scraping, doubtless for many other useful purposes.

Unlike the palæolithic celts, the neolithic celts were intended to be fitted with a handle. The commonest method of achieving this seems to have been by making a hole in one end of a long piece of wood, through which hole the axe-head was thrust, narrow end first. That this method was adopted there can be no shadow of doubt, for though in the bulk of cases the handles have disappeared from decay, yet in certain instances, such as that shown in Fig. 23, they remain to this day. Any person looking at this arrangement with a mechanical

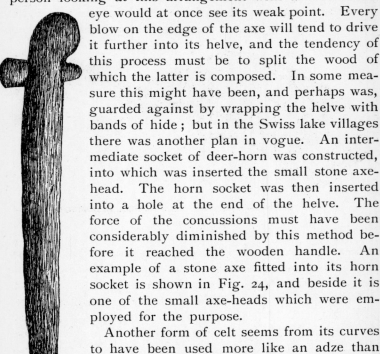

eye would at once see its weak point. Every blow on the edge of the axe will tend to drive it further into its helve, and the tendency of this process must be to split the wood of which the latter is composed. In some measure this might have been, and perhaps was, guarded against by wrapping the helve with bands of hide ; but in the Swiss lake villages there was another plan in vogue. An intermediate socket of deer-horn was constructed, into which was inserted the small stone axe-head. The horn socket was then inserted into a hole at the end of the helve. The force of the concussions must have been considerably diminished by this method before it reached the wooden handle. An example of a stone axe fitted into its horn socket is shown in Fig. 24, and beside it is one of the small axe-heads which were employed for the purpose.

Another form of celt seems from its curves to have been used more like an adze than an axe, and the fact that examples of this kind are found along the banks of the Thames may point to their having been used, as Dr. Haddon has shown, in New Guinea, for the hollowing of "dug-out" canoes. An implement of this type is shown in Fig. 25, and one can well imagine that it may have been fixed to a haft much as the New Guinea adzes now are. A bough is removed from a tree with a portion of the trunk adhering to it. Thus a **V**-shaped piece of

FIG. 23
HANDLED CELT
(Much reduced) Irish

wood is obtained, one limb being shorter than the other, and of course not attached to it at so acute an angle as that which is formed by the two limbs of the letter. To

FIG. 24. SMALL STONE CELTS

1. Set in reindeer-horn. 2. Separate stone Celt of same type
Swiss (⅔)

the shorter limb is lashed the stone head, secured in its place by bindings of cane and vegetable fibre, materials which would have probably been replaced in this country by strips of raw hide. The longer limb forms the handle.

Knives and knife-like implements naturally formed a large part of the output of the flint manufacturer, and

FIG. 25. FLINT ADZE (SIDE VIEW)
Thames at Chertsey (⅔)

were of the most diverse types.   No doubt in many instances sharp flakes without any further secondary work fulfilled admirably many of the purposes for which a knife is required.   The long, keen flakes of obsidian made in Mexico are said to have been used for sacrificial purposes, and are certainly sharp enough for cutting flesh.   But the

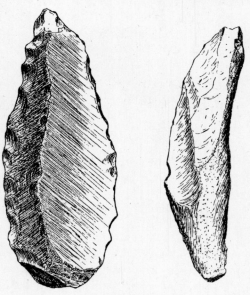

FIG. 26.   KNIVES (FLAT-BACKED AND TANGED)
Newhaven, Sussex (⅔ linear)

term knife as used here is applied to implements whose secondary working seems to have been undertaken for the purpose of turning them into tools useful for cutting and skinning purposes.   Two special varieties of these may first be dealt with—the broad-backed and the naturally handled.   The two types are shown in Fig. 26.   The example on the left of the figure belongs to the flat-backed variety.   Such an implement was made to hold in the

hand with the forefinger along the back. Take a tool of
this kind in the hand and shift it into different positions,
and it will at once be found how well adapted it is for the
purposes mentioned above. When held in this manner
the sharp cutting edge is downwards, and so arranged as
to be employed to the best advantage. A variety of this
type is the knife met with, at times in its handle, in the
Swiss lake villages. Here the back of the knife was
inserted into a piece of wood somewhat longer than itself,
and was secured in its socket by asphalt. The result was
a knife comparable, not to what we commonly call a knife
at the present day, but to the scrapers with which butchers
may be seen cleaning their blocks. The idea of this kind
of knife was the same as that of the broad-backed knife,
only that one was intended to have been held directly in
the hand whilst the other possessed a wooden handle.

The naturally handled knife is shown on the other side
of Fig. 26. This tool was evidently intended to be held by
its end and not by its back. Very possibly the end may
have been wrapped round with some vegetable fibre or
skin wrapping, for in Egyptian knives of this type that
method has been observed. Besides these two forms,
there is a distinct series of triangular knives, and there
are others not conforming to any of these types. In
further illustration of
the fact that primitive
man was quite ingeni-
ous enough to turn an
unusually shaped stone
to a particular use,
attention may be called
to Fig. 27. Here is an
implement made from
a piece of flint of a
curious shape. It was

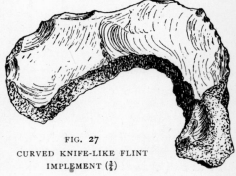

FIG. 27

CURVED KNIFE-LIKE FLINT
IMPLEMENT ($\frac{3}{4}$)

originally a **C**-shaped lump of stone. The hollow part makes a most excellent hold for the hand, whilst the sharply trimmed external edge, when the implement is thus grasped, is admirably adapted for the purpose of removing a skin from an animal.

Scrapers.—After skinning an animal it is necessary that the fat and other matters adhering to the inner aspect of the hide should be removed, if it is to be used for the purposes of a garment or a covering. For the purpose of this removal, neolithic man seems to have manufactured myriads of implements, which we call scrapers. In fact, these are, perhaps, the commonest of all the implements of the

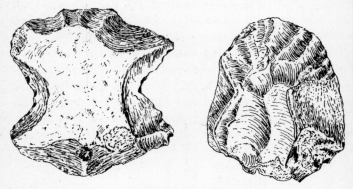

FIG. **28.** DOUBLE CONCAVE (L.) AND ORDINARY (R.) SCRAPERS
Icklingham (⅔)

period, omitting mere flakes which show us secondary working. Varying though they do in shape and size, there is a general similarity between all the convex scrapers, the type which we are now considering. Each has been made out of a flake detached from a block of flint. The surface of detachment, with its bulb of percussion, has been left untouched. At one end, or it may be at one side of the other, a bevelled edge has been produced by secondary flaking. This edge is generally semi-circular in its outline. Sometimes the scraper is long (Fig. 16), sometimes broad (Fig. 28 R.), the two forms sometimes called "finger" and "thumb" flints. In other cases (Figs. 29 and 30) the scraper is round and worked along the greater part of its border. These tiny "button" scrapers are rather a puzzle, for they are so small that it seems difficult to understand how they were employed.

FIG. 29. "BUTTON" SCRAPER
Lakenheath (1½)

It is obvious that they were of some use, otherwise they would not have been manufactured even in moderate numbers. Again, there is a form of scraper which is bevelled at the edge, the "side-scraper," a less common

FIG. 30. SCRAPERS
Mas d'Azil (⅓)

variety than the two first named. Some of the two commoner forms of scraper, being of considerable size, may probably have been used in the hand. Others may have been provided with a handle, for the Esquimaux, who use worked pieces of stone almost identical in character for the purpose of cleaning skins, insert these tools into bone handles. The *concave,* or as it is some-times called, "hollow" scraper (Figs. 28 L. and 31 L.), is

quite a different kind of tool.   Here the object was not to
clean the inside of a skin, but to shape off the roughnesses of a stick so as to convert it into an arrow-shaft—
for which reason this kind of scraper is sometimes called

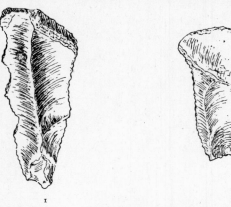

1   2

FIG. 31.   DOUBLE CONCAVE SCRAPER (L.) AND SAW (R.)
1. (L.) Lakenheath.   2. (R.) Icklingham (¾)

a "shaft-maker"—or to round an implement of bone—
a needle, or a borer—out of a splinter detached from the
bone of some large animal.   Hence in this class of
scraper we find one or more concave notches worked out
in the side of the stone or at its end; in fact, we come
back to the same implement with which we were con-
fronted amongst eoliths and palæoliths, but vastly better
worked.   Some of the most delicate of these implements
found in Ireland are so thin and fragile that one wonders
for what task they may have been designed.   Similar
examples have also occurred in Scotland.   Ireland provides a great variety of the ordinary kind of scraper, and
Mr. Knowles[1] has classified them as follows : (i.) side-
scrapers, the *râcloirs* of the French; (ii.) end-scrapers

[1] *Proc. Roy. Soc. Antiquaries of Ireland,* viii. 367.

divided into (*a*) those with circular curve, (*b*) those with elliptical curve, (*c*) oblique-ended, (*d*) broad or square-ended, (*e*) small-ended, (*f*) double-ended ; (iii.) toothed. Figs. 28 and 31 L. show two kinds of concave scrapers, both double, but in one case the two hollows are at opposite ends of the implements ; in the other they are side by side.

Arrow-heads of flint, and sometimes of other hard stones, are objects which always catch the eye of the public in a collection of neolithic implements, on account of the exquisite skill with which many of them have been turned out. These implements were not merely manu-

FIG. 32. FLINT ARROW-HEADS
Aberdeenshire (natural size)

factured during the Stone period, but found a market, if it may so be phrased, during the whole of the Bronze Age, and perhaps the Iron also. Hence we find them, as will be pointed out in a later chapter, in entombments belonging to the Metallic period. Several varieties have been recognised, which have been named leaf-shaped, lozenge-shaped, tanged, tanged and barbed, single-barbed and triangular. The characters of these types will be sufficiently indicated by the representations of them in Figs. 32–34. Stone arrow-heads are, of course, found in many parts of the world. Perhaps the most beautifully finished examples are those which were

G

manufactured in Oregon and in Prehistoric Japan. One
can hardly doubt that the prehistoric arrow-heads were
fastened on to their shafts in the same manner as that
which we know to have been adopted by savage races in

FIG. 33. ARROW-HEADS

1. Barbed, Aberdeenshire. 2. Tanged and barbed. 3. Single-tanged (¾)

modern times. The head is secured to the shaft by a
lashing of strips of hide, put on raw and then allowed to
dry in the sun. The result is a shrinkage which binds
head and shaft together wonderfully firmly. That such
a head with a strong bow behind it was capable of doing
effective work there is abundant evidence of the character afforded by Fig. 35.
This is a drawing of a
human lumbar vertebra, in
which is embedded a flint
arrow-head. As the missile
has penetrated the front of
the vertebra, it must have
pierced through the whole
of the abdomen, wall and
viscera, before reaching the
vertebral column in which
it has so firmly fixed itself.

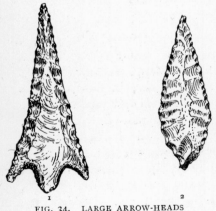

FIG. 34. LARGE ARROW-HEADS
1. Irish. 2. Thames at Hammersmith (¾)

Saws made of flint are recognisable by their carefully serrated edge (see Fig. 31 R.). These also seem to have been made after the age of metal had commenced. Canon Greenwell found seventy-nine of these implements in one barrow opened by himself.[1] *Borers, drills, punches,* and *fabricators,* need no very lengthy nor precise description, since their purposes are fairly well indicated by their names, and their appearances may be learnt from Fig. 36. With regard, however, to the last-named variety of objects, it ought perhaps

FIG. 35. FLINT ARROW-HEAD EMBEDDED IN HUMAN LUMBAR VERTEBRA
Grotte de la Tourrasse

to be stated that they are supposed to have been used for the purpose of making the finer flaking on neolithic implements (see p. 36). Fig. 36 is a good example of this class.

FIG. 36. BORER (L.) AND FABRICATOR (R.)
Avebury (½)

[1] *British Barrows,* p. 262.

Pigmy Implements (Fig. 37) form an interesting class which has lately attracted a good deal of attention. The Rev. R. A. Gatty[1] has described a number of varieties, and from this paper and from letters, which he has been good enough to send me, I extract the following points on this class of implements. The true pigmy implements met with on the Vindhya Hills, in India, and in England and elsewhere, seem to fall into four classes, all of which are exemplified in Fig. 37. These with the sizes of the smallest examples are as follows—

FIG. 37. PIGMY IMPLEMENTS
Top line, Scunthorpe; middle line, Vindhya Hills, India; lower line, Lakenheath (⅓)

Smallest Crescent	India $\frac{8}{16}$ in.	Scunthorpe	$\frac{6}{16}$ in.
Scalene	,, $\frac{10}{16}$,,	,,	$\frac{3}{16}$,,
Rounded and pointed	,, $\frac{10}{16}$,,	,,	$\frac{4}{16}$,,
Rhomboidal	,, $\frac{8}{16}$,,	,,	$\frac{6}{16}$,,

The scalene variety is the same as that called "trapéze" by M. de Pierpont, who has found them in Belgium. Besides these genuine pigmies there are also small implements such as the tiny arrow-head shown in Fig. 37 (top line, centre object) and in addition to this variety Mr. Gatty has also found tiny scrapers, convex and concave, knives, chisels, and points which may have been used for tipping blow darts. So small are some of these that sixty-four

[1] *Man,* Feb., 1902.

circular scrapers have been found which taken together weighed less than half an ounce. Of the so-called "Indian" varieties the remarkable point is that the forms in England and the forms in India are identical, a fact which, some have thought, points to a communication between these countries at a very early period. Others, on the contrary, only see in the resemblance a common result of a common need. The cutting edges show no secondary work, but the backs have in all instances been carefully retouched. The localities in which they have so far been found are not numerous in this country, but where they have been discovered they seem to exist in great numbers, and if accompanied by other implements—they are often found quite by themselves—then these implements seem to belong rather to early than late types of neolithic manufacture. Many suggestions have been put forward as to the purpose for which they were constructed. It is thought that they may have been used for tattooing, as barbs for arrows or harpoons, for arming fish-gigs, and for other purposes. This is a point which has not yet been cleared up, and perhaps never may be cleared up, but there can be no doubt that the group is a genuine and very interesting class of stone implements. In England Mr. Gatty has found these little tools in North Lincolnshire (Scunthorpe) on sand-dunes, and in the valley of the Don, near Bradfield. Dr. Colley March has found them on the Pennine Range, at an altitude of 1,300 feet. They have also been found at Lakenheath. As to the identity of all these and their belonging to the so-called Indian classes there is no doubt. Implements of the same kind, but perhaps belonging to the class of small tools, not the Indian varieties, have also been described from a kitchen-midden near Hastings, and from sand-dunes in Suffolk. Amongst the very numerous flint implements found at the Glenluce Sands, Wigtonshire, and at the

Culbin Sands, Elgin, there are many tiny implements, borers, scrapers, etc., but only a few of these—and perhaps these accidentally—agree in shape with the Indian forms. In France they have been discovered at Bruniquel and at Garanciéres (Seine et Loire), and have been divided by M. Thieullen into triangular or amygdaloid, concave crescentic, bevelled beak, cocked hat, disk, slice of melon, knife, piercer, diamond, cupola, and keel shapes. If the classification suggested above into Indian and other varieties be adhered to, it would appear that the French forms embrace both categories.

Instances of the overlapping of the latter Stone with the Bronze period have already been given in connection with the subject of bored-axes, arrow-heads, and saws, and a few more observations must now be made on the same point. Professor Ridgeway[1] has pointed out that in the Museum of the Royal Irish Academy there are stone axes which undoubtedly exhibit in the shape of their faces the influence of those made of metal, and he suggests that they may have been the property of poor men who could not afford the more expensive metallic article. Instances of the same kind are to be seen elsewhere, and particularly in the so-called ceremonial axes, made for show or for ritual purposes, and not for use. Some of these, which have been found in Denmark, are ornamented with raised lines, just like those on the bronze celts which they imitate. They are provided at one end, not at the centre, with a small hole, capable of receiving quite a thin stick. These were clearly made purely for show, and belong to the Bronze, or, perhaps, even to the early Iron Age. In other cases they are made of a stone so soft as to prove that no serious use was contemplated when they were manufactured. **Bracers** are flat pieces of stone, *e.g.* chlorite, pierced with two small holes at either end, and

---

[1] *Early Age of Greece.*

are supposed to have been worn on the wrist to shield
it against injury from the bow-string when shooting
arrows. These objects may belong to the Neolithic as well
as to the Metallic age. **Spindle-whorls,** sometimes called
Pixies' grindstones, used for winding the thread in the
operations of spinning (see Fig. 38), are very common
objects, belonging not merely, if at all, to the Stone Age.

FIG. 38. SPINDLE WHORLS ($\frac{1}{2}$)

Some allusion should be made to the fact that in some
districts many varieties of implements may be found,
whilst in others the range of examples is much more
limited. This has already been exemplified in the case of
the pigmy implements, generally found by themselves,
except at Lakenheath, a district where every archæological
find, from palæoliths to objects belonging to the Anglo-
Saxon period, has been made. On the Cotswolds, as
Canon Greenwell points out, few, if any, celts have been
found, though many arrow-heads have been picked up.
On the other hand, in Kent and Sussex, and, generally
speaking, in the district south of the Thames, arrow-heads
are rare, whilst celts are met with, at least in places, in
considerable numbers.

CHAPTER V

THE METALLIC AGE—COPPER—BRONZE

THE Italian archæologists describe, under the name of the Æneolithic period, an epoch when copper, in a pure and unalloyed condition, and stone were the materials out of which the implements of the time were manufactured. That such a stage was passed through, at least, in some parts of the world, there seems little reason to doubt, though it was probably not a universal experience. In his account of interments by cremation in Derbyshire, Mr. Jewitt[1] states, "In some instances I have found the lead ore, which occurs in veins in the limestone formation of Derbyshire, so completely smelted with the heat that it has run into the crevices among the soil and loose stones, and looks, when dug out, precisely like straggling roots of trees." He suggests that the discovery of lead may be traced to this accident, and one may at least offer the conjecture that the first acquaintance of man with copper may have come about in some similar manner. At any rate, as Mr. Gowland has pointed out,[2] the first ores found by man would be those off the surface of the ground or in the beds of streams. These would be mostly carbonates or oxides of the metal, even if at deeper layers they presented themselves as sulphides. It seems probable that copper may have been discovered

---

[1] *Grave-mounds and their Contents*, p. 31.
[2] *Archæologia*, lvi. 267.

independently in many different places and at different dates, though, no doubt, there were instances in which the knowledge of the metal was introduced to people unacquainted with it by persons of another district. On the date of the making of such a discovery, and on the character of the ore hit upon, hang several consequences. In the first place, the earlier the discovery of the metal the shorter the Stone Age in the district. Myres[1] thinks that Cyprus was the first place in the Mediterranean area in which copper was worked. Hence he points out that the Stone Age there was apparently very short, and that the Copper Age was contemporary with a large part of that of stone elsewhere. The copper Cypriote celts are, as he shows, plain, unflanged, and of shapes like those of stone, shapes few and simple, and showing little change of form throughout the series. Then, again, the occurrence or non-occurrence of a copper age seems to depend upon the character of the ore found in any given district. If a pure ore, the manufacture of objects in unmixed copper may be expected to have taken place before bronze makes its appearance. But if the ore is one in which copper exists together with some other metal capable of forming a bronze with it, then the stage of pure copper implements may be entirely absent. In Cyprus and Crete the metal is found pure, hence the first celts there are of copper, which can be hardened by hammering in an unalloyed condition. A copper age also existed in Spain,[2] and in America[3] many objects of wrought copper have been found, the Lake Superior copper mines in the States of Wisconsin and Michigan appearing to have been the centre of manufacture. In the neighbourhood of Lake Superior cutting implements of a form similar to those

[1] *Journal Anthrop. Inst.,* xxvii. 171.
[2] *Siret. L'Anthropologie,* iii. 385.
[3] Wilson, *Prehistoric Art,* 499.

of stone were made, though the author just quoted from does not lay claim to the existence of a distinct period of copper in America.

Coming to our own countries, there certainly is a distinct series of copper celts in Ireland, as has been proved by Coffey,[1] who has, moreover, shown that there is good reason for believing that they are the earliest forms, and not produced in a given district because in that district there was a lack of tin or other metal suitable for forming a hard alloy. At one end of the series, he says, are rude and heavy forms, which look backward to the stone axe, at the other forms which approach more and more closely the early bronze celts. England and Scotland, on the other hand, have been thought to show little evidence of any such stage. It has, in fact, been asserted that no such thing as a pure copper implement has been found in this country. Coffey, however, calls attention to four specimens discovered in England and the same number in Scotland. Other specimens found in barrows have turned out to be copper, though formerly thought to be bronze, but it must be admitted that so far the examples in this island proved to be pure copper are rare. Gowland has shown that the reason of this is that in England copper occurs with tin, just as in Hungary it occurs with antimony, either of which metals can be used to make a hard alloy with it. Hence the absence of a pure copper age in those countries. From this difference in the ores and resulting bronzes it has also been claimed that the discovery of the metal was made independently in a number of different countries. On the other hand, Sergi[2] claims that the knowledge originated in Cyprus and thence spread to a number of the countries around the Mediterranean. "In 1895," he

---

[1] *Journ. Anth. Inst.,* ii. 206 ; iv. 265.
[2] *Mediterranean Race,* p. 278.

writes, "I had already written that the origin of the use of metals in the Mediterranean may be found in Cyprus, the island of copper; thence its use was diffused through other Mediterranean regions, and through the Black Sea, and thence probably by the Danube into Hungary. To-day the fact that Cyprus was the centre of diffusion of copper and then of bronze throughout the Mediterranean and Europe generally, seems confirmed by new discoveries, and by explorers like Ohnefalsch-Richter and Myres, who have been able to show the contemporaneous existence, at least in part, of the Copper Age in Cyprus with the late Neolithic period in other regions; as likewise it seems to be shown that the primitive types of axes came from this island, and were diffused throughout the Mediterranean and Europe."

Montelius has divided the Bronze Age into five periods,[1] the *first* of which is characterised by implements made of pure copper or of copper with a very small admixture of tin. His classification depends upon the facts as they concern France, and his first period is estimated to have lasted from about 2000 to 1850 B.C. The celts are of types copied from those of stone; the sword is unknown; this was the period of dolmens and *allées couvertes*, and that to which a great many of the Swiss lake villages may be attributed.

The *second* period, lasting from 1850 to 1550 B.C., is one in which the bronze often contains as much as 10 per cent. of tin. The celts have straight borders, generally very slightly raised; triangular daggers were made, but no true swords; burial, as in the first period, was by inhumation.

The *third* period, 1550 to 1300 B.C., was characterised by celts with raised edges, palstaves, and swords. Inhumation and cremation were both practised.

[1] *L'Anthropologie*, xii. 609.

The *fourth* period lasted from 1300 to 1050 B.C., and the *fifth* from 1050 to 850 B.C., when the Early Iron Age may be said to have commenced. During these two periods the skill of artificers in bronze greatly increased, and many fine objects were constructed. The swords with horns to their handles and oval pommels were made during the latter part of this time. It must, of course, be borne in mind that any attempt to assign exact dates to such divisions as these can only be of a highly tentative character.

Objects of bronze have been found as isolated discoveries, as parts of the funeral gifts laid up with the remains of the dead in entombments, and in hoards, of which a few words must now be said. A hoard is a collection of bronze implements, with or without raw material, and a list of the principal discoveries of this class in England is appended to this chapter. Some of these hoards may have been temple-treasure, perhaps votive offerings, like the great collection discovered in Bologna in 1871. Here 14,800 bronze objects were brought to light in an earthenware vase. With them were also a few scraps of iron, showing, as did also the character of the bronze implements, amongst which were flanged, socketed, stopped, and looped celts, an axe with a transverse hole for its handle, chisels, gouges, horse-bits, fibulæ, etc., that the collection belonged to quite the end of the bronze period, perhaps about 1000 B.C. No hoards which can reasonably be assigned to this class seem to have been discovered in this country.

A second class of hoard was that secreted by some private person when obliged to leave his ordinary place of habitation for a time. Such temporary *caches* must often have been resorted to, and, no doubt, in many cases, on the return of the owner, the implements were disinterred and once more put to use. But in other cases

the hoard was never recovered by its original owner, and
has lain undisturbed and undiscovered to our own time.
A third group may be looked upon as the stock-in-trade
of a dealer, for the objects of which such hoards consist
are numerous, ready for use, and sometimes comprise a
number of implements of exactly similar size and shape.
The fourth class of hoard is that of the bronze-caster
himself, and consists of rough lumps of more or less pure
copper, worn-out implements ready to be remelted, and
sometimes the moulds in which the implements were to
be cast.

Of the private hoard, that discovered a few years ago
at Westbury-on-Trym [1] may be taken as an example.
This small collection, consisting of three celts and a very
remarkable bronze chisel, was found in the bank of the
Trym in a place called Coombe Dingle, not far from
which are remains of earthworks and other traces of an
early occupation. A hole in the bank of a stream is the
sort of place which would naturally be selected as a
temporary hiding-place. Of the manufacturer's stock-in-
trade class numerous examples might be given. At
Clohars-Carnoet in Finistere 203 bronze celts were found
together. Quite recently at Cwmdugold, near Machyn-
lleth, eighteen celts were found of three different sizes,
clearly an example of the same kind. Then there is the
great Dowris hoard, part of which is now in the British
Museum. This collection, apparently from the nature of
some of the objects comprised in it, belonging to a late
part of the period, contained trumpets, socketed celts,
tanged knives, razors, bells, a sword, spear-heads, and
other articles. Of the fourth class I may mention an example now in the Museum of the University of Birmingham. This example came from Hanwell in Middlesex,
and consists of about thirty pounds weight of nearly pure

[1] *Proc. Soc. Ant.*, xviii. 236.

copper.   The exact analysis, which I owe to the kindness of my colleague, Professor Turner, shows the following constituents in addition to copper :—

Sulphur	.	.	0·863 per cent.
Lead	.	.	0·079 ,,
Iron	.	.	0·038 ,,

Tin, antimony, zinc, and nickel, were tested for, but not found.   With the rough masses of which this part of the hoard was made up was a single imperfect socketed and ringed celt.   This appears to consist of bronze, but has not been assayed.

In the case of hoards of this class the rough masses of metal almost always consist of pure, or nearly pure, copper.   The tin which was to have been mixed with it was generally in the condition of cassiterite, which has been overlooked by the discoverers.

It is now time to give some description of the more important objects made in bronze, and in this chapter attention will mainly be paid to such examples as may be strictly confined to the bronze period proper.   Some other objects will find a place at a later period in connection with the account which will be given of the Early Iron Age and its manufactures.

Celts.—As in the case of neolithic implements, so here the most prominent and characteristic object is the axe-head or celt, of which several distinct varieties exist.

Flat Celts.—Axe-heads resembling in many particulars those of stone, and possessing neither flanged edges nor sockets for the reception of a haft, are generally considered to have been the earliest efforts at casting of the bronze period, and the copper celts already alluded to conform to this type.   Apart from the fact that man would be most

likely to make the new implement after the type of that
with which he was familiar, the difficulties presented in
the casting of such a tool would be much less than those
connected with a flanged or socketed implement.   In
fact, the simple flat celt
could be cast in a one-
sided mould either of
stone or of sand, and its
roughnesses afterwards
diminished by hammer-
ing or rubbing down.
In Fig. 39 will be seen
an example of this kind
of implement, an imple-
ment attached to its
handle in the same man-
ner as the neolithic celt,
that is, by being forced
through a hole in it.   It
will be noticed that the
cutting edge of this im-
plement is considerably
expanded. This is a char-
acteristic observable in a
very large number of

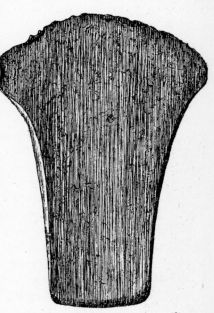

FIG. 39.   FLAT BRONZE CELT ($\frac{2}{3}$)

these objects, and may be looked upon as an early
departure from the stone type with straight sides.   These
celts are sometimes ornamented with patterns of a geometrical character, not effected in the casting, but produced by the action of a punch.

Flanged Celts.—The shape here does not differ in any
important respect from that of the flat celt with expanded
end, but there is a flange along each side of the implement, sometimes raised by hammering, sometimes pro-

duced in the casting. These are also at times ornamented with geometrical patterns not only on the faces, but on the flanges also. Sometimes there is a stop-ridge half-way down the head extending transversely between the two flanges. This seems to be a stage in the development of the next form.

Palstaves.—Sir John Evans limits the use of this term to two classes of implements. (i.) Winged celts with the wings hammered over so as to form what may be called external sockets to the blade. This kind of tool is rare in England, but Fig. 41 gives an example from Italy. The

idea of hammering over the edges is the same as that applied to the socketing of garden rakes and other tools at the present day, and may be seen applied also to a bronze arrow-head in the British Museum, the difference being that in the case of the last-mentioned objects the socket is single, whilst in that of the celt it is divided into two parts, one on either side of the blade. (ii.) Winged celts, with the portion of the blade which lies between the side flanges and above the stop thinner than that which is below. This is the common implement known by the name of palstave, and shown in Fig. 40. Sometimes it has a ring on one side for the purpose of enabling it to be lashed to the handle, and thus more securely fixed in position. The palstave is often ornamented with raised patterns of geometrical character produced in the casting. It may have been fixed at right angles to the handle by attachment to a portion of the haft placed in respect to the rest, as the handle of a walk-

FIG. 40
BRONZE PALSTAVE
Brittany (½)

ing-stick is to the stick itself. In this case the palstaff would have acted rather as an adze than an axe. Or it may have been fixed into the end of a straight stick, when it would assume the position occupied by the blade of a hoe or spade. It will be observed that in either case a portion of the blade was actually embedded in the handle, instead of the handle being embedded in it. In the first group the handle was embedded in the blade, but a part of the blade was also embedded in the handle. This form seems to have led up, as indeed it may easily have done, to the next class.

Socketed Celts.—Implements with a hollow recess for the reception of the handle, of which Fig. 42 is an example. That these are derived from the class last dealt with is shown by the facts that (*a*) a socketed celt has been found with its socket divided into two portions by a central septum, an obvious proof of descent from the winged celt with its wings hammered over, and (*b*) by the fact that the outside of the sockets of socketed celts are not unfrequently decorated

FIG. 41.
PALSTAVE, BRONZE
Italian (⅓)

FIG. 42. LOOPED AND SOCK-
ETED BRONZE CELT
Irish (¾)

H

with curved lines obviously representing the hammered-over wings of the earlier pattern (see Fig. 52 [4] and [10]). Such skeuomorphs, or forms of ornament demonstrably due to structure, afford valuable evidence of the derivation of the socketed celt, and may be compared with the linear and pellet ornamentation on the surface of the blades of palstaves, perhaps the skeuomorphs of a former method of attaching the blade to the handle by cords [1] (see Fig. 52 [7] and [10]). The socketed celt is met with under various shapes, may have a ring at the side, as in Fig. 42, and may be ornamented, indeed often is ornamented, around its neck with rings, perhaps the skeuomorphs of lashings, or upon its surface with linear and other raised patterns (see Fig. 52 [4] [7] [10]). Ornament produced by punches or hammers is almost entirely wanting, no doubt because the application of such kind of ornament to a hollow implement was difficult, if not inadvisable.

Miniature and Ceremonial Celts.—In the case of the neolithic celts, it was noted that small implements, evidently unintended for actual use, have from time to time been found, and the same is true of the objects of the later age with which we are now concerned. Celts made of bronze, but so thin as never to have been of any actual use, have been found by Mr. Hogarth in his excavations in the Dictyaean Cave in Crete. They have also been found at Dodona, at Hallstadt, and in Mexico. In some of these situations it seems unreasonable to doubt that their purpose was votive, but they may have been made, at times, for children's toys, or perhaps even for use as money, for which purpose similar objects are now in vogue on the West Coast of Africa.

Daggers.—The dagger, which, very probably, also served

---

[1] *Cf.* Haddon, *Evolution in Art*, p. 75 *et seq.*

the purposes of a knife, was an instrument early constructed after man had arrived at a knowledge of the use of bronze. Two distinct classes of dagger can be distinguished according to the manner in which the blade was attached to its handle, by tang or by rivets ; the latter appearing to be the more primitive implement. Of these, the earlier had thin flat blades, and were more or less triangular in shape, whilst later weapons were strengthened by a strong mid-rib, and sometimes presented some measure of ornamentation on the blade. Fig. 43 shows one of these daggers still attached to its original handle, an extremely rare example. The blade measures seven and a half inches, and the handle four. The latter overlaps the former by about an inch, and is secured to it by two bronze rivets about three-quarters of an inch in length. The handle is of horn. This object was found between nine and ten feet from the surface in a peat-bog near Castleisland in the County of Kerry.[1] Horn seems to have been a common material for the construction of the handle, and amongst other instances of its use, one may be quoted from Jewitt,[2] where the portion of the blade of a bronze dagger, found in a tumulus, presented near the rivet holes obvious signs of the grain of the horn which had originally been attached to it. Sometimes the handle was of bone or wood, like one described by Dr. Thurnam, which was held together by thirty rivets of bronze, and strengthened at the end by an oblong bone pommel fastened with two pegs. It was decorated by dots incised in the surface of the wood, forming a

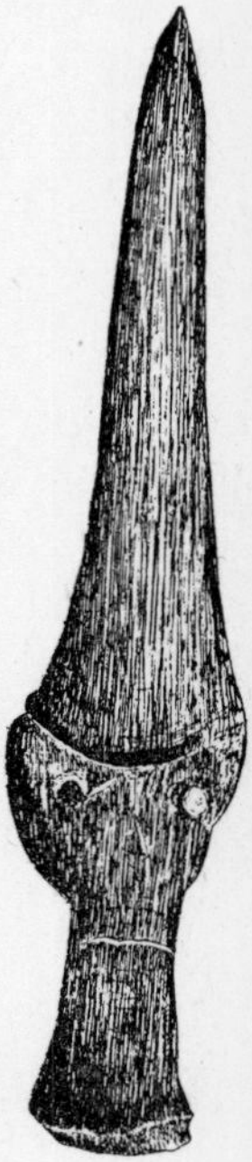

FIG. 43
BRONZE DAGGER
WITH HANDLE
Irish (¼)

---

[1] *Proc. Roy. Soc. Antiqs. Ireland,* vii. 423.
[2] *Grave-mounds and their Contents,* 24.

border of double lines and circles between the heads of the rivets. A still more elaborate handle, on which a Vandyke pattern was formed by thousands of small gold rivets, each with a head no larger than that of an ordinary pin, was described by Hoare.[1] Again, in some cases the hilt was made of bronze, and a few examples of this kind have been discovered in Ireland. Longer rapier-blade daggers have also been discovered. These, being of a later date than the shorter dagger, seem to form a kind of transition between it and the sword. Chapes or terminals to scabbards which may have belonged to daggers or to swords have been discovered, and in at least one case a complete dagger-sheath has come to light. This was found at Pilling Moss, measured eleven and a half by one and three-quarter inches, and had a bronze loop at the back through which a strap could be passed. Short scabbards like this may sometimes have been for swords, the upper portion having been constructed of wood, but the loop in this case seems to prove that we have the whole of the object, and that it was intended for a dagger and not for the longer implement.

Swords.—The leaf-shaped sword was certainly a weapon of the bronze period, though a late, rather than an early, specimen of work in that metal. There was a later bronze sword-blade which appears to have belonged to the Late Celtic period, but this was not leaf-shaped, but slightly tapering and with edges almost straight nearly to the point. The hilt was sometimes of bronze, and sometimes of plates of wood, or horn, or bone, riveted on to the metal. Those with hilts of bronze are rare in this country.

Spear-heads.—All the examples of this class, see Fig. 44, which have been found in this country, and which are

---

[1] *Ancient Wilts*, i. 202.

clearly recognisable as spear-heads, are cored, and have been made by persons thoroughly expert in the art of casting metal. Hence one may assume that they do not belong to the earlier part of the bronze period. Sir John Evans divides them into five classes, namely: (i.) Those which are simple and leaf-shaped, either long and narrow, or broad, and have holes in the socket through which to pass the rivets to fix them to the shaft. (ii.) Those which are looped, and have eyes on each side of the socket below, and on the same plane with the blade. Those are generally of the long, narrow, straight-edged kind. (iii.) Those with loops in the angles between the edge of the blade and the socket. (iv.) Those with side apertures and perforations through the blade. (v.) Those in which the base of each side of the blade projects at right angles to the socket, or is prolonged downwards so as to form barbs. In some cases the sockets of these weapons have been elaborately decorated with the chevron and other hatchings so characteristic of the art of the bronze period.

Other articles.—A host of other objects, made of bronze, are to be seen in museums of prehistoric archæology, and accounts of them may be sought for in the great work of Sir John Evans. It will only be possible here to enumerate a few of these, whilst some others, of the nature of personal ornaments, will be dealt with in a later chapter. Chisels, gouges, and saws are amongst the tools of this material; the latter class, however, being very rare, for up to 1885 only five

FIG. 44. BRONZE
SPEAR-HEAD
The Wrekin (½)

examples had come to light in this country.[1]   Mace-
heads, halberds, and sickles (see Fig. 45), trumpets,
bells, and shields may also be mentioned.   Allusion has
already been made to the fact that bronze arrow-heads

FIG. 45.   BRONZE SICKLE
Swiss Lake Village (⅔)

are of rare occurrence in this country.   This seems to be
the rule in all countries north of the Alps, where such
arrow-heads as have been found of this material appear
to belong to the late Celtic rather than to the bronze
period.   In Spain, metal arrow-heads seem to have been
in vogue from a very early period.   These range from
simple bars of copper, flattened and sharpened at one
end, to lozenge-shaped and triangular, tanged, and
tanged and barbed.   Montelius[2] states that many bronze
arrow-heads have been found in Egypt.   These may be
tanged, or barbed, or both, and some of them are
socketed, the socket being formed by the folding over of
the lower part of the blade.   An example of an arrow-
head of this kind found in France is in the British
Museum.   There is also found in Egypt a three-edged,
socketed, bayonet type, which is met with not only in
that country, but also in Arabia and in Sicily.

For a full account of the methods pursued in the casting
of the objects dealt with in this chapter, the reader must

[1] *Proc. Soc. Antiqs.*, xi. 12.   [2] *L'Anthropologie*, i. 44.

be referred to Sir John Evans' pages. Here it will not be possible to do more than to quote from them the summary given as to the various modes employed. Objects were cast—

(i.) In a single mould formed of loam, sand, stone, or metal, the upper surface of the casting exhibiting the flat surface of the molten metal, which was left open to the air. In the case of loam or sand castings, a pattern or model would be used, which might be an object already in use, or made in the desired form in wood or other soft substance.

(ii.) In double moulds of similar materials. The castings produced in this manner when in unfinished condition show the joints of the moulds (this may be noticed in Fig. 40). When sand was employed a frame or flask of some kind must have been used to retain the material in place when the upper half of the mould was lifted off the pattern. The loam moulds were probably burnt hard before being used. In many cases cores for producing hollows in the casting were employed in conjunction with these moulds.

(iii.) In what may be called solid moulds. For this process the model was made of wax, wood, or some combustible material, which was encased in a mass of loam, possibly mixed with cow-dung or vegetable matter, which on exposure to heat left the loam or clay in a porous condition. This exposure to fire also burnt out the wax or wood model and left a cavity for the reception of the metal, which was probably poured in while the mould was still hot.

The following list contains the hoards of bronze implements which have been found in this country, so far as they are within my knowledge. For the bulk of these I am indebted to the pages of Sir John Evans' work, and for the references to these its pages must be consulted.

The remainder have the references added to them. The hoards are arranged not according to their character, as has been done in the work just alluded to, but according to the plan pursued in this book, under the counties in which they have been found.

BEDFORD.—Wymington.

BERKSHIRE—
Hagbourn Hill.
Yattendon.

Wallingford.

CAMBRIDGESHIRE—
Burwell Fen.
Fulbourn Common.
Melbourn.
Meldreth.
Reach Fen.

Whittlesea.
Wicken Fen.
Wilburton Fen (*Proc. Soc. Ant.*, 1882, 112).

CHESHIRE.—Broxton.

CORNWALL—
Kenidjack Cliff.
Lanant.

Mawgan.
St. Hilary.

DEVONSHIRE—
Bloody Pool, South Brent.

Plymstock (Worth).

DORSETSHIRE.—Weymouth.

DURHAM—
Heathery Burn Cave.

Stanhope.

ESSEX—
Chrishall.
Greys, Thurrock (*Proc. Soc. Ant.*, xvi. 327).
Hatfield, Broad Oak (*id.* 96).
High Roding.
Panfield.

Romford.
Shoebury (*Proc. Soc. Ant.*, xiv. 174).
South Church, near Southend (*id.* xvi. 98).

GLOUCESTERSHIRE.—Westbury-on-Trym (*Proc. Soc. Ant.*, xviii. 237).

HAMPSHIRE—
Arreton Down, Isle of Wight.
Blackmoor.
Clothall.

Pear Tree, near Southampton (*Proc. Soc. Ant.*, xvii. 129).
Woolmer, New Forest.

HEREFORD.—Broadward.

HERTFORDSHIRE—
Cumberlow, Baldock.
Danesbury, Welwyn.

Westwick Row, Hemel Hempsted.

KENT—
Allhallows, Hoo.
Ebbsfleet, Isle of Thanet (*Proc. Soc. Ant.*, xiv. 309).
Haynes Hill, Saltwood.
Hundred of Hoo.

Isle Harty, Sheppey.
Marden.
Rochester.
Sittingbourne.

LANCASHIRE.—Winmarleigh, Garstang.

LEICESTERSHIRE.—Beacon Hill, Charnwood Forest.

LINCOLNSHIRE—
Flixborough.
Haxey.

Nettleham.
West Halton.

MIDDLESEX—
Bromley-by-Bow (*Proc. Soc. Ant.*, xix. 13).
Hanwell (Univ. Birm. Museum).

Hounslow.
Kemington.
Southall (*Proc. Soc. Ant.*, xvi. 327).

NORFOLK—
Carlton Rode.
Eaton.
Kelsdon Hall.

Reepham.
Stibbard, near Fakenham.
Stoke Ferry.

NORTHUMBERLAND—
Thrunton Farm, Whittingham.

Wallington, Alnwick Castle.

NOTTINGHAMSHIRE—
Newark (near).

Nottingham.

OXFORDSHIRE.—Burgesses' Meadow.

SHROPSHIRE—

Battlefield, near Shrewsbury.
Ebnall, near Oswestry.

Little Wenlock.
Porkington, near Oswestry.
Wrekin.

SOMERSET—

Edington, Burtle.
Heath House, Wedmore.
Quantock Hills.
Sherford, Taunton.

Taunton.
West Buckland.
Wick Park, Stogursey.

STAFFORDSHIRE.—Greensborough Farm, Shenstone.

SUFFOLK—

Exning.
Felixstowe (*Proc. Soc. Ant.*, xi. 8).

Martlesham.
Postlingford Hall, Clare.
Thorndon.

SURREY—

Beddington.
Beddlestead (*Proc. Soc. Ant.*, xviii. 285).
Farley Heath.

Kingston Hill.
Wandle River.
Wickham Park, Croydon.

SUSSEX—

Beachy Head, Eastbourne.
Hollingbury Hill, Brighton.

Wilmington.
Worthing.

WESTMORLAND.—Ambleside.

YORKSHIRE—

Bilton.
Cleveland.
Earsley Common.

Hotham Carr.
Roseberry Topping.
Weston.

CHAPTER VI

BONE IMPLEMENTS—ENGRAVINGS, CARVINGS, AND ART OF PRIMITIVE MAN—-ORNAMENTS

IMPLEMENTS OF BONE

SAVE where they are found with other undisturbed and undoubted relics of the period, there is often a difficulty in deciding whether a bone implement belongs to an early or a comparatively recent period. Take, for example, the pointed implements, made from a limb bone of some large animal, which are found along the Thames, and of which many have been discovered in the neighbourhood of Southwark Bridge. These might be a kind of spear-head of an early date, or they may, perhaps, even still more likely, be the points for the ends of the poles with which, in the Middle Ages, the skater propelled himself, on his bone skates, along the ice. But where implements have been found in caves mixed up with other objects of whose period there can be no doubt, as is the case in many instances, then we may at once accept them as belonging to that period. It is generally held as a fairly well-established fact that work in bone did not begin until a somewhat late period of the Palæolithic age, or at least that if it did, we have no relics left of an earlier date, which would be a somewhat strange thing had the industry really existed. Thieullen has, however, recently found at Chelles some worked pieces of bone which he believes to belong to the same very early

part of the Palæolithic age as the stone implements discovered in the same place. If this observation be corrobo-
rated, then we shall be obliged to assign an earlier date
for the known commencement of work in bone than has
hitherto been allowed. But at least this may be said, that
there is no evidence of any considerable amount of work
in bone until the period called by Mortillet the Magdalenian and described in Fischer's classification (p. 8)
as Papalian, from the Grotto du Pape at Bassempouy,
where characteristic objects in bone have been found.
As his classification chiefly depends upon the character
of the art, it will be dealt with more fully in the next
section of this chapter. Meantime, at this point it will
be convenient to consider some of the implements made
in bone and horn during this and the periods which succeeded it.

Harpoons.— Harpoons, or, as they are also called,
javelin-heads, form a characteristic series of objects of
the Magdalenian period in France, and have been found
also in British caves, such as Kent's Hole. But there
is a larger series available in France, and we are indebted
to the labours of M. Piette thereon for our knowledge
of the varieties and sequence of these objects.[1] The characteristic Magdalenian harpoon, he thinks, consisted of
two parts—a wooden shaft, and a head made of reindeer
or stag horn, provided with barbs on one or both sides,
which was attached to the shaft by a cord. During the
first, or equidian, portion of the Magdalenian period the
climate was dry and cold, there was no great amount
of water about, and, therefore, no great demand for
harpoons ; nevertheless, one fragment of what was probably a harpoon was found in the stratum belonging to
this date at Mas d'Azil. At a later date, when the rein-

[1] *L'Anthropologie,* vi. 283.

deer had become the prominent animal in the fauna, the climate was damper, and many harpoons appear. At first the butt-end of these was pointed, but this was open to the inconvenience that the cord attaching the head to the shaft could easily slip off. So the end was truncated, and still later a flange was made on either side of the shaft a short distance above the base, so as to give a good hold to the cord. This seems to have been the best and the latest type (see Fig. 46 *a*). In the later part of the Cervidian period, when the reindeer was gradually migrating north, the red-deer arrived. The man of the period endeavoured to manufacture, on the old lines, harpoons from his horns, but the result was not a success, because they were only hard on the out-side. It was obvious that some other plan would have to be tried, and consequently a kind of oval-flattened har-poon, with a hole at the

a   *b*

FIG. 46.   HARPOONS OF HORN
French (⅔)

base for the cord, and two rows of barbs, was devised (Fig. 46 *b*). On this followed various experimental forms, which narrowed themselves down to two types, found at Mas d'Azil in the stratum of the coloured pebbles. (1) An implement with a single row of barbs, with an oval or lozenge-shaped hole. This disappeared and left only (2) a

flat oval harpoon, with an oval hole and two rows of
pointed barbs almost parallel with the base (see Fig. 46 *b*)
and with no ornament to weaken it. This is found in
the shell-layer, though most of the bone implements in
that stratum have been destroyed by fire. The harpoon
is not found in the polished stone layers, for by this time
man had learnt how to make a fish-hook. From the
remains of some of the Swiss lake villages harpoons and
polished stone implements have been extracted together,
and it is possible that their use may have been simultaneous.

Javelins and Javelin-throwers.—It is possible that some
of the pointed implements of bone may have been the
heads of javelins, indeed, some of the objects called
harpoons by M. Piette, are described in the British
Museum Guide under the former name, and the wedge-
shaped butt is said to have been so constructed for the
purpose of fastening it into the shaft. So much do
opinions differ as to the use of the same object. At any
rate, there can be no doubt that javelin-throwers were in
existence, for one was found at La Madelaine ornamented
with carvings in the round of horses' heads, which in
general details quite resembles similar implements used
by the natives of Australia and the North-West Coast of
America for the purpose of increasing the leverage of the
arm in casting a spear.

Dress-fasteners.—These objects, of which an example
is shown in Fig. 47, were long known under the fanciful
name of " batons de commandement," or sceptres, and
were supposed to have been emblems of authority like a
Field-Marshal's baton. Schoetensack[1] has, however,
shown that they were a means of keeping together the

[1] *L'Anthropologie*, xii. 140.

cloak or skin robe, and that similar objects are used in that way by the Esquimaux to the present day. A thin cord, to each end of which was fastened transversely a little bit of stick, is brought round the neck over the robe. The

FIG. 47. DRESS-FASTENER
La Madelaine

two pieces of stick are then passed through the hole in the implement and the cloak is secured. Where there are several holes the object may have been to permit of the cloak being more or less closely brought together after the manner of the chain supplied with the modern Inverness cape.

Some of the simpler forms of " baton de commande-ment," unprovided with holes, have been identified with the " Pogamagan," or strikers, of the North American Indians, by a writer in *Nature*, who states that on the mural monument of Colonel Townshend on the south side of the nave of Westminster Abbey, there is a figure of a North American warrior with a pogamagan in his hand. Smaller dress-fasteners, made from the articulating end of a small animal bone, have been described by Green-well[1] and others. The object described and figured by the Canon was a calcined bone pin $1\frac{5}{8}$ inch long, with a large eye in the head a quarter of an inch in diameter, discovered in a barrow in the North Riding of Yorkshire.

[1] *British Barrows*, 352.

Needles.—These valuable implements, made of bone, have been found in the French caves and in Kent's Hole. A series with the implements used in their manufacture is exhibited in the British Museum, and figured in the Guide. From the bone selected for the purpose, a splinter was first detached, and this was then carefully rounded with the aid of a flint made after the pattern of a small-toothed concave scraper. The point was fashioned, and the whole of the needle polished, by a burnishing stone of sandstone. A pointed flint served as the drill for making the eye. In some cases the needles seem to have been made of a small round bone pointed and drilled. But it is clear that the points of these would not be as sharp or serviceable as those made from a splinter composed entirely of compact bone.

Picks or **hoes** have been found, not only in prehistoric workings such as Grime's Graves, but also in tumuli[1] in the excavation of which they may perhaps at times have been used. **Chisels** of horn have been found in the Swiss lake villages. Bone **arrow-heads** with traces of bitumen adhering to their bases, showing that this substance was used in attaching the head to the shaft, have been found in the same places. **Tweezers** of bone, perforated for hanging to the belt, were found by Bateman[2] in a barrow at Bailey Hill, in Derbyshire. **Borers** and implements like a small cigar, pointed at both ends, the use of which is rather doubtful, are other objects made of the same material.

ART OF THIS AND LATER PERIODS.

With the knowledge of bone as a workable article grew up a remarkable school of art, by no means one of the least interesting points in connection with this period of the world's history. The examples upon which our

---

[1] Greenwell, *op. cit.*, 231.   [2] *Ten Years' Digging,* 170.

knowledge of the subject is based have mainly been discovered in French caves; one instance, so far, alone having been afforded by this country. They have been carefully studied by M. Piette,[1] whose classification is given on p. 9. The period in question is called by him the Glyptic, and is divided into two epochs. (i.) Equidian, again subdivided into Elephantine or Ivory, and Hippic. The fauna was of the Mousterian character, and the works of art included sculptures in the round, bas-reliefs and engravings with cut-out contours. In part this epoch may be said to correspond to that known in another classification as Solutrean. (ii.) Cervidian, again divided into the reindeer and red-deer ages. Save that the reindeer, particularly in the first part of the time, existed in great numbers, and that there were also some circumpolar birds, the fauna of this period may be said to have closely corresponded to that of the present day. During this time were executed simple engravings. It was also the period of the manufacture of needles and of rounded harpoons of reindeer horn. Sculpture on ivory preceded that upon bone and horn, but the former chiefly characterises stations near the sea, the latter those of the mountains. If the sculptures and engravings on mammoth tusks and those in relief be excluded from what is usually known as the Magdalenian period, then what is left of it may be said to correspond to Piette's Cervidian epoch. The rounded statuettes of the Grotte du Pape at Bassempouy, which the author just quoted places at the earliest part of the Glyptic period, are figurines of female type, one of the most important being that called the Venus of Bassempouy and figured with other examples in *L'Anthropologie*.[2] Unfortunately only the abdomen, hip, and right thigh of this figure have come down to us. Both abdomen and buttocks are much accentuated, the latter being

---

[1] *L'Anthropologie,* v. 131 and vii. 2.   [2] vi. 129, pl. i.–vii.

I

of the steatopygous type. Another female figure has been carved to form the handle of a dagger. Here the breasts were long and pendent, but the details of parts of the figure had been sacrificed to the necessities of the purpose to which the work was to be put. In all, seven female figurines were found at Bassempouy, one at Mas d'Azil, and one at Laugerie Basse. They were not all of the heavy type of those just described. There was a second series,

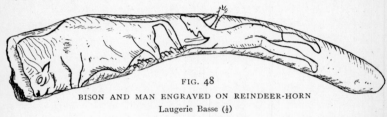

FIG. 48

BISON AND MAN ENGRAVED ON REINDEER-HORN
Laugerie Basse (½)

including the "figurine à la capuche," a statuette with a hood over the head, in which the figures were straight and thin, without protuberances and with very slight representations of flesh or muscle. Nude female figurines have been found in steatite at Mentone, and in marble at Troy, and on the Carian coast. It cannot, however, be said that all these are of anything like the same period, indeed, it has been suggested that the last-mentioned are crude imitations of the Chaldæan type of Astarte. Perhaps the subject of human representations may here be disposed of, though the cases to be cited do not all belong to this early period. The "femme au renne" was found at Laugerie Basse, and is an engraving in *champ-levé* on a piece of reindeer horn. The figure is that of a pregnant woman lying on her back beneath a reindeer. Unfortunately the head of the female and the fore part of the beast have been lost by an old fracture of the horn. The figure of a man chasing bison is shown in Fig. 48, the carving having been executed on a piece of reindeer horn. It was found at Laugerie Basse. The well-known figure of the man with eel and horses' heads, part of a dress-fastener, was discovered at La Madelaine. An inartistically executed profile of the head alone has also been discovered at Laugerie Basse. Poor as all these representations of the human form are, they are superior to those bas-reliefs which have been found on the stones of dolmens [1] and in a sepulchral grotto.[2] In these cases the face is reduced to the superciliary ridges and nose with small eyes. The breasts and sometimes the arms are represented. Similar figures, reduced to representations of the breasts, have been found on menihirion in Sardinia. Mention should also be made of the extremely rude figures, with girdles, discovered by Abbé Hermet and described by Cartailhac.[3] Some of these have beneath the girdles represented upon them what may be feet and legs, or may be the fringed ends of a stole-like garment. These figures, carved on

FIG. 49. HORSES' HEADS CARVED IN ROUND ON BONE
St. Marcel (⅓)

blocks of sandstone and about four feet in height, were discovered in Aveyron, France.

Returning now to the subject of the palæolithic works of art one may at once admit that, if he represented himself ineffectually, the man of the period was far more successful in his attempts to represent the animals which

[1] Cartailhac, *L'Anthropologie,* v. 147.
[2] De Baye, *L'Archéologie Préhistorique,* 159. Pl. i., ii., iii.
[3] *L'Anthropologie,* iii. 222.

he saw around him. Of these works of art many have been discovered embracing a wide range of subjects. Of mammals there are representations of the mammoth, horse (Fig. 49), reindeer (Fig. 50), cave-bear, urus, aurochs, deer, mountain goat, antelope, chamois, wild-boar, wolf, fox, lynx, otter, seal, walrus, and rabbit, besides some others which are as yet undetermined. Amongst fish, the salmon, eel (if it is not, as some suggest, a serpent), trout,

FIG. 50. REINDEER ENGRAVED ON STONE
St. Marcel (⅔)

and pike have been drawn. A representation of a swan was found at Laugerie Basse. The works are executed on pieces of bone or horn, or sometimes stone, and the graving-tool was evidently a sharp-pointed piece of flint. Amongst the most celebrated of these gravings are those of the mammoth, on a portion of mammoth's tusk, of the reindeer by a pool of water, on a piece of reindeer horn, and of the cave-bear on a flat, oval pebble of schist, all of which are well known from numerous representations in books dealing with the subject of prehistoric archæ-

ology.   For this reason it has been thought
better to give here a less well-known representation of the reindeer from St. Marcel
(Fig. 50).   M. Reinach[1] has recently pointed
out that all the animals, so far as we have
at present knowledge, represented on the
walls of caves or on pieces of bone, horn,
etc., are those which would be hunted or
fished for by a race of hunters and fisher-
men.   All the undesirable animals, such as
lions, tigers, etc.—for he believes the so-
called cave-bear of Bruniquel to have been
a badly-drawn ruminant—are wanting.   It
is suggested—but this, of course, is pure
theory—that the drawings may have been of
a magical character, and had for their object
the attraction of the species of game or fish
which they represent.   In addition to the
incised figures and those with cut-out outlines, the artist of the period attempted carvings in the full or half-round in the regions
of applied art.   Amongst these some of the
most interesting are the dagger handles.
Dagger and handle in these cases (see Fig.
51) were made out of one continuous piece of
reindeer horn, pointed at one end.   Two
examples may be mentioned, one of them,
that represented in the figure, a decided
success, the other certainly, to our ideas, a
failure.   In the first example the artist has
set himself the task of making an effective
and comfortable handle to a dagger of reindeer horn, which handle shall represent the
reindeer himself.   Now a reindeer is an

[1] *L'Anthropologie,* xiv. 257.

FIG. 51.   DAGGER,
REINDEER HORN

animal with branching horns, and our artist had first of all to think how they are to be disposed of. Hence he represented his reindeer running at full speed, head thrust far forward, so that the horns lie along his neck, where they are carved in high relief. The same pose enabled the artist to tuck the fore-legs well away under the body, so that they shall not project and make the grip uncomfortable. And it enabled him to throw the hind-legs straight out behind so as to merge with the blade portion of the dagger. It is important, of course, that the point where the handle merges into the blade shall not be weak. Hence the artist has carved the hinder part of the animal where he meets the blade in high relief, and not in the full round, as the anterior part is carved. The result is a dagger comfortable to handle, and a very remarkable piece of work for the time it was made and the tools with which it was executed. The other dagger handle was to represent the mammoth, not a very easy animal to work into a scheme of decoration, unless, perhaps, he had been carved on the handle in low relief. The artist, however, determined to try and execute him in the full round. He straightened the animal's tusks a bit, and brought them out along the blade, and so strengthens his junction. Thus he got out of one difficulty, but only to fall into another in connection with the legs. He could not well tuck these under the animal, and so he left them sticking straight out. The result is exceedingly inartistic, and ineffective too, for the implement when complete—the blade part has long been broken off—must have been most uncomfortable in the hand.[1] This part of the subject cannot be left without some notice of the remarkable series of

[1] Those desirous of thoroughly studying the interesting subject of the art of this early period may be referred to the valuable work by Wilson on *Prehistoric Art* published by the Smithsonian Institution.

coloured pebbles discovered at Mas d'Azil by M. Piette, and fully described by him in *L'Anthropologie*.[1] The layer in which these objects have been found passes insensibly into the shell layer, and the objects themselves are water-worn pebbles, coloured with peroxide of iron, probably mixed with fat or resin. The representations on the pebbles are divided into three groups. (1) *Numbers*, represented by (*a*) parallel bands, (*b*) circles or disks in lines, (*c*) oval disks placed tangentially to the edges of the pebbles. Sometimes the borders of the lines are even, sometimes fringed. In no case are more than eight lines or other figures present on any one pebble. (2) *Symbols*, (*a*) the equilateral cross or + figure, (*b*) the solar disk, (*c*) the Tau cross, T̄. (3) *Pictographs*, (*a*) serpentine bands, (*b*) ladder-like figures, consisting of a single upright with a number of bars crossing it, (*c*) tree-like forms, (*d*) the eye, (*e*) harpoons, (*f*) reeds, (*g*) wavy line. The most interesting point in connection with these objects is their apparent connection with early alphabets, a point on which Piette says, " Nine of the Mas d'Azil graphic signs are identical with characters in the Cypriote syllabary : Ko, mo, pa, lo, si, ve, sa, ti, ta. Eight of the same signs, of which some are also Cypriote, form part of the Aegean alphabet. Many ancient inscriptions from Asia Minor also, especially from the Troad, present characters re-sembling the pictures from Mas d'Azil. Recognising in the Cypriote and Aegean alphabets, or in the writing in use in Asia Minor before the Trojan War, the characters of Mas d'Azil, there is ground for believing either that the invasions from the west to the east carried into these regions at a very ancient period the writing used in Pyrenæan districts, or that the rudimentary writing of Mas d'Azil was in Prehistoric times the common patri-

[1] vii. 384. The accompanying portfolio of coloured figures gives a vivid idea of the whole series of finds.

mony of the Mediterranean littoral and the coasts of the Archipelago."

ART OF THE NEOLITHIC AND BRONZE PERIODS

No attempt can be made to enter in any detail into the art of these later periods, the decorative art, that is, for of the applied art of the late Celtic period some notice will be taken when that part of the subject is reached, but some comment must be made upon the contrast presented between the character of the older and the later forms of decoration. The former, whether those which have just been described, or the cavern decorations alluded to in an earlier chapter, consisted of graphic representations of animal and even of human life. Such representations are entirely wanting in the Neolithic period, and it is only in the latest examples of work in bronze that anything of the kind again appears. In place of these we find on the pottery of the Neolithic and bronze periods, and on the implements of the bronze, a wide range of ornament, but all of a geometrical character. It consisted of marks, lines or dots, impressed, incised, or raised, as a result of casting, in geometric forms, hatchings, zigzags, herring-bone work, chevrons, parallel lines and thumb-marks. Such geometric forms of design were not wanting during the Palæolithic period, but they are quite overshadowed by the predominance of graphic art. On harpoons and points of bone we find geometric forms, probably because there was little room for the graphic representations which were utilised where there was more space at the command of the artist. Fig. 52 shows a few of these geometric forms, of which forty-six are given by Wilson.[1] "The decorative art of the Bronze Age," says Wilson, "was but a continuation of that of the Neolithic period, and it is not impossible

[1] Plates 19 and 20.

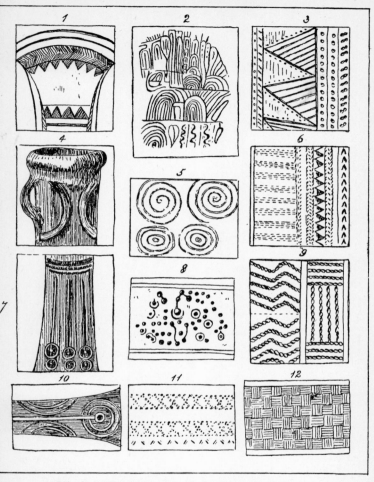

FIG. 52. NEOLITHIC AND BRONZE ORNAMENTATION

4, 7, 10. Ornament on bronze Celts
2. Dolmen of Gavr'Inis
3. Dots, lines and Vandyke on edge of bowl
5. Spirals and concentric circles (slab of stone),
    Eday, Orkneys
6. Herring-bone, dog-tooth, and twisted cord
    decoration (urn)

8. Cup-markings, single and encircled, Ross-
    shire
9. Twisted cord ornament (urn)
11. Crossed lines of small dots arranged in
    bands
12. Imitation of basket-work

that an investigation into the origin of some of the specimens in plates 19 and 20 (from which most of the selected
examples have been taken) would show them to have
belonged to the Bronze Age ; that is to say, the styles of
ornamentation of the two periods or ages were practically
the same, and the latter was but a continuation of the

FIG. 53.   CUP-AND-RING MARKINGS
Berwick

former, with such possible changes or additions as would
naturally grow." Amongst these forms of decoration
there is one to which some special attention must be paid.
These are the cup-and-ring markings which have attracted
the attention of so many observers, and as to the meaning
of which so many surmises have been made.   The nature
of these markings will be made sufficiently clear by Figs.
52 [5 8], and 53, and those who desire to pursue the subject further may be referred to the works mentioned in the
footnote.[1]

[1] Sir J. Simpson, "Archaic Sculptures"; C. Rau, "Observations on
Cup-shaped and other Lapidarian Sculptures in the Old World and in
America," Contributions to *North American Ethnology,* vol. v. ; Coffey,

Sometimes there are a series of cups without further ornamentation; sometimes the cups are surrounded by concentric lines; or, again, in addition to these there is a radial groove. "Cup marks," says Coffey, "are widely distributed in Europe. They have been recorded from France, Switzerland, Portugal, Germany, Austria, Denmark, Sweden, England, Scotland, and Ireland. Yet, with the exception of a few instances, cup-and-ring, or concentric circle sculptures, have not been recorded in Europe outside Sweden, Great Britain, and Ireland. The exceptions referred to are : a cupped stone near Bunsoh, Holstein, showing twenty-seven cups, three of which are surrounded by single rings; a cupped stone, stated to have existed near Mels, St. Gall, Switzerland, unfortunately destroyed, one of the cups of which was enclosed by two rings; some examples of cup-in-ring and cross-in-circle markings, in association with cup-marks, on rock-surfaces in the Eringerthal, Valais, Switzerland; an example of concentric rings on a rock-surface in the Meraviglie, Mentone; and two or three examples on a surface in Galicia." And he continues : "This narrow distribution of cup-and-ring cuttings is emphasised by the fact that cup-and-ring marks with radial gutters are absolutely confined to Great Britain and Ireland." A list of the localities in which these markings have been observed in this country will be found at the end of this chapter. The spiral ornament may perhaps have reached Europe through the Aegean from Egypt. It has been found on scarabs of the fifth dynasty in Egypt, and in others of the twelfth at Crete (2700–2500 B.C.).

"Origins of Prehistoric Ornament in Ireland," *Journ of Roy. Soc. of Antiq. of Ireland,* vol. iv. 349 ; v. 16, 195 ; vi. 34 ; and vii. 28.

PERSONAL ORNAMENTS.

Bracelets, torques, pins, and some other objects of bronze will be dealt with in a later chapter. Here it is only intended to call attention to one or two classes which can be satisfactorily dealt with at this point.

Gold.—An unusually large number of gold ornaments have been discovered in Ireland, and can be well studied in the collection of the Royal Irish Academy in Ireland. In a series of articles on this subject, the late Dr. Frazer[1] endeavoured to prove that all the ancient Irish gold was obtained abroad, and that everything in British and Irish history indicates Roman-Britain as its most available source. Ireland, he says, is not a land of gold; the small amount found in a small district of Wicklow was unknown beyond a hundred years ago, was soon exhausted, and differs in composition from that contained in our ornaments. These ornaments correspond remarkably in weight with multiples of Roman *aurei,* and closely as specific gravity. Britain became thoroughly drained of its gold, of which, like other Roman provinces, it must have possessed a considerable amount; this disappeared at the time when a number of captives reached our shores, and the value of one such captive is recorded as estimated at an "ounce of gold" by weight, not in the form of coins. If these views be correct, then the period of the gold ornaments would have to be set down as late. But there is abundant evidence that quite considerable quantities of gold have been obtained in Ireland, even in recent times.[2] Nor need we doubt that the source of the extraordinary amount of gold converted into ornaments[3] was purely native.

[1] *Proc. Roy. Soc. of Antiqs. of Ireland,* vol. vii.

[2] *Wakeman's Handbook,* p. 241.

[3] For list, see *Journ. Roy. Soc. Antiq. Ireland,* 1870–71, p. 509, and Catalogue of Gold Ornaments, R. I. A.

Jet.—Objects of this material have been found in *tumuli* in the shape of rings, buttons, and necklaces, the latter sometimes very elaborate pieces of work. Greenwell[1] describes one consisting of one hundred and thirty beads, and Bateman[2] gives an account of another (see Fig. 54) which consisted of four hundred and twenty bits, consisting of three hundred and forty-eight laminæ, fifty-four cylinders, and eighteen conical studs and perforated plates, the latter ornamented with punctured patterns.

Beads of **Amber** and of **Glass** also found in tumuli deserve mention in this place.

[1] *British Barrows,* p. 330.   [2] *Ten Years' Digging,* p. 24.

FIG. 54   JET NECKLACE

LIST OF CUP-AND-RING MARKINGS IN ENGLAND.

CUMBERLAND—

"Long Meg and her Daughters."   Cf. p. 199.
A circle near to this.

DERBYSHIRE.—High Hucklow.   In barrow.

DORSETSHIRE.—Came Down.   Cupped stones in a barrow.
(Warne, *Celtic Tumuli of Dorset*, p. 37.)

LANCASHIRE.—The Calder Stones.   Cf. p. 201.

NORTHUMBERLAND—

Beanley, near "The Ringses."
Bewick, double camp.
Cartington Fell.
Chatton Law Camp.
Chirnells Moor, near Rothbury.
Dod Law, near the double camp.
Ford Common.   In barrow.   (*British Barrows*, 403.)
Gled Law, near Dod Law.
Hunter's Moor, near Rowting Lynn.
Lord-in-Shaws Camp.
Morwick Mill, near.   Vale of Coquet.
* Rowting Lynn.
Stamfordham, near Black Haddon.   In barrow.   (*British Barrows*.)
Weetwood Bridge, near the camp.
Whitton Dene, near Rothbury.   (Cf. "Ancient Sculptured Stones of Northumberland," *Trans. Berwick Naturalists' Club*, v. 137.)

YORKSHIRE—

Claughton Moor.   Cupped stones in round barrow.   Cf. p. 171.
Kilburn Moor.   (*British Barrows*, 329.)
Way Hag, Ayton Moor.   (*British Barrows*, p. 342.)
Wykeham Moor.   Cf. p. 173.

CHAPTER VII

PLACES OF BURIAL—BARROWS LONG AND ROUND

"UNDERGROUND are all great treasures and wonderful things," says Rabelais, and his saying may be applied to the tombs and cemeteries of the bygone races of this country, so far as archæologists are concerned. For they have been most fruitful in affording information as to the habits of those who constructed and were deposited in them. As far as their physical characters are concerned, the examination of the skeletons exposed has taught us almost all that we know in that respect. And the custom of burying various things with the body of the departed, a custom perhaps based upon the idea that the gifts deposited would be useful to the spirit of the dead person in another world, has led to the storing up in burial mounds and graves of a varied series of objects, examples of which are preserved in many museums, objects which throw more light upon the position and habits of their former owners than perhaps any other discoveries which have been made. These "accompanying gifts" vary in number and character according to the race and period, and they will be dealt with more fully further on. The harvest of knowledge which has been gathered from the examination of burial mounds is so great that the information to be given here must necessarily be very much compressed and confined to the more important points. For further information reference may

be made to the works in the footnote.[1] Before turning to
the varieties of barrow two preliminary points have to be
dealt with.

Cremation and Inhumation.—As at the present day, so
in earlier ages, two methods of disposing of the bodies of
the dead were practised, ordinary burial or inhumation
and burning, with subsequent deposition of the ashes in
a grave mound, cyst, or urn-field.   The method of burial
by inhumation seems always and everywhere to have been
the earlier.   After it came a period when, as now, both
inhumation and cremation were practised at the same
time, the difference being perhaps due to racial, perhaps
to religious, distinctions.   But cremation never seems in
any place to have had the universal vogue that inhumation had before the introduction of the later method.
According to Sergi,[2] the former was the primitive method
of the Mediterranean race, the latter the introduction of
the Aryans.   On the comparative occurrence of the two
methods many statistics are available.   Thus in the
Etruscan tombs inhumation is the invariable rule.   In
Cyprus cremation is unknown, even in the Bronze Age.
Inhumation was also practised in Spain during the
copper and bronze periods, and it was the recognised
method of the Guanches.   On the other hand, cremation
was practised by those who constructed the terramare
of Italy and the well-tombs of Certosa, Bologna, and elsewhere where inhumation is almost unknown.   In the Rhoe-
tian cemetery of Vadena none but cremated bodies were
found.   In France and in the Swiss lake villages during
the stone period inhumation was the rule, cremation

---

[1] Greenwell, *British Barrows* and "Recent Researches in Barrows,"
Archæologia, lii. ; Bateman, *Ten Years' Digging;* Jewitt, "Grave Mounds
and their Contents"; Thurnam, papers on long and round barrows in
Archæologia, vol. xlv.   [2] *Mediterranean Race,* pp. 266 and 286.

K

coming in with the Bronze Age. In the cemeteries of Glasinatz and Hallstadt, belonging to the early Iron Age, both practices are met with. At Hallstadt, of 525 burials 455 were after cremation. In Britain both methods are met with during the Neolithic and bronze periods, the proportions varying in different parts of the country. Thus Greenwell says :[1] "In Derbyshire the proportion is slightly in favour of burnt bodies ; in Wiltshire burnt bodies are as three to one unburnt ; in Dorsetshire as four to one ; and in Cornwall cremation seems to have been by far the most common usage. In the counties of Denbigh, Merioneth, and Caernarvon cremation seems to have been almost universal. In Northumberland I have disinterred seventy-one bodies, and of these forty-five were after cremation, and twenty-six by inhumation—the proportion of burnt to unburnt bodies being, therefore, almost two to one."

Primary and Secondary Interments.—As to the meaning of the first of these two terms there can be no manner of doubt ; the primary interment was that of the first person or persons placed in the tomb. But there is more ambiguity as to the use of the latter term. Some of the tombs, as will appear shortly, were of the nature of family vaults, and were intended to be opened from time to time for the reception of fresh inhabitants. Such later interments might fairly be spoken of as secondary. But there are also in the grave mounds other burials of quite a different character. Sometimes a Saxon or a Roman interment is found somewhere in the superincumbent mass of earth, though the original mound, and the burial or burials which it contains, may be of the bronze period. This might also be spoken of as a secondary interment, and, in fact, is so spoken of. It might perhaps be better,

[1] *British Barrows.* Note on p. 22.

however, to confine this word to burials of the kind mentioned above, *i.e.*, burials of the same class but of later date, and to speak of the other variety as *alien* interments, *i.e.*, interments forming no part of the scheme of the original constructors of the mound and of a different period.

Varieties of Barrows.

We may now proceed to consider the various kinds of barrows met with in this country, and it will much simplify the matter if we compare the two leading varieties, long and round barrows, to two well-known methods of interment in the present day, the family vault and the single grave. The simile is not absolutely unassailable, but is sufficiently close, for the long barrow was a family or tribal burying-place, whilst the round barrow was, at least at times, heaped up over the remains of one person and not intended to be reopened for the introduction of further burials. In relation to this comparison it must also be remembered that our modern graves, though as a rule made for one interment, are sometimes used for two or even more. The long barrow is the earlier form, as it is the larger, and must, therefore, be first considered. It is the characteristic place of burial of the people of the later stone period, and the first form of artificial burial-place with which we are acquainted. But it must be freely admitted that so far we know nothing of the burial customs of the people of the earlier Stone Age, if, indeed, they had any.

Long Barrows.—The long barrow, whose special characteristics will shortly be detailed, was of two kinds, chambered and unchambered, and the former, as the more interesting of the two, may first be dealt with. If the first place of burial as well as the first place of habitation was a cave, it would not be surprising if man, when he emerged from his gloomy, natural shelters, made his first artificial homes and his first tombs on the model with which he was acquainted. As to the latter, at any rate this may be said, that the chambered tumulus, perhaps the earliest sepulchral monument existent, is an artificial cave or grotto, composed of great stones arranged so as to form a kind of cell. Such a cell may have been embedded in the earth, and covered up with no intention that it should ever again be disturbed, or it may have been placed on the surface of the earth and covered with a mound, with the same intention. A cell of this kind, which its builders closed up, as they thought, once and for ever, is properly called a *cist*, and that term should be reserved for such forms of interment. But at other times the intention was that the cell should be opened up from time to time for the introduction of further burials, and to this class belong the true chambered long barrows. In its simplest form the cell in such a barrow consists of three or more great stones reared up on end, and surmounted by another large flat stone, the "cap-stone," over all being placed a mound of earth. This cell or hut might be closed temporarily or permanently after the remains of the dead had been introduced into its interior by a further slab of stone forming a kind of door. Such a place of burial would form a unilocular tomb, though the loculus might have been intended for the reception of more than one body. But it is obvious that by making a kind of gallery of large stones, with transepts or chambers opening out of it, a multilocular burial-place, capable of accommodating a greater number of burials, perhaps of serving as mortuary chapels for a number of families, would result. An example of this may be studied in the plan of the barrow at Uley, in Gloucestershire (Fig. 55 [2]), and Stoney Littleton, Somerset (Fig. 55 [1]). At Uley there were four chambers opening

off the central avenue, the termination of which might be
described as a fifth. The avenue itself is entered by a kind
of low doorway (see Figs. 56 and 57), closed no doubt
originally by a slab of stone and with rough walls, curved
outwards on either side of it. There may have been only
a single pair of transepts, as was the case at Weylands
Smithy, or there may have been six, in three pairs, as at
Stoney Littleton. The horned cairns of Caithness seem
to belong to the class of barrow now under consideration.

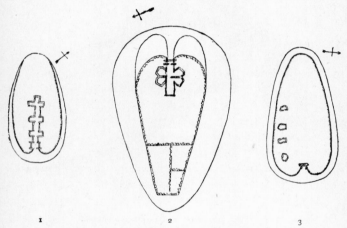

FIG. 55.   PLANS OF LONG BARROWS

1. Stoney Littleton, Somerset.   2. Uley, Gloucestershire.   3. Littleton Drew, Wilts

A second variety of chambered barrow is that in which
there is no central gallery, but the chambers are all
approached separately from the exterior of the tumulus as
in the case, for example, of the Rodmarton tumulus. In
a third form, perhaps not strictly a chambered barrow
in the restricted sense in which this word has been defined
above, the tumulus contains a series of cists, perhaps
never intended to be entered when once closed, but if to
be entered, then only approachable through the roof, so

to speak, that is, by removal of the top stone. Four cists of this kind were found in the barrow at Littleton Drew (Fig. 55 [3]), and others have been discovered in Wilts and Gloucestershire. A somewhat similar arrangement seems to have obtained in Arran, where the cairns have recently been most carefully examined and described by my friend Dr. Bryce.[1]

FIG. 56.   ENTRANCE TO LONG BARROW
Uley, Gloucestershire

It would be impossible within the limits of space to deal with the question of interments outside this country, but attention may here be called to the fact that the French *allées couvertes*[2] and the Hunnebedden of Holland[3] closely resemble the true chambered barrows of this island. The second form of long barrow, the unchambered type, is, according to Canon Greenwell, a variety due to the

---

[1] *Proc. Soc. Antiqs., Scotland,* July, 1902, and June, 1903.
[2] For a description of a typical example, see *L'Anthropologie,* i. 160.
[3] Franks, *Proc. Soc. Ant.,* 1872, p. 258, and *L'Anthropologie,* ix. 1.

difference in local circumstances and particularly to the supply of stone, and not of racial or chronological significance. The chambered barrows are met with chiefly in North Wilts and Gloucestershire, localities where large

blocks of stone of a kind suitable for the erection of such sepulchres abound. In South Wilts, in Dorset, in Yorkshire, and in Westmorland, the unchambered variety is found in districts where stone suitable for the construction of chambers is less easily to be met with. In the unchambered class there are sometimes walls in the interior of the mound, but no chambers or recesses as there are in the class first considered. The bones or ashes are embedded in the constituents of the mound itself and, remarkable to say, have sometimes been burnt *in situ*. In order

FIG. 57.   ENTRANCE TO LONG BARROW
West Kennett

to effect this the bodies or bones were arranged in a line, and the stones around them were built into a kind of flue, so that a draught might be created. For this purpose it was necessary that a vent should be constructed at the end opposite to that at which the fire was lit, and this has been identified in at least one case. Perhaps an example of each class may be briefly described before the general characteristics of long barrows are summed up. The chambered barrow at Uley (see Fig. 55) consists of a mound about 120 feet in length, 85 feet in its maximum breadth, and about 10 feet high. It was originally surrounded, like other long barrows, with a boundary wall, and its entrance, which is a low doorway, 2½ feet in height above the natural surface of the ground, is at the east end. The capstone of the doorway is 3 feet in length and 4½ inches in thickness. The gallery in the interior runs for a distance of 22 feet from east to west. It is 5 feet high and 4½ wide. Its sides are formed of large slabs of stone set edgeways, the spaces between being filled with smaller stones. The roof is formed of large flat slabs. As already mentioned, there are two transepts on either side. As an example of the other class, the barrow at Scamridge (Greenwell, ccxxi.) may be cited. The mound here was 165 feet in length, 46 feet in breadth at the west end, and 54 at the east. In height it rose from 7 feet at the west to 9 feet at the east end. It contained a wall about 5 feet from the exterior on the north side, which may have run the entire length of the barrow, and with this exception and another to be mentioned in a moment was composed of oolitic rubble, clay, and earth. This further exception was along the central line of the barrow, where the mixture of stone and earth above alluded to gave way to a line of oolitic rubble, amongst which were deposited the remains of fourteen bodies, the component parts being scattered about in a confused manner. This disorder was not due to secondary disturbance of the barrow, but was the original manner in which the bones were laid down. At the eastern end of this line of bones there were evidences that a fire had been lit for purposes of incineration. It had been intended that its action should penetrate along the whole line, hence the arrangement of the bones in the midst of loose rubble, which might act as a flue. As a matter of fact there was a regular gradation from much to little burnt bones. At the east the bones had disappeared and the oolite had been converted into lime, whilst at the west the bones were untouched by fire. This condition of affairs has been observed in other barrows of the same class. Canon Greenwell thinks that the manner of carrying out the burning was in this wise:[1] "The bodies sometimes in a complete state, at other times fragmentary and the bones disjointed, were laid at or above the level of the natural surface on a thick layer of clay, or, as in this case (*i.e.* a barrow at Westow, E.R., Yorks), on a pavement of flagstones; upon them were placed, as here and at Rudstone, turfs or earth, and upon that again stone; there do not appear, in all cases, to have been any intervening turfs, the stone itself lying immediately upon the bones. Wood was placed amongst, alongside, and underneath the stone, the evident remains of it, in the shape of charcoal, being found abundantly in some parts; and in others, where charcoal is wanting, it is probable that the intense burning had consumed the wood too perfectly for any remains beyond a white ash to be left. Over and upon this covering deposit of stone was then thrown up the ordinary material of the barrow." At some point, but where is not quite clear, the wood was fired with the intention that all the bones in the tumulus should be consumed, or at least, perhaps it should be put, purified by the influence of the flames.

Where cremation has not taken place, the bodies are either buried in a contracted position, or the remains of many skeletons may be mixed more or less promiscuously together. In the Wilts barrows these remains are gener-

[1] p. 495.

ally found in a stratum of black earth, whose blackness is not due to the influence of fire, below the great mass of earth, flint, etc., of which the bulk of the tumulus is composed. Partly in the same layer, and partly above it, have been found the remains of oxen and other animals, perhaps the relics of the funeral feast. In the floors of these barrows and scooped out in the surface-chalk, have in a number of instances been discovered pits from one to two feet in depth, and from two to three feet in diameter. The object of these is very obscure, since they have never been found to contain human bones, but we may conclude that they were of some ceremonial importance. It will have already been noticed that the bones of the dead are often mixed up in a confused manner, and it may be added that parts of skeletons are not infrequently missing. This is not due to the barrow having been opened and the bones disarranged after the flesh had disappeared from them. It is a condition which is met with in obviously undisturbed mounds. Hence it is clear that the bones were deposited as we find them, that is, that the flesh had been removed from them before they were laid in the grave. On this fact has risen a suggestion that our predecessors in this land were, like many other savages, cannibals. Whether this be true or not, it is an unnecessary hypothesis, for the state of affairs can be quite well accounted for by supposing that these barrows were ossuaries, erected from time to time over a number of bodies whose bones had been allowed to accumulate until a sufficient number, or a convenient time, seemed to warrant their final deposition. To the points already given the following general remarks upon long barrows may be added. Both kinds differ from the round variety in several ways, which will shortly be considered, but of which one must here be mentioned, namely, that they occur in isolated positions and not in groups.

As their name signifies, they are very much longer than they are broad ; they almost always run east and west, and the east end, which is that where the interments most commonly are found, is broader and higher than the west. In the case of the unchambered barrows there is usually a ditch on either side of the mound, but not continued round its ends. In the chambered variety this is quite frequently absent, and in its place is to be found a dwarf wall, sometimes interspersed with small ortholiths or standing stones (see Fig. 58). Moreover the interior of the chambered barrow may have dry walls intersecting it apart from those which form the cells for the reception

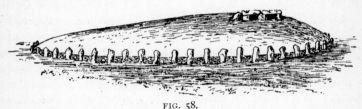

FIG. 58.

RESTORATION OF LONG BARROW AT WEST KENNETT WITH PERISTALITH

of the bodies (see Fig. 55²). And in some cases (*e.g.* the Tinglestone, near Avening, Glos.) a monolith or menhir has been found on, or, as at Ablington, Glos., in the barrow itself. The skulls of the primary interments in these barrows are always dolichocephalic (see p. 304) or of the long variety. The accompanying gifts are few, and consist of flint implements and rough pottery. No trace of bronze has been found in any of them. In France and Scandinavia barrows of the same class have been found to contain objects of gold, and stone implements in abundance, thus forming a contrast to their English brethren. Alien interments, Anglo-Saxon, Roman and pre-Roman, have been found in the superincumbent masses of earth covering in the primary burials of the long barrow. There has been much controversy as to the origin of the chambered barrow. Was it derived from the primitive house, or did the beehive house grow out of the tomb? It is certainly suggestive to find that the Lapps of the extreme north of Scandinavia use a mound-hut closely resembling a tumulus. "Here," says Mr. A. Evans, "are the ring-stones actually employed in propping up the turf-covered mound of the dwelling, and there is the low entrance-gallery leading to the chamber within, which, in fact, is the living representative, and at the same time the remote progenitor, of the gallery of the chambered barrow."

Round Barrows.—Barrows with a more or less circular base-plan, which occur, as a rule, in groups, are very much more numerous and widely distributed than the long variety. Even in Wilts, where there are, or have been, sixty long barrows, these, according to Thurnam, are only as one to thirty-five as compared with the round barrows, which amount to nearly 2,000 in number.

Though all more or less circular, a number of varieties have been described and arranged into the following classes by Thurnam :—[1]

ROUND BARROWS (*Bronze Period*).

1. Bowl-shaped barrows
   - *a.* Simple bowl-barrows.
   - *b.* Trenched bowl-barrows.
   - *c.* Composite bowl or oval barrows.

2. Bell-shaped barrows
   - *a.* Simple bell.
   - *b.* Twin.
   - *c.* Triple.

3. Disc-shaped barrows
   - *a.* Simple—with flat area.
   - *b.* With one, two, or three small central tumuli.
   - *c.* With one low mound nearly covering the area.

[1] *Archæologia,* xlii. 168.

The bell variety is distinguished from the bowl by having a ditch around it, and the disc from both by its resemblance to a circular shallow dish inverted. The "Druid" barrow, of Stukeley, belongs to this category, and consists of one or more very small mounds with a circular bank surrounding them at some distance. The following general account relates to all these classes, for we have no evidence as to any reason for the varieties of shape, nor does it appear that they are of racial or chronological value.

Structure of the Barrow.—Commonly the primary interment was made in a grave excavated in the ground, over which was heaped up a mound of earth gathered from the

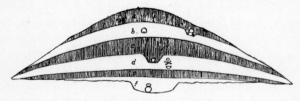

FIG. 59. SECTION OF BARROW WITH SUCCESSIVE INTERMENTS

immediate neighbourhood. Here the interments might end, but it was not uncommon for others to be added, so that several layers or strata may be met with, some or all of them containing later burials. Fig. 59 gives a section of a tumulus examined by Warne and described in his *Celtic Antiquities of Dorset*. It is one of a group of six on Lord's Down, in the parish of Dewlish. It was eighty-two feet in diameter and fourteen feet in height. Here a cavity (*f*) had been cut in the chalk, to contain the primary interment in an urn. The cist was packed with flints and chalk-rubble, the latter extending for some distance beyond its limits. On the chalk rubble was a layer of earth (*e*), and above this a second layer of chalk-rubble (*d*) containing an interment. After the mound had reached this point a further cist was cut in it, in which an interment took place, a fresh layer of earth (*c*) being then added. Above this again was a further layer of chalk-rubble (*b*) and a final layer of earth (*a*), and in both of these strata were interments. Thus there were three layers of chalk-rubble, and the same number of earth, alternating with one another, and each of them containing an interment. Around the barrow was sometimes a ditch, sometimes a ring of standing stones. This was possibly a "ghost-hedge," and like the rings of stone and trenches sometimes found inside the fabric of the barrow, is always interrupted at one or more points. In the floors of the wold barrows are sometimes found the same strange pits already mentioned in connection with the unchambered long barrows of the south-western part of the island. These pits are generally filled up with the ordinary constituents of the mound itself, but they may contain fragments of animal, or, but rarely, human bone, charcoal, potsherds, or burnt earth and stones. They are not usually in close contact with the bodies, and no satisfactory explanation of their purpose is as yet forthcoming. The remains of animal bones are found in numbers in the substance of many barrows, and may represent the relics of the funeral feast. Amongst the bones thus discovered have been those of the red-deer, goat, sheep, horse, pig, and different kinds of oxen. Bones of water-voles are very common in Derbyshire barrows and are found elsewhere, but these are the remains of animals which have burrowed into the mounds and made their hybernacula there. The human bones have often been found gnawed by these animals, and the remains of one of them was found inside a human skull in a barrow. Perhaps the bones of the badger and the fox may have at times been introduced in the same manner. They are found, and so are those of the (probably wild) cat, hare, pigeon, and polecat. The dog has been found buried with his dead master, not merely in British mounds, but in various parts of the world.

A remarkable feature of the round barrows is the finding of fragments of flint and of pottery strewn, evidently of set purpose, throughout the earth of which they are composed. It is impossible to doubt that some ceremonial significance attached to this deposition of shards, and perhaps the recollection of the pagan ceremony lingered in the custom alluded to in *Hamlet* of placing such objects in the graves of suicides, for the sacred observance of one religion may be transmuted in another into a ceremony of disgrace.

Disposition of the Bodies.—The round barrows contain bodies which have been cremated and others which have been inhumed, nor is there any evidence to show that one or other method was the earlier. Indeed, there is abundant reason to believe that both methods were practised at the same time, and Canon Greenwell even cites one case in which a burial after cremation and a burial by inhumation seem to have taken place simultaneously in the same mound. We may gather, then, that the condition of affairs was much as it is now, when the method of interment is determined by the wish of the relations, or by the directions of the dead person.

When the body was unburnt it was generally laid in the grave in a contracted, very rarely in an extended, position. There is sufficient evidence to show that the body was sometimes interred in its clothes, whether of skin, or of wool, or of coarse cloth. Where the body was burnt the ashes may have been laid upon the ground, or placed in a cinerary urn—the common method of disposal, or under an inverted urn. The primary interment may have been single or multiple. Fig. 60 shows the skeletons of a mother and child surrounded by a number of fossil echini. In a barrow at Goodmanham (Greenwell, lxxxv.) the calcined bones of two infants, who may be presumed to have died at about the same time, are the sole occupants of a barrow. Greenwell, Bateman, Hoare, and Warne, all record cases in which husband and wife have been buried together.[1] A man, a woman, and two children, presumably a family, have been found simultaneously interred.[2] Greenwell is inclined to believe that many of the cases of multiple interment, simultaneous in character, are cases where wives, children, servants, or all of these, have been immolated with the chief, or head of the family, a custom so common that it would be almost surprising if no evidence of it were met with in the past history of this country.

Burnt or unburnt, the body, or what remained of it, was sometimes deposited in the barrow without any protection from the earth which was to be heaped upon it. In other cases some form of protection was afforded, an urn being generally provided in cases of incineration. Sometimes the head alone was shielded, either by two pieces of stone placed in a ∧-shaped manner over it, or by being embedded in gravel before the rough stones of the tumulus were heaped up over the body. Sometimes a cist was excavated for the body, and this cist may have been lined with stones or with wood, and roofed. A hollowed trunk of a tree sometimes has been used as a

[1] "Two skeletons lay side by side, evidently those of a man and a woman—the bodies touched each other—the head of each leaned towards the other, so that the foreheads touched so intimately that the blade of a knife could not be pressed between them. The right arm of the man lay across his breast, that of the woman by her right side, over which his left arm was crossed, apparently to clasp the left hand of the woman, whose arm was bent in that direction across the body."—Warne, *Celtic Tumuli of Dorset.* [2] Bateman, *Ten Years' Digging,* 78.

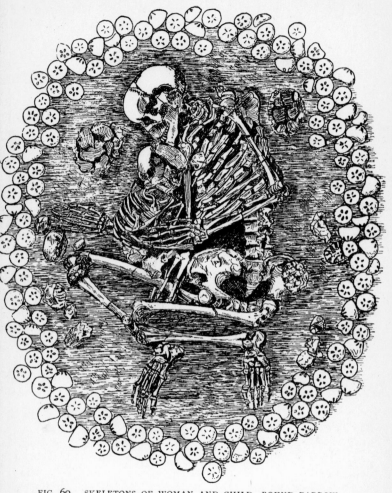

FIG. 60.   SKELETONS OF WOMAN AND CHILD, ROUND BARROW
Dunstable Downs

(*By kind permission of W. G. Smith*)

L

coffin, or a similar receptacle has been formed from boards. In one case given by Greenwell the remains lay on a wooden platform, in a cavity formed in the clay and itself lined with planks, the idea apparently being to keep the body from the wet. A chamber of the beehive type has also been found in the centre of a barrow for the reception of the body. In certain cases no trace of human remains has been found in a barrow, though implements and perhaps pottery may have been brought to light. By some writers such mounds have been looked upon as cenotaphs, but as Greenwell rightly points out, the idea which gives rise to the erection of a cenotaph is one which belongs to an age more artificial than we can suppose that to have been which saw the construction of the round barrows. What is far more likely is that, owing to some peculiarity of the soil, the entire of the human remains have become decomposed, only the imperishable stone implements entombed with the body remaining. Alien interments may be met with in the case of round barrows as in that of their long predecessors.

Accompanying Gifts.—The objects buried with the dead in the long barrows were, as we saw, very few in number ; in the round variety the condition is just the reverse. Implements of stone and bronze, the latter of early types, pottery, ornaments of gold, amber, and jet, with other objects, are found with the skeletons or ashes of the dead. The pottery will be dealt with separately in its own place, and no special description of the other objects need be given, since many of them have already been touched upon in previous chapters. A few further points may be mentioned here. Gold has not been found in any great abundance in English barrows. Hoare cites instances from six barrows in Wilts, and perhaps this is the largest number which could be claimed by any county. The whole number of finds is but small, and the character of the articles found is not imposing. Evidently there was no great introduction of this metal into the country during the period of the construction of the round barrows. Amber, jet and glass beads, and ornaments, have been found, but not with any great frequency. The necklace drawn in Fig. 54 is an example of work in the second of these materials. Pottery, implements of stone and of bronze, form the most numerous classes, and the discoveries in these directions have afforded most valuable information to the students of prehistoric archæology. Raddle, a substance of which there is no doubt that primitive man was very fond, has been found, as in a barrow opened by Bateman,[1] where there was discovered a flat piece of sandstone rubbed hollow on one side, and a round piece of raddle or red war-paint, which, from its abraded surface, must have been in much request, probably for colouring the skin of its former owner. Where this substance has been found in tumuli it seems to have been always associated with well-made flint implements.

Flint and steel for the making of fire have also been found in tumuli, the latter being represented by a nodule of pyrites, and both it and its fellow flint showing signs of use. Similar objects have been found in Saxon graves on the Continent.[2] They have also been buried with the dead by Lapps.

Pottery.—The important subject of pottery can only be touched upon here, but some mention must be made of the characteristic features of this work and the varieties of vessels met with in the barrows of the Neolithic and bronze periods. So far no definite evidence is forthcoming that pottery was made during the Palæolithic

[1] *Ten Years' Digging,* 168.
[2] De Baye, *The Industrial Arts of the Anglo-Saxons,* p. 96.

period, in fact, Mortillet lays down the law that in France and in England there are no remains of pottery belonging to that time, if indeed pottery was then manufactured. During the bronze and Neolithic periods, however, plenty was made, and there is no great difference between that belonging to the earlier and later dates. In the bronze period the articles were for the most part smaller, with thinner walls and finer paste. The ornamentation, though on the same scheme and consisting of geometric figures, was lighter, and the patterns were more artistic. There are more cups, dishes, and plates, but the differences are of a minor character, and, with the note just given, the same description will suffice for the work of both periods.

The pottery was always made by hand, that is to say, without a wheel, that useful invention having come in with the late Celtic period. It was burnt, but in an open fire and not in a kiln. In most examples, and in all those of any considerable size, small stones have been mixed with the clay of which the vessel was compounded. It was never glazed with a true glaze, though many drinking cups have a kind of polish upon them. It is clear that this was intentionally produced, and the method adopted was probably that of rubbing the vessel, when the clay of which it was composed had partly dried, with a piece of hard stone or perhaps with a bone implement. There are never any signs that colour was applied as a decoration.

It was almost always ornamented, and the patterns on it were of a geometrical, never of a biomorphic, character. Moreover, the patterns were almost always sunk into the clay, the use of raised bands being rare. A common method of effecting the ornamentation was to impress a twisted thong upon the moist clay either in continuous bands as in Fig. 61, or in shorter lengths as in Fig. 63, where a kind of herring-bone pattern has been thus produced. In other cases ornamentation has been produced by impression of the point of the finger or by making geometrical figures in lines or rows of dots with the point of some sharp instrument. Sometimes, though rarely, the vessels are provided with feet; covers also are very rare. Ears or lugs sometimes occur, and these may be either pierced or unpierced; the latter, according to Greenwell, belonging to a later date. There may be four pierced or four unpierced ears; in the vessel represented in Fig. 62 there are eleven vertical piercings, opening both above and below, within the cavity. A cup with a single handle, capable of admitting one finger only, has been discovered in a barrow.

The quality of the pottery varies a good deal, and wide differences may be observed between the examples in the same interment. "It is no uncommon occurrence," says Greenwell, "to find in the same barrow, and under circumstances which show that the several vessels are the product of the same period, some which evidence considerable skill, whilst others might have been made by the veriest tyro in the trade."

Four classes of vessels have been met with in connection with interments. With the exception of the cinerary urns, as to the purpose of which there can be no doubt, since the burnt remains of the dead are found in them, the names which have been given to these objects are of a more or less fanciful character. Still, as they serve a purpose in dividing the specimens into definite classes, they may continue to be used until some better nomenclature is accepted.

(i.) The most common objects are those known as *Food Vessels*, which have been found in association with both burnt and unburnt bodies. They are from three to eight inches in height, and vary considerably in shape. Commonly they are more or less conical below, with a parallel-sided upper portion or even a contracted mouth. Knobs or ears are often found around the shoulder of the vase, and they have been ornamented freely in the manner already described.

(ii.) *Drinking Cups* are met with in considerable numbers, but not so commonly as the first-named variety. Commonly they fall into one or other of two classes, though exceptional forms are met with. The first type narrows from the mouth to a point generally somewhat above the middle. From this the vessel swells out, again to taper at the base. The second type, the lines of which are less flowing and graceful, is rounder at its lower portion than the first, and from the upper part of this segment the sides expand, without any curvature until they reach the mouth.

FIG. 61. CINERARY URN (PLAIN PATTERN)
Durrington (height, 13½ inches)

FIG. 62. CINERARY URN
Woodyates (height, 18½ inches)

(iii.) *Cinerary Urns* (Figs. 61 and 62) are the largest examples of pottery met, ranging in height from five inches to three feet. The breadth at the widest portion

is generally equal to the height.   In shape they generally
form two truncated cones, the larger forming the basal
portion, the smaller the upper.   Where the cones meet
the upper forms an overhanging ring, a very characteristic
feature of all shapes of cinerary urns.   The ornamentation
is often confined to the upper cone, but may extend below
it.   A less common form of urn, met with in Dorsetshire,
is almost tub-shaped.   Fig. 62 represents a large urn 18½
inches in height and 15½ inches in diameter at the top.   It
was found in a barrow at Woodyates, and has the overhanging rim.   The upper part is ornamented with rows of
diagonal, impressed-cord lines enclosed within vertical
lines of the same, so as
to form a herring-bone
pattern.   Round the
shoulder is a line of
thumbnail-shaped cord
impressions.   It is in
the Devizes Museum.

(iv.) *Incense Cups* are
always found with burnt
bones, and may per-
haps have been cinerary
urns for the remains of
infants.   They often ex-
hibit the feature, rare in
other kinds of pottery, of
perforations.   They are
generally of finer clay
than the other varieties,
and of small size.   Sometimes they have a kind of
grape pattern upon them
(Fig. 64).   Fig. 63 is an
incense cup of thick

FIG. 63.   PART OF "INCENSE" CUP.
Winterbourne Stoke (height 1½ inches)

FIG. 64.   "INCENSE" CUP, GRAPE PATTERN
Normanton, Wilts (height, 2¾ inches)

coarse clay with two perforations, and marked with cord ornamentation.

It appears that all the varieties described above were made for sepulchral purposes, for the ordinary domestic pottery, as far as we know it, was dark-coloured, hard-baked, and perfectly plain and without ornament.

LIST OF BARROWS IN ENGLAND.

(With regard to this list, it has not always been found possible to determine from the Ordnance Map whether a given mound is a long or a round barrow. All those stated to be long may be taken to belong to that class. The remainder are almost entirely round barrows, but it is possible that amongst them may also be included some examples of the other class. Moreover, since the nature of a mound can only be told by excavation, since Romans and Saxons threw up barrows very like to those of the bronze and Early Iron period, and since rubbish heaps, natural hillocks, and foundations of windmills have sometimes been taken for barrows, it cannot be guaranteed that all the objects contained in this list are sepulchral in their nature ; but this at least may be said, that all of them have been claimed as barrows, and many, if not most, of them have been proved to be such. No attempt has been made to include in the list all the round barrows of the country, but it is hoped that the facts given may afford some idea of the distribution of sepulchral mounds of the pre-Roman period throughout England. Some references, here as elsewhere, have been given to the literature of the subject. The reader is asked also to refer to the general statement as to these lists made in the Preface.)

BEDFORDSHIRE—

Leighton Buzzard.
Wing, near Leighton Buzzard.

BERKSHIRE—

Bearwood. In a wood near Wokingham.
Blewbury, 1½ S. of. Seven barrows. 2 S. of, is another near a square camp.

BERKSHIRE (*contd.*)—

> *Brimpton, several large circular barrows.[1]
> Childrey.[1]
> Kingston. Lisle Park, N. of.
> *Lambourn,[1] $1\frac{1}{4}$ E. of. Two. $1\frac{1}{4}$ S.W. of. One. (In one a half nodule of pyrites found.)
> Letcomb Bassett.[1]
> Newbury, $1\frac{1}{4}$ S.W. of. Four.
> Upper Lambourn, $1\frac{1}{2}$ N.E. of. Twenty. Contents in British Museum.

BUCKINGHAMSHIRE—

> "Adwell Cop.," $\frac{1}{2}$ S.E. of Adwell.
> Great Kimble, near the church (Ro.-Brit. pottery, *Proc. Soc. Ant.*, xii. 340).
> Horsenden, $1\frac{1}{4}$ S.E. of. Two.
> Icknield Street, along the line of. The most important group is at Eddlesborough.
> "Thornborough Mounds," 2 E. of Buckingham. Two.
> West Wycombe, $2\frac{1}{2}$ N.W. of. Two.
> *White Leaf Hill, near.

CAMBRIDGESHIRE—

> "Chronicle Hills," $\frac{3}{4}$ N.E. of Thriplow. Three large barrows (*Gent. Mag. Lib. Arch.*, i. 88).
> "Copley Hill," $\frac{3}{4}$ E. of the Gogmagog Hills.
> Five Hill Field, near Royston (*Archæol.*, xxxii. 357).
> "Moulton Hills," near Bourn.
> Muttilow Hill (Burnt Bones, Jewitt, 35).
> "Wormwood Hill," $\frac{1}{4}$ S. of Vandlebury.

CHESHIRE—

> Alderley Park. Two.
> Codlington.
> Cotebrook, 1 N. of.
> Goostrey, 1 E. of. Three.
> *Eddesbury Hill. Near this are "Glead Hill Cob," "Castle Cob," and "The Seven Lows."
> Withington Hall, $1\frac{1}{4}$ W. of. Three.

[1] *Archæologia*, lii. 1.

CORNWALL—

Angrowse Mullion. (Bronze dagger, urn, and piece of pyrites.)

Ballowal, St. Just.   Karn Gluze.

Boscregan.   Karn Leskys and Karn Creis.   (Pottery and burnt bones, Borlase.)

Bossiney.

Braddock Down, near Bodmin Road Station.

Castle Down, near St. Columb Major.

Harlyn Bay.   Late Celtic interments in cists.

Pennance, near St. Ives.

Resparvel Down.

Rillaton.   (Contained a gold cup.)

Samson Island (Scilly).   (Opened 1862.)

Tregaseale, St. Just.

Treloe Down.

Trevalgue.   (Perforated axe-hammer.   *Archæol.*, xliv. 423.)

(For further notices of Cornish barrows, see Borlase, *Archæologia*, xlix. 181, and Nænia Cornubiæ.)

CUMBERLAND—

Long.

   *Peelohill, near Bewcastle.   "Cairn o' the Mount."

Round.

Arthuret (perhaps eskers).

Aspatria, Beacon Hill.

   *Aughertree Fell.

Barnscar.   Many cairns (unexamined).

Bewcastle, "Murchie's Cairn."

Binsey, summit of.

Blencarn.

Blindcrake, between this place and Redmain, "The Grey Barrow" at Isell.

Boothby.

   *Broadfield, Inglewood Forest, near Highhead Castle.

Castle Carrock, near Brampton.   (*British Barrows*, 379.)

Cockermouth, near.   "The Toot Hill."

Dunmail Raise.

CUMBERLAND (*contd.*)—

> Eamont.
> Egremont Common.
> Fishers Cross.
> Friars Moor.
> Geltsdale, Coldfell.
> Gillalees Beacon.
> Graysonlands, Glassonby. (Bronze Age interments in tumulus with circle. *British Barrows*, 7. *Proc. Soc. Ant.*, ii. xviii. 321.)
> Hallbank Gate.
> Harras.
> Hartside, Benty Hill. "Old Anthony's Chair."
> Keswick, Latrig.
> Kirkoswald, Parks Tumulus. (Bronze.)
> Kirksanton, near Millom.
> Knock's Cross, Port Carlisle.
> *Newton Regny.

DERBYSHIRE—

> Bakewell, 1 E. of. On Calton Pastures. Five tumuli.
> Blake Low. Longstone Edge.
> Brassington, near. "Minning Low." (Jewitt, p. 54.)
> Brushfield Hough, in Monsal Dale.
> Bunkers Hill, near Arbor Low.
> Elton Moor. (Pyrites.)
> Eyam Moor. Six tumuli.
> Flax Dale. (Internal circles of stones surrounding urn with burnt bones.)
> Grinlow, near Buxton. (*Proc. Soc. Ant.*, ii. xv. 419.)
> Gunton, near Buxton. (*ib. ib.*)
> Hartington, near. "Carden Low." (Bronze dagger.)
> Hitter Hill. (Jewitt, 16.)
> Hollinsclough, 1¾ N.E. of.
> Kenslow.
> Melbourne, near. "Knowle Hills."
> Middleton-by-Youlgrave. "Borther Low." (Bronze celt.)
> Parcelly Hay, near Arbor Low.

DERBYSHIRE (*contd.*)—

  Parwich Moor.   (Bronze dagger and celt.)

  Pilsbury, near Hartington.   "Castle Hill Barrows," and
    "Wolf's Cote Barrows."

  Stanton Moor.   (Covered vase, *Archæol.*, viii. 62.)

  Stoney Middleton, 1¼ S. of.   Three tumuli.

  Stoop High Edge, 3¼ S.S.E. of Buxton.   (*Proc. Soc. Ant.*,
    ii. xvi. 261.)

  Thirkellow Frith, 3 S.S.W. of do.   (*Ib.*, xv. 419, and
    xvi. 261.)

  Tissington.   (Jet ring.   Jewitt, 176.)

  (For full list of lows in Derbyshire, see Bateman, *Ten
    Years' Digging*.   Jewitt, *Grave Mounds*, may also be
    consulted.)

DEVONSHIRE—

  Black Down, Symondsborough.

  Broadbury, between Okehampton and Holsworthy.

  Cosdon Beacon, Dartmoor.

  Farway, many barrows.

  Hookner Tor.   Several cairns, one with ring of upright
    stones.

  Sidmouth, near.   Broad Down.

  Stanborough Camp.   (Opened 1799.)

  Western Beacon.

  (See Page, *Exploration of Dartmoor*.)

DORSETSHIRE—

  (This county contains a very large number of barrows.
    Only a few of the most important sites have been in-
    cluded in this list.)

  Long.

    Bere Regis.

    Chettle.

    Eastbury, near.

    Gussage, near.   Long barrows.

    Litton Cheney, 1 E. of.

    Pimperne.

    Tarrant Hinton.

    *Wor Barrow.   (Pitt-Rivers, *Excavations*, iv.)

DORSETSHIRE (*contd.*)—

Round.

> Bincombe Barrows. Many tumuli, one, opened 1784, contained bronze dagger.
>
> Bradford Down.
>
> *Bridehead, near. ("For sight of barrows not to be equalled in this world."—Stukeley.)
>
> Busbury Rings, within the area of the camp.
>
> Came Down. (Stones with concentric circle markings covered two burials after cremation.)
>
> *Chalbury, near. "Rimbury." (An urn-field, not barrows, the necropolis, perhaps, of the adjacent town of Chalbury. Urns, etc., in the Dorchester Museum.)
>
> Deverel Barrow, near Dewlish.
>
> East Chaldon, near. "The Five Marys."
>
> Eggardon Hill.
>
> Fontmel Down.
>
> Grimstone, ¾ N. of.
>
> Handley, near. Many tumuli. (Some examined by Pitt-Rivers, *Excavations,* ii. Bronze.)
>
> Litton Cheney.
>
> Longbredy. Disc barrows.
>
> Long Bury Barrow, near Gillingham. (*Said* to be Danish.)
>
> Milborne Stileham.
>
> Pimperne.
>
> Puddletown Heath. Many tumuli.
>
> *Stowborough. "King Barrow." (Opened 1767. Tree coffin, remains of body wrapped in deerskin.)
>
> Tarrant Hinton, near.
>
> Tollard Royal, near. Woodcuts.
>
> Winterborne Kingston.
>
> Winterborne Steepleton. (Pierced greenstone axe.)
>
> Woodyates. Disc barrows.
>
> Woolsbarrow, Bloxworth Heath.
>
> Worgret, ½ N.W. of.

> (See Warne's *Celtic Tumuli of Dorset,* also his map and that of Pitt-Rivers. Also *Archæologia,* xxx. 327.)

DURHAM—

Long.

Copt Hill, Houghton-le-Spring. (Cremated burial of Stone Age, with alien Bronze Age interment.)

Round.

Bradley, near Ryton. (Contracted body in cist.)

Eggleston in Teesdale. (Fosse and circle of stones, "The Standing Stones.)

Hetton. "The Fairies' Cradle." (Cairn of stones containing urn.)

Ryton, to N. of Churchyard.

Sacriston, near Durham. (Unburnt body in cist with cup.)

Sherburn Grange. (Cist with contracted body.)

Silksworth, Steeple Hill. (Unburnt body and urn with burnt bones of child.)

Sunderland, near. Hambleton Hill. (Barrows with urns containing burnt bones.)

Sunderland, near. Tunstall Hill. (Cist with unburnt body.)

Treindon Grange. (Urn with burnt bones.)

Wardon Law, below it is a small barrow.

Westow. (Cist with contracted body and flint knife.)

ESSEX—

Aldham, near Colchester. Near the Church House.

Askesden, near Saffron Walden. In Plesh Wood.

Chadwell, near Romford.

Hockley, near Rochford. "Plumboro' Mount."

Lawford, near Mannington. Near the Church. (Opened middle of last century, contained black pottery.)

Maldon, near Beeleigh Abbey.

Messing, near Colchester. In Podswood.

Navestock.

Northey Island, on the Marshes.

Rowhedge, or East Douyland. Near the old Church.

Shoebury. (Late Celtic urn-field, not tumuli, *Proc. Soc. Ant.* ii. xvi. 259.)[1]

Sturmere, near Sudbury. Two tumuli.

Theydon Bois, near Epping. Three tumuli.

[1] I have thought it well to include the late Celtic burial-places in this list.

GLOUCESTERSHIRE—

Long.

Ablington. (Opened 1854.)

Avening, near. With menhir on it "The Tinglestone."

Avening Barrow.

*Belas Knapp, above Winchcombe. (Contained thirty-eight skeletons, see Mrs. Dent's *History of Winchcombe.* Unfortunately almost ruined by boys since opened.)

Bisley, 2 N. of. Two barrows at the village of Camp.

Bisley, 2 E. of. Edgworth Barrow.

Bisley, 1 E. of. "The Giant's Stone Barrow." (Almost entirely removed.)

Bisley, N. of. Througham Barrow. (Chambers used as pigstye.)

Bourton-on-the-Water, near. Cold Aston.

Boxwell. Leighterton Barrow. (Opened 1700, burnt and unburnt interments.)

*Brimpsfield, Buckholt Wood. "West Tump." (Contained twenty skeletons.)

Cheltenham, 3 S. of. On Shurdington Hill. "Crippett's Barrow." (*Archæologia* xlii. 201.)

Cirencester, 5 N.W. of. Duntisbourne Barrow. (Central part gone, ends resemble and have been taken for round barrows.)

Cirencester, in "Quern's Field," close to amphitheatre. (See Buckman's *Corinium.*)

Duntisbourne Abbots. "Hoarstone tumulus." (Composed of loose quarry stones. Contained eight or nine bodies.)

Farmington, within the entrenchments of Norbury Camp.

Lower Swell. In "Cow Common Field." (Opened in 1867, skeletons, flints, and pottery. *British Barrows,* 445, and Rolleston, *Collected Works,* i. 353.

Minchinhampton Common. "Whitfield Tump." Remains of barrow.

Nailsworth, 1½ S. of. Lechmore Barrow, nearly destroyed.

Nailsworth, 2 N.W. of. Bown Hill Barrow. (Opened 1863, skeletons, etc. *Proc. Cots. Field Club,* iii. 109, v. 279.)

GLOUCESTERSHIRE (*contd.*)—

Nympsfield. (Opened 1862, skeletons, flints, pottery. *Jl. Anthrop. Soc.*, s. i., iii. 66.)

North Leach, 2 S. of. At Crickley Barrow. Two barrows.

North Leach, 4 N.W. of. Haselton Barrow. A second close to it.

North Leach, 2 S.E. of Lodge Park.

*Notgrove, 1 N.W. of. In the "Poor's Lots." (Opened by Witts, see his book *ut infra.*)

Prinknash Park. In Pope's Wood. "Idol's Barrow."

Randwick, 2 N.W. of Stroud.

Rodmarton. "Windmill Tump." (Opened 1863, skeletons, flints, pottery. *Archæol.*, ix. 367.)

Selsley Hill. "The Toots."

Stow-on-the-Wold, 3 miles from, in Eyford parish. (*Brit. Bar.*, 514.)

*Uley, near the camp. "Hetty Pagler's Tump." (Contained nearly 30 skeletons and an alien (Rom.) interment. *Archæol.*, xlii. 201. This tumulus can be entered and examined, but the key of the enclosure must first be obtained.)

Upper Swell. (Skeletons, flints, pottery. *Brit. Bar.*, 524.)

Willersey, in the camp. (Nature rather doubtful.)

Withington, 1 S. of.

Round.

Witts (*Archæological Handbook of Gloucestershire*, a book which, with its accompanying map, will be found indispensable to any person working at the early history of the county) enumerates 126 of these. The following are among the most important.

Avening Copse. "The Oven." (Burnt bones and flints.)

Bisley. "Money Tump." Two others between this and Lypiatt Park.

Cheltenham, 4 S. of. Near the "Air Balloon" public-house. Three barrows.

Cheltenham, 2 S. of. Dry Heath Field.

Dowdeswell, 1 S. of. Foxcote.

Dursley, 2½ S.E. of. Symonds Hall Farm. Two. Another on Symonds Hall Hill.

Lower Swell. "Cow Common." Eight barrows. (*Brit. Bar.*, 445.)

M

GLOUCESTERSHIRE (*contd.*)—

    Leckhampton Hill, near camp.

    Lower Swell, 2 W. of.   Picked Morden.

    Nailsworth, 1 S.E. of.

    Thornbury, 1¼ S. of.   Near the "Ship" Inn.   Two.

    Tormarton, 1 S.E. of.   Three.

    Turkdean, 1 S.E. of.   Three at Leygore Farm.

    Snowshill. (Bronze. *Archæol.*, lii. 1.)

HAMPSHIRE—

   Long.

    Barton Stacey, 1¼ S. of.   Two.

    Clanfield, 1 E. of.   On Clanfield Down.

    Winchester, on St. Giles Hill.

   Round.

    Andover, Road from Winchester to, 6½ N.W. of Winchester.   One on either side of the road.

   *Baughurst Common. Several.

    Beauworth, 1 S. of.

    Brightstone Down, I. of Wight.

    Broughton. (Urn with burnt bones.)

   *Burghclere, 1¼ S. of. "The Seven Barrows." (Burnt bones, flints, pottery, one bronze pin. *Proc. Soc. Ant.*, ii. x. 18.)

    Cheriton, ½ E. of. Two.

    Gorley Common, 1½ S.E. of. "Black barrow." Oval tumulus.

    Itchenstoke Down. Several. One 1 W. of Abbotstone, and one in Abbotstone Wood.

    Mitcheldever. One in Cranbourne Wood and two on Down. 2 W. of Mitcheldever Tunnels.

    New Forest. One near Stony Cross, another in Berry Lodge Walk.

    Petersfield, ½ E. of. On Heath Common. Nine.

    Petersfield, Butser Hill. Several.

    Preshaw, 1½ N. of Preshaw House.

    Sydmonton, ¾ S. of.

    Winchester, 1½ S.W. of. On Compton Down.

    Winchester, 2 S.E. of.

    Woolmer, Several.

HEREFORDSHIRE—

    Bucton Corn Mill, W. of.

    King's Pyon (?).

    Leintwardine, ½ W. of.   Two.

    St. Weonard's.

    Walford, near Brampton Bryan.

    Whitchurch, 1 S.W. of.   Three.

HERTFORDSHIRE—

    Great Amwell.

    Hitchin.   (Opened 1806 and 1816.)

    Royston.

    Therfield.

    Widford.

KENT—

    Long.

    Chilham.   "Julaber's Grave."

    Round.

    *Aylesford.   British urn-field, not tumuli. (*Proc. Soc. Ant.*,
        ii. xiii. 18.)

    Benstead.

    Bourne Park.

    Dover, near. (Burnt bones and pottery. *Archæol.* xlv. 53.)

    Ewell.   In Lousyberry Wood.

    Eythorne.

    Folkestone.   Sugar Loaf Hill.

    Greenwich Park.

    Iffin's Wood, near Canterbury (*Archæol.* xxx. 57.)

    Isle of Harty.

    Queenborough.

    Shorne. (*Proc. Soc. Ant.*, ii. xviii. 73.)

    Sibertswold.   "Rupert's Butts."

    Stowting.   "Mountain Hill."

    Thanet.   "Hackendon Banks."

    Wye.   "The Giant's Grave."

    Walmer. (Bones and flint chips, *Proc. Soc. Ant.*, ii.
        v. 31.)

LANCASHIRE—

>Bannishead Mire, near Coniston. Ring-mound.[1]
>Bleaberry Haws, near Coniston. Ring-mound.[1]
>Goathwaite Moor, near Coniston. Ring-mound.[1]
>High Haume, Ireleth. "The Beacons." Sepulchral (?)
>Kirkby Ireleth. Ring-mound.
>Todmorden. Pottery, burnt bones, bronze implements, and jet. (*Reliquary*, ix. 276.)
>Torver Beck. Ring-mound.
>Torver Hare Crag. Ring-mound.
>Urswick, near. Birkrigg Common.
>Weeton Lane Head, near Birkham.

LEICESTERSHIRE—

>Hallaton, ½ W. of. "Castle Hill." (Early Iron Age).
>Kibworth Beauchamp, N. of.
>Ratcliffe-on-the-Wreak, ½ S. of. Shapley Hill.

LINCOLNSHIRE—

>Ash Hill, ½ S. of Swinhope.
>Broughton. (Flint in urn of burnt bones.)
>Bully Hill, ½ S.E. of Tathwell. Six.
>Burgh-le-Marsh.
>Cleatham, ½ N.W. of.
>Dowsby, ½ N. of.
>Fordington, ¾ S. of Ulceby.
>Revesby, N.E. of. Two.
>Scunthorpe, near.
>Walton-le-Marsh, ½ N. of "Castle Hill."

MIDDLESEX.—Hampstead. "Boadicea's Grave." (Probably early bronze. *Proc. Soc. Ant.*, ii. xv. 240.)

MONMOUTHSHIRE.—Risca, 1 N. of.

NORFOLK—

>Bircham. (Gold beads.)
>Broome Heath, ¾ E. of Ditchington.
>Cressingham. (Amber, gold, bronze.)

---

[1] *i.e.* a low bank of earth or stones forming a small circle. Probably sepulchral. See *Archæol.* iii. 415.

NORFOLK (*contd.*)—

> Roughton, N. of.
> Rushford, 1 W. of.   " The Seven Hills."
> Salthouse, 1 S. of.   Eight.
> Weybourne, ½ W. of.

NORTHAMPTONSHIRE—

> Grafton Regis.
> Kings Sutton.   " The Lows."
> Longman's Hill, in Pitsford Parish.
> Northampton, meadows near.
> Northampton, " Danesbury Camp." (British Cemetery, not tumuli, of perhaps first century B.C.)
> Woodford, near Thrapston.

NORTHUMBERLAND—

> Alwinton.   (*Brit. Bar.* 422.)
> Ashington.   (Cists with urns.)
> Bamborough Castle, near.   (*Brit. Bar.*, 413.)
> Broomlee Lough, ¾ S. of.
> Broom Ridge.
> Carham.   (Unburnt body with bronze dagger.)
> Chatton, near.   (*Brit. Bar.*, 412.)
> Chesterhope Common, 1¼ W. of Sweethope Loughs. (Gold beads.   *Brit. Bar.*, 436.)
> Cheswick.   (Unburnt body with bronze dagger.)
> Coldsmouth Hill, near Kirk Newton.
> Doddington.   (*Brit. Bar.*, 410.)
> Eglingham, 2 N.W. of.   Thirteen.   (One with circle of stones.   *Brit. Bar.*, 418.)
> Ford Common.   (Flints and pottery.   Stones with cup-markings.   *Brit. Bar.*, 403.)
> Haltwhistle, near.
> Haltwhistle, 1 N. of.   Eight.
> Holystone.
> Ingram, 1½ W. of.
> Kirk Whelpington.   (*Brit. Bar.*, 433.)
> Nether Witton, ½ N.W. of.
> North Sunderland.   (Bones of a girl and three drinking-cups.   *Trans. Berw. Nat. Club.*, iv. 428.)

NORTHUMBERLAND (*contd.*)—

> Otterburn, 1 N.W. of.
>
> Ovingham. (*Brit. Bar.*, 437.)
>
> Plessy. (Many burnt bodies in urns.)
>
> Rothbury. Cartington Fell. (One with circle of stones. *Brit. Bar.*, 428.)
>
> Seghill. (Quartzite celt in cist with infant body.)
>
> Stamfordham, near Black Haddon. (Stones with cup-markings.)
>
> Warkworth. (*Archæol.*, lii. 1.)

NOTTINGHAMSHIRE—

> Blidworth, 1 E. of.
>
> Oxton, 1 N. of.
>
> Potters Hill, near South Collingham.

OXFORDSHIRE—

> *Long.*
>
> > Lyneham. (*Proc. Soc. Ant.*, ii. xv. 404.)
>
> *Round.*
>
> > Ash Hall Barrow, near Ash Hall on the Akeman Street.
> >
> > Chadlington, 1¼ E. of.
> >
> > Henley Park, ½ N. of Henley-on-Thames.
> >
> > Mixbury, ½ W. of.
> >
> > Shutford, 1 S. of.
> >
> > Wytham. (Burnt bones, flints, bone fibula. *Brit. Bar.*, 352.)

SHROPSHIRE—

> Beguildy, ½ N.W. of.
>
> Corra, ¾ S. of.
>
> Felindre.
>
> Hope, ½ N. of.
>
> Little Wenlock, ¾ N. of.
>
> Longmynd, "Robin Hood's Butts," and other tumuli.
>
> Ludlow Racecourse, "Robin Hood's Butts."
>
> Marton village, E. of.
>
> Prees, 1½ N.E. of.
>
> Rushbury.
>
> Wrekin, The.

SOMERSET—

    Long.

      Nempnet, " Fairy's Toot." (Chambered.)

      Orchardleigh. (Chambered.)

     *Stoney Littleton. (Chambered. *Archæologia,* xix. and xxxviii.)

    Round.

      Dundry Hill.

      Priddy, on Mendip. "Priddy Nine Barrows."

      Priddy, on Mendip. Ashen Lane. Eight.

      Sigwell. Twin and Round Barrows. (Bronze. Rolleston, *Sci. Papers,* i. 440.)

STAFFORDSHIRE—

      Brundlow, near Sheen. (*Proc. Soc. Ant.*, ii. xv. 428.)

      Earl's Sterndale, near. "Hitter Hill." (Opened 1862, skeletons and urns.)

      Elford, near. "Robin Hood's Butts."

      Harlington. Many tumuli on the hills near.

      Roylow, near Sheen. (*Proc. Soc. Ant.,* ii. xv. 419.)

      Tissington, near. "Sharp Low."

      Tixall Heath. "The King's Low" and "The Queen's Low."

      Uttoxeter High Wood. "Toot Hill."

      Wetton Long Low. Twin Barrow. (Jewitt, *Grave Mounds,* 36.) (? really a long barrow.)

SUFFOLK—

      Aldborough. Six tumuli opened 1862.

      Fornham St. Geneviéve.

      Risby Heath.

      Warren Hill, near Mildenhall. (Eighteen deer-antlers over the body. *Jl. Suff. Inst. of Arch.,* iv. 289.)

SURREY—

      Addington, near. Thunderfield Common. Twenty-five.

      Coulsdon, near. Farthing Down.

      Elstead, near.

      Frensham Common.

      Pattenham Heath.

      Westcott, $1\frac{1}{4}$ W. of.

SUSSEX—

       Alciston, near. Many.

       Graffham, $1\frac{1}{4}$ S.W. of.

     *Hove, near Brighton. (Tree coffin, stone axe, bronze knife, amber cup. *Suss. Arch. Coll.*, ix. 120.)

       Kingby Bottom.

       Lewes, Downs near. Many.

       Rottingdean, $1\frac{1}{2}$ N. of.

       Treyford, $\frac{3}{4}$ S. of. "The Devil's Jumps." Five tumuli.

       West Burton, $\frac{3}{4}$ S.W. of.

WARWICKSHIRE—

       Brinklow.

       Compton Verney, near. Tachbrook. Knightlow Cross.

       Coombe Abbey, $\frac{1}{2}$ N. of.

       Hartshill, W. of. "Key Abbey Mound."

       Seckington.

       Wolstone. Near the Fosse Way.

WESTMORLAND—

    Long.

     *Crosby Garrett, Raisett Pike. (Burnt bodies and alien interments. *Brit. Bar.*, 510.)

    Round.

       Ashfell, Kirby Stephen.

       Askham. Cairn with ring of stones. (*Br. Bar.*, 400.)

       Brackenber Moor.

       Crosby Garrett. Cairns. (*Br. Bar.*, 386.)

       Crosby Ravensworth. (*Ib.*, 396.)

       Dufton Church.

       Gamelands, Orton.

       Great Asby Scar. (*Br. Bar.*, 396.)

       Kirby Stephen. Six barrows, one contained tree-coffin with bronze bowl, perhaps post-Roman. (*Br. Bar.*, 382.)

       Ravenstonedale. (*Ib.*, 393.)

       Shap, Raftland Forest.

       Warcop. (*Br. Bar.*, 385.)

WILTSHIRE—

Long.   Unchambered.

Examined by Cunnington and Hoare, and described in
Ancient Wilts, and by Thurnam, *Archæologia*, xlii. 161.

Arne Hill.

Bishops Cannings.

Boreham.   "King's Barrow."

Bratton.

Brixton Deverell.

Corton.

"Druid's Head," near.

Easton Hill.

Figheldean.

Fittleton.

Fyfield, near Pewsey.   "Giant's Grave."

Heytesbury.   "Bowls Barrow."

Horton.

Knook.   Two.

Knowl Hill.

Normanton.

Norton Bavant.

Scratchbury.

Shalbourne.

Sherrington.

Stockton.

Stonehenge.   Two.

Tilshead.   "White Barrow."

Tilshead.   East.

Tilshead.   Old Ditch.

Tilshead.   Lodge.

Tinhead.

Warminster.

Willesford.   "Ell Barrow."

Wilsford.

Winterbourne Stoke.

Long.   Chambered.

East Kennett.

Lanhill.   "Hubba's Lowe."

WILTSHIRE (*contd.*)—

> Littleton Drew. "Lugbury."
> Luckington. "Giants Caves."
> Monkton. "Millbarrow."
> Oldbury.
> Rockley.
> Temple Farm.
> Tidcombe.
> Walker Hill. "Old Adam," or "Adam's Grave."

Round.

> Very numerous. Hoare (*Ancient Wilts*) describes 465 as opened by himself. The following list contains some of the more important localities—
> Aldbourn. Sugar Hill Down. (*Archæol.*, lii. 1.)
> Allington, 1 N. of. "Kitchen Barrows."
> Alton Priors, N. of.
> Avebury, neighbourhood of. Many.
> Bishops Cannings Down.
> Bratton.
> Brigmilstone. (Flint and pyrites found.)
> Cherhill Downs.
> Cliffe Pypard, near Uffcott.
> *Collingbourne Ducis. (Burnt body in hollowed tree-trunk with stag's-horn hammer.)
> Deverills. Many near these villages.
> Everley.
> Hinton Down. (*Archæol.*, lii. 1.)
> Little Durnford. (Covered vase found.)
> Rushmore, near. (Examined by Pitt-Rivers, vol. ii. of *Memoirs*. Bronze.)
> Stonehenge. About 300 in vicinity.
> Tan Hill. (Jet ornament. *Archæol.*, xliii. 510.)
> Upton Lovell. (Bronze pin and perforated stone axe.)
> Warminster, Cop Head. (Fragments of stag's horn.)
> Wilsford. (Bronze celt.)
> Winterbourne Monkton. (Flint implements and jet.)
> (Full information as to this class of barrow in Wilts will be found in Thurnam's paper, *Archæol.*, xliii. 285.)

WORCESTERSHIRE—

Kidderminster Foreign.

Spring Grove, between Kidderminster and Bewdley. "The Devil's Spadeful."

YORKSHIRE—

The barrows in this county are very numerous, and many of them have been opened and described by Canon Greenwell. The figures in brackets after certain of the examples indicate the page in *British Barrows* at which the description occurs. Those marked thus †† are dealt with in *Archæologia,* lii. 1.

Long.

Ebberston (484).

Gilling (550).

Kilburn (501).

Kilham (553).

Market Weighton (505).

Over Sitton (509).

Rudstone (497).

Weston (490).

Willerly (487).

Round.

Acklam Wold. (Burnt and unburnt bodies. Food vessel with cover.)

Ampleforth Moors. Many.

Ayton Moor, Way Hag. (Cup-marked stones.)

Bempton, Metlow Hill. † ¾ N. of Danes' Dyke. (Flints.)

Binnington (179). Flints and pottery.

Bishop's Burton. Several. (Flints and pottery.)

Butterwick (186). (Bronze axe.)

Cherry Burton (279). Four.

Claughton Moor. (Contained stones with cups and circles.)

Cleveland.

Cold Kirby (336).

Cowlam (208, bronze in three, seven others, some with flints).

Danby Moor. Many. One has a ring of stones.

Yorkshire (*contd.*)—

Driffield, Moors near. Many. Objects from them in the Driffield Museum. The Danes' graves are late Celtic. *Journ. Anth. Inst.*, 1903, 66.

Duggleby. Howe Hill Barrow (*Journ. Anth. Inst.*, xxii. 3).

Egton (334). "William Howe." (Jet beads. "Three Howes." (Burnt bones and a flint.)

Etton (282). Seven.

Ferry Fryston (371).

Fimber. (Jet necklace.)

Fimber, on wolds near. (Barrow with oaken coffin.)

Flying Dales. Several.

Folkton (271). †

Ganton (169). Flints and pottery.

Gilling (343). Six.

Goathland, "Simon Howe."

Goodmanham (286). Thirty-eight. (One contained covered vase, another jet necklace and earrings.)

*Gristhorpe. (Oak coffin, bronze knife. Objects in Scarborough Museum.) †

Harpham. (Flints.) †

Helperthorpe. (191–203.) (Flints, bronze, alien interment in one.)

Heslerton (141). Three barrows. Here formerly long barrow, destroyed 1868.

Hunmanby. Two. †

Hutton Buscel (357). "The Three Tremblers," and others.

Hutton Cranswick. (Perforated canine of wolf. Proc. Yorks. Phil. Soc.)

Ilkley, near. Many.

Kilburn (339). (In one a number of cup-marked stones.)

Kilham. "Danes Graves." (Early Iron Age. *Proc. Soc. Ant.*, ii. xvii. 119.)

Kirby Grindalyth (140).

Kirby Underdale (132). (With alien Saxon interments. Flints and burnt bones.)

Langtoft (204). (Pottery.)

Langton (136). (Several interments. Bones, beads, pottery.)

YORKSHIRE (*contd.*)—

    Londesborough (331).

    Lythe. †

    Market Weighton.   Many near.

    Melmerby Common.   (Bone Fibula.)

    Newbold, N. of.   Five opened 1877 (*Proc. Soc. Ant.*, ii. vii. 321).

    Over Sitton (336).

    Potter Brompton Wold (160).   Five.   (Flints, pottery, burnt and unburnt bones.)

    Rudstone (229).   Nine barrows.

    Runwick and Staithes, cliffs between.

   *Rylston (374).   Scale House.   (Interment in hollowed oak-tree.   Clothes of corpse.)

    Sherburn (145).   Several barrows.   (Pottery, flints, stone implements.)

    Skipwith Common.

    Slingsby (347).   Thirteen.   (In one a bone fibula.)

    Thwing (256).   Near this is "Willy Howe," a large barrow opened in 1857, and again by Greenwell. †

    Weaverthorpe (192).   Flints.

    Welburn (356).

    West Tanfield, near Ripon.   "Centre Hill."   (Oak coffin, flints, and pottery.)

    Willerby (130).   Nine.   (Flints, pottery.) †

    Wykeham Moor.   (Cup-marked stones.)

    (Further notes in *Gentleman's Mag.*, lxii. 84, and lxiii. 16 ; and in Ord's *History of Cleveland.*)

CHAPTER VIII

MEGALITHIC REMAINS : DOLMENS—CISTS—CIRCLES —ALIGNMENTS—MENIHIRION

SINCE many of the megalithic monuments are un-doubtedly of a sepulchral nature, and it is highly probable that all of them may be of that character, they naturally fall into place after the burial mounds considered in the last chapter. Monuments of this character have been most elaborately classified by Lukis [1] in a paper which should be studied by those working at the subject.

Dolmens.—The skeleton of one kind of long barrow—the chambered variety—as we saw in the last chapter, consisted of a cell or cells constructed of great stones. If the earth or stones of which the mound or cairn consisted be removed, the skeleton will remain behind exposed, and is then called a dolmen (daul-maen, table-stone). Mr. Gowland would enlarge the definition so as to make the term connote also monuments of the same kind still embedded in their mound, and would thus define the class of objects now under consideration : Stone burial cham-bers, generally of rude megalithic structure, larger than cists, whether covered by a mound or not. In popular parlance, however, the dolmen or Druid's Altar or cromlech —the last two misleading names—is an uncovered struc-

[1] *Archæologia,* xxxv. 232.

ture of stones, made up of two, three, four or more slabs standing upright and supporting a large flat stone, the "cap-stone." (See Figs. 65 and 66 and Fig. 67, which gives a view of the double dolmen at Plas Newydd or Anglesea Castle, Isle of Anglesea). Sometimes there may have been a stone floor, but oftener there is no trace of anything of the kind. Sometimes, though rarely, the dolmen is double, as in the Anglesea example. Or—if indeed this should be classed amongst dolmens—there may be the remains of several chambers as at Weyland Smith's Forge on the Berkshire Downs, where the remains of a chambered tumulus lie uncovered in the interior of a little copse. It has been suggested by some, notably by Fergusson,[1] that some of these monuments were never covered with a mound, but were always sub-aerial. This is an opinion, however, which has never met with general acceptance, and may now be said to be without supporters. That so many of these structures should have been stripped of their superincumbent mound is certainly remarkable, but that some of them have been exposed in recent times is no less true. For example, the dolmen at Lanyon, in Cornwall, the cap-stone of which is believed to weigh fifteen tons, was entirely covered with earth until the beginning of the last century, when the soil was carted away by a farmer who wished to utilise it for the improvement of his land. There was no idea that the mound was other than a natural one, until one hundred cartloads of earth had been removed, when the cap-stone began to appear. When all the earth had been carried away the dolmen was fully exposed. Some broken urns and bones were found inside, but it had evidently been rifled years before. Again at Cnocan, near Mallow, in County Cork, the stones of a cairn were removed gradually for the purpose of road-mending, thus exposing a fine dolmen

[1] *Rude Stone Monuments.*

FIG. 65. DOLMEN

"Devil's Den," near Marlborough

FIG. 66. DOLMEN

Bodowr, Anglesea

containing a skeleton with a bronze sword and other objects. The agriculturist has never had very tender feelings towards the relics of antiquity when they have seemed suitable for any of his purposes, though as late as 1859, in the Isle of Man, a farmer has actually been known to offer up a heifer in sacrifice, to prevent any

FIG. 67. DOUBLE DOLMEN
Plas Newydd, Anglesea

harm befalling him in consequence of the opening of a tumulus on his land. It is unfortunate that similar or any motives have not restrained other early depredators.

"Farmer Green," said Stukeley, in 1710, removed the stones from a long barrow near that at West Kennett "to make mere-stones withal," *i.e.*, boundary stones, probably the boundaries of his sheep-walks. This wretch was the great destroyer of the Avebury avenues and circles, and, according to Thurnam, was probably responsible for the removal of the peristalith which originally encircled the

N

West Kennett barrow. To disinterments of this kind we owe the existing uncovered dolmens of the country. These single cells, covered or uncovered, vary considerably in size. Perhaps the smallest in these islands is that at Bodowr, in the Isle of Anglesea, which will just about accommodate one person in a crouched position. (See Fig. 66.) From this we ascend to the larger Kit's Coty House, to the great dolmen at Pentre-Ifan, and—though monuments of this size are unknown in England—to constructions of the magnitude of that at New Grange, near Drogheda, or the Chamber of Giants at Om, near Copenhagen. In this last there is a passage three metres in length which leads into a large chamber, spacious and high enough for twenty people to walk about in it. The walls, like those of the passage, are formed of large, rough stones, flat and erect. The spaces between them are carefully filled with small stones placed one upon another. The roof of the chamber is formed of large slabs long enough to rest upon the tops of the standing stones. Over this is still the earthen mound, but suppose it removed, and we should have a dolmen—in the common acceptation of the term—of enormous size. Dolmens are known in many parts of the world. They are numerous in Brittany, and here, according to Lukis,[1] they are always included in a mound of stone, or earth, or both. Out of one hundred and fifty dolmens in this district there are only eighteen about which there is no trace of a barrow. In some of these cases, too, there are still the remains of the passage which led to the interior, a passage which would have been quite useless had the structure always been sub-aerial and free-standing. Part of the mound still exists which covered the dolmen near Corancez, in the district of Chartres, an example with a cap-stone fifteen by ten-feet-six in size.[2] The Breton dolmens nearly all have

[1] *Proc. Soc. Ant.*, 1872, 366.   [2] Lewis, *Journ. Anth. Inst.*, 1890, 68.

openings between the south and the east of the compass,
and where there are avenues they are oriented in the same
way. Similar structures are met with in Spain and in the
North of Africa, Algiers, and Tunis, where, however, they
appear to be inferior in excellence of construction to those
of Europe.[1] They are found in Turkey, Syria, Palestine,
India, Japan,[2] and also in Corea, but here rarely, and only
in the south part, where they are of a class intermediate
between the cist and the true dolmen. In Ireland they
exist in extraordinary numbers. According to Borlase[3]
there are: Certain dolmens, 780; chambered tumuli, 50;
uncertain, 68; total, 898. There are actually 163 in the
county of Sligo alone. It has, in fact, been suggested[4]
that there was a dolmen-building race which made the
circuit of the world, passing through Europe and Asia,
and everywhere leaving behind them monuments identical
in form. For Sergi, however, the dolmens of Europe and
Africa are all the product of his Mediterranean race.

Cistvaens.—The cist, cistvaen (cista-maen, stone-chest),
is perhaps best looked upon as a small variety of dolmen,
from which it differs not only in size, but also, according
to Greenwell's view, which we may take to be correct, that
the dolmen was intended to be reopened from time to
time for later burials, whilst the cist was closed up once
for all. The term is generally applied to a box-like tomb
formed of stones, and originally covered with a mound,
though, like the dolmen, it may have in later times been
robbed of this protection. Within the cist may have been
placed a body burnt or unburnt, or less frequently, the
remains of a burnt body in an urn. It is very difficult to
ascertain what relationship in point of time the dolmen

---

[1] See Sergi, *passim*, also Carton, *L'Anthropologie*, ii. 1.
[2] Gowland, *Archæologia*, lv. 439.   [3] *Dolmens of Ireland*.
[4] Bertrand, *De la Distribution des Dolmens*, etc., Paris, 1860.

and the cist bore to one another. The stone bed or coffin may have grown into the vault, or the vault may have diminished into the bed. In Brittany both kinds have been found in close relation, perhaps the smaller in distinct subordination to the larger. Whichever came first it seems fairly clear that there was a time when both were being constructed. Perhaps position or wealth, or even personal caprice, may have been the only determining factor in the choice between the two methods of interment.

Circles.—Here we approach a much more difficult problem, and one on which a vast amount of writing has been expended. In consonance with the general idea of this book little notice will be taken of the theories which have been brought forward to explain the stone circles of this and other lands. Here the main object will be to explain the classes and structure of these objects. For further information readers may be recommended to consult the works mentioned in the footnotes.[1] That some of the circles were sepulchral in character there can be no sort of doubt, and with this class we may first deal before discussing those as to whose nature some still feel a hesitation. (1) *Circles composed of cists.* There can, of course, be no doubt as to the nature of this form of circle. Near Port Erin, in the Isle of Man, there is an example of this

[1] Some idea of the mass of literature on the subject may be gained from the statement that Mr. Jerome Harrison's valuable and careful *Bibliography of Stonehenge and Avebury*, *Wilts Arch. and N. H. Soc.*, xxxii. 1, runs to more than one hundred and sixty pages. This may be consulted, as well as the following: Fergusson, *Rude Stone Monuments*, though many of the theories there put forward are now exploded; Evans, *Archæological Review*, ii. 312, a most important paper; various articles by Lewis in *Jour. Anthrop. Inst.* In the author's little book, *Life in Early Britain*, will also be found a summary of the theories up to the date of its publication. See also Colley March, *Trans. Lanc. and Chesh. Antiq. Soc.*, 1888, and Lockyer and Penrose, *Proc. Roy. Soc.*, 452.

kind in the Meayll Circle.[1]   This circle, which is placed
near three little prehistoric villages, each consisting of
four to sixteen hut-circles, consists of six symmetrically
arranged sets of cists, each a tritaph, *i.e.* two tangential
and one radial.   There is some evidence that a cist formerly
existed in the centre of the circle.   The floor of each cist
was paved with flat stones, and all the interments were
after cremation.   There were two to five urns in each
tangential cist, or in the proximal end of the radial.   This
circle had two openings in it, one to the north and one to
the south.   According to Jewitt,[2] there is a somewhat
similar circle in the Channel Islands, but I know of
nothing like it in England.   (2) *Circles composed of stones
formerly enclosing a tumulus.*   Whether it may have been
for the purpose of supporting the mound, or of indicating
that it was a place under tabu, or of serving as a " ghost
hedge " to keep the unruly spirits of the dead within
bounds, there is no doubt that a peristalith, or low enclosure of stones, often surrounded a funeral mound.
This arrangement, which has already been alluded to
in the previous chapter, is not confined to this country.
Pausanias, writing in the second century A.D., mentions
the interest with which he examined the grave of Aegyptus,
because Homer had alluded to it, and he describes it as a
mound of earth of no great size, and enclosed in a circular
kerbing of stones, an account which he also gives of other
tombs.   In a great many cases, as, for example, in that of
the great barrow at West Kennett (see Fig. 58), it is the
ring of stones which has gone, whilst the mound remains,
for the stones are available for many purposes from road-
mending upwards.   But in some instances it is the mound
which seems to have disappeared, and the circle is then
left behind as a ring of low and often prostrate stones.

[1] See Herdman and Kermode, *Trans. Biol. Soc. Liverpool,* October 13th,
1893.   [2] *Op cit.*, p. 78.

(3) *Circles composed of stones formerly contained within a barrow.* The hedge of stones was sometimes included within the substance of the mound itself, instead of forming a low wall around its base externally. Such a circle is described by Bateman[1] in a barrow near Cawthorn Camps in the North Riding of Yorkshire. "By cutting," he says, "from the north towards the centre, we uncovered some flat stones, set upright in the ground, which on further examination were found to be part of a complete circle, seven yards in diameter, standing about two feet above the natural level, and enclosing a grave." This, as he points out, is what would have been called a "Druidical circle" had the earth all been removed from the stones. The Flax Dale barrow, described by Jewitt,[2] is another example of the same kind of thing. Greenwell[3] found a circle of chalk stones with an opening on the east side, which had a radius of thirty feet, and was enclosed in a mound eighty feet in diameter. It is obvious that by the removal of the earth such a circle would be exposed, and present the appearance with which we are familiar in the smaller stone circles of the country. It is probable that to this and the class immediately preceding it most of these objects belong. (4) *Small circles, with central interment, without mound.* Excavations made in the interior of small circles have sometimes revealed the existence of interments, though there was no mound or trace of mound left. This must not be taken as implying that there never was a mound, but that we have no evidence of the existence of any such feature in these particular cases. An example of this kind is recorded by Bateman[4] on Stanton Moor, where, "near the Andle Stone, we noticed a small circle of six stones, four of which were upright and two prostrate, the diameter being about twenty feet." On digging

---

[1] *Op. cit.*, p. 207.
[3] *Op. cit.*, p. 145.
[2] *Op. cit.*, p. 71.
[4] *Op. cit.*, p. 84.

in it it was found that "a grave had been dug for the reception of three or four cinerary urns and as many incense cups." Fragments of calcined bones were found. A most remarkable double, concentric circle of wooden posts, enclosing a central interment, has recently been found at Bleasdale, near Garstang. In other cases, however, careful examination has failed to reveal the existence of any traces of a burial within the circle. Such, according to Mr. Collingwood,[1] is the case at Sunken Kirk, near Swinside, the third largest circle in Cumberland. Here the results of a searching examination were entirely negative. There were no traces of interments, nor of ancient fires, nor was there any tumulus, or any remains of a tumulus, in the interior of the circle.

In respect of all these circles connected with interments —and the same is true of the larger class which has yet to be dealt with—one special point requires notice, and that is their incompleteness. There is always an interruption in the circle, as there is in the ditch which includes a barrow. In the case of the larger circles this interruption may be looked upon as a doorway or entrance, but in the case of the enclosed circles, those which were buried in the material of the mound, if a gateway at all, it can only have been intended for the use of the spirits of the departed. Whatever its idea or intention, it is there, and Canon Greenwell, who calls attention to it, notes the similarity of idea with that of the penannular ring, when that shape is not required by the exigencies of use, and with that of the frequently interrupted circles which are met with in the case of cup and circle markings on rocks.

Passing now to the *Great Circles* like Stonehenge and Avebury, can we say anything as to the sepulchral character of these? According to some they are purely religious edifices, though, like many of our modern churches,

---

[1] *Proc. Soc. Ant.,* ii. xix. 98.

surrounded by a cemetery, as was the case at Stonehenge, where there are three hundred barrows in the immediate vicinity. But beyond this, according to another idea, which may well be the correct one, the great circles are actually derived from sepulchral monuments. "The stone circle," says Mr. Arthur Evans, "that originally performed a structural function in early dwellings and in certain barrows, by propping up the superincumbent mass of earth, becomes itself an independent feature in sepulchral ritual. It separates itself from the mound to form a huge circle of monoliths, surrounding it at an even distance ; or it may fulfil a ritual purpose by itself, apart from any central mound or chamber." The same writer states it as his opinion that the component parts of such circles, namely, the circle itself, the avenue of stones which leads up to it, imperfect at Stonehenge, though better marked at Avebury, and the central dolmen, wanting at Stonehenge, are all of them amplifications of the simplest sepulchral forms. The circle is an enlarged version of the ring of stones placed round the grave mound ; the dolmen represents the cist within it ; the avenue is merely the continuation of the underground gallery which leads to the sepulchral chamber, which remains as a ritual survival when, owing to cremation or other causes, the galleried chamber to which it led has itself been modified away. He also thinks that the central object of Stonehenge was probably a sacred oak-tree, "the Celtic image of Zeus," according to Maximus Tyrius. Stonehenge is perhaps the latest of these monuments ; it is, at any rate, the only one in which there is evidence of dressing or workmanship as applied to the stones of which the monument is constructed. Mr. Arthur Evans did not hesitate to place it at quite a late date, holding that it belongs "to the same age as the latest class of the round barrows by which it was surrounded—a class of barrows which it would not be safe to bring down beyond the approximate date of 250 B.C." On the other hand, since the article from which this quotation has been taken was written, an opportunity for a more complete investigation of the circle has been afforded, and has been conducted under the guidance of Mr. Gowland, whose discoveries seem to show that it was erected at the very end of the Neolithic period, when bronze was just becoming known, but was still unutilised for the purpose of making implements.[1] Stonehenge consists of the following parts : (i.) a shallow ditch and bank, which opens out at one point into an avenue flanked by a ditch and bank on either side ; (ii.) a ring of hewn local sarsen stones, with imposts mortised to them ; (iii.) a ring of less perfectly hewn, diabase pillars ; (iv.) an ellipse of hewn sarsen trilithons, with mortise and tenon connections ; (v.) an ellipse of less perfectly hewn diabase pillars ; (vi.) a single recumbent rock of different character from the rest. The plan, which Mr. Gowland has kindly permitted me to reproduce (Fig. 68), is the result of his recent survey. It shows the standing and recumbent stones, differentiating between "sarsen" and diabase, but not the ditch, which is too far distant to come into a plan on this scale. The portions marked "excavations" are the places examined during the operations for raising the stone described in Mr. Gowland's paper in *Archæologia* cited above. The igneous, or "blue" stones, were formerly regarded as strangers brought from a distance, but Professor Judd has recently examined them, and believes that they are ice-borne boulders, the relics of a former drift deposit. He also thinks that they were probably commoner formerly than now, and that, perhaps, an accidental abundance of them at or near Stonehenge may have helped to determine the selection of this site. In the examination recently

[1] *Man*, 1902, 6 and 16 ; *Archæologia*, lviii. 38.

made it was found that the dressing of the stones had not
been accomplished with the aid of metal tools as was
formerly thought. " The tabular structure of the 'sarsens,'
and their great inequality of hardness, makes very little
working necessary. They seem to have been broken to
shape by alternate heating and chilling, and by the use of
the heavy mauls; but their preliminary dressing took
place at a distance, and all that can be seen at Stonehenge are the grooves pounded out by the mauls and
the traces of the sideward blows by which the intervening ridges were obliterated. The 'blue-stones' show no
grooves, but also no such careful shaping as the 'sarsens.'
The surface tooling was effected by hammer-stones."
(Gowland.) The tools found during the excavations were
of several classes : (i.) haches, longer or shorter ; (ii.) an
intermediate type much chipped and blunted : (iii.) hammer-
axes ; (iv.) intermediate types of hammer-stones with
traces of an edge. The four types thus described were
all of flint, unhafted, and too brittle for use on "hard
sarsens " or " blue-stones," though they would have been
serviceable for working the softer varieties. (v.) Regular
hammer-stones of quartzite, more or less chipped, from
one to six pounds in weight; (vi.) quartzite mauls, with
two well-defined faces, and traces of a waist, as if to hold a
rope; these weighed from thirty-seven to sixty-four pounds,
and are similar to the great stone mauls used in Japan,
which are raised and let fall by ropes held by several men,
whilst another man directs their aim by a wooden handle.
The mode of erection of these great stones has often
excited curiosity. Those of the outermost circle, thirty
in number when the circle was perfect, are each sixteen
feet in height and three and a half feet distant from one
another. The stones of the great trilitha of the ellipse
gradually rise in height to twenty-five feet, the stature
of the tallest. The diabase pillars are only about six feet

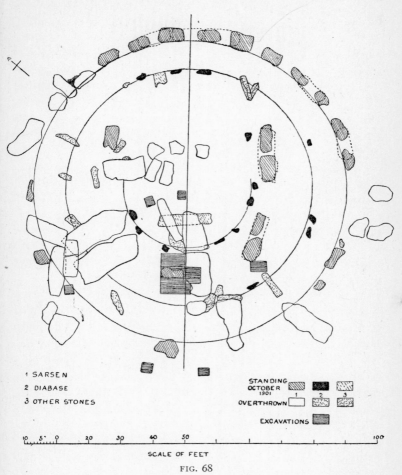

1 SARSEN
2 DIABASE
3 OTHER STONES

STANDING
OCTOBER
1901

OVERTHROWN

| | 1 | 2 | 3 |

EXCAVATIONS

SCALE OF FEET

10 5 0   20   30   40   50   100

FIG. 68

PLAN OF STONEHENGE

in height.   As regards the problem of their setting up,
Mr. Gowland remarks : "It differed in different cases, for
the 'recumbent stone,' twenty-five feet long, went only
four feet into the ground, while the 'leaning stone,' twenty-
nine feet long, went eight feet down.   The reason is
obvious, for the two stones were set up as a pair to carry
a lintel in the most important part of the whole structure.
The shorter stone, therefore, being set less deep, had a
more elaborate base, and, to gain base, was only dressed
on the parts which showed above ground.   The leaning
stone was erected by (i.) excavating a pit with three
vertical walls and one sloping rim on the side next the
stone ; (ii.) raising the head-end of the stone by levers
and timber packing till its foot slid down the sloping rim
into the pit ; (iii.) hoisting it from about fifty degrees into
an erect position by ropes ; (iv.) securing it in its place by
the smaller 'sarsens' which support its oblique lower
surface.   Similar leverage is customarily employed in
Japan with trunks of trees, and many rope-ends each
pulled by one man.   The 'recumbent' stone, on the other
hand, was (i.) supported at its foot-end on a low wall of
small 'sarsens'; then (ii.) tipped upright, as above,
against two large 'sarsens' placed in front ; then (iii.)
packed tight, as above, with disused mauls."   On one
stone a stain of copper oxide was discovered, from which
it is concluded that that metal was known though not
employed in the execution of the work.   From what we
know of the date of the commencement of the Bronze Age
in this country, then, the date of the circle may be set
down at somewhere between 2000–1800 B.C.   An attempt
has been made to work out the date on the hypothesis that
the circle was a temple for sun-worship, a view held by
Mr. Lewis, who points out that of twenty-one circles in
South Britain nineteen have a special reference to the
N.E. and nine to the S.E.   To the N.E. of Stonehenge

is the detached stone known as "The Friar's Heel." Lockyer and Penrose working on these lines obtained a date of 1680 B.C. with a possible error in either direction of two hundred years.

All that remains of Avebury shows us that when it was in its prime it was a far more imposing edifice than

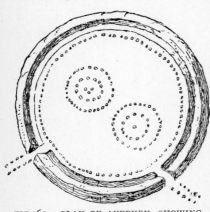

Stonehenge, and that Aubrey was right in saying that it as far surpassed that erection as a cathedral does a parish church. It has, however, been so much despoiled by "Farmer Green" and other depredators that it requires a plan and some imagination to form any sort of an idea of what it must originally have looked like. The great rampart and fosse are still there, and form, perhaps, the most striking of the

FIG. 69. PLAN OF AVEBURY, SHOWING FOSSE, CIRCLES AND AVENUES AS THEY PROBABLY EXISTED

existing parts of the temple. They enclose an area of twenty-eight and a half acres, and have a diameter of 1,200 feet. The depth of the fosse is still forty feet, and as it is inside the rampart it is evident that its purpose was not defensive. Within the ditch was a circle of rough stones—unlike Stonehenge, the stones here are quite unhewn—which encloses two circles, each with a smaller concentric circle in its interior. In the centre of each pair of circles there appears to have been an arrangement of stones called a cove. These points will be seen indicated in Fig 69, where also it will be observed that the commencement of two avenues is represented. One of these is still sufficiently obvious, and leads in the direction of West Kennett, of the existence of the other there is more doubt.

A few notes concerning some of the other circles in this country will be given in the list at the end of the chapter, and attention may be called to the figure showing the set of circles at Stanton Drew (Fig. 70). Before

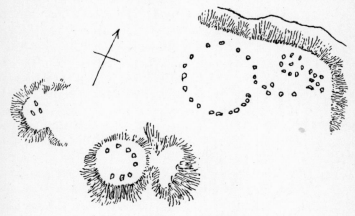

FIG. 70. PLAN OF STONE CIRCLES
Stanton Drew

leaving this for the next group of megaliths, however, attention must be called to a quite different form of circle met with in Cornwall. Here encircling walls of large stones, set on edge and with earth between them, are found as the fence around groups of hut dwellings; these are, of course, in no way akin to the circles which have lately been engaging our attention.

Alignments.—Rows or avenues of stones are often associated with stone circles, as we have just seen to be the case at Avebury. In this country this class of monument is best seen on Dartmoor, though the objects there are almost insignificant when compared with the avenues of Carnac in Brittany. On Dartmoor[1] there are thirty-eight stone rows, of which twenty-five are associated with circles. In its typical and complete form, in fact, the Dartmoor row begins with a circle and ends with a menhir. Within the circle is very commonly, though not always, a barrow or a cistvaen. The circles are free-standing, and have never been the supports of a mound. The most celebrated are the Merivale rows, of which the north avenue commences with a circle around a menhir. The south avenue ends with a menhir at each end, and has a circle twelve feet in diameter midway. This circle once enclosed a cistvaen. To the north-west of the rows is the great menhir, with the remains of a small circle around it, and also the fragments of a row. The great circle, which is near by, is fifty-four feet in diameter, and at present isolated. It may, however, very probably have been connected with the other works by an avenue now destroyed. At Callernish[2] there is a similar conjunction of circle and avenues. The circle is forty-two feet in diameter, and single lines of four or five stones each extend E., S., and W. from it. Somewhat E. of N. there are two longer lines, one of nine and one of ten stones. The ends of these lines are 294 feet from the centre of the circle, *i.e.* just seven diameters of the circle.

Menihirion.—The menhir, or standing stone (Figs. 71 and 72), is as ancient an institution as it is world-wide, and, in the shape of obelisks and monuments, persistent. Such stones, as indicated in the section immediately preceding, are sometimes met with in conjunction with other varieties of megaliths. Sometimes, as at the Tingle-

---

[1] For an account of these objects see Worth, *Cornwall Roy. Inst. Jour.*, xii. 76.

[2] Lewis, *Cornwall Roy. Inst. Journ.*, xiv. 378, and *Proc. Roy. Soc. Ant. Ireland,* ix. 268.

FIG. 71.   THE KINGSTONE
Rollright, Warwickshire

stone barrow, the menhir is on the mound, sometimes it is, as at Ablington, inside the chamber of burial, sometimes it is embedded in the substance of the mound itself. Again, the menhir may be quite isolated and independent of other ancient remains.   Perhaps this is the most

o

common occurrence. In this country they are not usually of great size, that at Clun, for example, measures eight feet in height, six and a half feet in width, and eight inches to a foot in thickness. In Brittany menihirion exist of much greater size, for that at Dol is twenty-eight

FIG. 72. MENHIR
Woeful Dane's Bottom, Gloucestershire

feet above the soil and sixteen feet below. The great menhir of Men-er-H'roeck at Locmariaquer was sixty-four feet high before it was shattered by a stroke of lightning. These stone pillars sometimes bear cup-and-ring markings. Occasionally they are perforated, as in the case of the Mên-an-Tol in Cornwall and the menhir at Woeful Dane's Bottom in Gloucestershire. (Fig. 72.) In this last case, however, the perforations are small and natural, but may still have added to the importance, perhaps to the sanctity, of the stone in the eyes of its erectors. Perforated menihirion occur also in Ireland[1] and Cyprus.[2]

LIST OF DOLMENS IN ENGLAND

This list includes a few cistvaens, which are specially indicated.

BERKSHIRE—" Wayland Smith's Cave." Remains of chambered dolmen in clump of trees, on downs near White Horse and Icknield Street. (*Archæol.* xxxii. 312.)

CORNWALL—

Ballowal.

Bosporthennis.

Caerwynen.

Carn Kenidzhek, near St. Just.

Chapel - carn - Brea, St. Just. (Also cist.) (Small dolmen in mound.)

*Chûn Cromlech, near the Land's End.

Crouza Downs, St. Keverne. "The Three Brothers of Grugith." (Cistvaen.)

Hawkstor, near the Stripple Stones.

*Lanyon Quoit, Boswavas Moor. Upset in 1815, but restored in 1824, though not as it originally stood. (*Archæol.* xxxii. 314.)

Mulfra Quoit, near Lamorna Cove. (Ruined.) One mile from this is another ruined dolmen.

Pawton, St. Breock. (Small dolmen in a mound.)

Pendarves Quoit, near Camborne.

Sancreed. (Small dolmen in mound.)

St. Columb Major, 1 S.E. of. (Ruined.)

Tregiffian, St. Just.

Trevethy Quoit, near St. Clear.

*Zennor Quoit, near St. Ives.

[1] *Proc. Roy. Soc. Ant. Ireland*, vi. 158; Wakeman's *Handbook*, p. 14.
[2] *L'Anthropologie,* vi. 158.

DERBYSHIRE—

Minning Low.

Ringham Low. Chambered tumulus. (Jewitt, p. 70.)

Taddington, near. "The Five Wells." Chambered tumulus. (*Ib.*, p. 69.)

DEVONSHIRE—

Archerton, Dartmoor. Cistvaen.

Brown Heath.

Cawsand Beacon. Cistvaen.

Coryton Ball. Ruined dolmen.

Grims Grove. Ruined dolmen.

Harter Tor.

Hound Tor Down.

Lake Head Hill. Two cistvaens.

Lundy Island.

Merivale Bridge. Ruined dolmen.

Morte Point, near Ilfracombe.

*"The Spinster's Rock," near Drewsteignton.

Trowlesworthy Tor.

Yar Tor, near Buckfastleigh. Cistvaen.

(See also list of Megalithic remains *infra*.)

DORSETSHIRE—

Carlben Circle, near, on the Bridport-Dorchester road. (Ruined.)

*"The Grey Mare and Her Colts." Gorwell, Blackdown.

"The Hellstone." On Ridge Hill, above Portisham. (Restored.)

Two Gates, on the Roman Bridport-Dorchester road.

HEREFORDSHIRE.—"Arthur's Stone." Moccas, near the Dore Valley.

KENT—

"The Countless Stones," near Aylesford. (Apparently remains of a chambered tumulus.)

*"Kit's Coty House," near Aylesford. (*Archæol.* ii. 116.)

MONMOUTHSHIRE.—Newchurch, near Caerwent.

NORTHUMBERLAND.—Alnwick Deer Park. Cistvaen of Bronze Period.

OXFORDSHIRE—

> Enstone, near. "The Hoar Stone." (Ruined.)
> Steeple Aston, near. "The Hoar Stone."
> Rollright. "The Whispering Knights." (Partly ruined.)

SOMERSET—

> Stoke Bishop.
> Wellow. Dolmen in mound. (*Journ. Anth. Inst.* xi. 118.)

WESTMORLAND.—Brougham. Moorhouse Farm. Cistvaen with contracted body. Food and drink vessels.

WILTSHIRE—

> *"The Devil's Den." Clatford Bottom, near Marlborough.
> "The Hareholes." Two cistvaens at Lockeridge.
> Nettleton, near Castle Combe.
> West Kennett. Dolmen in mound. Ruined. (*Archæol.*, xlii. 213.)

LIST OF OTHER MEGALITHIC REMAINS IN ENGLAND

CHESHIRE.—"The Bridestones." On Cloud Hill, near Congleton. Remains of circle and avenue.

CORNWALL—

> Boscawen-un. Circle.
> Bolleit. Circle.
> Carwen. Circle and enclosures.
> *"Dawns Men." (Stone Dance.) "The Merry Maidens." Circle of nineteen stones, near Lamorna Cove.
> Duloe circle, near St. Keynes. Probably enclosing ring of a cairn.
> Fernacre, near Garrah. Circle 140 feet in diameter; forty-five out of fifty-five stones still standing.
> "The Giant's Staff." Menhir 12 feet high, near Pentewan.
> *"The Hurlers." Three intersecting circles near the Cheesewring. (*Arch. Journ.*, 1862.)

CORNWALL (*contd.*)—

*"Mên-an-Tol," or "The Crick Stone." A holed stone, the centre of three monoliths. The hole is 21 × 18 inches on one side, smaller on the other. The stone is 3 feet 9 inches in height.

"The Merry Maidens." Circle on Carn Kenidzhek, near St. Just, 72 feet in diameter.

Newtown, near St. Buryan. Two holed stones.

*"The Nine Maidens." Boskednan. Circle 72 feet in diameter.

"The Nine Maidens." Crows-an-wra, near the Land's End. Nineteen stones forming a circle 81 feet in diameter.

"The Nine Maidens." On St. Breock Downs. Eight stones, formerly nine, forming an alignment 262 feet long.

Pridden, near St. Buryan. Menhir and Roundago. (*Proc. Soc. Ant.*, ii. vi. 500.)

"The Old Man," or "The Fiddler." On St. Breock Down, near "The Nine Maidens." Menhir 7½ feet high.

"The Pipers." Trewoofe, near St. Just. Two monoliths 320 feet apart, and 13½ and 15½ feet high respectively.

Stannon Down, near Bodmin. Circle of seventy-six stones, 134 feet in diameter.

"The Stripple Stones." Hawkstor, near Bodmin. Circle (five erect, eleven fallen) 148 feet in diameter.

Tregaseale, St. Just. Two circles.

"The Trippet Stones." One mile from "The Stripple Stones," on a moor near Carbilly. Circle (nine erect, four fallen), 105 feet in diameter.

CUMBERLAND—

Ainstable. Circle.

Burn Moor, near Eskdale. Circles. (*Proc. Soc. Ant.*, ii. xii. 92.)

Dacre, Yamonside. Circles. (Perhaps natural.)

Dalston, Chapel Flat. Circle.

*"Grey Yauds." Circle. Cumwhitton, King Harry Fell. (Nearly destroyed.)

*"Keswick. Circle.

CUMBERLAND (*contd.*)—

> Kirk Santon. "The Standing Stones," called "Giants' Graves," and two small circles.
>
> Lamplugh, Stockhow. Circle.
>
> *"Long Meg and her Daughters." Half-mile N. of Little Salkeld. Circle with cup-and-circle markings. There is a second small circle, which formerly had a cairn in its centre. Cup-and-circle markings here also. (*Proc. Soc. Ant.*, ii. x. 310.)
>
> Studfold Gate. Reported remains of stone circle.
>
> *Swinside, Sunkenkirk, near Millom. Circle. (*Proc. Soc. Ant.*, ii. xix. 98.)

(NOTE.—The circles at Annanside, Gutterby Kirkstones, and the Standing Stones at Hall Foss, all of which were near Whitbeck, have been destroyed.)

DERBYSHIRE—

> *Arborlow, Youlgrave. Circle with ditch and rampart. (*Archæologia*, vii. 112 ; lviii. part 2 ; *Man*, 1903, 133, 145.)
>
> Beeley Moor, above Chatsworth. Circle.
>
> Derwent, 1¾ S.E. of. Circle.
>
> Eastmoor, near Ramsley Lodge. Circle.
>
> Eyam, 1½ N. of, on Eyam Moor. "Wet Withins." Circle. (*Man*, 1903, 135 ; *Jl. Anth. Inst.*, 1874.)
>
> Froggatt Edge. Circle.
>
> Hathersage, near. Two circles with tumuli.
>
> "Marl Wark." 2¼ miles W. of Dore. Circle.
>
> "The Nine Ladies," Stanton-in-the-Peak. Circle. (*Archæologia*, vi. 112 ; *Man*, 1903, 136.)

DEVONSHIRE—

> Assycombe. Cairn and row.
>
> *"The Bair Down Man." Menhir, near Princetown.
>
> Batworthy. Three circles and rows.
>
> Bellaford Tor. Circle and cistvaen.
>
> Bisworthy. Circle.
>
> Brown Heath, near Erme Head. Avenue and circle enclosing dolmen.
>
> Challacombe Down. Four rows of stones with menhir.
>
> Cholwich Town. Circle and avenue.
>
> Cocks Tor. Circles and rows.

DEVONSHIRE (*contd.*)—

Conies Down. Cairns and rows.

Cordon. Triple rows.

Coryton Ball. Seven parallel rows of stones.

Down Tor. Circle, row, and menhir.

Drewsteignton.

Drizzlecombe. Three circles and row.

*" The Grey Wethers." Two circles under Sittaford Tor.

Glazecombe. Circle and row.

Grimsgrove. Circle and cistvaen.

Harford, near Ivybridge. Circle and cistvaen.

Hound Tor. Circle with cistvaen.

*" The Long Stones." Scorhill Down. Circle.

Loo Hill, near Sidford. Menhir.

*Merivale Bridge. Three circles, two avenues, and a menhir.

" The Nine Maidens," or " The Nine Stones." Belstone Tor. Circle.

Raybarrow. Circle.

Ringmore. Circle.

Shavercombe. Circle with cistvaen.

Sherberton.

*Shuffle Down. Five rows of stones, with " The Long Stone," a menhir, also pounds.

Stalldon Moor. Circle with avenues.

Throwleigh. Circle.

Tolch Gate. Circle and avenues.

Trowlesworthy Tor. Avenues and single row with circles.

Yardsworthy. Circle, row, and menhir.

Yar Tor. Many lines of stones.

(NOTE.—The megalithic and rude stone remains of Dartmoor, including Pounds and the different objects mentioned above, are very numerous, and some are very difficult to place. For further information, see a paper in *Cornwall Roy. Inst. Journal*, xii. 76, also Page, *An Exploration of Dartmoor*, and Baring Gould's *Book of Dartmoor*.)

DORSETSHIRE—

" The Broad Stone." Fallen menhir, on roadside, near Winterborne Abbas.

DORSETSHIRE (*contd.*)—

> Carlben Circle, near Longbredy Gate. Stones almost entirely buried. A few isolated stones near by.
>
> Kingstone Russell, near. Menhir.
>
> "The Nine Stones." Small circle near Winterborne Abbas.
>
> Osmington Hill. Small circle with remains of avenue.
>
> *Tenant Hill, near Kingston Russell Farm. Circle.

GLOUCESTERSHIRE—

> "The Hoar Stone." Menhir, near Lower Swell.
>
> Marshfield. Remains of circle.
>
> *"The Tingle Stone." Menhir standing on a barrow near Avening.
>
> "The Whittle Stone." Menhir, near Lower Swell.
>
> *Woeful Dane's Bottom, near Minchinhampton. Menhir.

HAMPSHIRE—"The Long Stone." Menhir, near Brixton, Isle of Wight.

KENT—

> Addington Park. Two circles with (?) remains of dolmens.
>
> Coldrum Farm, near Addington Park, on a hill. Circle with dolmen.
>
> Ryarsh, Gold Piece Field.
>
> White Horse Hill, in Poundgate or White Horse Wood. At this place and Ryarsh are blocks of stone which may have formed part of an avenue connecting the above-mentioned circles with Kit's Coty House, which is six miles distant.

LANCASHIRE—

> *Birk Rigg, near Bardsea. Circle with enclosure and tumulus. (*Archæologia*, liii. 418.)
>
> Bleaberry Hawes (*ib.*).
>
> *Bleasdale, near Garstang. A remarkable double circle of *timber*, with a central interment containing calcined bones.
>
> "The Calderstones," near Liverpool. Arranged in a circle, but probably remains of a dolmen. Cup-and-circle markings (see a paper on them by Herdman).
>
> Knapperthaw, near Lowick. Remains of a circle.
>
> Rusland Whitestock. Menhir.

LEICESTERSHIRE—Charnwood Forest, near the Monastery. Doubtful circle, perhaps natural.

NORTHUMBERLAND—

Alnwick Park. "The Longstone." Menhir.

Cartington, near Debdon House. Part of circle.

Doddington. Part of circle.

"The Duddo Stones." Grindon Rig. Part of circle.

"The Five Kings." Vale of Coquet. Part of circle.

Flodden. Menhir.

Humbleton. Menhir.

"The Hurl Stone," near Lilburn. Menhir.

Lordenshaw Camp, near. Rothbury. Avenues.

*"The Poind and his Man." Two monoliths and two barrows were here in 1718. One monolith has been removed.

*Roddam, near. At the Three Stone Burn. Remains of a circle. Three upright, twelve fallen stones.

Matfen. "The Standing Stone," near Corbridge. Menhir.

Swinburn, Chollerton. Menhir.

Yeavering. Menhir.

OXFORDSHIRE—

"The Devil's Quoits." Three large stones near Stanton Harcourt.

*Rollright. Circle. Close by are (1) a partly ruined dolmen, "The Whispering Knights," and (2) a menhir, "The King's Stone"; the latter just across the boundary in Warwickshire. (See an admirable account by A. Evans in *Folk Lore*, vi. 5).

SHROPSHIRE—

Clee Hill, near Abdon Burf. Circle and menhir. "The Giant's Staff."

*Clun Valley, near Whitcott Keysett. Menhir.

*"Mitchell's Fold." Circle near Stapeley Hill.

Marshpool. Circle near Stapeley Hill.

Stapeley Hill, summit of. Small, nearly buried circle.

"The Whetstones," near Stapeley Hill. Possibly remains of circle.

SOMERSET—

"Hauteville's Quoit," near Stanton Drew. Circle.

*Stanton Drew. Circles. (*Proc. Soc. Ant.*, 1883, 347.)

WARWICKSHIRE—

*"The King's Stone," near Long Compton, and close to the Rollright Stones in Oxfordshire. Menhir.

Wardington. "The Hoar Stone." Menhir.

WESTMORLAND—

Crosby Ravensworth. "Druid Circle." Circles.

Gamelands, near Raisbeck Hall. Orton. Circles.

*Gunnerfield, near Shap. Circles with cairns. (See Carlisle vol. *Proc. Arch. Inst.* and *Proc. Soc. Ant.*, ii. x. 319.)

*"Karl Lofts" and "The Guggleby Stone," near Shap. Circle and avenues. (See *Gent. Mag. Lib. Arch.*, ii. 72.)

Leaset Wood. Clifton Dykes.

Lowther Scar, near Bempton. Circle.

Moor Divock, Askham. Circles. Also "The Copstone." Menhir.

Ravenstonedale, Rotherbridge. Circle.

WILTSHIRE—

*Avebury. Circle with ditch and avenue. Near this is Silbury Hill, an artificial mound of great size; nature still undetermined. (*Archæol.* xxv. and Lord Avebury's *Prehistoric Times.*)

"Longstone Cove." Two stones only remaining between Beckhampton and Avebury.

*Stonehenge. (See references in pp. 183–190.)

West Kennett. Remains of circles.

NOTE.—The circle on Overton Hill, East Kennett, has been destroyed.

YORKSHIRE—

"The Bride Stones." Bilsdale. Circle.

"The Bride Stones." Doedale. Circle.

"The Bride Stones," near Grosmont. Circle.

"The Bride Stones." Sleights Moor, near Whitby. Circle.

Cloughton, $\frac{3}{4}$ N. of. Circle.

YORKSHIRE (*contd.*)—

"Danby Long Stone." Menhir, near the ancient village on Danby Moor.

*"The Devil's Arrows." Three stones near Borough-bridge. (*Proc. Soc. Ant.*, ii. vii. 134.)

"The Lad Stone," near Greetland. Menhir.

*"The Rudstone." At Rudstone-on-the-Wolds, near Bridlington. Menhir.

Simon Howe, near Goathland Mill Station. Three upright stones.

"The Standing Stones." $1\frac{3}{4}$ S.W. of Robin Hood's Bay, on Flyingdales Moor.

"The Wolf's Fold." Beacon Hill, near Slack. Circle.

CHAPTER IX

EARTHWORKS—CAMPS—DYKES

SCATTERED all over the face of the country, though
in much greater numbers in some districts than in
others, are a large variety of earthworks of a defensive
character. From the great size which they sometimes
reach, and the commanding positions which they frequently occupy, these memorials of the past attract, and
have always attracted, a considerable amount of attention.
It is only, however, of late years that any attempt has
been made to arrange them in a scientific manner, and
to assign dates to them on any other grounds than those
supplied by the imagination. In looking through the
pages of guide-books and the older county histories, one
notes that such a camp has been assigned to the Britons,
a second to the Romans, and a third to the Danes; but
for the truth of such assignations no evidence as a rule is
forthcoming. Shape used to be relied upon as a criterion,
the circular camps being considered British, the rectangular Roman, and the oval Danish. This is now
known to be a fallacious test, for, though many of the
rectangular camps are of Roman origin, any hard and
fast division like the above is misleading, and must be
abandoned. To give but one example : Pitt-Rivers has
shown by excavation that three rectangular camps—the
South Lodge, Handley Down, and Martin Down entrenchments, are all of the bronze period, and, therefore,

belonging to the class commonly called British.[1]   There is only one way of dating an earthwork, and that is by trenching and excavating it, and examining the objects thus brought to light.   This lesson, together with the proper method of carrying out such an examination, is one of the debts which the science of prehistoric archæology owes to the late General Pitt-Rivers.   Any person who visits the magnificent collections which he has left behind him at Farnham, and there studies the series of models descriptive of the excavations which he carried out, will readily understand that the process of examining an earthwork thoroughly is a somewhat lengthy and expensive one, and will not be surprised to find that so far it has only been applied to a few examples.   It will be a long time before any large number of earthworks can be examined in this careful manner, and it must, consequently, be a long time before any accurate classification of such objects can be undertaken.   Thanks, however, in large measure to the labours of Mr. Chalkley Gould and a committee of which he is chairman, steps are now being taken to make some sort of a division and census of earthworks in this country.   The classification which he has adopted roughly divides the objects under consideration into those which are probably pre-Roman, those which may be Roman, and those which are almost certainly post-Roman.   Actually the classification is by shape, but roughly it works out somewhat in this manner.   To the last group, which may be at once disposed of, belong the moated mounds and mounds with base-courts, formerly supposed to be the buhrs of the Saxon period, but now thought, with greater probability, to be of Norman construction.   These form a quite distinct class, and cannot be confused with the pre-Roman earthworks by any person who has examined an example of each.   The same may

---

[1] *Excavations*, vol. iv.

be said of the moated farmstead enclosures, many of which are clearly mediæval, though some may be of earlier date. There are various other objects, however, which more closely resemble the earthworks with which we are concerned in this chapter, and of which some mention must be made. The true Roman camp seems usually to have been rectangular, and to have possessed four entrances, one on each side, which entrances were not, as a rule, supplied with the elaborate outworks met with in many of the more important earlier fortresses. When we come across a construction of this kind we may at least strongly suspect that it is not of pre-Roman date. Then there are circular enclosures with ditch and mound, but with the former *inside* the latter, of which examples exist at Blois Hall and Thornborough in Yorkshire. These remind us of the arrangement already noted at Avebury, and are perhaps more probably religious in their character than military. The Cornish "rounds," which may have been enclosures for the purpose of games, form a separate class, and so also, of course, do the Roman amphitheatres, of which a few exist in this country. Then, especially in the northern parts of the country, where earthworks of all kinds are peppered so thickly over the hills, we have to distinguish from the earthworks in which we are now interested others which, though they have been set down by the older antiquaries as belonging to this class, may well be the tun-garths of early settlers, or pele-garths or mediæval enclosures, or even the villages of the sixteenth century during the period of the Scottish raids. Finally we have to distinguish between the true camp and the fortified town or oppidum, often a difficult, even an impossible task. In the case of a village like that at Woodcuts, fully described by Pitt-Rivers, or like that at Chalbury, near Weymouth, though there are embankments and ditches, yet they are not of a pronounced character, and are evidently so subsidiary to the pit-dwellings which they surround that we may fairly call such a collection of earthworks a village. But let us take, on the other hand, the case of such a fortress as Worlebury, near Weston-super-Mare. Here there is no question as to the strength of the fortifications, which are powerful enough to place it in the first rank of fortresses. Yet, on the other hand, within the enclosure are about one hundred pits, small certainly as places of habitation, perhaps only the cellars or storehouses of wigwams erected above them, but still giving evidence that this earthwork was a regular place of habitation. The same might be said about other earthworks which have been carefully examined, Winkle-bury, for example. These we must certainly speak of as fortified towns, or oppida, because they contain places of habitation. It is very dangerous to lay down laws about matters which have been so imperfectly investigated at present, but perhaps one may venture the surmise that there were three classes of earthworks more or less over-lapping one another. There was the strongly fortified hill-camp, intended as a place of resort in an emergency, but not as a place of habitation. It was a place to which the inhabitants of the valleys betook themselves with their families and their herds when attacked by enemies, but a place reserved for such occasions, and, perhaps on account of its bleakness, or of its want of water, unsuitable, and unintended for any protracted occupation. Then there was the village, surrounded by low banks and ditches, of little use for purposes of defence, but subserving other ends, perhaps as cattle-folds, or means of drainage. And finally there was the third class where, because the local climate, the water supply, and the general topographical conditions were all favourable, the town was also a camp, and served the purposes both of a habitation and a fortress.

The second class does not come under consideration here, but is reserved for the next chapter. Here we are chiefly concerned with the defensive earthwork, the object commonly called in this country a "camp," whether with, or without, enclosed hut-circles, and with that portion of this subject which relates to earthworks of the pre-Roman period, the so-called British camps. As a matter of fact, this title ought to be dropped as misleading, and that of pre-Roman earthworks adopted, since it commits us to less than the other. Certainly many of these works are of the bronze period, but there can be little doubt that in this country, as certainly in France, some of them were originally constructed in the Neolithic age. Here again the impossibility of deciding without excavation must be insisted upon, and at the risk of being tedious a further example may be cited, in illustration of the unexpected results which may follow a proper investigation. "Cæsar's Camp," near Folkestone, which the country people, in the time of Lambarde, "ascribed to King Ethelbert, the first godly king of this shyre," which Wright considered to be the site of a Roman Pharos, and which has been believed by many to have owed its construction to that race, whether the Pharos theory was right or not, turns out on examination to have been almost certainly a construction of the Norman period.[1] Lastly, mention must not be omitted of the fact that many of these fortresses have been used by different races, and altered from time to time to suit the ideas of their several occupants. Old Sarum, for example, which was probably pre-Roman in its inception, was certainly afterwards a Roman fortress, a Saxon burh, a Norman stronghold, and a Mediæval city. To take another example where the successive occupations have been fewer : on Hod Hill, in Dorsetshire, there is a large pre-Roman camp, which was afterwards occupied by the

[1] *Archæologia*, xlvii. 429.

P

Romans themselves. Probably they found the enclosure too large for the number of troops occupying the place ; at any rate they cut off a small corner at the point best designed to watch over the Vale of White Hart, and used it as their place of occupation. The alterations have not always been the same, but the history of this earthwork is that of many others throughout the country. Others have been occupied at still later dates. According to tradition, the almost certainly pre-Roman earthworks on Woodbury Hill, in Worcestershire, were occupied by Owen Glendower and his French allies under Montmorency, and here they were encountered by Henry IV. and his son. Hambledon Hill, close to Hod Hill, was, during the Civil War, occupied by nearly 2,000 "Clubmen," under the leadership of Mr. Bravel, Rector of Compton. They were driven from this fortress by Cromwell and Desborough on August 4th, 1645. Perhaps, even yet, these earthen fortresses have not seen the last of actual use in warfare.

Having thus cleared the ground, we may proceed to turn our attention to the task of classifying and describing the earthworks with which we are now concerned, those, namely, which there is some reason for thinking may be pre-Roman, or, perhaps it may be better put, which there is no good ground for believing not to be pre-Roman.

Such earthworks may be provisionally arranged under three headings—Promontory, Hill, and Plateau forts— and each of these must now receive consideration.

Promontory forts.—These strongholds (Fig. 73) may be defined as fortified places which, being already strong in their natural defences on one or more sides, have only been furnished with embankments in a portion of their circuit. The name of promontory forts has been given to this class by Westropp,[1] who points out that the type

[1] "The Ancient Forts of Ireland," *Trans. R. I. A.*, xxxi. Also separately published.

occurs in Greece and elsewhere round the Mediterranean,
and is found in Dalmatia, at Rügen in the Baltic, in
Switzerland, France, and the British Isles. There is no
reason to suppose that there is any relation of derivation
between the forts in these different localities, since the
plan is one which might readily occur to any person,
given suitable topographical conditions. The term used
is a convenient one, as it enables us to group together,
not merely the so-called "cliff-castles," which are protected on one or more sides by the sea, but also those
inland examples which occur upon spurs of hills. So
that in this class we have two obvious subdivisions, coast
and inland.

(i.) **Coast examples.**—These fortresses have been constructed on projecting headlands by the simple process
of cutting off the approach from the land by one or more
lines of embankment. Along the whole coast of Cornwall, Borlase[1] states that there is scarcely a high piece of
cliff or promontory which does not bear on its rough
crest some landmark of the Prehistoric time. Many of
these are cliff castles. One of the best of these is on
Trevalgue Head. Here a narrow passage cuts off a
small island from a promontory on the mainland. The
first line of defence is on the mainland itself, and consists of a ditch and rampart, the latter averaging about
8 feet in height. Beyond this, at the narrow extremity of
the promontory, are the following defences : (i.) a ditch
8 feet deep and 12 feet wide ; (ii.) a rampart 20 feet broad
and 10 feet high ; (iii.) a second ditch also 12 feet wide ;
(iv.) a second rampart 20 feet high and 30 feet wide ; (v.)
a third ditch 10 feet wide, hewn out of the solid rock ;
and (vi.) of a third rampart 10 feet high. The narrow
piece of land on which these are constructed averages

[1] *Archæologia*, xliv. 422.

from 80 to 100 feet in breadth. On the sea side of these defences is a chasm 25 feet wide and 55 feet deep. At full tide this is entered by the sea, which converts the fortress itself into an island. On the other side of the chasm and on the island itself is a further rampart 20 feet high by 30 feet thick. Still further across the island is the final piece of defence, cutting off what we may call the citadel, in the shape of a rampart 12 feet high on its outer side. Many rude chippings of flint have been found in this embankment, perhaps a clue to its date. From this castle no less than three others of similar type, Trevarrian, Bedruthan, and Park Head, may be seen, so thickly are these fortifications scattered along the Cornish coast. Similar castles are found on the West Coast of Ireland and in France. A good example in the latter country is that at Castel-Meur, Cléden, Finistère.[1] In this case the base of the promontory is defended by three ramparts and ditches. Within the enclosure were ninety-five rectangular habitations, sunk in the earth and lined internally with walls of dry stone. Early iron implements were found in them. As to the age of the Cornish and Irish cliff-castles it is impossible to speak. Nor is it easy to say whether they were the work of the natives or of invaders making a temporary stay in the country. The fact that in some places these forts occur on harbour-less points, and that they resemble so closely other forts inland, would lead one to conclude that, in some cases at least, they may well have been native fastnesses and not merely temporary camps thrown up by sea-borne invaders. One of the largest fortresses of this kind is that formed by Flamborough Head, where it is cut off from the mainland by the great entrenchment two and three-quarter miles in length, which is called the Dane's Dyke.

[1] *L'Anthropologie*, i. 401. For a further note on French camps, see the same journal, xiii. 84.

The entrenchment is double, and is provided with projections, or breastworks, at certain points. Here, again, we have no certain knowledge of the date of the work. The entrenchment is called the Dane's Dyke; the portion of the head cut off by it is called Little Denmark; and General Pitt-Rivers thought that this line of fortification, and others to the west of it, were successive constructions of invaders who had arrived by sea and fortified themselves, from time to time, in the process of driving further inland the native tribes. Canon Greenwell expresses some doubt of this, and the point must be regarded as at present unsettled.

(ii.) **Inland examples.**—The inland promontory fort is exactly on the same lines as its seaside brother, save that it relies for the defence of one or more of its sides on the steepness of the escarpment of a hill or on a precipice. Where the unembanked side or sides were not absolutely precipitous, it is probable that they were defended by a palisade of wood, all trace of which has, of course, long disappeared. Fig. 73 gives an example of this kind of fortification as exemplified in the great camp on Bredon Hill, Gloucestershire. On two sides, where the escarpment of the

FIG. 73. CAMP
Bredon Hill, Gloucestershire

hill is steep though not precipitous, there are no signs of any entrenchments. This projecting nose of ground is defended on the remaining side by an angular pair of entrenchments, separated from one another by a considerable distance and perhaps of different dates. Within the inner line is a singular mass of stone, "The Bambury Stone," concerning which many theories have been spun. It is simply a huge block of the local oolite, but whether the hollow in which it lies, by the excavation of which the block has become visible, is natural or artificial is uncertain. In the inner rampart of this camp have been found Roman pottery and coins, sufficient evidence, it seems, to permit us to believe that it was occupied for a time by that people, who may have constructed this line of defence. Probably the outer rampart at least is of earlier date. A few worked flints have been found on the hill in the neighbourhood of the camp, but apart from the objects mentioned there is singularly little to help us to assign to it a date. Mr. Westropp states that the promontory forts on the spurs of inland hills in this country are especially abundant in Yorkshire, along the Esk Valley from Guisborough to Whitby. Eight or nine of these spurs are fortified, sometimes with a single rampart of earth, sometimes with a core of loose stones, more rarely with a facing of dry masonry of large blocks; in a few cases several fosses and mounds occur. The fort on the third spur from the west has a double earthwork with a ditch, and farther back three earthworks and two fosses. In the rear of these is a ring-fort; still further back a single mound crossing the ridge. Then a mound across two-thirds of the ridge from the west, and another overlapping it from the east, running down the eastern slope to a bog. These forts have been found to contain articles of bronze, but the tumuli which are mixed up with them seem to have mainly exhibited objects of stone.

One cannot help being struck with the small size of some of these inland promontory forts, and wondering what their purpose can have been. On the promontory of Stinchcombe Hill, above Dursley, in Gloucester, for example, there is a very small portion cut off by three lines of entrenchment. Near by, but not included in the ramparts, is a row of pit-dwellings. The portion of the hill which is cut off is so small that it can hardly have been of any use as a place of refuge for the inhabitants of these pits. Possibly some of these small forts may have been signalling stations.

Hill - forts.—Fortresses whose lines are determined by the shape of the summit of the hill on which they are placed. These include some of the most characteristic of the objects commonly spoken of as British camps. They have been very fully treated by Pitt-Rivers,[1] whose military training rendered him a peculiarly valuable witness on such subjects. He sums up the special characters of this particular group of camps under the following heads: (i.) The entrenchments occupy the whole summits of the eminences on which they stand. (ii.) Considerations of the supply of water and fuel are invariably sacrificed to the occupation of the strongest features of the country. He has never come across an earthwork with a well in it. Here one may pause to note the puzzling fact that these hill-forts seem in almost all cases to have been singularly badly off for a water supply. Some have supposed that the inhabitants brought up water from some neighbouring source, though it has never been explained how this could have been done if the fortress was at all closely invested. Others think that there may have been wells which have now been filled up. Or again, it has been suggested, and this from what we know of the

[1] "Hill-Forts of Sussex," *Archæologia*, xlii. 27.

physical conditions of the country is not improbable, that the springs may then have been much higher than they now are. But there are cases where any supply of this kind seems to have been always impossible. Perhaps some use may have been made of catchment basins and dew-ponds, or perhaps the absence points to the fact that the earthern forts were not intended for prolonged occupa-

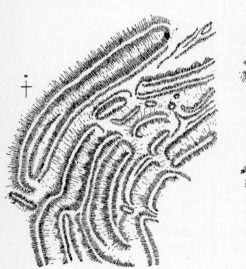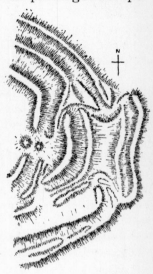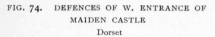

FIG. 74. DEFENCES OF W. ENTRANCE OF MAIDEN CASTLE
Dorset

FIG. 75. DEFENCES OF E. ENTRANCE OF MAIDEN CASTLE
Dorset

tion, but merely for temporary protection in case of a sudden raid. (iii.) The strength of the ramparts corresponds inversely with the natural strength of the position. (iv.) The ditch, which was generally on the outside of the rampart, has been noticed occasionally on the interior. This is a more common arrangement, however, in those earthworks which seem to have been constructed for religious or spectacular purposes. (v.) Outworks were thrown up on commanding sites within two or three hundred yards of the main work. (vi.) The ramparts at the gateways were increased in height, and sometimes thrown backwards so as to form a re-entrant angle, and thus obtain a cross-fire upon the causeway over the ditch. The extreme complexity of the arrangement of the earthworks at and near the places of entrance

FIG. 76. BRITISH CAMP
Herefordshire Beacon, Malvern

is, it may be pointed out, one of the important characteristics of this and the next class of forts. No better example could be desired than the entrances to Maiden Castle, near Dorchester, in Dorset, shown in Figs. 74 and 75. The extraordinary complexity of the banks may be likened to the fingers of two hands, interlocking with one another. Another form of breastwork, defending the entrance, will be noticed in the plan of Yarnbury, in Fig. 78. In the case of the Sussex forts, Pitt-Rivers points out that circular erections, with intervals between them, have been placed in the neighbourhood of the

entrance for the purpose of guarding it. In the case of
the special group, with which he was dealing, the inhabitants of the camps were lodged in pit-dwellings, and
the interior of the ramparts was found to be strewed with
flint flakes of artificial manufacture. As an example of
this kind of fortress, the great camp on the Herefordshire
Beacon, one of the Malvern Hills, of which a view is
given in Fig. 76 and a plan in Fig. 77 may be cited. Here
the outer earthworks include a large portion of the hill,
though the central portion, or citadel, is very small in

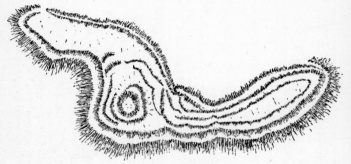

FIG. 77.   PLAN OF BRITISH CAMP
Herefordshire Beacon, Malvern

comparison with the extent of the outer fortifications.
Objects belonging to the bronze period have been found
in the neighbourhood of this camp, but its exact date is
as yet unsettled. Though the term earthworks has been
frequently used in connection with the class of object now
under consideration, it must not, therefore, be supposed
that fortresses with rude stone walls are on that account
excluded. A place like Worlebury, whose ramparts are
mainly of stone, differs in no essential respect from one
like Malvern, where earth has been the material employed
for the embankments. The builders of these fortresses
used the materials that came most easily to hand, and

when we talk about earthworks we must remember that the term is not, in all cases, strictly accurate.

Plateau forts.—This class of fortifications differs chiefly from the last in that the embankments by which it is surrounded are not adapted to the outlines of the top of a hill. The ground on which they are placed is high, but

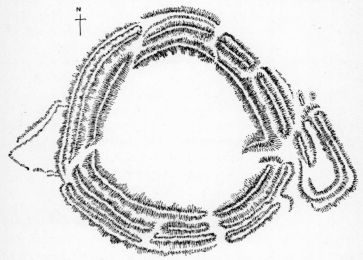

FIG. 78.   PLAN OF YARNBURY CASTLE
Wilts

the area immediately around may be almost or quite flat. Take the case of Yarnbury, of which a plan is given in Fig. 78. This camp occupies, it is true, an elevated position on Salisbury Plain. To reach it one has to ascend considerably, but when one arrives in its neighbourhood there is a long stretch of almost flat ground surrounding the earthwork itself. In fact, it lies on a plateau, and has thus no natural defences, such as belong to both the classes of fortresses which we have so far been considering. It must, therefore, depend upon the height of its banks and the depth of its ditches, together with the intricacy of its entrances, for the protection denied to it by nature. Mr. Gould is inclined to think that earthworks of this class are perhaps later in date than the other varieties, but as has been already pointed out, there is only one unfailing test of period, and that has not been applied as yet to any forts of this kind.

Dykes.—From the group of objects now to be considered must first be excluded those lines of entrenchment which, though called dykes, were constructed, like the " Dane's Dyke " on Flamborough Head, for the purpose of converting a promontory into a fortress or a camp. Such dykes are somewhat different in purpose, if identical in construction, from those now to be considered, and they have already been dealt with in an earlier portion of this chapter. The more or less lengthy lines of entrenchment, with which we are now concerned, are met with in many parts of the country. In certain districts they exist in great numbers, Warne, for example, enumerating no less than twenty-five in Dorsetshire, in his list of the antiquities of that county. Some, at least, of these seem to have been utilised as tribal boundaries, even if they were not originally constructed for that purpose. McKenny Hughes,[1] dealing with Offa's Dyke, one of the most important of these works, at one period the boundary between the Briton and the Saxon, inclines to the view that it is really made up of a number of works, possibly of the Roman period, which were subsequently united together to form a tribal boundary. This dyke, near to, and parallel with, which is another known as Watt's Dyke, runs in an approximately straight line. As the present boundary between England and Wales is tortuous, the dyke is sometimes in one country,

[1] *Archæologia*, lii. 465.

sometimes in the other. It can be well studied as it crosses Shropshire on the hills in the district of Clun. A still greater dyke is the Wans Dyke, in the south-west of England, which possesses a total length of eighty miles. Commencing on the banks of the Severn, it passes through part of Somerset, crosses the Avon, first at Warleigh, near Bathford, and afterwards at Benacre, near Melksham. It passes through Spye Park, and across the Wiltshire Downs by Shepherd's Shore, an excellent place to study it. Thence it makes its way towards Inkpen, in Berks. According to Stukeley and Guest,[1] this dyke was one of four lines of defence successively constructed by the Belgae in their northward advance, the other lines being Combe-Bank, Bokerley Dyke, and a dyke north of Old Sarum. This view has, however, been upset by the investigations made by Pitt-Rivers.[2] He shows that the Wans Dyke, contrary to what was once believed, is a work of Roman or post-Roman date, though he does not decide whether it is Romano-British or Saxon. The Bokerley Dyke in Wilts is about four miles in length, and belongs to the same period as the Wans Dyke. Its extremities, like those of some other dykes yet to be mentioned, seem to end "in the air," that is, without abutting upon any natural object of support, such as a river or a lake. In considering this and many other problems in connection with the early occupation of this country, one cannot be too careful to keep in mind the differences between our present physical geography and that of the earlier period. All that we know points to the fact that there were then far greater and more numerous forests than now. The greater part of Warwickshire, for example, was covered with the forest of Arden, a fact which explains the dearth of prehistoric objects in that county. Denbighshire was covered with forest up to a

---

[1] *Origines Celticae*, ii. 201.   [2] *Excavations,* vol. iii.

comparatively recent period. The great forest of Anderida in the south extended in a belt for many miles.
Swamps must have been much more common, and
marshy places and fens, for the climate was wetter, and
the streams must have been much clogged by pieces of
wood and the dams of beavers. Forests, such as then
existed, almost impenetrable, and the haunt of savage
wild beasts, and swamps must have offered greater
obstacles to the advance of troops than mountains, rivers,
or even narrow seas. In fact, we know that it was the
forest of Anderida which, for so long a time, cut off the
inhabitants of Sussex from attack on any side but that of
the sea. In the case of the Bokerley Dyke, Pitt-Rivers
has shown that it extended across an open place between
two forests, so that its ends were by no means without
support. In the eastern counties there are several important dykes lying across the course of the Icknield
Way. Of these the Roman Way, shown by Hughes[1] to
be really a dyke and not a road, the Fleam Dyke and the
Devil's Ditch are right across the Way, whilst the Black
Ditches, farther east, cross what may have been a bye-
road from it. Ridgeway[2] has shown that it was probably
in the neighbourhood of these dykes, and most likely
near the Fleam or the Devil's Ditch, that the Romans,
under P. Ostorius Scapula, defeated the Iceni, as related
by Tacitus.[3] The Devil's Ditch is about eight miles long.
The bank is 18 feet above the level of the country, 30 feet
above the bottom of the ditch, and 12 feet in width at the
top, whilst the ditch itself is 20 feet wide. Now all these
dykes seem to end "in the air," like the Bokerley Dyke,
but, like it, this idea is dispelled when the circumstances
of the time at which they were constructed are considered.
If the plan annexed be examined (Fig. 79), it will be

[1] *Camb. Review*, May 6th, 1885.   [2] *Proc. Camb. Ant. Soc.*, xxxiii.
[3] *Annales*, xii. 31.

noticed that a great deal of the land now inhabited was
at the period in question either fen or forest, and the
dykes extend between these two. The Roman Way does
not quite touch the fen, though it starts from the forest.

But there are two
small subsidiary
dykes connected with
it, one at Cherry
Hinton, the other at
Fen Ditton, which,
in some way or an-
other, no doubt made
up the deficiency.
The Fleam Dyke
and the Devil's Ditch
both abut upon one
or other of these sup-
ports, and the Black
Ditches run between
the River Lark and
the forest.

If Ridgeway is
right in his view,
these dykes are pre-

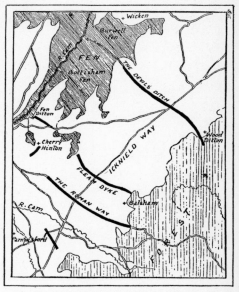

FIG. 79.   CAMBRIDGESHIRE DYKES

Roman, and of an earlier period than the western dykes
previously mentioned. In examining ditches of this kind
it must not be forgotten that there are many lines of entrenchment in the country which are not prehistoric, or
even belonging to an early period of history, but are
mediæval, or, it may be, post-mediæval. Thus there is
a ditch which runs along the summit of the Malvern Hills
from end to end, dividing Herefordshire from Worcestershire, which is called the "Shire Ditch," or the "Red Earl's
Ditch." There seems little doubt that this was cut by
Gilbert de Clare, Earl of Gloucester, to separate his own

forest of Malvern, which he had as dowry with his wife, the daughter of Edward I., from the possessions of the Bishop of Hereford. Other lines of entrenchment may perhaps be referred to the period of the Civil War. But much doubt must rest upon all dykes until their date has been decided by the use of the pick and shovel.

LIST OF EARTHWORKS

The following list is quite of a tentative character. It has been compiled from County Handbooks, archæological surveys, the Ordnance Map, and other sources, and I have to express my grateful acknowledgments to Mr. Chalkley Gould, who has looked through it and given me many suggestions. At the same time I am fully aware that it must contain many errors of omission and of commission. I hope that it includes all the most important examples in the country, but I fear that it may also include some examples which are not pre-Roman, and perhaps even others which have disappeared altogether. In spite of this I have thought it well to publish the list. It may at least serve as a groundwork for a more complete and accurate attempt in the future, and a complete list of earthworks is a thing very much to be desired. Where the word (Ro. ?) is added, it is doubtful whether the earthwork is one altered or originally constructed by the Romans.

BEDFORDSHIRE—

> Biggleswade, near.   Old Warden.
> "Cæsar's Camp," near Sandy.   Oval.
> "Maiden Bower," near Dunstable.   Circular.
> "Wanlud's Bank," near Leagrave.   Many gold British coins found near.

BERKSHIRE—

> "Alfred's Castle."   W. side of Ashdown Park.   Circ. 2 entrances.
> Aston Upthorpe, W. of.   Oval.   (? Danish.)
> Badbury Hill. $1\frac{1}{4}$ N. of Coleshill.   Circ.

BERKSHIRE (*contd.*)—

"Cæsar's Camp," East Hampstead.   Irreg.
"Chirbury."   1½ S. of Hinton Waldrish.   Oval.
"Grimsbury Castle."   In Grimsbury Wood, 1½ N. of Cold Ash.   Irreg.   1 ent.
Lambourne, near Ashbury.
Little Wittenham, ½ S. of.   Oval.
Lowbury Hill.   2 S. of Blewbury.   Square with tumulus.
Maidenhead Thicket.   Quadrilateral.
Newbury, near.   Bussock.
Newbury, near.   Borough Hill.
Newbury, near.   Overborough.
"Perborough Castle."   1 S. of Compton.
"Sigsbury."   1 S. of Letcombe Regis.   Circ.   1 ent.
*"Uffington Castle."   ¾ S. of Woolstone.   S. of "White Horse."   Irreg.   1 ent.
"Wallbury."   ½ W. of Wood Hay.

BUCKINGHAMSHIRE—

*Bulstrode Park.   Irreg.   2 ent.
Chesham, 2¼ N.E. of.   Circ.
"Cholesbury."   Oval.   (? Danish.)
"Danesborough," near Bow Brickhill.
*"Desborough Castle."   E. of West Wycombe.   Oval.
Great Missenden.   Quadrilat.   (? Roman.)
Harlington, ½ S. of.   Circ.
Keep Hill, near Wycombe.
Lee, ¾ N.E. of.
Shepley Church End.
West Wycombe.   Circ.
Whelpley Hill, ½ E. of

CAMBRIDGESHIRE—

"Arbury."   1 N. of Cambridge.
"Belsars Hill Camp."   1¼ N. of Rampton.   Circ.
"Vandlebury."   Entrenchment on Gogmagog Hills.
Wimblington, 1¾ E. of.   (Possibly Roman.)

Q

CHESHIRE—

"Bucton Castle," near Staleybridge.

"Camp Hill," near Whitmore Station.

Helsly Hill, near Frodsham.

"Kelsborough Castle," near Kelsall.

"Maiden Castle." Bickerton Hill.

Oakmere. Delamere.

CORNWALL—

Earthworks and cliff-castles very numerous in this county. The following is a selection only.

"Blackaden Rings," near Menheniot.

"Black Head, The." St. Austell. Cliff-castle.

Bodmin, near Tregoar. (Roman coins found.)

Braddock. Entrenchments in Largin Wood.

"Bury, The." ½ W. of Week St. Mary. Oval. (? Roman.)

Caddan Point. Cliff-castle.

"Cadsonbury." 1½ S.W. of Callington. Oval. 2 ent.

"Caer Bran." ¾ S.W. of Sancreed.

"Caer Dane." ½ E. of Perranzabuloe.

"Castel-an-Dinas," near Penzance.

"Castel-an-Dinas." 2 S.E. of St. Columb Porth. (Contains two tumuli. Traditionally hunting-lodge of King Arthur.)

"Castle Canyke." 1 W. of Fletcher's Bridge. Circ.

"Castle Dour," near Fowey.

Castle Downs, on. Circ.

"Castle Gotha," near Phœbe's Point, St. Austell.

Cheesewring, near the.

*Chûn Castle. Rough stonework.

"Crellas, The." Bodenaar.

Delabole Station, ¾ S.E. of.

"Demeliock Castle." 2¼ E. of Port Isaac.

Dodman, The. Cliff-castle.

"Dingerein Castle," or "Geraint's Castle." Gerrans Bay.

"Dunmeer Castle," near Dunmeer Bridge. Irreg. Oval.

Egloskerry, 1 W. of.

Germoe. 1 N.E. of. Two camps.

CORNWALL (*contd.*)—

"Giant's Castle."   St. Mary's Island, Scilly.

Goonhilly Downs.   Quadrilateral.

Grampound, 1 S.E. of.   Golden Farm.   Irreg.

Grampound, ½ N.E. of.   On the St. Austell road.

Grampound, 1 W. of.   On the Truro road.

Grampound, 1 N. of.   Near left bank of Fal.   Quadrilat.

"Great Dinas," near Manaccan.

"Kilbury Rounds," near St. Mabyn.

Kilkhampton.   Five camps in the immediate neighbourhood.

Ladock, ½ E. of.

Ladock, 1½ S.E. of.

"Lescudjack Castle," near Penzance.

Linkinhorne, ¾ S.W. of.   Circ.

"Little Dinas," near Manaccan.

Luxullian, ½ S. of.

Mawgan, ½ E. of.

Mevagissey, near.   Turbot Point.

"Padderbury," near Menheniot.

Pellynt, ¾ N.E. of.

*Pencarrow.   Circ.

Pengold, ½ S.E. of.

Pengold, 1 S.E. of.

"Penhargate Castle," near Dunmeer Bridge.

*"Perran Round," near Perranporth.   (? Amphitheatre.)

Port Isaac Road Station, ½ E. of.

Poundstock, 1 E. of.

"Prideaux Warren," near St. Blazey.

Quethiock, 1 N. of.

Rame Head.   Cliff-castle.

"Redcliff Castle," near Bodruthan.

"Resongy Round," near Penzance.

"Resugga Castle," near Grampound, on the left bank of the Fal.

St. Columb Porth, N. of.

St. Denis, ¼ N. of.

St. Endellion, ½ W. of.

St. Enoder, ¾ E. of.

CORNWALL (*contd.*)—

St. Eval, ½ S.E. of.

"St. Syth's Beacon," near Michaelstow.

Tintagel. Cliff-castle.

"Trecroben Castle," near Lelant. On Trecroben Hill.
Rampart of large stones and earth.

*"Treryn Dinas." Cliff-castle near Penzance with logan
stone.

Trevalgue Head. Cliff-castle. (*Archæol.* xliv. 422.)

Truen, near Penzance. A "round" 125 feet in circumference.

Truro, 1½ E. of.

Truro, near. 1 S. of Newbridge.

"Upton Castle," near Five Lanes. Circ. rampart, with
rectang. enclosure within.

"Warbstowbury." ¼ W. of Warbstow Cross. Circ.
1 ent. Contains a long mound called "King Arthur's
Grave."

West Looe, 1 N.E. of.

CUMBERLAND—

Aughertree Fell, near Irebay. Three circular camps.

*Bewcastle. Probably originally British.

Bothel Crags, on. Camp Hill. (? Roman.)

"Caermote." N. of Bassenthwaite Lake, near Bewcastle.

*"Caerthanoc." Soulby Fell.

"Castle How." W. side of Bassenthwaite Lake. Circ.

Crewgarth. Five-sided. Date uncertain, may be mediæval.

Dovenby Hall, near Bridekirk. Three oval ewks. Date
doubtful.

*"Dunmallet," near Ullswater. Double-ramparted hill-fort.

Hayton Castle Hill.

Lazonby, 2½ W. of. Circ. 1 ent.

Lazonby, 2¼ W. of. Circ. 1 ent.

"Maiden Castle." Burnmoor.

Newton Regny. Oval.

Overwater. Quadrilat.

Ponsonby, E. of. Infell. Five-sided. Date uncertain,
may be mediæval.

"Shoulthwaite Castle." Shoulthwaite.

CUMBERLAND (*contd.*)—

Snittlegarth. Quadrilat.
Tower Tye, Naworth. Circ.
Triermain, Watch Hill. Circ.

DERBYSHIRE—

Ashbourne, 5 N. of. Parwich. Ro. coins found.
Bolsover.
Calton, near Chatsworth.
*"Carlswark." Hathersage Moor.
Castleton, 1 N.W. of. Mam Tor.
Combe Moss. Possibly altered by Romans.
Cronkstone Hill. Peak.
"Dove Holes," near Buxton.
Fin Cop.
Harthill Moor, Banks on.
Hathersage Village. Circ. (? Danish.)
Markland Gripps. Elmton.
Mouslow, near Glossop.
Pilsbury.
Standerton.
Taddington.

DEVONSHIRE—

The following is a selection from the many earthworks
in this county.
Bampford Speke, 1½ S. of. Oval.
Barnstaple, 1½ N.E. of. Square.
"Beacon, The." ½ N.W. of Martinhow.
"Blackdown Camp." ½ W. of Hazelwood. Oval.
"Boringdon Camp." On N. edge of Cann Wood.
Braunton Barrows. Near Saunton Down.
Brayford, 1½ N.W. of. Oval.
*"Cadbury," near Exeter. Late Roman objects found
1848.
"Castle Dyke." Ugbrooke Park. Probably first Brit.
then Ro.
*Clovelly Dykes. Irreg. quad. (Brit. and later Ro.)
Coombe Raleigh, 1½ N.E. of. On Dumpton Hill. Oval.
1 ent.

DEVONSHIRE (*contd.*)—

*"Cranbrook Castle." 2½ N.E. of Chagford. Circ. rampart of stones and earth.

"Dane's Castle," near Exeter. (Perhaps Danish.)

"Dupley Castle." 1 N.E. of Newton St. Patrock.

Durniford.

Dembury, ½ S.W. of. Oval.

Dolbury, near Silverton.

Hawksdown Wood, In. 1¾ S.E. of Colyton. Irreg.

Heywood Wood. 1¼ S. of Chulmleigh. Circ.

High Peak, near Sidmouth. Charcoal, bones of ox, deer, etc. Flint implements and coarse pottery found.

*"Hembury," near Honiton. Oval. Certainly at some period Roman. Ro. coins and lar found. Perhaps Moridunum. But probably Brit. in origin.

*"Hembury," near Buckfastleigh. Irreg. oblong. Bronze celt and sling-stones found.

*"Hembury." In N. of county, 1¾ N.E. of Payhembury. Oval. 1 ent.

"Henbury Castle." 2 S. of Buckland Brewer.

"Henwell Castle," near Parracombe.

Ideford, 1½ E. of. Circ.

Kentisbury Down.

Malborough, ½ N. of. Irreg.

"Membury," near Axminster.

Milber Down. 1 S.E. of Newton Abbot.

Milton Abbot, 1 E. of.

"Musbury," near Axminster. Remarkable entrance defences.

"Old Barrow," near Countisbury. Quad. with rounded angles.

Parracombe, 1 N. of.

*"Prestonbury." On Prestonbury Common. Oval.

*"Sidbury Castle." ½ W. of Sidbury. Large store of sling-stones found 1864.

"Shoulsbury." Shoulsbury Common, Challacombe. Square.

"Stanborough." 1 S. of Halwell. Circ.

"Stockland Great Camp." 1¼ N.E. of Colleigh. Irreg.

Stoke Gabriel, 1 S.E. of.

DEVONSHIRE (*contd.*)—

Stoke Rivers, $\frac{3}{4}$ E. of.

Stratton, 1 N.E. of.

Stratton, 1$\frac{1}{2}$ N. of.

"Voley Castle." 1$\frac{1}{2}$ N.W. of Parracombe.

Widworthy, $\frac{1}{2}$ S.E. of.

"Woodbury Camp." 1$\frac{3}{4}$ W. of Dartmouth. Oval.

"Woodbury Castle." 1$\frac{1}{4}$ E. of Woodbury. Irreg.

"Wooston Castle." 3 from Moreton Hampstead.

DORSETSHIRE —

Abbotsbury, near. Wears Hill.

*"Badbury Rings," near Sturminster Marshall. The "Mons Badonicus" of Guest.

Banbury Hill, near Okeford Fitzpaine.

Buckland Newton, 2 S.E. of.

"Buzbury Rings," near Tarrant Keynston. Circ.

"Cattistock Castle." Cattistock. (? Ro.)

Cerne Abbas, near. Two camps.

"Coney's Castle," near Wootton Fitzpaine.

Cranborne Chase. Two camps in Bussey Stool Wood.

"Dungeon, The." 1$\frac{1}{2}$ E. of Middlemarsh.

Eggardon Hill, near Powerstock. With hut-circles.

*"Flower's Barrow," near Lulworth.

Gallows Hill, near Wool.

*Handley Hill. Bronze or early Ro. (Pitt-Rivers, *Excavations*, iv.)

*Hambledon Hill, near Iwerne Courtney. Probably first Brit. then Ro.

*Hod Hill, near Stourpaine. Brit. with small Ro. enclosure in N.W. corner. Hut-circles.

"Lambert's Castle," near Marshwood. D-shaped.

*"Maiden Castle," near Dorchester. Perhaps the Dunium of Ptolemy. At first Brit. Certainly at one time Ro. Remarkable entrance defences.

Minterne Magna, $\frac{1}{2}$ N. of.

Morden Heath.

Nettlecombe Tout, near Milton.

Ower Heath.

Pillesdon Pen. Oval.

DORSETSHIRE (*contd.*)—

    Pimperne Down, on.

    "Poundbury," near Dorchester.   Possibly Pre-Roman.

    Powerstock.

    *"Rawlsbury."   On Bulbarrow Hill.   Irreg. circ.   Iron anchor and other iron and bronze objects found. (*Archæol.*, xlviii. 115.)

    Rings Hill, Worbarrow Bay.

    *"South Lodge Camp."   Rushmore.   Bronze.   (Pitt-Rivers, *Excavations*, iv.)

    "Spettisbury Rings," or "Crawford Castle," near Spettisbury.   Circ.

    Shipton Beacon.   Irreg.

    "Weatherbury," near Milborne Stileham.

    Woodbury Hill, near Bere Regis.   Irreg. circ.

    "Woolsbarrow."   On Bloxworth Heath.

DURHAM—

    "Castle Hill."   Bishopton.   Possibly prehistoric, but certainly occupied by Roger Conyers, twelfth century.

    "Castle, The."   Hamsterley, $1\frac{1}{4}$ N.W. of.   Rampart of cobble-stones.

    Cockfield Fell.   Small square earthworks, probably prehistoric.

    "Maiden Castle," near Durham.   Old Elvet.

ESSEX—

    *"Ambresbury Banks."   Epping Forest.   Excavated. British.

    Asheldham, near Burnham.

    "Grymes Dyke," and other ramparts near Lexden.

    Loughton.   Epping Forest.

    "Pitchbury Ramparts."   Great Horkesley.

    Pleshy.   The outer work possibly British.

    Prittlewell.   Smither's Farm, near Southend.

    Ring Hill.   2 from Saffron Walden.

    South Weald, Brentwood.

    "Wallbury Camp." $\frac{1}{2}$ W. of Little Hallingbury.

"Abbey Camp." Alveston. Oval. 1 ent.

Ablington, near Bibury. 1 ent.

Amberley, near Minchinhampton. Many pit-dwellings in and near.

Batsford, near Moreton-in-Marsh. Quadril. Ro. coins and other antiquities found.

Beckford. 2½ N.E. of Winchcombe. Irreg. A spring near, with covered approach.

"Birdlip Camp." ½ N. of Birdlip Hill. Flint arrow-heads.

"Blackenbury," or "Brackenbury," or "Becketsbury." 2 S. of Dursley. 2 ent. Many pit-dwellings near. (*Proc. Soc. Ant.*, ii. x. 325.)

Blaize Castle, Henbury. Irreg. Many Ro. coins found here.

*"Bloody Acre Camp." Tortworth Park, Cromhall.

"Bury Hill Camp." Mangotsfield. Irreg. 1 ent.

Caerwood, Tidenham.

*Cam Long Down. Many pit-dwellings near. Many flints found.

"Castle Bank." Saintbury. Round barrow within.

"Castle Tump." Stow Green, Coleford.

Charlton Abbots. Circ. 1 ent.

Cleeve Hill Camp.

Clifton. St. Vincent's Rocks. Nearly destroyed. Probably at one time Roman. Traditionally the British Caer Oder.

Combesbury Camp. Tidenham. Circ.

"Conderton Camp." Bredon Hill. Irreg. oval. 1 ent. (? Danish.)

Condicote. 3 N.W. of Stow-on-the-Wold. Almost obliterated.

Coopers Hill. 2 W. of Birdlip.

Crickley Hill. 1 N. of Birdlip.

Dowdeswell. Two camps.

Dyrham Camp. 3 S. of Chipping Sodbury. Close to site of Battle of Deorham.

Elberton. Irreg. quadril.

Eubury, Condicote.

Gloucestershire (*contd.*)—

*"Godwin Castle," or "Painswick Beacon," Painswick. Irreg. Ro. relics.

*Haresfield. Brit., with separate portion entrenched by Ro.

Hazelwood Copse. 1 S.E. of Nailsworth. Many worked flints found near.

Horton Camp. 3 N.E. of Chipping Sodbury.

"Kemerton Camp." Bredon Hill. Ro. pot. and coins. Contains the "Bambury Stone." An ancient *cache* of wheat discovered here.

King's Weston Camp. Henbury. Indistinct.

Leckhampton. 2 S. of Cheltenham. Bronze and flint implements. (*Archæol.* xix. 171.)

Little Dean. 1½ N.W. of Newnham.

Lydney. Close to Ro. villa. Many Ro. coins. Perhaps originally Brit.

Lydney. ½ mi. from last. Ro. coins, etc. Probably first Brit. then Ro.

Meon Hill. 6 S. of Stratford-on-Avon. Irreg. 394 iron sword-blades found here in 1824.

*Minchinhampton. Includes nearly 600 acres.

"Norbury." Farmington.

"Norbury." Colesbourn.

*Nottingham Hill. Cleeve. Brit. and Ro. coins.

Oldbury-on-Severn. S. of Oldbury Pill.

Oxenton Hill.

Prestbury. 2 from Cheltenham. Traces of stone foundations within, probably mediæval.

Ranbury Camp. 4 E. of Cirencester.

Randwick. 2 N.W. of Stroud.

"Ring Outpost, The." Cleeve Hill.

"Salmonsbury." Bourton-on-the-Water. Rectang. Ro. relics and 120 iron sword-blades. Perhaps originally Ro.

*Sodbury. Rectang. Probably Ro.

Sowdley. 2 W. of Newnham.

Stinchcombe Hill. Small earthworks at end, near pit-dwellings.

"Toots, The." Oldbury-on-Severn. Many Ro. coins found.

Towbury. Twyning.

GLOUCESTERSHIRE (*contd.*)—

> Trewsbury. 3 S.W. of Cirencester.
> *"Uleybury," near Uley-cum-Owlpen. Ro. coins and worked flints found.
> "Welshbury." 3 N. of Newnham.
> Willersey. Remains of long barrow in camp.
> Windrush. Circ. 1 ent.
> (For further notes, see Witts' *Archæological Handbook of Gloucestershire.*)

HAMPSHIRE—

> "Balksbury," or "Folksbury," near Andover.
> Basingstoke, 1 N.W. of.
> "Beacon Hill Camp," near Burghclere. Hut-circles.
> "Buckland Rings." 1 N. of Lymington. Irreg. cir.
> Buriton, 1½ W. of. Irreg. Probably Ro.
> Bury Hill, near Andover.
> "Cæsar's Camp." Aldershot. Ro. coins.
> "Cæsar's Camp." Crondall. 100 Merovingian gold coins found near it in 1828.
> Chilworth, 1 S.E. of. Circ.
> Christchurch, 1½ N.W. of. St. Catherine's Hill. Irreg. and circ. ewks.
> "Danebury." 1 N.E. of Nether Wallop. Circ. 1 ent.
> Egbury Hill. Pentagonal.
> Ellisfield. Circ.
> "Hengistbury," near Christchurch.
> "Lidbury Ring." 1¾ E. of Middleton. Probably Brit. then Ro.
> Lydmorton, ¾ S. of.
> Mortimer Heath, Silchester. Square. (? Ro.)
> *Old Winchester Hill. Ro. lamp and coins. Perhaps originally Ro.
> *Quarley Hill. 1 S.W. of Quarley. Oval. 1 ent.
> Sherfield English, 1 N.E. of.
> Sherfield-upon-Loddon, ½ N.W. of. Oval. 1 ent.
> Stockbridge.
> "Norbury Ring." ½ N.W. of Stoke Charity. Circ.
> *Sydmanton, ½ S.W. of. Ladle Hill.
> *Tatchbury Mount. 2 N.E. of Tolton. Oval.

HAMPSHIRE (*contd.*)—

    Upper Clatford, ½ W. of. Bury Hill. Circ. 2 ent.
    *"Walbury." ½ N. of Coombe. Irreg.
    Winchester. St. Katherine's Hill. Probably Ro.
    "Winklesbury Circle." Vallum of flints.
    Worldbury Mount. A "White Horse" here, not ancient.
    "Tunorbury." Hayling. Circ.

HEREFORDSHIRE—

    Aconbury Camp. ½ W. of Aconbury. Oval. 1 ent.
    Ashton, near Eye in Pyon Wood.
    Aymestrey, ½ N. of. Irreg.
    Bach Camp. Kimbolton.
    Bradnor Hill Camp. Kington.
    Brandon. ¾ S. of Leintwardine. Irreg. 1 ent. Probably Ro.
    "Capler Camp." 1 S.E. of Fownhope. In Capler Wood.
        Oval. 1 ent.
    Coxwall Knoll. ½ N. of Brampton Bryan.
    Credenhill Park Wood, In.
    *"Croft Ambrey." 4 W. of Orleton.
    *Deerfold, near Wigmore. Circ.
    "Dinefor Camp." 1 S. of Billingham. Oval. (? Ro.)
    "Eaton Hill Camp." Foy.
    "Ethelbert's Camp." ¾ S. of Dormington. Irreg. (? Ro.)
    Fownhope Park. Cherry Hill. ½ N. of Fownhope. Oval.
        1 ent.
    Garmsley. 1½ E. of Bockleton. Oval.
    *Herefordshire Beacon. Malvern Hills. Irreg.
    *Holly Bush, or Midsummer Hill. Malvern Hills. Irreg.
    Ivington. 1¾ N.W. of Hope-under-Dinmore. Irreg.
    "Kilbury Camp," near Ledbury. Irreg.
    "King's Cellar, The," or "Sutton Walls." 1 N.E. of
        Moreton-on-Lugg. Said to be a Mercian Palace.
    Little Doward Camp, near Whitchurch.
    "Oldbury Camp." Much Marcle.
    Pentwyn Camp. 2 W. of Brilley. Circ.
    Pudleston, 1 W. of. Irreg.
    "Risbury Camps." ½ S. of Humber. Oval.
    Ruckhall Camp, near Eaton Bishop.

HEREFORDSHIRE (*contd.*)—

    Uphampton Camp. Docklow.

    Walford, near Ross.

    "Wall Hills." 1 W. of Collington. Oval. Spear, arrowheads, pot, worked flints.

    Walterstone, $\frac{1}{2}$ E. of. Circ. 2 ent.

    Wapley Hill, $\frac{1}{4}$ S. of Combe. Irreg. 1 ent.

    Westington Camp, Grendon Bishop.

    "Vineyard, The." Haffield.

HERTFORDSHIRE—

    "Aubreys," or "Aubury," near Redbourn.

    Beech Bottom, near Sandridge.

    "Cleigh-hangres," near Watton.

    "Ravensborough Castle." Hexton.

    "Slad, The," near Wheathamstead.

    St. Albans. Ewks. Nearly parallel with Ro. wall of Verulamium.

HUNTINGDONSHIRE—

    "Bulwark Fort, The." Earith.

    Bury, S. of.

KENT—

    Alkham.

    Bigbury Camp, near Canterbury.

    "Castle Rough." Milton.

    Chilham. $\frac{1}{2}$ S.E. of. Entrenchment supposed to be Brit.

    "Clubberlubber." Swanscombe.

    Coldred. Rectang. 2 ent. (? Ro.)

    Darenth, near Green Street Green.

    Holwood, Keston.

    Kingston. (? Ro.)

    Knowlton.

    Maidstone, $1\frac{1}{2}$ S. of.

    Offham, 1 E. of.

    Ospringe.

    Queenborough Camp. Rectang. (? Ro.)

    "Roman Codde." Kingsdowne, near Walmer.

    Westerham. Camp in Squerries Wood.

    (See Archæological Survey and list by Flinders Petrie in *Archæologia Cantiana*, xiii.)

LANCASHIRE—

Beadle Hill, near Burnley.

Birkrigg. (C.)

Bleaberry Hawes. Torver. (C.)

" Bucton Castle." Mossley.

Castercliff, near Colne.

" Castle Steads," near Walmesley.

" Dykes, The." 2¼ E. of Burnley.

" Eusdon Fort," near Burnley.

" Foula." Urswick, Holme Bank. (C.) Foundations of walled enclosure.

Hawkshead Hall Park. (C.)

Heathwaite Fell Stone Rings. (C.)

" Mount, The." Holton, near Lancaster. Querns, etc., found.

" Ringstones." Worsthorne.

Scrow Moss Coniston. (C.)

Stonyhurst Park.

Torver Beck. Bannishead Moor. (C.)

Trawden. 2 S. of. Circ.

*Urswick, Great. Oval stone-walled enclosure.

Warton Crag.

Whalley.

(C. enclosures with earth and stone banks, the period of which is not very certain. Described by Cowper, *Archæologia*, liii. 389.)

LEICESTERSHIRE—

Beacon Hill. Bronze celts and armlets found.

Billesdon.

Breedon Hill.

Barrow Hill, near Great Dalby.

" Bury Camp," near Ratby.

LINCOLNSHIRE—

Billingborough, ¾ S.E. of. Rectang. (? Ro.)

Burnham, near Barrow Haven. (? Danish.)

" Castle Hills." Gainsborough. Said to be British, then Danish.

" Countess Close." Alkborough. Rectang. (? Ro.)

LINCOLNSHIRE (*contd.*)—

"Dam Close." S.W. of Willoughby. (? Ro.)

Hallington, near. Orgarth. (? Danish.)

Honington, ½ S.E. of. Rectang.

Kingerby.

"Manwarings, The," near Swineshead. (? Danish.)

North Kyme, near Heckington. (? Ro.)

Revesby.

"Round Hills," near Bassingthorpe. Circ.

"Three Castles." ¾ S.E. of Barrow Haven. Irreg. Said to be British, then Danish.

"Yarborough Camp." 1 N.E. of Melton Ross. Rectang. Probably Ro. Many coins found.

MONMOUTHSHIRE—

Bishton, near.

Caerleon, 1 N.W. of. The Lodge Farm. (? British, then Ro.)

"Coed-y-Bunedd." ½ N. of Bettws Newydd.

"Craig-y-gaercyd," near Llancayo, N.W. of Usk.

Kemeys Inferior, S. of. Two camps.

Kemeys Inferior, N. of.

Llangwm, 1 S. of. Oval. (? Ro.)

Llangwm, ¾ N. of.

Llanhennock, 1 N.E. of.

Llanishen, 2½ W. of. Irreg.

Llantilio Crosenny, 1½ S.E. of.

Llanvihangel Crucorny, 2 N. of.

Llanvair Discoed, 1 E. of.

Newport, 1¼ W. of. (? Ro.)

Portskewet, Coast near. (? Ro.)

Raglan, 1½ W. of.

Risca, 1 N. of. Oval. 1 ent.

St. Bride's, near Netherwent.

Tintern, 1 S.W. of.

"Twyn-y-gaer." 2 N.W. of Llanvihangel Crucorny.

NORFOLK—

"Castle Hill." Entrenchment E. of Huntworth.

Fakenham Camp.

Tasburgh Camp.

NORTHAMPTONSHIRE—

    Arbury.

    Borough Hill, Daventry.

    Cotton Camp. $\frac{3}{4}$ E. of Little Addington.

    East Farndon. Entrenchment.

    *Hunsbury Hill. $1\frac{1}{4}$ S.W. of Northampton. Circ. Late Celtic, as proved by excavation. Objects in Northampton Museum.

    "Larches, The." $1\frac{1}{4}$ N.E. of Farthingstone. Entrenchment.

    "Rainsborough Camp." Newbottle. Oval. 2 ent. Ro. coins.

    Thenford, 1 N. of. Irreg.

NORTHUMBERLAND—

    The earthworks in this county are extremely numerous. A selection of the more important is here given, and, on account of their number, the plan of placing named camps in alphabetical order has here been departed from, and all are classified according to the place nearest to them.

    Alnham, $\frac{1}{2}$ W. of. On Castle Hill. Circ. 1 ent.

    Alnmouth, N. of. Irreg. quad.

    Alnwick. (i.) Near tower in Park. Oval. (ii.) Close by this and to S. of it. (iii.) 1 S. of this "Black Chesters."

    Alwinton, N. of. Two camps.

    Bamburgh. (i.) $1\frac{1}{4}$ S.W. of, on West Hill. Irreg. (ii.) 1 S.W. of, on Crook Hill. Irreg. oval. (iii.) 2 S. of, on Pigdon Hill. Irreg. (iv.) On Cat Crag.

    Barrasford, near Moneylaws.

    *Beanley Moor. "The Ringses." With hut-circles.

    Belford. (i.) $\frac{1}{2}$ N.W. of. "Derry Camp." Quad. (ii.) On Chapel Hill. (iii.) On the Kyloe Hills.

    Bellingham. (i.) $2\frac{1}{2}$ S. of. "Garret Holt Camp." Circ. (ii.) 2 S.E. of. Irreg. 1 ent. (iii.) $2\frac{3}{4}$ S.E. of. Rectang. (iv.) $1\frac{1}{4}$ N.W. of, in Riding Wood. Oval.

    Bewick Hill. $1\frac{3}{4}$ N.E. of Eglingham. *(i.) Double Camp, with hut-circles. (ii.) 1 mile from this, near Blaw-Weary.

NORTHUMBERLAND (*contd.*)—

Birtley, near. (i.) Birtley Shields Green. (ii.) Birtley West Farm. (iii.) High Shields Green. (iv.) Mill Knowe.

Bolam. (i.) On Old Stale Hill. (ii.) On Huckhoe.

Bolton. (i.) "The Guards." (ii.) On Jenny's Lantern Hill.

Bowmont Hill. 1 S. of Mindrum. Irreg. oval.

*Broughlaw, near Ingram. With hut-circles.

Bucton Moor. 1 W. of Bucton. Two circ. camps.

Caistron, near Hepple.

Callaly. On Castle Hill. One rampart consists of squared stones set in lime. (? Brit., then Ro.) Two other camps near here. (i.) High Houses. (ii.) Rabbit Hall.

*Carry House Camp. 1 S. of Countess Park. Hut-circles.

Catcleugh Plantation. Irreg.

Chatton, ½ E. of. On Chatton Law. Circ. and others.

Chillingham. Hebburn Crags, E. of.

Cochrane Pike. 1¼ S. of Ingram. Oval.

Cornhill, near Campshill.

Doddington, near. *(i.) Dod Law. Double Camp. (ii.) Fenton Hill. 1 N. (iii.) "The Ringses." (iv.) Several others near here.

Downham Village. (i.) E. of, on Camp Hill. Oval. (ii.) ½ N.E. of. "Moneylaws." Oval.

East Ord, ½ N.W. of, at Canny Bank.

Elsdon. (i.) ¾ S.W. of. Irreg. (ii.) 1½ S.W. of, at Raylees. (? Ro.)

Flodden, near the Linthaughs.

Gunnarton. *(i.) "Moneyhill." Mound with ramparts and fosses. *(ii.) One on each side of Gunnar Heugh, with rough stone walls. Hut-circles near. (iii.) 1 N. of Gunnarton Nick, "Pity Me Camp."

*Hare Haugh Hill. 1½ S.E. of Holystone. Oval. 2 ent.

*Hare Hope Hill, near Humbleton, in Monday Cleugh, on Standrop Hill. Irreg. quadrilateral.

"Harelaw." ¾ S.E. of Mindrum. Circ.

Hartleyburn Common, near Lambley Station. Rectang. 1 ent.

Hepple, behind Swindon Hill. "Soldiers Fauld."

R

NORTHUMBERLAND (*contd.*)—

Holystone, ½ W. of, near Campville Farmhouse.

Howick Burn, near mouth of. Circ. Ro. coins.

Ilderton. (i.) On Ilderton Dod. Rectang. (ii.) Rose-
den Edge. Octagonal. Hut-circles.

Ingram, near. (i.) 1 S.E. of. On Castle Knowe. Circ.
3 ent. (ii.) On Old Fawdon Hill. (iii.) Wether Hill.
(iv.) Gibbs Hill. (v.) Chubden Hill. (vi.) Knock Hill.
(vii.) Ewe Hill. (viii.) Reaveley Hill.

Kirk Newton, near. (i.) Little Hetha. (ii.) Great Hetha.
(iii.) Sink Side. (iv.) Fawcett Shank and others.

*Kirk Whelpington. Several camps in neighbourhood.

*Linhope Farne, 4 mi. from Ingram. (i.) "Greaves Ash,"
with many hut-circles. (ii.) Near this "The Chesters,"
also with hut-circles.

*Lord - in - shaws. Many hut - circles. Near Rothbury.
(Greenwell, *British Barrows*, 430.)

Matfen, near. On Grindstone Laws. Circ.

Middleton Hill, near Wallington. (? Ro.)

Long Framlington. On Hall Hill, near Heatherwick's
Well. Rectang. 1 ent.

Norham, near Twizell Bridge. "Haly Chesters." Quadril.

Otterburn. (i.) 1 N.E. of, on Colwell Hill. Circ. 1 ent.
(ii.) Fawdon Hill.

Plashetts, near, on Haw Hill.

Rothbury. (1) "Old Rothbury," N.W. of. Circ. (ii.)
½ W. of, at Westhills. Circ. Others in neighbourhood.

*Rowting Lynn.

Swinburn, near. (i.) On Reiver Crag. (ii.) On Oxhill.
(iii.) On Blue Crag.

Swine Hill, on Watling Street, near Ridsdale. Rectang.
(? Ro.)

Thorneyburn, near.

*Tosson, Great. Burgh Hill Camp.

Trewhitt. "Roberts Law."

Unthank, near Berwick. Three Camps.

Warden. (i.) W. of. Circ. 1 ent. (ii.) N.W. of, on
High Warden. Circ. 1 ent.

Weetwood Bridge, near Wooler. Stone balls and querns
found.

Northumberland (*contd.*)—

Whalton, ¾ N.E. of. (i.) "Dead Men's Graves." (ii.) Near this a second, larger.

Wooler. (i.) ½ W. of. "Green Castle," or "Maiden Castle," or "The Kettles." Irreg. quad. Hut-circles. Ro. coins found. (ii.) "Cup and Saucer Camp." S.W. of Humbleton Mill. Several others in the neighbourhood.

*Yeavering Bell. Hut-circles. Many flint implements found here.

(Information respecting many of these camps and other antiquities of the county may be found in Tomlinson's *Comprehensive Guide to Northumberland*.)[1]

Nottinghamshire—

Egmanton, 1 S.W. of. (? Danish.)

Rinshill, near.

Oxfordshire—

Chadlington, 1 N.W. of.

Chalcombe Lodge, near.

Chastleton, ¾ S. of. Irreg. rectang. (Rollestone's *Sci. Papers*, i. 224.)

Crowell. (? Ro.)

Evenley, 1 S.W. of.

Idbury, ½ S.W. of.

"Maiden Bower," near Steeple Barton.

Nether Worton, ½ N.E. of. Oval.

North Leigh, 1 S.E. of, in Eynsham Hall Park.

"Rainsborough Camp." ½ S. of Charlton. Circ. 1 ent.

"Round Castle." ¼ E. of Begbroke.

Sarsden, ¾ S. of.

Shutford. ¾ S. of Madmarston Camp. Circ.

Swallcliffe, near Blacklands. (Ro. coins found. Perhaps first Brit.)

Wigginton, 1¼ N. of. Tadmarton Camp. Circ. 1 ent.

Wigginton, ½ S.W. of the last Camp.

---

[1] "Arthur's Round Table." Soney Rigg, near Plashetts, perhaps similar to those ewks mentioned in note to Yorkshire ewks.

SHROPSHIRE—

"Abdon Burf." On Brown Clee Hill. Irreg. circ.

"Banks, The." 1 S. of Wem. Rectang. (? Ro.)

Belan Bank. ½ S. of Kinnerley.

"Berth, The." ¾ N. of Eyton.

"Billings Ring." 1¼ N.W. of Edgton.

"Bodbury Ring." ½ N.W. of Church Stretton. Circ.

Brockton, 1 N.W. of. Irreg. circ.

Burrow Wood. ½ W. of Hopesay. Irreg.

"Bury Ditches." 2 N.E. of Clun.

"Bury Walls." 2 S.W. of Hodnet. (Ro. coins found.)

"Caerbre," near Chirbury.

*"Caer Caradoc," near Church Stretton.

*"Caer Caradoc," near Clun.

"Caer-Din Ring." 1¾ S.W. of Church Town.

"Castel Brogynton." In Brogynton Park, near Oswestry.

*"Castel-Bryn-Amlwg." 1¾ N. of Felindre, in Clun Valley. Circ.

"Castle Ring." Slitt Hill. Irreg.

"Castle Ring." ½ S. of Snailbeach.

*Caynham, ½ N. of. (? Ro.) The Chastel Key of the thirteenth century and perhaps the Kair Key of Henry of Huntingdon.

"Cefn-y-Castel." On the Breidden Hills.

Church Town, ¾ S.E. of. Irreg. oval.

"Clee Burf." On Brown Clee Hill.

Clun, near. (i.) 1 N.E. of. Irreg. (ii.) 1¼ S.W. of. (iii.) ½ S. of. (See also "Bury Ditches" and "Caer Caradoc.")

"Coed-y-Gaer." 1¼ N.E. of Llansilin.

Coxwall Camp. (Partly in Herefordshire.)

"Ditches, The." ½ S. of East Hope.

Longnor, 1¼ W. of. Irreg. (? Ro.)

Minsterley, ½ E. of. Gallows Hill. (? Ro.)

Moel-y-Golfa, Breidden Hills.

Newcastle, N. of. Irreg. (? Ro.)

Nordy Bank. ½ E. of Clee St. Margaret. Irreg. 3 ent.

Norton Camp, near Stokesay. (? Ro.)

*"Old Oswestry," or "Hên Dinas." ½ N. of Oswestry.

SHROPSHIRE (*contd.*)—

Pontesbury, ½ S. of.   Circ.

Pontesbury, ½ S.E. of.   Oval.   1 ent.

Pontesford Hill.   Oval.

Priestweston, 1¼ S.W. of.   Irreg.

Ratlinghope Hill.   Irreg.

"Ring, The."   ¾ S. of Pontesbury.

"Robury Ring."   1 N. of Asterton.

*Roden, 1¾ W. of.   Irreg. circ.

Ruyton-of-the-Eleven-Towns, 1½ S. of.   Irreg.

Snead, ½ N.E. of.   Two irregular camps.

Titterstone Clee.   1 W. of Cheney Longville in Warthill
    Plantation.   Irreg.

*Wrekin, The.

SOMERSET—

Banwell, ½ E. of.   Oval.   (Agrimensorial cross in it.
    Coote, *Romans of Britain*, p. 101.)

Bath.   Lansdowne Hill.

Bathampton Camp.   1 E. of Bath.   Irreg.

"Bats Castle."   ¾ S. of Dunster.   Quadril.   2 ent.   (?Ro.)

Blackers Hill.   1 N. of Ashwick.

Blaise Hill.

Bleadon Hill, near Hutton.

"Borough Walls," or "Bower Walls," near Rownham
    Ferry on Avon.   (*Archæol.*, xliv. 428.)

Bourton, 2½ N. of.   On Park Hill.   Irreg.

Bourton, 2½ N.W. of.   Irreg.

Brean Down.   With hut-circles.

Brent Knoll.   Irreg.   Ro. coins.

"Brewers Castle," near Dulverton.

Broomfield, ¾ N. of.

Burrington, ¼ S. of.   Rectang.   1 ent.

"Bury Castle," near Selworthy.

*"Cadbury Camp."   N. of Sutton Montis.   Irreg.   Ro.
    coins.   Traditionally the Camelot of Arthurian legend.

"Cadbury Camp," near Tickenham.   Oval.   Loose stone
    ramparts.

"Cadbury Camp," near Yatton.

"Caer Badon," near Claverton.

Somerset (*contd.*)—

"Castles, The." Bathealton. Ro. coins.

*"Castle Neroche." Buckland St. Mary. British, afterwards Roman.

Charnwell, near Sigwell.

Clatworthy. ½ N.W. of. Oval.

Countesbury.

"Cow Castle," on Exmoor.

*"Danesborough." Stowey.

*"Dolebury," near Churchill. Oval, stone-walled. A square camp, probably Roman, within its enclosure.

Dowsborough. 1¼ S. of Holford. Oval. 1 ent.

Dundon Hill. Irreg.

Dunster, ½ S.W. of. Circ.

"Elworthy Barrows." Brendon Hill.

*Hamdon Hill. Irreg. British ewks, of which N.E. portion was altered by Romans. *Archæol.* xxi.; *Proc. Soc. Ant.*, ii. xi. 86.

"Jack's Castle," near Bruton.

"Kenwalch Castle," near Stavordale.

"King Alfred's Fort." ¼ N. of Borough Bridge.

Kingsweston Hill, near Henbury.

"Maesbury Castle." 1¼ W. of Oakhill. Oval. 2 ent.

"Maesknoll." ½ N. of Norton Malreward.

*Norton Fitzwarren.

"Ponter's Ball," or "Wall," near Glastonbury.

Sigwell. (Rollestone, *Sci. Papers*, i. 440.)

"Solisbury Camp," near Swainswick. Irreg. The Mons Badonicus of Earle.

Stantonbury Hill. ½ N. of Stanton Prior. Irreg.

Stokeleigh, in Leigh Woods, opposite Clifton. Irreg. (*Archæol.* xliv. 428.)

Stonesbury Camp, on Exmoor.

Stoney Stratford, 1 N.E. of. Oval.

Tedbury Camp, near Mells. Irreg.

"Trendle Ring," near Bicknoller. Circ.

Wadbury Camp, near Mells.

Wick Rocks, near Bath.

Wiveliscombe, ¾ E. of. Irreg.

SOMERSET (*contd.*)—

> *"Worlebury," near Weston-super-Mare. Late Celtic, contains many pits, stone-walled.
>
> Yarlington, W. of.
>
> (See *Proc. Somerset Arch. & N.H. Soc.*, v. 38.)

STAFFORDSHIRE—

> Arley Wood. Remains of ewk. (? Ro.)
>
> "Berth, The," near Whitmore. (? Ro.)
>
> "Bury Ring." 2 S.W. of Stafford.
>
> "Castle Old Fort," near Over Stonnal.
>
> "Castle Ring." Beaudesert Old Park. Irreg. 1 ent.
>
> Kinver Edge. Quadrilat.
>
> "Knaves Castle," near Brown Hills.

SUFFOLK—

> "Castle Yard." ¼ E. of Bramfield.
>
> Clare Camp. N. of the town.
>
> "Warbanks," near Cockfield. Possibly British.

SURREY—

> Albury, near. On Farley Heath. (? Ro.)
>
> "Anstiebury," near Dorking. Circ. Flint implements found in and near.
>
> Ashstead, 1½ N. of. On Ashstead Common. 2 ent.
>
> Byfleet, 1½ E. of.
>
> "Cæsar's Camp." Wimbledon Common. Circ. 2 ent. (*Archæol.* xxxii. 450.) Wantonly destroyed in 1875.
>
> "Cæsar's Camp." St. George's Hill, Weybridge.
>
> "Cardinal's Cap, The." Caterham on the White Hill.
>
> "Castle Hill." Hascombe. Quadrilat.
>
> "Castle Hill," near Godstone.
>
> "Elderbury." St. Anne's Hill, near Chertsey.
>
> Farley Heath. Slight remains. Aubrey's "Roman Temple." Many early British and Roman coins found.
>
> Holmbury Hill, near Ockley. Rectang.
>
> Leatherhead, ¾ N.E. of. Irreg. rectang. (Ro. tiles and coins found 1859.)
>
> Tilford, near. (i.) Hillyfield. (ii.) Long Town. (iii.) Kinchill.
>
> Warlingham, 1½ E. of.

Sussex—

Amberley, 1 S.E. of.

Beltout, above Berling Gap.   (A.)

*Brighton Race Course.   White Hawk Hill.   (A.)

"Broyle, The."   Near Chichester.

"Castle, The."   Newhaven.   (A.)

"Chanctonbury Ring." $\frac{3}{4}$ W. of Wiston.   (A.)

Chichester, 4 N. of.   St. Roches Hill.   (A.)

*"Cissbury."   Worthing, $2\frac{1}{2}$ N. of.   Oval, contains many
pits.   A flint-factory.   (A.)   (*Jl. Anthrop. Inst.*, v.
1876; *Archæol.*, xlv. 337; Rollestone, *Sci. Papers*, i.
409.)

"Devil's Dyke Camp." $\frac{1}{2}$ S. of Poynings.

"Ditchling Beacon." $\frac{1}{2}$ S.W. of Westmeston.   Irreg.
(? Ro.)   (A.)

Edburton, $\frac{1}{4}$ S.E. of.   Circ.

Fulking, 1 S. of.   (? Ro.)

"Goosehill Camp." $1\frac{3}{4}$ W. of West Dean.   Circ.

Graffham, $1\frac{1}{4}$ S.W. of.   Entrenchments.

"Harrow Hill." $2\frac{1}{4}$ E. of Burpham.   Circ.

Highdown.   4 S.W. of Cissbury.   (A.)   Bronze implements found (*Proc. Soc. Ant.*, ii. xviii. 386).   Late
Celtic.

"Hollingbury Castle." $1\frac{1}{2}$ N. of Brighton.   (A.)   Bronze
celt, torque and armillae found.   (*Archæol.* xxix. 372,
and xlvi. 423.)

Kingston-by-Sea, $1\frac{3}{4}$ N. of.

"Lingfield Mark Camp," near E. Grinstead.   British
Oppidum.   (*Proc. Soc. Ant.*, ii. xiv. 33.)

"Mount Caburn." $\frac{1}{2}$ N. of Biddingham.   Circ.

Piecombe Street, $\frac{1}{2}$ N. of.   Circ.   2 ent.

Ranscombe, W. of Mt. Caburn.   (*Archæol.* xlvi. 423.)

Saxonbury Hill.   2 N.E. of Rotherfield.   Oval.

Seaford, near.   (A.)

"Trundel, The."   1 S.E. of West Dean.   Circ.

(For Sussex Hill Forts, see *Archæologia*, xlii. 27.   Those
marked (A.) above are included in this paper.)

Warwickshire—

Ashorne, near.   In Oakley Wood.   Irreg.

Barmoor.

WARWICKSHIRE (*contd.*)—

    Beausale, near Wroxall.

    Brinklow. Irreg. oval.

    Brownsover. Irreg.

    "Danesbank," on Cappa Hill.

    Loxley, Red Hill.

    "Mount, The," near Beoley.

    "Mount, The," near Cheswick Green, Monkspath Street.

    Nadbury Camp, on Edge Hill.

    Oldbury, near Hartshill.

    Solihull Lodge.

WESTMORLAND—

    Bampton Grange.

    Brackenber, near Appleby.

    Clifton, W of.

    Great Asby. Several camps in neighbourhood.

    "Grig Hall, near Kendal." Also three other earthworks.

    "Grimes Hill," N. of Kirby Lonsdale.

    Haweswater.

    Kirby Stephen. Two ewks.

    Laithwaite Crags.

    Milburn, 1 E. of.

    Newbiggen, 2 E. of.

    Oddendale.

    Ortonscar.

    Orton. Two ewks.

    Sandford, near Appleby. Two ewks.

    Stainmore. Two ewks.

    Troutbeck, near Ambleside. Two ewks.

    Shap, S. of.

    Tirril.

    ("Arthur's Round Table," near Penrith, appears to be a mound like those mentioned at the end of the Yorkshire ewks.)

WILTSHIRE—

    *"Barbury Castle." On Barbury Down, near Hackpen Hill. Oval. 2 ent. Possibly the Berranbyrig of the Saxon Chronicle.

    "Battlesbury Camp." 1½ E. of Warminster. Irreg. 2 ent.

WILTSHIRE (*contd.*)—

Bradenstock-cum-Clack.

*" Bratton Castle," near Edington.   Below this a " White Horse," restored.

" Bury Camp."   ½ S. of North Wraxall.

" Bury Hill."   1¾ W. of Purton Stoke.   Oval.

Brixton Deverill, 1½ E. of.   Rectang.   2 ent.

Casterly Camp.   ½ N. of Great Bedwyn.

" Castle Ditches."   1 S.E. of Tisbury.

" Castle Rings."   1 N.W. of Donhead St. Mary.

" Chiselbury."   2 N.W. of Broad Chalke.

" Chisenbury Camp."   ¾ N.E. of East Chisenbury.

" Church End Ring."   1¼ S. of Wylye.

Clay Hill.   2 W. of Warminster.   Irreg.

" Codford Castle."   ½ N.E. of Codford St. Mary.

" Coniger, The."   E. of Stonehenge.

Dean Station, near.

" East Castle."   ½ S. of Hanging Langford.

*" Figsbury Ring."   1 S.E. of Winterbourne Earls. Unusual internal ditch.

" Fosbury Camp."   On Haydown Hill, near Vernham's Dean in Hants.

" Groveley Castle," near Little Langford.

" Hanging Langford Camp."   1¾ S. of Wylye.

Kingston Deverill, 1 S.W. of.   Rectang.

Knap Hill.   1 N.E. of Alton Priors.

" Knook Castle."   1½ W. of Chitterne St. Mary.

" Lidbury Camp."   On Littlecote Down, 1 S.E. of Chisenbury Camp.

Martin, 2 W. of.

*" Liddington Castle."   1 E. of Chisledon.   Oval.

Martinsell Hill, near Marlborough.

" Membury."   1½ E. of Aldbourne.

Milk Hill.   1 N.W. of Alton Priors.

" Oldbury Castle."   ¾ S.E. of Cherhill.

*" Old Sarum."   (British, Roman, Saxon, Norman, and Mediæval city.)

Odstock, 1½ S. of.

" Ogbury."   E. of Durnford.

WILTSHIRE (*contd.*)—

"Oliver Castle." On Roundway Hill, near Devizes.

Orcheston St. Mary, 2½ E. of. Two concentric rings.

"Ramparts, The," near Stonehenge. Stukeley's "Vespasian's Camp." Perhaps later Ro. Outer ramparts seem to be of different date from inner.

"Ringsbury Camp," near Purton.

"Robin Hood's Bower." In Southfield Wood, 1½ S. of Warminster.

"Rybury." 1 N.W. of Stanton St. Bernard. Oval.

*"Scratchbury Camp." 1 S.E. of Battlesbury. Irreg. 3 ent.

"Sidbury Hill." 1¼ N.W. of North Tidworth. Br. celt found on slope of hill. (*Proc. Soc. Ant.*, ii. 1882, 227.)

"White Sheet Castle." 1 N.E. of Stourton.

Whitsbury, N. of.

"Wick Ball Camp," near Teffont Magna.

*"Winklebury." ½ S.E. of Berwick St. John. (Pitt-Rivers, *Excavations*, ii.)

Woodford, 1 S.E. of.

*"Yarnbury." On Berwick Down. N. of Steeple Langford. Circ. 1 ent.

WORCESTERSHIRE—

Berrow, near Martley.

"Gadbury Bank." W. of Eldersfield. Irreg. Oval.

Hanbury. Ro. coins found.

Spetchley Park. Round Hill.

Woodbury Hill. 1 W. of Witley Court. Irreg. 1 ent.

*Wychbury Hill. S.E. of Pedmore. Irreg. 1 ent.

YORKSHIRE—

*Almondsbury Camp, near Huddersfield.

Argam, 5 N.W. of Bridlington. Line of entrenchment like that on Flamborough Head.

Austerfield, near Bawtry. (? Ro.)

Bridlington. On the Wolds W. of are several camps, some probably British, others Roman.

"Castle Dyke." 1¼ S.W. of Aysgarth.

YORKSHIRE (*contd.*)—

"Castle Dyke." N.W. of Ripon.

*"Castle Hill." Skipsea.

"Castle Stead," near Pateley Bridge. (? Ro.)

*"Dane's Dyke, The." Double entrenchment, probably of the bronze period, fortifying Flamborough Head.

Gisburne.

Highcliff Nab. S. of Guisborough.

Kirklees Park, near Cooper's Bridge. (Traces only.)

Lee Hill. N. of Slack. Circ.

North Grimston, 2 E. of. (? Ro.)

Norton, near.

"Studfold Rings." ½ N. of Ampleforth.

Swale R. and Tees R. Between these are many camps, dykes, and entrenchments, for which see *Archæologia*, vi.

Swine in Holderness.

(At Blois Hall, near Ripon, at Thornborough, and near Penistone, are circular ewks, surrounded by a mound and *inner* trench, like that at Avebury, but without any standing stones. The nature of these ewks is unknown, but it can scarcely have been military, judging from the position of the ditch. Perhaps they were religious in their origin.)

LIST OF DYKES

(Some of those included belong to a period later than that commonly called prehistoric.)

BUCKINGHAMSHIRE—

"Grim's Dyke," near Prince's Risborough.

CAMBRIDGESHIRE—

"The Devil's Ditch." Fens at Reach to woodlands at Camois Hall, near Wood Ditton.

"The Balsham or Fleam Dyke." Fen Ditton, by Great Wilbraham and Fulbourne to near Balsham.

"The Bran Ditch." Fen called Melbourn Common to Royston, ending at Haydon, in Essex.

"The Brent Ditch." Pampisford to Abingdon Park.

"The Roman Way."

CORNWALL—
"The Giant's Hedge." From Trelawne to an earthwork on Bury Down.

CUMBERLAND—
"The Bishop's Dyke," dividing parishes of Crosby and Irthington.

DORSETSHIRE.
Warne enumerates twenty-five. The most important are—
*"Bokerley Dyke."
"Coomb Bank." W. of Spettisbury.

ESSEX—
"The Bran Ditch," entering from Cambridgeshire.

GLOUCESTERSHIRE—
*"Offa's Dyke."
"Bagendon Earthworks. Dykes 3 N. of Cirencester.

HAMPSHIRE—
"The Devil's Dyke," near Andover.

HEREFORDSHIRE—
*"Offa's Dyke."
"Rowe Ditch," Pembridge. 1 mile long.

HERTFORDSHIRE—
"Grim's Dyke," on Berkhamstead Common.
"The Bank," in the parish of Cheshunt.
Great Berkhamstead, through North Church and Wigginton parishes to the north of the camp at Cholesbury.

LANCASHIRE—
Bleaberry Haws, dyke $\frac{1}{2}$ mile long.
Bacup, $\frac{3}{4}$ N. of.

NORFOLK—
"Bunn's Bank," Attleborough.
"The Devil's Dyke," S. of Narborough.
"Fen Dyke," near Grime's Graves.

NORTHUMBERLAND—
"Awd Dyke," Brands Hill.
"Black Dyke." Crosses Roman wall S. of Brownlee Lough.

OXFORDSHIRE—

> "Grime's Dyke," or "The Devil's Ditch," between Mongewell and Henley, eleven miles in length.
>
> "Medlar's Bank," near and parallel to last, about fourteen miles long.

SHROPSHIRE—

> *"Offa's Dyke."
>
> *"Watt's Dyke." Nearly parallel with the last, and about two miles to its east. An extensive but less important dyke.

SOMERSET—

> *"Wansdyke."

WILTSHIRE—

> *"Bokerley Dyke."
>
> "Grim's Dyke," in S. part of county.
>
> "The Roman Dyke." Shiftway Coppice, Rushmore. Roman or Romano - British. (Pitt - Rivers, *Excavations*, i.)
>
> *"Wansdyke."
>
> "The Old Ditch." On Salisbury Plain.

WORCESTERSHIRE—

> Pendock, near.

YORKSHIRE—

> Vale of Pickering, many on the N. side of.
>
> "The Roman Rig." Between Sheffield and Mexborough, on the ridge of hills left of the Don.
>
> Between Catterick on the Swale and Gainford on the Tees (*Jl. Arch. Inst.*, vol. vi.)
>
> "The Double Dykes," on Ampleforth Moors.
>
> The Scanridge Dykes at Ebberston and on the West Riding Moors in that district.
>
> From Richmond on the Swale to Barford on the Tees.

CHAPTER X

EARLY PLACES OF HABITATION—PIT-DWELLINGS—
HUT-CIRCLES — SOUTERRAINS — DENE-HOLES —
BEEHIVE HOUSES — PILE-DWELLINGS — CRAN-
NOGES—TERRAMARE

SO far as we know, the earliest places of habitation of
man were caves, grottos, rock-shelters, and other
natural, if only partially efficient, protections from
the wind and the weather. Of these sufficient has been
said in previous chapters, and they need not further be
alluded to. But in later times—in most cases probably,
in much later times—there were other forms of prehistoric
dwelling-place, of which remains are still in existence,
which will form the subject of this chapter. Many of
these were, if not originally connected with the late Celtic
period, at least occupied during it. Since this period has
yet to be dealt with, in dealing with them we are to some
extent trenching upon the province of another chapter.
There is reason for supposing, however, that the original
construction of some of the villages was considerably
earlier than would seem to be indicated by the discovery
therein of objects belonging to their latest occupants.
When Macaulay's New Zealander visits this country, he
will not, if he is an instructed person, estimate the date
of the foundation of Westminster Abbey by the latest
monuments which it contains.

In Belgium, the Abbé Gaillard has divided the neolithic

stations—other, of course, than those of a lacustrine character, with which we are not at present concerned—into
two classes, which he calls respectively *cités agrestes* and
stations à ciel ouvertes. The former are collections of
underground habitations, in which the hearth was situated
six feet or so below the level of the surface of the ground;
the implements which belonged to the dwellers in such
pits are to be found, as one would expect, at some distance
below the soil. Of the dwellings of the second class no
trace has been left, for, according to the writer just cited,
the people of such stations lived in tents. Their occupation, then, of any given spot is only obvious from the
implements and pottery found thereat. In Belgium the
dwellers in tents were less skilful in polishing stone than
their pit-dwelling relatives (perhaps successors), and the
pottery which they used was coarser and less ornate. It
is perhaps not necessary to pin ourselves down too closely
to the meaning of the word tent ; if we admit that it may
be used to include other temporary above-ground resi-
dences, made, for example, of boughs, sods of turf and
the like, then it is probable that the same classes of stations
may be recognised in this country. There are spots where
great quantities of neolithic flakes and other traces of work
in flint are to be found, without any evidence, in the near
neighbourhood at least, of pits or huts for the dwellings
of the workers. In such cases it is not unreasonable to
suppose that tents or other temporary above-ground huts
were their dwelling-places, and that all traces of these
have now disappeared. Of the other, or underground,
habitations we have plenty of remains, and it is these
that we must first of all consider.

Pit - dwellings.—Pit - dwellings, "hut - circles," the
"British villages" of the Ordnance maps, are the
remains of habitations occupied, we can now say with

certainty, in the Neolithic period. Pitt-Rivers thought that a careful examination of sites of this kind might prove that they all belonged to the late Celtic period, into which similar collections of habitations, such as that at Woodcuts, undoubtedly extended, if, indeed, they did not originate at that time. Later investigations have not confirmed this view, and the excavations in Kent by Mr. Clinch,[1] and in Dorset by Dr. Colley March,[2] have settled the point that these structures were in use in the Premetallic period. Filled up as they now are with rubbish, nearly to the level of the surrounding ground, they look like dimples on the surface of the earth, and the shallow depressions thus formed are scarcely to be noticed, save by the trained eye. When examined, it would appear that the method of their construction has been somewhat as follows. First a hole was excavated in the ground twelve to thirty feet in diameter and three to six in depth. Sometimes the earth which was removed in making the hole was heaped up in a ring round its mouth, thus deepening the cavity and forming a wall which would prevent surface water from pouring into the pit. The walls of the pit were sometimes, as at Hurstbourne, Hants, rudely pitched with stones. From the centre of the floor it is probable that in many cases the trunk of a tree was erected as a pillar for the support of the roof. Where the pit was of any considerable diameter, the presence of some central support for the roof would seem to have been indispensable. The roof itself, we may suppose, was formed by a number of boughs of trees fixed peripherally into the mound surrounding the pit and meeting centrally at the pillar which emerged from it. After the boughs had been placed in position they would have been covered over

---

[1] *Journ. Anthrop. Inst.*, s. ii. ii. 124.
[2] *Proc. Soc. Ant.*, ii. xviii. 258.

S

with turfs removed from the surface of the ground (see Fig. 80). In one of the Kentish pits upwards of nine hundred fragments of flint, including cores, flakes, and waste chips were found, the evidence derived from them

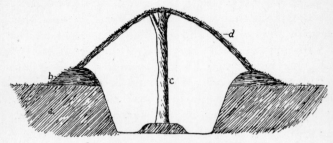

FIG. 80.   IDEAL SECTION OF PIT-DWELLING

a. Natural soil.   *b*. Bank of same heaped up round pit.
c. Central support of roof.   *d*. Roof of turfs and branches.

and from other points being conclusive that this was a neolithic workshop.   In the Eggardon pits examined by Dr. Collie March no trace of any metallic object was discovered.   The same is true of those examined by Dr. Stevens at Hurstbourne and of the pits at Stand-lake, Oxon., of which there is a model in the Ashmolean Museum at Oxford.   These were examined by Akerman and Stone, but at a period when the science of examin-ing such structures was in its infancy.   Hence Pitt-Rivers thought that further examination might lead to the discovery of metal in this village.   In the light of the observations which have just been recorded, how-ever, this is more doubtful than when the General wrote. Besides the larger pits in the Kentish group, wherein we may suppose the men of the period lived, there were smaller excavations, in which only traces of fire were to be found. From this it would appear that in this locality it was the custom to use separate cooking-pits, in which animals may have been roasted whole—a custom which, as we know, obtains and obtained amongst many savage races. The method of construction of the pit was not quite the same in all cases. At Fisherton, for example, in the Wylye Valley, Wilts, there is a group of pits, of which models may be seen in the Devizes Museum. Here a shaft, some three feet in diameter, was sunk into the earth for a depth of from seven to ten feet. At some distance below the surface of the earth this shaft was expanded to a diameter of from five to seven feet, so that a kind of bottle-shaped cavity was formed in the earth, the neck of which was uppermost. The resemblance to a bottle was increased by the fact that in some cases the floor of the pit, formed of the chalk in which the excavation was made, was elevated in the centre, like the "kick" in the bottom of a wine-bottle. These pits to some extent resembled the dene-holes, which will shortly be described.

Later Pits in Ramparted Villages.—In the case of the village at Woodcuts, so laboriously examined by Pitt-Rivers,[1] there was a very complicated system of ditches and ramparts, as will be seen from the plan shown in Fig. 81. From the shallow nature of the former, it seems possible that these were designed more for purposes of surface drainage than for that of protection, and perhaps solely with the former object in view.

In the pits contained within these ramparts were found pottery, including Samian ware, bronze and iron implements and Roman coins, clear evidence of a late date of occupation. These pits had apparently not been made for purposes of habitation, but as storehouses, or perhaps as refuse-pits. What is most remarkable is that they were also used for purposes of burial. In two villages at Woodcuts, 191 of these pits were examined, and in them were found twenty-eight skeletons. Such pits were of a smaller

---

[1] "Excavations in Cranbourne Chase," vol. i. of *Memoirs*.

diameter than those of the habitable class. Models of this village and of the excavations, showing where the different implements and skeletons were found, are in the Museum at Farnham, and here, also, are the remains and objects which were discovered in them. At the village itself, the ramparts and ditches are still quite distinct, and some of the pits which were cleared out, as well as the mouths of two deep wells discovered during the excavations, are yet to be seen. Similar villages have been described by Haverfield[1] in the upper valley of the Thames, near Wallingford, Dorchester, Oxford, and Eynsham. Here the pits are partly wells, seven or eight feet deep, partly rubbish-holes, partly burial-places ; one, so large and irregular that it can hardly be called a pit, was found to contain over a hundred bushels of lime. The trenches, two to five feet deep, and two to three feet wide at the top, and V-shaped below, seem principally to represent the foundations of wattle and daub, or mud walls once surrounding various enclosures. These enclosures vary widely in shape and size. Some are circular, with diameters that range from 24 to 145 feet. Others are purely rectangular or rhomboidal, and these are in general at least as large as the larger circles ; in some cases, indeed, we may have in them the lines of roads or field-walls. In several cases the circular and rectangular areas intersect, as if different in date. All the walls appear to have been mud or wattle and daub ; no traces of flint, or brick, or stone walls were noticed, nor even the footing courses which are almost invariably found in more modern mud walls. Late Celtic pottery and fragments of Samian were found in these pits, with other objects. Haverfield thinks that we have here a village, or something like a village, the inhabitants of which were engaged in pastoral, and possibly in agricultural pursuits. The circular enclosures,

[1] *Proc. Soc. Ant.*, s. ii. xviii. 10.

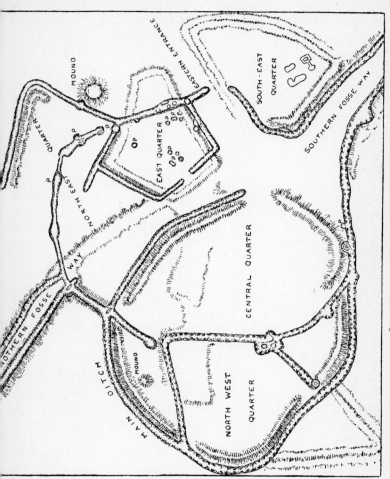

FIG. 81. PLAN OF PART OF WOODCUTS VILLAGE

PP. Pits

the late Celtic urns, the burials, may denote that the village existed before the Roman Conquest, or, at any rate, before Roman civilisation spread over Oxfordshire. The rectangular enclosures may be, with the Samian and Romano-British pottery and other such things, the introduction of the second or third century of our era.

Hut-dwellings have been found within stone wall enclosures in the Furness district, and described by Cowper.[1] At High Hugill, near Windermere, in Westmorland, the site of the settlement consists of an enclosure, two sides of which are angular and two rounded. It was encompassed by the foundations of a wall or rampart, which has been, in places, 14 feet in width. The foundations were apparently formed by stones set on edge, the space between which was probably filled in with smaller stones. Within this enclosure are sundry ill-defined lines of division walls, courts, and hut-dwellings, one or two of which are circular, and measure about 7 feet and 13 feet in diameter.

At Mill Riggs, Kentmere, Westmorland, the settlement occupies a small terrace flanked by a cliff on the east, and is oval in form, measuring 240 feet north and south, 160 feet across its wider end at the north, and 140 feet at the south, where it narrows. The walls seem to have been 7 to 10 feet thick, but they are now chiefly to be traced by their foundations. It is suggested that they were not of solid construction, but were faced by stone and filled up inside with softer stone, as was probably the case at the settlements at Urswick, near Dalton-in-Furness, and Hugill, the spot described above. There were four entrances in all, placed on the south-east, west, north, and north-east sides, but it is not certain that all these were ancient. The interior of the settlement is subdivided by cross walls, the use of which was perhaps for

[1] *Archæologia*, liii. 409; *Proc. Soc. Ant.*, ii. xvi. 253; xviii. 265.

penning cattle. There are also six or seven hut circles. These are rounded mounds of earth and stones raised four feet or so above the level of the soil outside. The diameter of these huts is 15 to 25 feet internal measurement, and their doorways are placed to the north-west. Cowper is careful to distinguish these settlements from others in the same district, which are quadrangular in shape. The Furness sites, he thinks, with their irregular courts and groups of cairns, and with the absence of rectangular buildings which they show, were the homesteads of primitive communities, while the quadrangular structures seem to have been self-contained farms, almost certainly of post-Roman date. The late Bishop Creighton[1] conveys a warning as to mistaking, on account of their shape, all circular excavations for early remains, and at the same time gives a picture which may enable us to form an idea of what the early dwellings of this kind were like and how their occupants may have lived in them. Speaking of the mediæval period on the Borders, he says, "The houses of the peasants were huts of clay, frequently with the floors scooped out so as to resemble the beehive huts of primitive times. They were thatched with straw and were mere shelters against the weather. They contained no furniture, save perhaps a few wooden stools; the beds were litters of straw. There was nothing to tempt the cupidity of the plunderer, and the destruction of the house was not worth the time it would take. The common way of doing mischief was to fire the thatch, when the fire caused the walls to crumble. To prevent this loss the Borderer, if he had time, tore down the thatch of his house when a raid was announced, then he gathered his cattle and drove them to a place of safety. His wife walked by his side, carrying all the accumulated wealth of the family in a few personal ornaments which

[1] "Carlisle," in the Historic Towns Series.

hung around her neck." Not very different perhaps may have been the flight of the occupants of some group of pit-dwellings to the fortified camp in their neighbourhood at the news of the approach of some hostile tribe.

The Romano-British village at Wetton, in Stafford-shire,[1] had its huts in rows or streets, and the precise position of each was indicated by a pavement of rough limestone, which had formed the floor. This remained either entire or in part. Sometimes the spot was shown by a sunken surface covered with ashes or charcoal and broken pottery, the teeth, bones, and horns of animals that had been used for food, burnt stones, and other vestiges of human occupation. The discovery of iron and bronze implements here, with Roman coins, leaves no doubt as to the period of this settlement.

An instance of the existence of pits within a strongly fortified place must conclude this section of the chapter, and may be taken from the discoveries made at Worle-bury, near Weston-super-Mare. In this camp,[2] and chiefly towards the eastern end of it, are nearly a hundred shallow pits. As the diameter of these is seldom more than six feet, and as some of them are much smaller, so much so as to make it even difficult to sit down in one in a cramped position, it can scarcely be supposed that they were intended as living-places. They were probably cellars or storehouses, and, as at Woodcuts and else-where, burial-places, for in the course of their excava-tions the explorers of these pits found parts of eighteen skeletons. The largest pit of all was six feet deep, tri-angular in shape, its sides measuring 6, 9 and 10 feet respectively. The pits are hollowed out of the rock where it is soft and easily removable. Besides the skeletons of men and bones of animals and birds, much

---

[1] Bateman, *Ten Years' Digging*, 194.
[2] See Knight, *The Sea-Board of Mendip*, 111.

rude pottery, flint, bone and bronze objects, glass beads, and spearheads and other things made of iron were found. No Roman objects were discovered, so that we may provisionally place these pits at an early part of the early Iron age.

Souterrains and Dene-holes.—Subterranean dwellings, of a more elaborate character than those already described, are not common ; indeed, are almost unknown in this country, though there are souterrains in connection with some of the ancient Cornish villages. In Ireland such underground chambers are common in the "raths" or forts, and are sometimes found apart from them. At Killala,[1] for example, there are a series of underground chambers and passages of considerable size. The Scotch "Eirde houses," "weems," or "Pict's houses," are of a similar character; indeed, the resemblance of the Cornish, Scotch, and Irish examples seems clearly to point to a common origin. Others have been found in France, Hungary, and elsewhere. The most interesting structures of this type met with in England are the dene-holes, of which some account must now be given.[2] These subterranean chambers are reached by a vertical shaft of some depth, which appears to have been, at least in some cases, lined with flint stones where it passed through the Thanet sand—no doubt a somewhat treacherous stratum—to reach the subjacent chalk in which the chambers themselves were excavated. The special feature of these excavations is that each consists of a primary chamber from which others branch off, as shown in the annexed plan (Fig. 82). One system of chambers sometimes communicates with another, and thus a most complicated group of rooms is produced.

---

[1] *Journ. R. Soc. Ant. Ireland,* viii. 191.
[2] For full account of the exploration of these, see *Essex Naturalist,* December, 1887.

In other cases quite thin walls separate one set of chambers from another. In exploring the pits at Hangman's Wood, near Grays, Essex, bones of the horse, ox, sheep, dog, and badger were found, as also some human bones. Pottery, some of it mediæval and some British, but in no great quantity, was also discovered. One of the most interesting finds was a piece of Niedermendig lava, once part of a stone for grinding corn. It seems more probable that these excavations were of the nature of storehouses than living-places. Underground dwellings have also been discovered in the Isle of Portland,[1] which are really subterranean beehive huts, completely walled in with flat stones overlapping inwards, until they leave an opening at the crown of 16 inches in diameter. This opening has generally been found to be covered with a slab. Over all was the soil about a foot in thickness. The height of these chambers was about 8 feet, though in one case it was 12 feet, and the width at the bottom was from 10 to 12 feet. In one instance twin chambers were found, communicating with one another by a passage at the base 2 feet in height by 2 feet 6 inches in width. Skulls and bones of domestic animals, corn-crushers, a celt and flint flakes, with other stones and blackened wheat, have been found in these chambers. It still remains doubtful whether they were storehouses or dwelling-places. The evidence at present forthcoming certainly seems to point to the former conclusion. Somewhat similar constructions have recently been discovered at Waddon, near Croydon.

FIG. 82.   GROUND PLAN OF TWO CONNECTING DENE-HOLES

[1] Damon, *Geology of Weymouth*, etc., 164.

Flint implements and Romano-British pottery were discovered in them.[1]

Beehive Houses.—Take such an edifice as the last, and instead of burying it in the earth, erect it on the surface of the ground, and place its entrance at the side, and not at the top, and the result is the beehive house, a well-known object in Ireland. The tumbled-down remains of such huts may be seen in the "cittiau" of Braich-y-Dinas, on Penmaenmawr. Examples are also met with in Cornwall, for example, at Chysoyster. These buildings, being made of rough stones, uncemented together by mortar, are of course very liable to tumble down. The principle on which they are constructed is that of advancing each course of stones a little nearer towards the centre of the hut than that immediately below it. As a result the walls gradually slope inwards until they meet at the top, the whole forming a figure like the old-fashioned straw bee-skep, from which their name is derived.

Pile-dwellings.—To give anything like a complete account of the pile- and other lake-dwellings of the prehistoric period within the limits of this book would be an impossible task. Only the most prominent facts can be mentioned here, and those who desire to pursue their studies further may be referred to the books mentioned in the footnote.[2] In the first instance it may be said that the idea of the constructors of all these villages was to surround their places of habitation with water. A similar idea occupied the minds of the mediæval castle-builder, and of the constructors of the terramare. But the end was achieved in a different way in the two cases. The

[1] *Reliquary*, ix. 71.
[2] Keller, *Lake Dwellings of Switzerland ;* Munro, *The Lake Dwellings of Europe*, and *Ancient Scottish Lake Dwellings ;* Bulleid, *Account of the Lake Village at Glastonbury.*

lake-village was an artificial island, of one sort or another, in the midst of a natural sheet of water. The moat of the castle, or homestead, or terramare, was an artificial lake formed around a building on the dry land. The result was the same, though the method by which it was arrived at was different.

The first method was that adopted by the constructors of the lake-villages of Switzerland, and of the crannoges of Ireland and Scotland; but here again each went to work upon somewhat different lines. The builders of the *lake-villages* followed a plan which is still practised in New Guinea. How it is carried on there may be gathered from the account given by Haddon.[1] In the first place a series of long poles pointed at one end were gradually worked into the bed of the lake. When a sufficient number of these were securely in position, a platform of wood was erected upon them, and on this platform log-houses, for the accommodation of the makers, were constructed. The platform and its houses may have then been connected with the shore by means of a gangway, and the task was completed. A very large number of villages of this kind have been discovered in different parts of the Continent. According to Mortillet there are in Switzerland 160 such settlements, and of these no less than 51 are in the Neuenberger See. There are 32 in France, 36 in Italy, 11 in Austria, and 46 in Germany. At Staffis, in the Neuenberger See, there are two villages of the Bronze period, near together; one of them only measures a few square metres, whilst the other is over two hundred metres in length, and nearly fifty metres wide. The great settlement of Morges, in the Lake of Geneva, is 360 metres in length, and 30 to 45 in width; its area, in fact, is more than 10,000 square metres. The villages, then, vary considerably in size, and they

[1] *Head-Hunters: Black, Brown, and White.*

also vary in date. Some of them are of a comparatively early period in the Neolithic age, or at least disclose implements which would lead one to come to that conclusion, for the stone hatchets which are found are small and imperfectly polished. Moreover, they are made of serpentine, diorite, sausaurite, and other materials easily accessible. The pottery, too, is coarse and cylindrical, and shows no trace of ornamentation. In the greater number of the lake-villages of Switzerland implements of a better class are found, amongst them large perforated hammer-axes made of tough stone such as jade, chloromelanite, or nephrite. The pottery also speaks of a higher skill, for it is ornamented with various geometrical figures, dogtooth, rows of dots and shaded triangles. In yet another series, articles of bone, of copper, and of bronze are met with, accompanied by still more richly ornamented pottery. The facts just mentioned go to prove that this class of village was in use over a long period of time. In the valley of the Mandel, Belgium,[1] a village has been discovered, supported upon many piles of oak, in which have been found flint implements, objects of bone and bronze, pottery, and a coin of Trajan. From this we learn that this particular village—and the same may be true of others—had been the home of men for many generations.

In the case of the *crannoge*, so common in Ireland and Scotland, and utilised in both countries up to so very recent a period, instead of rearing a platform upon piles, an artificial island was constructed by heaping brushwood, stones, and other matters together in a selected spot on the floor of the lake and driving piles into its floor around the heap so as to prevent its being washed away by the action of the waves. By this means an artificial, but approximately solid platform was formed,

[1] *L'Anthropologie*, xii. 558.

upon which the houses were erected, and this again was connected with the shore by means of a gangway. Near Clones, in Ireland, is a crannoge which has been very carefully investigated with the following results.[1] Part of this crannoge consisted of a small natural shoal of marl, which had been supplemented by laying down three or four superimposed layers of tree-trunks, some eighteen inches in diameter—birch, oak, and fir. Beneath these was a layer of earth and stones. The remaining portion of the crannoge rested on the bed of the lake and consisted of (i.) a layer, the lowest, of bracken, fern, and moss; (ii.) branches of oak and blackthorn and hazel with large stones in places. In this layer were both horizontal logs and perpendicular piles; (iii.) clay and gravel. In the construction of the entire crannoge metallic implements had been used, and in it were found implements of stone, bronze, iron, bone, and wood, also pottery, glass, and a leather dagger-sheath.

So far, it must be admitted, the discoveries of this class in England have been few, and, with the exception of the remarkable discoveries at Glastonbury, not very important. Duncombe[2] has described a number of piles in the river Costa, near Pickering, Yorks, which appear to have belonged to a construction of the Swiss nature. Bones of various animals and fragments of pottery have been found in the bed of this stream. Near Hedsor, Bucks,[3] an oak floor about four inches in thickness, supported upon piles of oak and beech, varying in diameter from five to nine inches, was found, under about 2 feet 6 inches of alluvium and six feet of peaty soil. The principal and larger piles were about five feet apart, and the small thickly studded between them. Pottery and iron objects were found in the excavation of this village, the construction

---

[1] D'Arcy, *Journ. Roy. Soc. Ant.*, *Ireland*, vii. 205.
[2] *Journ. Anthrop. Inst.*, i. 151.   [3] *Proc. Soc. Ant.*, ii. xvi. 7.

of which, owing to the difficulties met with in the exploration, has not been very clearly made out. Pitt-Rivers called attention to the existence of piles in beds of peat seven to nine feet deep, near London Wall and in Southwark. The articles found near them were for the most part Roman, but some of the bone implements were of a rude type.

The most interesting and the most carefully examined object of this class is the village near Glastonbury, most of the things found in which are to be seen in the Museum in the little town itself. The peat-moor where it lies was once a mere, and here an artificial platform of clay and timber had been constructed and surrounded by a stockade composed of a palisade of piles from three to nine inches in diameter, and from nine to eleven feet in height, between which was a kind of rough hurdle-work. On this platform was a series of huts, each about twelve to fourteen feet in diameter, constructed of wattle and daub, with a stone hearth in the centre, and a few stones in front of the door—which was about three feet in height—by way of threshold. As one might expect, a foundation of timber and clay was not of a very stable character, and must gradually have sunk so as to render the huts uncomfortably damp. No doubt it was on account of this fact that it was found necessary from time to time to raise the level of the floors by the addition of fresh wood and clay. As the old hearthstones seem always to have been left behind, we have a guide to the number of times that the operation of raising the floor was necessary, and find that it took place no less than nine times in the case of one hut, whilst others show four, five, or six superimposed hearths. A remarkable series of objects in metal—particularly a bronze bowl made familiar by the reproductions of it which have been constructed— glass, and wood have been discovered in this village.

Indeed, one of the interesting things about the village is the evidence which it presents as to the carpentry of the period, as well as the love of art which existed. The peat having preserved the timber, which in so many other places has decayed, we know that their bowls—there is a model of one of these in the British Museum which admirably exemplifies this point—and even the waggon wheels were decorated with scrolls and patterns of a flamboyant character. Mr. A. J. Evans[1] thinks that the whole series of remains was accumulated within a definite period of not very extensive duration, which closed before the days of Roman contact. On the other hand, the relics do not belong to the earlier style of the "late Celtic" fabrics in Britain, as illustrated by the Arras chariot-burials in Yorkshire, but might be referred to the first and second centuries before Christ, though some belonged to a date coming very close to the period of Roman influence. A typical form of fibula or safety-pin, on the other hand, is identical with specimens found in association with Ptolemaic coins of the second century before Christ, in the Illyro-Celtic cemetery of Gurina, in the Gailthal. The remains at Glastonbury thus represent the results of the second wave of Belgic or East Gaulish conquest in this island. Other contemporary aspects of the same culture are seen in the Aylesford cemetery, associated with imported Italo-Greek vases, and in the Oppidum or fortified settlement at Hunsbury, near Northampton. The relics found in the well-known camp at Worlebury, Weston-super-Mare, show the same culture under a military aspect in this western district; but in the Glastonbury village the population was apparently unarmed and peaceful.

Terramare.—Although no instances of this kind of

---

[1] *Journ. Anthrop. Inst.*, s. ii. i. 188.

T

village has been discovered in this country, or indeed outside of Italy, a brief reference may be permitted to them here. A moated enclosure with pile-dwellings inside it, such was a terramare. The moat, fed by a canal, and crossed by a bridge, surrounded a heaped-up rampart, within which was an enclosure. So far the arrangement differs in no important way from the moated enclosures of this country, but of a much later date. But in our moated enclosures there is generally a mound or earthen keep. In the terramare the enclosure was occupied by a number of huts built on a platform which was itself supported on piles, but on piles driven into the dry ground, and not into the bed of a lake. No doubt this kept the huts dry, and may also have been convenient for the herding of cattle in the same enclosure. The relics found within the terramare show that they belonged to the Bronze period.

LIST OF VILLAGES IN ENGLAND

In the following list all classes above mentioned are included, differentiation being made where possible. Where no statement to the contrary is made the pit-dwelling or British village is meant. Only a selection of sites is included in this list.

BEDFORDSHIRE—

    Blowsdown, E. of Dunstable.
    Dunstable Downs, near Dagnal.
    Dunstable Downs, near the Five Knolls.
    Luton, Warden Hills.

BERKSHIRE—

    Little Coxwell, ½ E. of.
    Long Whittenham (Rom. Brit.)

BUCKINGHAMSHIRE—

    Hedsor. Pile-dwellings. (*Proc. Soc. Ant.*, ii. xvi. 7.)

CUMBERLAND—

> *Birker Fell, Barnscar.   With sepulchral cairns.
> Bootle Fell.
> Brampton, near, Castle Carrock and Cardonnock Pike.
> Caldwell, near, Carrock Fell.   Doubtful.
> Gillalees Beacon, Lower Brow.   Doubtful.
> Thelkeld, Wanthwaite Crags.   Old settlement, examined without very definite results.
> Thwaites Fell.

CORNWALL—

> Bodinnar.   With subterranean passage.   (See *Proc. Soc. Ant.*, ii. iv. 161.)
> Bodmin Moor.   Brockabarrow Down.
> Bodmin Moor.   Browngelly Downs.
> Bodmin Moor, near Fox Tor.
> Bodmin Moor.   Garrow Tor.
> Bodmin Moor, near Leskernick Hill.
> Bodmin Moor.   Rowtor Moor.
> *Bosporthennis.   Beehive Hut.
> Calvanack, near. $1\frac{1}{2}$ S.E. of Croft Michel.
> Carn Brea, near.
> Chapel Enny.   Ref. as Bodinnar.
> *Chysoyster.   Ref. as Bodinnar.
> Croft Michel, $\frac{3}{4}$ S. of, near Camborne.
> Mullyon, near Kynance Cove.   (*Proc. Soc. Ant.*, ii. xvii. 79.)
> Newbridge, near.   3 E. of St. Just.
> Old Busullow, near Morvah.
> Sancreed, $1\frac{1}{2}$ S.W. of.
> Smallacombe Down, Bodmin Moor.   " Smallacombe Enclosures."   Pottery and worked flints have been found here.
> Twelve Men's Moor.

DEVONSHIRE—

> (Very numerous, the following being the most important.)
> Archerton.
> Bellever Tor.

DEVONSHIRE (*contd.*)—

Brent Moor.

Brown Heath, near Erme Head.

Cawsand Beacon.

Dunnabridge Pound, Dartmoor. Walled enclosure containing "The Judge's Chair." Group of stones. Nature doubtful.

*Grimspound, near Hameldon Tor. Walled village with hut circles.

Harford Moor.

Harter Tor.

Haytor.

*Kestor.

Lakehead Circle, near Postbridge.

Leighon Tor.

Manaton, near. Walled enclosure, perhaps a cattle-pound.

*Merivale Bridge, Dartmoor. "The Plague Market," or "Potato Market."

Metherall.

Mis Tor, between it and Cock's Hill.

Rolls Tor, or Roose Tor, near. (Flint implements found here.)

Shaugh Moor.

Shell Top.

Shilstone Pound.

Shuffle Down.

Stannon Hill.

*Teigncombe Common. The Round Pound and the Square Pound.

Trowlesworthy Tor.

Yar Tor, near Buckfastleigh.

DORSETSHIRE —

(Very numerous, the following being the most important.)

Cattistock. (i.) ½ N.E. of. (ii.) 1½ E. of.

Cerne Abbas. (i.) 1¾ W. of. (ii.) ¾ N. of. (iii.) ½ S.E. of, on Black Hill.

DORSETSHIRE (*contd.*)—

> *Chalbury, near Weymouth, surrounded by fosse and vallum. "Rimbury," close by, seems to have been the necropolis of this village.
> Chettle, 1 S.W. of.
> Eggardon Hill.   (*Proc. Soc. Ant.*, ii. xviii. 258.)
> Farnham, 1¾ S.E. of.
> Grimstone, ¾ N. of.
> Hinton Parva, ¾ N. of.
> Hod Hill.
> Maiden Newton, 1¾ E. of.
> *Portland (dene-holes). Cf. Damon's *Geology of Weymouth*.
> Puddlehinton, ¼ S. of.
> Plush, ½ S.E. of.
> Shillingstone, 1 S. of.
> Sydling St. Nicholas, ½ S.E. of.
> Tarrant Hinton.   (i.) 1 W. of.   (ii.) 1¼ S.W. of.
> Tenant's Hill, near the stone circle.
> Turnworth, 1 N.W. of.
> West Compton, 1 E. of.
> Winterbourne Kingstone, 1 S.W. of.
> *Woodcuts, near Tollard Royal. (Excavated by Pitt-Rivers.   See text.)

ESSEX (dene-holes)—

> East Tilbury.
> *Grays, near.   Hangman's Wood.
> Little Thurrock.

GLOUCESTERSHIRE—

> Cam Long Down.
> Minchinhampton, near Amberley Camp.
> Selsley Hill, in the area of the camp.
> *Stinchcombe Hill, near the Drakestone.
> *Westridge Hill, near Wotton-under-Edge.

HAMPSHIRE—

> Burghclere, ½ S.W. of.   In camp.
> On Brighstone Down, S.E. of Calbourne, Isle of Wight. Eight villages.

HEREFORDSHIRE—
> Holly Bush Camp, on Malvern Hills, S. of.

KENT—
> Addington Park, Hayes Common. (*Proc. Soc. Ant.*, ii. xii. 258.)

LANCASHIRE—
> Dunnerdale Fell. (C.)
> Heathwaite Fell. (C.)
> Monk Coniston Moor.
> Seethwaite Stone Walls. (C.) (C. = Cowper, *Archæologia*, liii. 409.)

NORFOLK—
> Aylmerton. "The Shrieking Pits."
> Beeston Heath. "Hills and Holes."
> Sheringham.
> Weybourne.
> Wretham Mere, near Thetford. (Lake-dwellings. See *Norf. Arch.*, vii. 355.)

NORTHUMBERLAND—
> Beanley. Near and in "The Ringses."
> Bewick, at the Double Camp.
> Brough Law, near Ingram.
> Carry Hill Camp, near. (*Archæologia*, xlv. 355.)
> "The Chesters," near The Breamish.
> Colledge, Valley of, near Kirknewton.
> Colwell Hill Camp, near.
> Earle Dene, near Earle.
> Fawcett Shank, near Kirknewton. (*Trans. Berw. Nat. Field Club*, 1861 and 1862.)
> *Greaves Ash, near Linhope Farne. Greenshaw Hill.
> Gunnar Heugh Valley, near Gunnarton.
> Hartside Hills.
> *Hawsden Burn, by. Near Brand's Hill. (Cheviots.)
> Humbleton Hill.
> Ilderton, Roseden Edge.
> Ingram Hill.
> Keilder.
> *Lord-in-Shaws, near Rothbury.

NORTHUMBERLAND (*contd.*)—

Megrim's Knowe, near The Breamish.

Middleton Hill, near Wallington.

Snear Hill.   (Cheviots.)

Swint Law, near Yeavering Bell.

Thorngrafton, near Haltwhistle.

West Hill, near Rothbury.

Wooler, at Kettles Camp.

Yeavering Bell.   (Cf. ref. to Greaves Ash.)

OXFORD—

Chadlington Downs, near Chipping Norton (dene-holes). (See Essex Report, *supra*.)

*Standlake.   Explored 1857.   (See *Archæologia*, xxxvii. 363, and also reprint of lecture by Boyd-Dawkins in *Gents. Mag. Lib. (Arch.)*, i. 301.   Objects obtained are in the Ashmolean Museum.

SHROPSHIRE—

Pike's End, Lyneal-cum-Colemere.   Possible Lake-village.   (*Proc. Soc. Ant.*, ii. xix. 140.)

SOMERSET—

Brean Down.

*Worlebury.

STAFFORDSHIRE—

Borough Holes, near Wilton.

SUFFOLK—

Barton Mere, 3 N.E. of Bury St. Edmunds.   Said to be Lake-dwellings, but very doubtful.

SURREY—

Croydon.   Waddon, near.   Subterranean beehive chambers.   Flints and Ro.-Brit. pot.   (*Reliquary*, ix. 71.)

Leatherhead, near.   Pottery, charred wheat, etc.   (*Proc. Soc. Ant.*, ii. xviii. 253.)

SUSSEX—

Cissbury, west slope of area.

Goodwood.   "The Trundle."

Hollingbury.

Kingby Bottom, near Lavant.

Wolstonbury.

WESTMORLAND—

Crosby Ravensworth. Ewe Close, Oddendale.
Crosby Ravensworth. Howarcles.
Great Asby Scar.
Holborn Hill.
*Hugill High House, Windermere. (*Proc. Soc. Ant.*, ii. xvi. 253.)
Kentmere. (*Ib.* ii. xviii. 265.)
Kirkby Lonsdale. (*Tr. Cumb. and Westm. Antiq. Soc.*, vii.)
Knype Scar, Bampton.
Langdale, Harbyn Ring.
Lowther Woodhouse.
Moor Witherslack, Harnburn Rigg.
Urswick, near Dalton-in-Furness. (*Archæol.*, xliii. 409.)

WILTSHIRE—

(Very numerous. The following are the most important.)
Barford St. Martin, N. of. Hams Hill Ditches.
Berwick St. John, ½ E. of.
Bower Chalk, 1 S.E. of.
Broad Blumsdon, ½ N.E. of. "Castle Hill."
Chitterne St. Mary, W. of. Two settlements.
Durrington Walls. ½ S.W. of Durrington.
*Fisherton Delamere.
Fyfield Down.
Great Ridge Wood, S. of. Four settlements.
Hindon, ¾ N.W. of.
Huish Hill, ½ E. of Huish.
Imber, ½ N.W. of.
Longbridge Deverill, S.W. of.
Marden, ¼ N.E. of.
Marlborough, 1½ N.W. of.
Martinsell Hill.
Monkton Down, 1¼ E. of Winterbourne Monkton.
Ogbourne St. George, N.E. of. Several settlements.
Pewsey Down.
Rotherley. Explored by Pitt-Rivers. (See vol. ii. of his *Excavations*.) Romano-British.

WILTSHIRE (*contd.*)—

Rushmore.   (Do. vol. i.)   Romano-British pits.

Sherrington, 3 W. of.

*Steeple Langford Downs.   (*Brit. Arch. Jl.*, 1862, 22 and 117.   *Archæologia*, xxii. 430.)

*"Stockton Works," 1¼ S.W. of Stockton.   Ro.-Brit. pottery.   Ro. coins.

Stonehenge, 2 W. of.

Swallow Cliffe, 1 S. of.

Tilshead, 2¼ E. of.   "Church Pits."

Westbury, ¾ N.W. of.

Wootton Rivers, 1 N.W. of.

YORKSHIRE—

Blakey Moor.   1¾ W. of Rosedale.   Stone Haggs.

Blayshaw Bents, near Stean.

Danby Moor.   (Date and use very doubtful.)

Egton, moor near.

Goathland.   "Killing Pits."   Very probably only kilns.

Rudstone, near the.

*Scarborough, Wolds near.   Many dwellings.

Skipwith Common.

Lake-dwellings—

Barmston.   (Bronze.)

Gransmoor.   (Bronze.)

Pickering.   (*Jl. Anthrop. Inst.*, s. ii. i. 151.)

Ulrome.   (Bronze.)

CHAPTER XI

THE LATE CELTIC OR EARLY IRON AGE

IT has already been shown that there was a considerable overlap between the Stone and the Bronze age. The Bronze age also overlapped that of Iron; indeed, the Stone probably overlapped it too, for it is most probable that objects such as the elaborate perforated stone hammers (see Fig. 83) were used long after the metals were in common employment.

The discovery of iron was, some would have us believe, due to its being found in a nearly pure state in meteoric masses; others think that it may have arisen from pieces of rich iron ore becoming accidentally embedded in

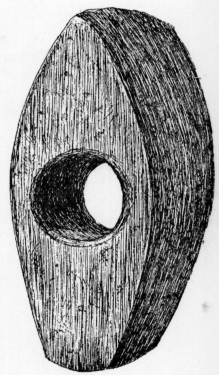

FIG. 83. PERFORATED STONE AXE-HAMMER.
Irish (⅓)

the domestic fire, the burning embers of which would easily reduce them to the metallic state. Or again, perhaps primitive man, who had already ascertained that metallic copper could be obtained from certain stones, made experiments with other stones, with the result that he lighted upon iron.[1]

Ridgeway[2] is of opinion that iron was discovered by the Celts, and certainly the objects of the Early Iron age in this country appear to have been made by a Celtic race, whose track can be traced across Europe from the Mediterranean to Britain. The most important stations so far discovered in which objects of the Early Iron age have been brought to light are on the Continent, and some mention must be made of them before the objects belonging to this period in England are dealt with. The stations in question are those of Hallstadt and La Téne ; according to Montelius[3] the succession and dates of these periods may be arranged as follows :—

Hallstadt, i. 850—600 B.C.   Period of transition from bronze to iron, which might be also called the last (or, according to his classification, sixth) age of bronze.

Hallstadt, ii. 600—400 B.C. ⎫
La Téne, i. 400—250 B.C. ⎬ Iron.
La Téne, ii. 200—150 B.C. ⎪
La Téne, iii. 150 B.C.—A.D. ⎭

The lake of Hallstadt, near which are the cemeteries from the excavation of which so much has been learnt about this period, is situated in the midst of the Austrian Alps. Nearly one thousand graves have been opened there, and the examination of these has disclosed the fact

---

[1] Gowland, *Archæologia*, lvi. 302.

[2] *Early Age of Greece*, from which other opinions cited in this chapter, under the name of this author, are taken.

[3] *L'Anthropologie*, xii. 609.

that burials were sometimes by inhumation, sometimes by cremation, and sometimes by partial cremation; that is to say, that whilst the greater part of the body was inhumated, some portion, perhaps only a very small part of the body, was separated from the rest for the purpose of being subjected to the action of fire.

With the remains of the dead were deposited, as accompanying gifts, their weapons and ornaments. The swords show the gradual transition from bronze to iron, for some are entirely of the former metal, some have iron blades and bronze hilts, and others are forged from iron alone. These weapons are all leaf-shaped, and do not gradually taper to their end, but are brought abruptly to a kind of triangular point. The handgrip is large in all of them, a point of contrast with the relatively small size of this part of the earlier bronze weapon. Spears are very common, and are almost all made of iron. The axe-heads tell the same tale as the swords. Some are of bronze— socketed and flanged ; a larger number are of iron ; one has its cutting edge of iron, whilst the shaft-bed and flanges are of bronze. It was found in a tomb together with an iron dagger, provided with a bronze handle. Two helmets, many plates of bronze, bosses of circular shields, are other objects of a martial character which have been brought to light. Amongst the ornaments none are more numerous nor more important than the brooches, of which several as a rule were found in each grave. They belong to two classes: (i.) those of the safety-pin type, and (ii.) those formed by bending a single piece of round wire into two spirals, one at either end, so as to form two discs, the so-called "spectacle-fibulæ." These had sometimes an iron, more often a bronze, pin. Pins, rings, armlets, spirals, chains, and beads of gold, bronze, amber, and glass, with other objects, should be added to the list of ornaments buried with the dead of Hallstadt.

La Téne is a place, near the village of Marin, to the north of the Neuenberger See in Switzerland, which was, according to Ridgeway, undoubtedly an oppidum of the Helvetii. Here the admixture of the two metals, which was noticed at Hallstadt, is no longer discoverable. The swords, the spear-heads, and the axes are all of iron. The swords are from thirty to thirty-eight inches in length, the handles forming from four to seven and a half inches of this. They have a double-edged blade, which usually possesses a mid-rib. The edges are parallel, or nearly so, almost to the extremity, which ends in a rounded point, if such a term may be allowed.

Attached to the heel of the blade is a curved ridge, which on its concave aspect adapts itself to the upper end of the scabbard. This last was sometimes wholly of bronze, sometimes provided with scapes of that metal, and in either case at times considerably ornamented. The shield was oblong. Many agricultural implements were used by the inhabitants of this oppidum, sickles, scythes, shears—a very characteristic object—rakes, and ploughs, and all were made of iron. The pins, which are made of bronze or iron, are characterised by the double-sided spiral winding of the head, and particularly by the extension of the pin-trough, which is bent backwards towards the shoulder-piece. But the points of greatest interest in connection with the race and culture of which La Téne is the name-site, are the pottery and the style of ornament. For with this civilisation for the first time the potter's wheel enters into this country. This point will be more fully dealt with in a few pages, where the scheme of ornament which belongs to it will be more particularly considered. At present it may be stated that it is specially characterised by a form of scroll, of a flamboyant type, and believed to have been derived from the palmetto of the Greeks. Figures of animals, with arabesques and flourishes, masks of human faces and other ornaments were applied to their vessels and to other articles in common employ. Enamelling also seems to have been a discovery of this people, and the chief countries in which it was practised were England and France.

We may now turn to the consideration of the objects belonging to this period which have been discovered in our own country. In the last chapter as much has been said as space will permit concerning the villages belonging to this stratum of culture. Having called attention to them, we may next consider the question of interments, before passing under notice some of the individual objects discovered in the villages, or with the remains of the dead.

The " Dane's Graves "[1] is the local name of a burying-ground of the Late Celtic period, near Kilham, East Riding of Yorkshire. The interments here were by inhumation, and in a contracted position.

One of them was a "chariot-burial," that is to say, the chariot of the dead man had been buried with him, but not, it would appear, since there were no horses' bones discoverable, the animals which had been accustomed to drag it. Two snaffle-bridle bits of iron were found, also several rings and ornaments of bronze. From the position of the objects in the grave it seems that the wheels must have been taken off the body of the chariot and laid upon their sides. The body of the car was deposited upon them, and the trappings of the horses laid beside them. One of the bodies in this grave had some personal ornaments, amongst them two bosses, originally connected with the fastening of the belt, which were made of white shell set in thin bronze sockets. In this connection it may be noted that in another grave was found a pin whose head was wheel-shaped, with four spokes, perhaps a representa-

---

[1] *Proc. Soc. Ant.*, ii. xvii. 119.

tion of a chariot wheel. This pin, which was made of bronze, was also inlaid with fragments of white shell. Other chariot-burials have been found at Arras[1] and Beverley. At the former place in one such interment the whole of the chariot, together with its horses, had been buried with its former owner. In two others at the same place only the wheels of the chariot had been laid with the dead man, perhaps as sufficiently representing the entire object. At Beverley the same state of things was found, for there also remains of two wheels and an iron bit were the only objects discovered, even the bones of the interred body having completely disappeared. Other interesting objects found in the Arras interments—some of the spoils of which are in the York, some in the British Museum— are iron mirrors. Before leaving the subject of chariot-burials, mention may be made of the fact that they occur on the Continent in the La Téne stratum. At Nanterre,[2] for example, in France, an interment of this class has recently been described. Here the horses had been buried with their master, as their bones as well as their trappings and parts of the tyres of the wheels were found in the grave. The metallic objects were partly of iron, partly of bronze.

A group of barrows of the period now under consideration was opened by Greenwell at Cowlam, in the East Riding of Yorkshire. [3]

By far the most important series of interments, however, which have so far come to light are those at Aylesford, described in an elaborate paper by Mr. A. J. Evans.[4] In this cemetery the cinerary urns were placed in shallow pits no great distance below the surface of the ground, and with no mounds heaped up over them. With the

---

[1] Greenwell, *British Barrows*, 454.   [2] *L'Anthropologie*, xiii. 66.
[3] *Brit. Barrows*, 208. See also note on p. 50 in the same book for further instances of interments of this class.   [4] *Archæologia*, lii.

urns were placed smaller vessels and other objects. The
pits described by Mr. Evans formed an irregular ellipse
and represented, in his opinion, a group of interments
belonging to the same family. He also points out that
this cemetery fits on to a widespread group of "urn-
fields" containing cremation interments as this did, the
first appearance and dissemination of which in central
and northern Europe goes *pari passu* with the diffusion
of the Early Iron age culture, and the final triumph of
iron over bronze. There are certain slight differences,
a tendency to place several cinerary urns in the same
grave, and a reduction in the number of the accessory
vessels placed with that containing the ashes themselves.
This urn-field belongs to the period which preceded the
Roman invasion of Britain ; its immediate antecedents
are to be sought in the Belgic parts of Gaul, but may
be ultimately traced to an extensive Illyro-Italic province
and to a southern branch of the urn-field group character-
ising the Early Iron age of east-central Europe. It
appears that the main portion of the cemetery was occupied by the "family-circle" type of interments, associated
with objects characteristic of the Late Celtic culture. But
on the outskirts were other interments, with relics of an
earlier civilisation, which seems to show that this site was
utilised, not only by the later Celtic people, who had introduced from Gaul these new sepulchral methods, but also
by the representatives of the race who had occupied this
country before their arrival, and that the two races lived
side by side in its neighbourhood. Or, of course, the
invaders may have made use of a cemetery which had
previously been formed by the earlier race.

Pottery.—Turning now to the objects found in this
cemetery and to other objects belonging to the same
period as that with which it is connected, we may first

pay attention to the pottery. This differs in several respects from the earlier pottery, of which some mention has been made in chapter vii. In the first place, it is thrown on a wheel, and not hand-made, as in the other case, and here, of course, we touch a cardinal point of distinction. Then, in the next place, the paste is much finer. In the older style of pottery fragments of stone and grit were mixed with the clay of which the vessels were built up. These are almost entirely wanting in the later pottery, though occasionally small grains of quartz may be made out. The clay is of much finer quality, and the burning has been better carried out. As a general rule the internal colour of the pottery is of a light brown colour, though occasionally it may be of a pale brick shade resembling some Roman vases. The surface seems in almost all cases to have been coated with pigment. This, which is black and shining, was probably formed from charcoal very finely pounded, a method employed in the case of Gaulish vases of a contemporary period. When this pigment has worn away, the outer surface is left of a dark brown colour.

No one would apply the word graceful to the heavy pottery of the earlier period, but it is a term that may well be used of that with which we are now concerned. The contours of the vases, says Mr. Evans, from whose paper the facts here given have been collected, are often of real elegance, and the finer among them are provided with well-turned pedestals. Amongst their most characteristic features are the raised cordons or ribs, generally defined by two lateral grooves by which they are accompanied, and which divide the body into zones. Sometimes these zones are themselves decorated with finely incised sloping lines, and at times other linear ornaments, such as zigzags and sprays, have been drawn with a blunt point. At times, again, the whole side of the vessel is

U

covered with comb-markings that give it the appearance of basket-work or of the grain of wood. This kind of ornament is perhaps borrowed from the older form of pottery, for there the forms and ornaments of the basket-work in which it had its origin are reproduced with certain modifications and additions. The Aylesford class of pottery seems to extend over the whole of south-eastern England, examples having been found at Elveden, in Essex, and elsewhere. It has also been found in Dorset-shire, including the Isle of Portland, at Northampton, and at Hunsbury close by.

Buckets or Situlæ.—One of the most remarkable and beautiful objects in the Aylesford find was a bronze-plated pail, composed of wooden staves, bound together with three bronze bands, the two lower of which were destitute of ornament. The upper band, which encircled the rim of the bucket and carried the handle, was ornamented with *repoussé*-work representations of animals and scroll-like ornaments. The handle, which was movable, was made of iron plated with bronze. It was ribbed in several places, and was connected with the pail itself by an attachment, on either side, shaped like a human head, bearing a sort of crested helmet. As for the decorations on the upper band, these are of two kinds, foliated and zoomorphic, and an examination of them has led Mr. Evans to enunciate some very interesting views as to their connections. Fig. 84[1] shows a quintuple scroll resembling, in all but the number of its parts, a design found on a scabbard at La Téne itself. A comparison of this with other La Téne sheaths leads him to believe that this ornament is really a modification of the upper volutes of a Greek anthemion or palmette. In Fig. 84[2] is shown another of the foliated ornaments from this bucket-rim. Here in the centre is a circle of volute petals.

Above and below it are foliated scrolls, with a general resemblance to those in the other figure. The "circle" represents in fact one of the star-like flowers, sometimes rendered as volutes, which on Greek bronze vases and other ornamental metal-work often appear encircled by the sprays of arabesque foliage, serving at times as offshoots for a palmette. The animals, with curved horns, which

1   2

FIG. 84. LATE CELTIC ORNAMENT

form the remaining ornaments of the rim of the pail, have their bodies facing one another, but their heads turned back to back. The tails are bifid. This is not an uncommon *motif* in archaic Greek and Oriental art. Sometimes the bodies, placed as they are in this case, have but a single head. This type has been explained as being due to a primitive attempt at perspective, the intention being to show both sides of an animal in a single front view. Animals of a monstrous character with one head and two bodies are not by any means unknown, and perhaps it may be suggested that the sight of such a monstrosity may in the first instance have given rise to this peculiar form. If so, it is not the only debt that mythology and art owe to teratology. A further example of late Celtic ornament is given in Fig. 85. The "Marlborough Bucket," now in the Devizes Museum, was found by Sir Richard Colt Hoare, in St. Margaret's Mead, Marlborough, and contained burnt human bones. It was classed by its finder as

FIG. 85. FRAGMENT OF LATE CELTIC ORNAMENT

Roman, and by Wright[1] as Saxon, but it appears to belong to the same class as the situla at Aylesford, and, thinks Mr. Evans, may be recognised as an article of Armoric fabric imported into southwestern Britain. If so, it would be an additional witness to the trade connection which seems to have existed between the western tract of Gaul and the opposite coasts of our own island, of which the finds of Gaulish coins of the Channel Islands, or of Armoric type in Devonshire and Hants, have already supplied interesting evidence. The fir-wood, of which this bucket was made, has perished, and its place is now taken by modern staves. The sides are quite vertical, therefore the iron hoops which held the staves together would not "bind," and the vessel was probably not intended to contain liquids. A thick hollow bar of iron crossed the top of the bucket, and was fixed into the ends of two staves projecting above the rim. This was apparently intended not as a handle, but to fasten down a lid of wood, of which traces were found adhering to the under side of the bar. Two drop-handles of iron were fastened to the sides. The decoration consisted of three broad bands of thin bronze, fastened to the wood by round bronze-headed nails of iron. Fragments only of these bands remain, but they were covered with *repoussé* ornament of grotesque animal forms and human heads.[2] The side-curls attached to some of the heads on the

---

[1] *Celt, Roman and Saxon,* 400.
[2] Catalogue of Devizes Museum, No. 387.

bucket seem to have been derived by direct descent from the early Phœnician bowls and situlæ found in the tombs of Palestrina and elsewhere.

Bowls.—A group of bowls of this period has been described by Romilly Allen,[1] who finds in their ornamentation a link between the flamboyant ornament of the Pagan Celtic metal-work and the spiral ornament of the Celtic MSS. and sculptured stones. Their mountings, in the shape of small circular enamel discs, have often been looked upon as personal ornaments. Objects of this class were found in a grave at Barlaston, in Staffordshire, and described as portions of a Saxon helmet, by Jewitt.[2] The grave in this case was cut in a solid Red Sandstone rock, and at one end there was a recess containing the remains of a bowl with three very beautifully enamelled plates, each provided with a hook. The bowls to which these and other similar objects belong have the following peculiarities: (i.) A concave fluted moulding just below the rim. (ii.) Hooks for suspension by means of rings, with zoomorphic terminations projecting over the rim. The lower portions of the hooks, which are fixed to the convex sides of the bowl, are in the form of circular discs, or of an oval with the lower end pointed, or of the body of a bird. (iii.) Champlevé enamel decorations, either on the lower part of the hooks or on separate pieces of metal of various shapes attached as mountings to the bowl. (iv.) A ring on a disc fixed to the bottom of the bowl, which is corrugated to give it additional rigidity, with, in some cases, strengthening ribs round the sides of the bowl in addition. The bowls now under consideration seem to belong to the end of the Late Celtic period and the beginning of the Saxon. Other bowls of bronze, but unprovided with the enamel ornaments described above,

[1] *Archæologia*, lvi. 39.   [2] *Grave Mounds*, p. 258.

were common in the Late Celtic period, and perhaps one of the best known of them is that which was found in the Glastonbury village, and of which fac-similes are now to be purchased. This bowl was furnished with projecting bosses by way of ornament.

Swords.—The sword and sheath shown in Figs. 86 and 87 were found on the moors of Catterdale, at the head of Wensleydale, Yorkshire, and described by the late Sir A. W. Franks.[1] The remarkable feature about it is that it still retains considerable portions of its handle, these remains being of thin bronze, probably once attached to horn or hard wood. The blade is of iron. The sheath, which, unlike the blade of the sword, is in a good state of pre-servation, is of bronze. The front is comparatively plain, but the back is strengthened by a band of bronze, of which the upper part spreads out into a pierced triangular plate. At about two-fifths of its length it widens into a very prominent loop, through which no doubt a belt or rather cord or chain was passed. The end of the sheath, the total length of which is twenty-three inches, is protected by a solid bifurcate chape. In the paper just mentioned an account is given of the various swords of this class which had then been dis-

[1] *Archæologia*, i. 251.

FIG. 87.
LATE CELTIC
SWORD-
SHEATH

FIG. 86. LATE
CELTIC SWORD

covered ; a class found as far west as Ireland and as far east as Hungary, as far north as Scotland and as far south as the Apennines. In general character all these swords resemble one another, their length varying from 3 feet 6 inches to 1 foot 8 inches. The ends are fairly sharp, though not as pointed as the bronze swords which preceded them. The tangs are of tolerable length, so as to fit into a handle of good size. The handles, which have rarely been preserved, were formed in a few instances either entirely or partly of bronze, but more usually they were made of some material which has perished, probably of wood. The sheaths are, in England, often made of bronze, more rarely of iron. The loops for suspension are, in one variety, very prominent and half-way down the sheath. In another and commoner variety they are less prominent and at the upper end. The tops of the sheaths are frequently straight, though more generally ogee-shaped, and fitting into a corresponding curved bar in the handles. Franks divided these weapons into three classes, viz. (i.) Bronze sheaths with bifurcate ends and very large loops half-way down the backs, found only in England and Scotland. (ii.) Sheaths with broad rounded ends and the loop towards the upper part, found both in England and abroad. (iii.) End of the sheath more pointed, and strengthened with a peculiar heart-shaped termination, found in England and Ireland, but more common on the Continent.[1]

Shields.—Two kinds of bronze shields have been discovered in this country, round and oblong. The latter are placed in the British Museum amongst the objects belonging to the Late Celtic period, a position which

---

[1] For a further example of the first class see a paper with illustration by Greenwell, *Proc. Soc. Ant.*, ii. xvi. 4.

no one would dispute. The former are classed amongst the ordinary bronze objects, but will be described here for purposes of contrast with the other variety, which, there is no reason to doubt, they preceded.

Of the *round* variety there are several specimens in the British Museum. Two of these were found in Wales on Moel Siabod and at Rhyd-y-Gorse, near Aberystwith, respectively,[1] and have concentric circles of raised moulding, with concentric bands composed of rounded knobs between them. Two others found in the Thames are similar in character, but the mouldings and the knobs are much bolder and the number of rows of both is much smaller. In the Welsh examples there are twenty rows of studs, whilst in those found in the Thames there are only four.

The remains of another circular shield, but this time found in connection with Late Celtic objects, was discovered at Grimthorpe, Yorkshire, and was classed by its describers as Anglo-Saxon.[2] On the breast of the skeleton lay a mass of decayed wood, a quantity of ferruginous dust — probably all that was left of the handle and inside fittings of the shield—and remains of decomposed leather. On these lay two thin plates of bronze, and the umbo or boss of the same metal. The plates of bronze are not much thicker than writing paper, measure $12\frac{1}{2}$ inches from point to point of the semi-circles which they form, and are $3\frac{3}{4}$ inches in width in the middle. They have a raised pattern around their border. This shield appears, then, to have been made of wood, faced with plates of bronze and with a bronze umbo, covered or backed with leather and perhaps provided with an iron handle and fastenings. Other round shields have been found in Scotland and in Ireland as well as in this

[1] *Archæologia*, xxii.
[2] Mortimer, *Reliquary*, ix. 180; Jewitt, *Grave Mounds*, 245.

country.[1] Descriptions of some of them will be found in Evans' work [2] and in Ridgeway's chapter on the Round Shields.[3] In the latter work it is pointed out that the round shield with a central boss is characteristic both of the Achean and the Hall-stadt folk, and that bronze shields of the type mentioned above all possessed a backing of leather. A lining of leather has, in fact, survived in some of the bronze shields of Etruria. In Ireland, at least, these defensive weapons seem to have been used in the early Christian period, for sculptured upon one of the crosses at Kells, co. Meath, are armoured figures with round shields.[4]

Of the *oblong* shields there are two very beautiful examples in the British Museum, a portion of one of them being shown in Fig. 88. This shield was found in the Thames, near Battersea. It is 2 feet 6½ inches in length, and curves inwards at the sides. It has a central boss, a

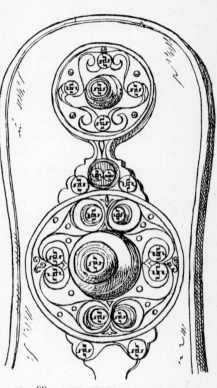

FIG. 88. LATE CELTIC BRONZE SHIELD
British Museum

[1] Round shields of thin bronze, with alternating ridges and rows of knobs, also a snake-ornamented shield, are to be seen in the Edinburgh Museum of Antiquities. [2] *Ancient Bronze Implements.*
[3] *Op. cit.*, 453. [4] Wakeman's *Handbook*, 229.

very marked feature, ornamented with what looks like a modified swastika. The remainder of the shield is decorated with wavy patterns and ornaments, relieved with red enamel.

The other shield, which was found in the River Witham, is oval, and measures 3 feet 8½ inches in length. It has in its centre a much decorated boss, in the middle of which are set some fragments of coral, and other pieces of the same substance are near to it. When it was first found this shield was further decorated with the figure of a boar with very much elongated legs. A drawing near the shield shows what this figure looked like, but it does not appear precisely how it was worked upon the shield. Both of these shields may be referred to the La Téne culture, and probably belonged to Belgic warriors.

Brooches.—Ridgeway points out that[1] the primitive safety-pin, which is the foundation form of brooches with a catch, was a development from the simple pin, which itself was probably preceded by and derived from a thorn, and, as he aptly notes, the two Irish words for a brooch, *eo* and *dealg*, both mean a thorn, just as in German we get *dorn*, with the signification of the pin of a brooch. "For greater security," he proceeds, "someone with a progressive mind bent up the pin after passing it through the garment and caught the point behind the head. The inventor, or someone else wishing to get a better hold for the point of the pin, gave the pin a complete turn, and thus produced the spring." Once this point had been reached, development produced the numerous patterns of fibula or safety-pin of the Late Celtic and succeeding ages. There is, however, a very important difference between the Late Celtic fibula and its Roman

[1] *Op. cit.*, "The Brooch," p. 552.

successor. The former is made of one piece of metal, and the head has not to be fixed by a hook. On the other hand, the Roman fibula, as found here and elsewhere in the Roman provinces, is made in two pieces. The pin and the spring are separate from the bow, and are provided with a hook to catch the loop of the spiral. A brooch of the La Téne pattern, the characters of which have been given in the first part of this chapter, has been found in Britain, and an example from Suffolk is figured and described by Ridgeway in his chapter on the subject. Some of these brooches were ornamented with enamel, as, for example, one in the Ashmolean Museum at Oxford, which bears a fly with blue enamelled wings. The brooch represented in Fig. 89 was found in the Thames at Datchet. It is made of bronze, and is ornamented with seven beads of amber and three of blue glass. It is believed to belong to the period with which this chapter deals.[1]

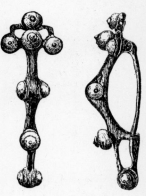

FIG. 89

LATE CELTIC BROOCH ($\frac{1}{2}$)

Armlets and Torques.—Fig. 90 shows an elaborate torque intended to be worn round the neck, found in a gravel-bed at Perdeswell, near Claines, Worcestershire. Only a portion of the object was discovered, but its vertebrated pattern closely resembles a bronze armlet found by Greenwell in a Late Celtic barrow at Cowlam. Torques were sometimes made of gold, and one found near Holywell, in Flintshire, is now at Eaton Hall. It weighs twenty-eight ounces, and is forty-four inches in circumference. The armlets, which were of smaller size,

---

[1] *Proc. Soc. Ant.*, ii. xv. 191, with coloured figure.

were intended to be worn, not on the wrist, like a bracelet, but higher up above the elbow.

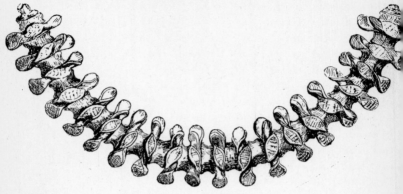

FIG. 90.   PART OF BRONZE TORQUE
Perdeswell, Worcester

Horse-trappings.—Many objects belonging to this period must be omitted, from considerations of space, but mention must be made of the bits, rings, head-ornaments, and other objects connected with the harness of the chariot horses.   Objects of this class may well be studied in the collections from the Polden Hills in Somersetshire, and from Stanwick in Yorkshire, which are exhibited in the British Museum.

Enamelling.—Mention has several times been made of the application of this beautiful art to ornaments and objects of daily use, and it may once more be pointed out that the art was introduced into this country by the Late Celtic people.   In the British Museum there are examples of its application to brooches, armlets, and horse-bits, as well as to some larger objects.   Red, blue, and yellow are the chief colours made use of.

CHAPTER XII

PHYSICAL REMAINS OF PREHISTORIC MAN

TO deal adequately with the subject of this chapter would require a book not less in size than the present manual. This chapter must, therefore, be looked upon as a mere note on the subject, inserted because to omit any mention of the kind of men who made the objects described in the preceding pages would be to leave a gap which ought in some way, however inadequate, to be filled.

Of the remains of men belonging to the palæolithic stratum of culture there are but few, and these few are in many cases still doubtfully attributed to that epoch. In fact, the changes of view which have taken place as to the position of what are generally regarded as the most ancient skulls make it very difficult to lay down any laws which are not in danger of modification by further alterations in scientific opinion. It is not so many years ago, for example, since the skulls found at Cro-Magnon were believed to be palæolithic, and they are classed as possibly belonging to that period in so recent a book as Taylor's *Origin of the Aryans*. Yet at the present date these skulls are held by many to be certainly neolithic, whilst no one probably would assign to them an earlier position than that of the Mesolithic period. Deniker [1] considers that seven skulls have been found which certainly belong

---

[1] *The Races of Man*, Eng. Trans., 310 *n*.

to the Mousterian period, namely, two from Spy (Belgium), and one each from Eguisheim (Alsace), Olmo (Val d'Arno, Italy), Bury St. Edmunds (England), Podbaba (Bohemia), and Predmost (Moravia). To this period he thinks that possibly the following skulls may also be assigned: Neanderthal (Rhenish Prussia), Denise (Auvergne), Harcilly-sur-Eure (Eure), La Truchére (Saone), and Tilbury (England). Three skulls seem undoubtedly to belong to the Magdalenian period, viz. Laugerie-Basse, Chancelade (Dordogne), and Sordes (Landes). With these may perhaps be classed the Engis, Bruniquel, and Sargels skulls. Amongst the mesolithic or early neolithic skulls, as to whose exact position there may still be considered to be some doubt, are those of Cro-Magnon (Dordogne) and Baoussé-Roussé (Maritime Alps), the six so-called Mentone skulls, those from Furfooz (Trou-de-Frontal, Belgium), Solutré, Grenelle, and others. Of some of these, and of other skulls of an early date, some notice must now be taken, but before doing so it will be necessary to mention briefly the lines upon which craniologists work in determining the differences between individual crania and groups of crania. The method adopted in the past, and still in full operation, has been to take certain measurements of length, breadth, etc., and to construct from them certain indices, affording matter of comparison between different skulls. Of all these indices the most commonly employed is that known as the "Cephalic Index," by which the relations of length and breadth are estimated. Any person looking at the drawings of the two skulls shown in Figs. 91 and 92, and especially at those drawings which show the top view of the skull, or *norma verticalis*, can scarcely fail to notice that one of them is much longer than it is broad, whilst the breadth of the other approaches more nearly to its length. In other words, it is more nearly circular than the skull with which

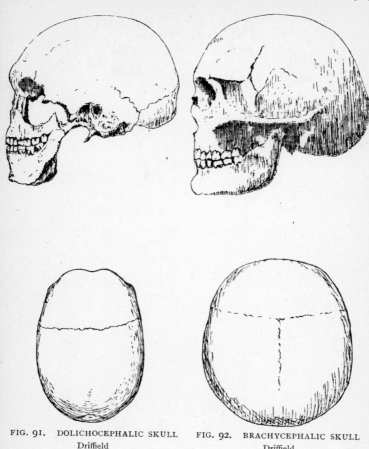

FIG. 91.   DOLICHOCEPHALIC SKULL   FIG. 92.   BRACHYCEPHALIC SKULL
Driffield   Driffield

it is being contrasted.   In order to ascertain more exactly
the relations between length and breadth than can be done
by merely looking at the skulls, two measurements are
taken.   The first of these is from the centre of the forehead (glabella) above the root of the nose, to the prominence
at the back of the skull (inion, or external occipital pro-
tuberance).   This gives the maximum length.   The second

is at right angles to the first, and is taken at the point of maximum breadth, which may be nearer to the front or back of the skull, according to its shape. The length is multiplied by 100 and divided by the breadth, the result being the index required. Various divisions of skulls, according to the results given by this method, have been suggested, though all agree that there are three main classes, namely, long or dolichocephalic, intermediate or mesaticephalic, and short or brachycephalic crania. Broca's division is as follows :—

Skulls with index below 77·7 . Dolichocephalic.
Above this and below 80 . . Mesaticephalic.
Above 80 . . . . Brachycephalic.

Besides this index there are others relating to the orbit and many other parts of the cranium, which cannot be touched upon here. Another method of measurement is to take the cranial capacity in cubic centimetres by filling the skull with shot or millet seeds, and measuring the amount which it is capable of containing. In addition various angles are measured with a view of estimating, amongst other things, the amount of the projection of the lower part of the face (prognathism and orthognathism), though less importance is assigned to this particular observation than was once the case. A more recent method of comparison of skulls which, though as yet in its infancy, may revolutionise the subject of craniology, is the natural system of Sergi.[1] Here the entire contour of the skull is taken into consideration, and not merely isolated measurements from point to point. So far the difficulty in connection with this system has been that it comprises a series of forms which have to be estimated by eye. So far as the leading types, when characteristic specimens are selected, are concerned, there is not much

[1] *Specie e Varietà Umana*, "The Mediterranean Race," etc.

difficulty about this. But the intermediate types, and those on the borderland, may easily be assigned to one class by one observer, and to another by a second. An attempt to estimate these differences, and arrange the skulls in Sergi's classes by means of geometrical figures, has recently been made by Wright,[1] and in some such direction, no doubt, the problem of arranging these forms so as to be truly comparable by all observers will be solved.

Passing now from these prefatory observations to the consideration of the skulls themselves, it will be well to review the features of some of the examples at present believed to belong to the earliest periods. This must be done at somewhat greater length than will be necessary in connection with those undoubtedly belonging to the Neolithic and Bronze periods.

Palæolithic. — Amongst the skulls belonging to the earliest periods, that which has of late years attracted the greatest amount of discussion is that found at *Trinil*, in Java, by Dr. E. Dubois.[2] For this a new family, that of Pithecanthropus, has been formed by its discoverer. At the present moment, however, it must be admitted that there is so much divergence of opinion as to this skull, that it is impossible to base any arguments upon it. At the same place as the skull, but at twelve to fifteen metres from it, was found a femur, or thigh-bone, and also in the same neighbourhood a molar tooth. It has been assumed by the discoverer and by some others that all these remains belonged to the same individual. Though this is possible, it is by no means certain, nor can it ever be proved, and this fact adds greatly to the difficulty in deciding as to the character of the skull. There is no doubt that the femur

---

[1] *Man*, August, 1903.

[2] *Pithecanthropus erectus, eine Uebergangsform aus Java*, Batavia, 1894.

X

is that of a human being, and the disease from which its possessor suffered is a perfectly well recognised one. The molar tooth, though very large, is almost certainly human. As for the skull, which is the real crux, the opinions of scientific men who have examined it are very much at variance. Virchow declared that it was pathological, but that distinguished man had rather a tendency to take that view of certain early skulls, for he came to the same conclusion as to the Neanderthal example. At the same time other men of science have held the same opinion respecting the Trinil skull, and Sir William Turner, without expressing the view that it is pathological, has pointed out that the skull of a microcephalous idiot presents a frontal flattening very analogous to the Javan example. The theory that the condition is pathological, and due to an early synostosis or junction of the sutures is not one which can at present be ruled out of court.

Then there is the view held by Sergi,[1] a very skilled craniologist, that the skull is that of "an animal with some human characteristics, but, in my opinion, it is not man nor the intermediary type; it is a higher type of the other anthropomorphic species."

To this may be added Deniker's[2] opinion that the owner of the skull was "a being more closely related to man than to the anthropoid apes, or even a man of a race inferior to all existing ones."

Perhaps scientific opinion in this country would find itself most in agreement with Cunningham's[3] view that Pithecanthropus, to give him his discoverer's title, cannot represent a transition animal between man and any of the existing anthropoids, since he stands in the direct line of

[1] *The Mediterranean Race*, 201.
[2] *The Races of Man*, 360.
[3] *Nature*, February 28th, 1895.

human divergence in the genealogical tree, as will be seen in a graphic manner below.

European Races	1,550 c.c. cranial capacity.
Low Races	1,250 c.c. cranial capacity.
Pithecanthropus	1,000 c.c. cranial capacity.

Chimpanzee, 350 c.c. cr. cap.

Gorilla and Orang, 500 c.c. cranial capacity.

If, however, the skull can be called human, and if it is not pathological, it is certain that it is of considerably lower type than that of any other race or healthy individual as yet known. The figure 93 annexed [1] shows the curve of the vault of the skull in this example, as compared with the curves of a chimpanzee on the one hand, and with those of the Spy and Cro-Magnon skulls on the other.

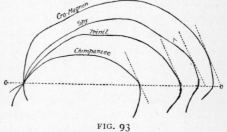

FIG. 93

CURVES OF VAULTS OF VARIOUS SKULLS

It is perhaps a misnomer to speak of this as a palæolithic skull, but its importance and the great amount of interest at present attaching to it warrant the devotion of more space to its consideration than can be accorded to the other examples which still remain for description.

The **Neanderthal** skull was once as great a bone of contention as that which has been last discussed. It was considered to be simian in its type; it was thought to be pathological; and many were the dissertations written and opinions expressed about it. It was found near

[1] After Manouvrier, *Bull. Soc. d'Anthropologie*, 1896, 438.

Dusseldorf with two femora, two humeri, and some other fragments. It is characterised by its huge superciliary ridges and by the flatness of the forehead. It is dolichocephalic, and though considered when first discovered to be of a much lower character than the skull of any known race, is now recognised as differing but little from the skulls of some low races (*e.g.* Australians). It is without doubt the skull of a human being, removed by a great gap from the anthropoid ape.

The **Spy** skulls belong to two nearly perfect skeletons of a man and a woman which were found in a cavern in the Namur district of Belgium, together with implements of the Mousterian period. Here again we have a dolichocephalic skull with retreating forehead and enormous superciliary ridges. The height of the skull is intermediate between that of the Neanderthal and an ordinary modern skull of European type.

The **Galley Hill** skeleton was found at a depth of eight feet in the pleistocene high-level gravels of the Thames, with palæolithic implements and remains of extinct mammals. It may have been the skeleton of a neolithic man interred in this position, and such is the opinion of such authorities as Sir J. Evans and Boyd-Dawkins. Others, however, believe it to be the skeleton of a man contemporary with the implements and remains with which it was found. The skull is very dolichocephalic, with low forehead and prominent superciliary ridges, points which bring it into series with the Neanderthal and Spy examples.

In contrast with these is the **Rossillon** skeleton, found by Abbé Tarnier in the Ain Department, France.[1] In the sixth and most ancient layer in the grotto examined was found a skeleton, the bones of which had been coloured with red ochre, like those of Mentone and other

[1] *L'Anthropologie*, vi. 314.

ancient remains. The skull in this case is sub-dolicho-cephalic, has no signs of inferiority such as low forehead, and does not show the prominent superciliary ridges of the Neanderthal class. One would be disposed to look upon this as being a skeleton of later date, but the nature of the excavation seems to leave no doubt as to its position as a palæolithic example. It may well, however, be of the Magdalenian period, whilst those above described seem to belong to the much earlier Mousterian era.

The **Laugerie-Basse** skulls and skeleton, without any reasonable doubt, belong to the Magdalenian age. The skeleton is that of a male, whilst both the older skulls belonged to females. All are dolichocephalic. The cranial capacity of the male and of one of the females is above the average of the present day, whilst that of the other female is very low, only 1,100 c.c.

The **Chancelade** skull is also of the same period. It was found in the Dordogne, and is dolichocephalic and well formed.[1] It will be noticed that all these skulls without exception belong to the dolichocephalic group. So also does the Cro - Magnon skull, which we may perhaps look upon as belonging to the transition period, perhaps to the early neolithic era.

Neolithic.—The skeletons of the people of this period and of the next in this country are numerous, and have been very fully studied, so that we can form a very fair idea of what the physical characteristics of the race were. In this country the greatest number of skeletons examined have been those from Wilts and Gloucester, but others have been investigated from other parts of this island. The skulls belonging to this period and found in the long barrows are dolichocephalic, like those described

[1] For further notes on skulls of the Palæolithic period see Keane, *Ethnology*, pp. 144 *et seq.*

in the previous section. The foreheads were not low, on the contrary they were well formed, and did not present the beetling brows characteristic of the Neanderthal type. The jaws were small and well shaped. The stature perhaps averaged about five feet and a half inch. The bones, generally speaking, were slender, often with a well-marked ridge on the back of the femur and a flattening of the tibia, from which we gather that they were those of a people active on their feet, probably constantly engaged in the chase.

Bronze.—Here again there is no lack of skulls and skeletons, and the descriptions of them are many. In the barrows of this period we find two classes of skulls, long and broad. The former may be those of the earlier people, the latter those of a race which had invaded the country. Or the collocation may be explained without supposing the arrival of a different race, but these are points into which it is impossible to enter here. Suffice it to say that the skulls regarded as typical of this period are brachycephalic, of large size and with well-formed brow. There are salient ridges above the eyes, but these are not the monstrous projections of the Neanderthal type. One gains the idea that the cast of countenance of the possessors of these skulls must have been much more fierce and commanding than that of the milder race which preceded them. They were also taller, their average stature being about five feet five inches, a measurement which, in fact, exceeds the stature of the present inhabitants of this country. Dr. Thurnam, from his examination of the bones of these two races, has also come to the conclusion that the average age at the time of death was higher than that of the preceding race. That of the Neolith, in his opinion, was forty-five, that of the man of the Bronze period fifty-five.

APPENDIX

LIST OF MUSEUMS CONTAINING OBJECTS DEALT WITH IN THIS BOOK

THIS list of museums has been compiled for the use of persons visiting different parts of the country who may desire to study the objects described in this book. Considerable trouble has been taken to ascertain the special features of interest in each collection, and it is hoped that no important museum has been omitted. In a few cases where the interest of the collection lies chiefly in the Roman series, or where there are important objects belonging to this period, the fact has been indicated in the table. The symbol × shows that objects are present, – that they are absent. The same symbols have been used to indicate that a catalogue or guide is or is not published.

	Stone.	Bronze.	Late Celtic.	Catalogue.	Special.
BEDFORDSHIRE—					
Bedford, Lit. and Sci. Inst.	×	×		–	
BERKSHIRE—					
Reading * . . .	×	×		×	Roman, from Silchester.
CAMBRIDGESHIRE—					
Cambridge, Arch. Mus.* .	×	×	×	–	
,, Woodwardian Mus.	×	–	–		
Wisbech . . .	×	×		–	
CHESHIRE—					
Chester . . .	×	×		–	Important Roman series, with Catalogue.

	Stone.	Bronze.	Late Celtic.	Catalogue.	Special.
CORNWALL—					
Penzance . . .	×	×		—	
CUMBERLAND—					
Carlisle . . .	×	×	×	—	
Keswick, Fitz Park . .	×	×		—	
DERBYSHIRE—					
Derby . . .	×	—	—	—	
DEVONSHIRE—					
Exeter . . .	×	×		—	
Plymouth Institution .	×	×			
DORSETSHIRE—					
Dorchester * . . .	×	×	×	—	Rimbury objects.
Farnham ** . . .	×	×	×	—	Objects described in Pitt-Rivers' *Memoirs.*
DURHAM—					
Ushaw College . .		×		—	
ESSEX—					
Colchester Castle . .	×	×		×	Fine Roman series.
GLOUCESTERSHIRE—					
Bristol . . .	×	×	×	—	
Cirencester . . .	×				Fine Roman series, with Catalogue.
Cheltenham College . .	×			—	
Gloucester . . .	×	×	×	—	
HAMPSHIRE—					
Newport, Isle of Wight .	×	×		—	
Ryde, Isle of Wight . .	×	×		—	
Winchester . . .	×	×		—	
HEREFORDSHIRE—					
Hereford . . .					

	Stone.	Bronze.	Late Celtic.	Catalogue.	Special.
KENT—					
Canterbury . . .	×	×	×	—	
Dover . . .	—	×	—	—	
Folkestone . . .	×	×	×	—	
Maidstone . . .	×	×	×		Eoliths.
LANCASHIRE—					
Blackburn . . .	×	×		—	
Manchester . . .	×	×		—	
Stonyhurst College . .	×	×		—	
LEICESTERSHIRE—					
Leicester . . .	×	×	×	—	
LINCOLNSHIRE—					
Lincoln . . .	×	×	×	—	
MIDDLESEX—					
London, British Museum **	×	×	×	×	
,, Guildhall . .	×	×	×	×	
,, Nat. Hist. Mus., South Kensington	×				Type series of Eoliths.
,, Society of Antiquaries	×	×	×		
NORFOLK—					
Norwich . . .	×	×	×	×	
NORTHAMPTONSHIRE—					
Northampton . .	×	×	×	—	Late Celtic series from Hunsbury.
NORTHUMBERLAND—					
Alnwick Castle . .	×	×		×	Catalogue for private circulation only.
Newcastle-on-Tyne . .	×	×			Important Roman series, with Catalogue.

.	Stone.	Bronze.	Late Celtic.	Catalogue.	Special.
NOTTINGHAMSHIRE—					
Nottingham . . .	×	×	—	—	
OXFORDSHIRE—					
Oxford, Pitt-Rivers ** .	×	×			
,, Ashmolean . .	×	×	×		Important Late Celtic series.
SHROPSHIRE—					
Ludlow . . .	×	×		×	
Shrewsbury . . .	×	×		—	Important Roman series from Viroconium.
SOMERSET—					
Bath, R. Lit. and Sci. Inst.	×	—	.	—	
Glastonbury* . . .			×		Objects from Lake-village.
Taunton . . .	×	×	×	×	Objects from Worlebury.
SUFFOLK—					
Bury St. Edmunds, Moyses Hall . . .	×	×	×	×	
Ipswich . . .	×	×		×	
SURREY— . . .					
Godalming, Charterhouse School . . .	×	—	—	—	
Guildford . . .	×	—	—	—	
SUSSEX—					
Brighton . . .	×	×		×	
Chichester . . .	×	×		—	
WARWICKSHIRE—					
Birmingham, University .	×	×	—	—	
Warwick . . .	×	×		—	
					.
WESTMORLAND—					
Kendal . . .	×	—	—	—	

	Stone.	Bronze.	Late Celtic.	Catalogue.	Special.
WILTSHIRE—					
Devizes * . . .	×	×	×	×	Colt Hoare Collection.
Marlborough College .	×	×	—	—	
Salisbury, Blackmore Museum.**	×	×	×	×	Perhaps the most valuable series of stone implements for the student in England.
WORCESTERSHIRE—					
Worcester . . .	×	×		—	
YORKSHIRE—					
Driffield, Mortimer Museum	×	×	×		
Giggleswick School . .	×	×	×	—	Objects from the Victoria Cave, Settle.
Hull	×	×		×	
Keighley . . .	×	—		—	
Leeds	×	×		—	
Scarborough . . .	×	×		—	Gristhorpe objects.
Sheffield . . .	×	×		×	
Whitby . . .	×	×		—	
York * . . .	×	×	×	×	Arras objects. Most important Roman series.

INDEX

PLYMOUTH
WILLIAM BRENDON AND SON, PRINTERS

THE ANTIQUARYS BOOKS

Demy 8vo. 7s. 6d. net each.

" The 'Antiquary's Books' makes an excellent commencement in the first volume. It is in outward respects a shapely demy octavo in scarlet cloth, well printed, illustrated with thirty or forty plates."—*Pall Mall Gazette.*

" The publishers have been fortunate in securing the services of the Rev. Dr. Cox, one of the most learned and painstaking of antiquaries, as general editor of the series. Antiquarian books too often are as dry as matchwood, but there is no reason why they should be so, and the present volume abundantly testifies to this."—*Birmingham Post.*

MESSRS. METHUEN are publishing a series of volumes dealing with various branches of English Antiquities.

It is confidently hoped that these books will prove to be comprehensive and popular, as well as accurate and scholarly ; so that they may be of service to the general reader, and at the same time helpful and trustworthy books of reference to the antiquary or student. The writers will make every endeavour to avail themselves of the most recent research.

The series is edited by the well-known antiquary, J. Charles Cox, LL.D., F.S.A., Member of the Royal Archæological Institute, Corresponding Member of the British Archæological Association, and Council Member of the Canterbury and York Record Society, and of the British Numismatic Society. Each book is entrusted to an expert in the selected subject, and the publishers are fortunate in having secured the services of distinguished writers.

A special feature is made of the illustrations, which will vary, according to the requirements of the subjects, from 50 to 150. Some are in colour. The type is large and clear, the length of each volume is about 320 pages.

ENGLISH MONASTIC LIFE Third Edition
By ABBOT GASQUET, O.S.B., D.D., Ph.D., D.Litt.
With 42 Illustrations, 5 Maps, and 3 Plans.

" This delightful book, so full of quaint learning, is like a painted window, through which, if one looks, one may see the old world of the Middle Ages as that world must have shown itself to a monk."—*Daily News.*

" Curiously interesting and highly instructive."—*Punch.*

" An extremely interesting summary of the laws which governed the religious and domestic life in the great monasteries."—*Yorkshire Post.*

REMAINS OF THE PREHISTORIC AGE IN ENGLAND
By BERTRAM C. A. WINDLE, Sc.D., F.R.S., F.S.A.,
Professor of Anatomy and Anthropology in the University of Birmingham
With 94 Illustrations by Edith Mary Windle

" It gives a tabulated list of such remains ; divided into counties, and subdivided into earthworks, barrows, camps, dykes, megalithic monuments, and so on, with detailed explanations ; to these are added a list of museums in which specimens of prehistoric remains are preserved. Confining himself almost entirely to accepted facts in the science of archæology, the Professor devotes no more space to what he describes as theory spinning about the dates of various epochs than is necessary to present the subject with completeness, especially on its geological side. Mrs. Windle's excellent illustrations throughout the volume add greatly to its value."—*Yorkshire Post.*

THE OLD SERVICE-BOOKS OF THE ENGLISH CHURCH. By CHRISTOPHER WORDSWORTH, M.A., AND HENRY LITTLEHALES
With 38 Plates, 4 of which are in Colour

"It is infinitely more than a fascinating book on the treasures of past ages. It is the history of the making of a great and living book. The illustrations are most beautifully reproduced."—*St. James's Gazette*.

"Scholars will find that its pages are thoroughly trustworthy. The introduction yields a great deal of unusual knowledge pertaining to the subject. The illustrations are exceptionally numerous and creditable in execution for a book of moderate price, and are reproductions in facsimile from English originals. All save two are, we believe, given here for the first time."—*Athenæum*.

CELTIC ART IN PAGAN AND CHRISTIAN TIMES
By J. ROMILLY ALLEN, F.S.A.
With 44 Plates and 81 Illustrations in the text

"Unquestionably the greatest living authority on the Celtic Archæology of Great Britain and Ireland, he writes as only a master of his subject can. An admirable piece of work."—*St. James's Gazette*.

"The letterpress and pictures are remarkably good throughout: both author and publishers are to be congratulated on the issue of so attractive and useful a book."—*Athenæum*.

SHRINES OF BRITISH SAINTS
By J. CHARLES WALL
With 28 Plates and 50 Illustrations in the text

"The present volume may be said to be of a slightly more popular character than that on 'Old Service Books,' but the same wide research and careful compilation of facts have been employed, and the result will be, to the general reader, equally informatory and interesting."—*Academy*.

"The shrines have for the most part passed away. What they were like may be learned from this volume."—*Manchester Guardian*.

"This is a good subject and one that is well handled by Mr. Wall."—*Athenæum*.

ARCHÆOLOGY AND FALSE ANTIQUITIES
By ROBERT MUNRO, M.A., M.D., LL.D., F.R.S.E. F.S.A. Scot.
With 18 Plates, a Plan, and 63 Illustrations in the text

"The author passes in review the more conspicuous instances of sham antiquities that have come to light since the beginning of the second half of the last century in Europe and in America."—*Westminster Gazette*.

"He provides us with an account of all the most famous attempts made by sinful men to impede the progress of archæology by producing forged antiquities; and he points out a number of examples of the way in which Nature herself has done the felony, placing beneath the hand of the enthusiastic hunter of remains objects which look as if they belonged to the Stone Age, but which really belonged to the gentleman next door before he threw them away and made them res nullius."—*Outlook*.

THE MANOR AND MANORIAL RECORDS
By NATHANIEL J. HONE. With 54 Illustrations

"This book fills a hitherto empty niche in the library of popular literature. Hitherto those who desired to obtain some grasp of the origin of manors or of their administration had to consult the somewhat conflicting and often highly technical works. Mr. Hone has wisely decided not to take anything for granted, but to give lucid expositions of everything that concerns manors and manorial records."—*Guardian*.

"We could linger for a long while over the details given in this delightful volume, and in trying to picture a state of things that has passed away. It should be added that the illustrations are well-chosen and instructive."—*Country Life*.

"Mr. Hone presents a most interesting subject in a manner alike satisfying to the student and the general reader."—*Field*.

ENGLISH SEALS
By J. HARVEY BLOOM, M.A., Rector of Whitchurch
With 93 Illustrations

"The book forms a valuable addition to the scholarly series in which it appears. It is admirably illustrated."—*Scotsman.*

"A careful and methodical survey of this interesting subject, the necessary illustrations being numerous and well done."—*Outlook.*

"Presents many aspects of interest, appealing to artists and heraldic students, to lovers of history and of antiquities."—*Westminster Gazette.*

"Nothing has yet been attempted on so complete a scale, and the treatise will take rank as a standard work on the subject."—*Glasgow Herald.*

THE ROYAL FORESTS OF ENGLAND
By J. CHARLES COX, LL.D., F.S.A.
With 25 Plates and 23 Illustrations in the text

"A vast amount of general information is contained in this most interesting book."
Daily Chronicle.

"The subject is treated with remarkable knowledge and minuteness, and a great addition to the book are the remarkable illustrations."—*Evening Standard.*

"The volume is a storehouse of learning. The harvest of original research. Nothing like it has been published before."—*Liverpool Post.*

THE BELLS OF ENGLAND
By CANON J. J. RAVEN, D.D., F.S.A., of Emmanuel College, Cambridge
With 60 Illustrations

"The history of English bells, of their founding and hanging, of their inscriptions and dedications, of their peals and chimes and carillons, of bell legends, of bell poetry and bell law, is told with a vast amount of detailed information, curious and quaint."—*Tribune.*

"The illustrations, as usual in this series, are of great interest."—*Country Life.*

THE DOMESDAY INQUEST
By ADOLPHUS BALLARD, B.A., LL.B., Town Clerk of Woodstock
With 27 Illustrations

"In point of scholarship and lucidity of style this volume should take a high place in the literature of the Domesday Survey."—*Daily Mail.*

"Replete with information compiled in the most clear and attractive fashion."
Liverpool Post.

"The author holds the balance freely between rival theories."—*Birmingham Post.*

"Most valuable and interesting."—*Liverpool Mercury.*

"A brilliant and lucid exposition of the facts."—*Standard.*

"A vigorous and independent commentary."—*Tribune.*

PARISH LIFE IN MEDIÆVAL ENGLAND   Second Edition
By ABBOT GASQUET, O.S.B., D.D., Ph.D., D.Litt.
With 39 Illustrations

"A rich mine of well-presented information."—*World.*

"A captivating subject very ably handled."—*Illustrated London News.*

"A worthy sequel to the Abbot's scholarly work on monastic life."—*Liverpool Post.*

"Essentially scholarly in spirit and treatment."—*Tribune.*

THE BRASSES OF ENGLAND
By HERBERT W. MACKLIN, M.A., St. John's Coll
Cambridge. President of the Monumental Brass Society
With 85 Illustrations

Monumental brasses occupy an almost unique position amongst the material records c the later middle age and of the renaissance in England. Widely distributed in time an place, and numbering several thousands, they have been strangely neglected by the historia and the general antiquary, though they have long been the object of a special cult an possess a not inconsiderable literature of their own.

The President of the Monumental Brass Society here treats of Brasses from the huma and historic, as well as the technical, point of view. His twelve chapters trace the rise an decline of the art of brass engraving from the reign of Edward I to the Caroline Decadence Architectural Ornament and Foreign Workmanship occupy separate chapters, and anothe of some importance is devoted to the Mediæval Clergy of England, with appendices on th Religious Orders and the Universities. Numerous lists of examples are a prominent featur of the book, and every period is illustrated from tracings, rubbings, and photo-lithographs.

CHURCH FURNITURE
By J. CHARLES COX, LL.D., F.S.A., & A. HARVEY, M.B

In these pages far fuller accounts than have yet been attempted are given, from th earliest examples down to the end of the seventeenth century, of such extant objects a altars, altar-stones, holy tables, altar rails, sedilia, aumbries, piscinas, holy water stoop Easter sepulchres, gospel lecterns, pulpits, both of wood and stone, hour glasses, candlestick chests, and poor-boxes. Particular attention has been bestowed upon screens, stalls, bencl ends, and seats. Fonts and font-covers are treated with considerable fulness. A shor account is given of altar-plate, including pyxes, censors, and paxes. Among the exception curiosities of later days, the several instances of those remarkable instruments, th "vamping horns," are set forth, and various noteworthy examples of early royal arms an Tables of Commandments are specified. Tentative lists, classified according to date, a: given of the known examples of these different objects of Church furniture throughou England. The illustrations are numerous, and for the most part original, or specially draw for this work.

These Volumes will follow

FOLK-LORE IN EARLY BRITISH HISTORY
By G. LAWRENCE GOMME, F.S.A.

THE ROMAN OCCUPATION. By JOHN WARD, F.S.A

CASTLES AND WALLED TOWNS OF ENGLAND
By ALFRED HARVEY, M.B.

ENGLISH HERALDRY. By T. SHEPARD

GUILDS OF LONDON. By GEORGE UNWIN

SCHOOLS IN MEDIÆVAL ENGLAND
By A. F. LEACH

ENGLISH COSTUME. By GEORGE CLINCH

THE MEDIÆVAL HOSPITALS OF ENGLAND
By MISS ROTHA M. CLAY

OLD ENGLISH INSTRUMENTS OF MUSIC
By F. W. GALPIN, M.A., F.L.S.

OLD ENGLISH CUSTOMS AND CEREMONIES
By F. J. SNELL, M.A.

METHUEN & CO., 36 ESSEX STREET, LONDON, W.C.

A CATALOGUE OF BOOKS PUBLISHED BY METHUEN AND COMPANY: LONDON 36 ESSEX STREET W.C.

CONTENTS

SEPTEMBER 1907

A CATALOGUE OF

MESSRS. METHUEN'S
PUBLICATIONS

Colonial Editions are published of all Messrs. METHUEN'S Novels issued at a price above 2s. 6d., and similar editions are published of some works of General Literature. These are marked in the Catalogue. Colonial editions are only for circulation in the British Colonies and India.

I.P.L. represents Illustrated Pocket Library.

PART I.—GENERAL LITERATURE

Abbott (J. H. M.). Author of 'Tommy Cornstalk.' AN OUTLANDER IN ENGLAND: BEING SOME IMPRESSIONS OF AN AUSTRALIAN ABROAD. *Second Edition. Cr. 8vo. 6s.*
A Colonial Edition is also published.

Acatos (M. J.). See Junior School Books.

Adams (Frank). JACK SPRATT. With 24 Coloured Pictures. *Super Royal 16mo. 2s.*

Adeney (W. F.), M.A. See Bennett and Adeney.

Æschylus. See Classical Translations.

Æsop. See I.P.L.

Ainsworth (W. Harrison). See I.P.L.

Alderson (J. P.). MR. ASQUITH. With Portraits and Illustrations. *Demy 8vo. 7s. 6d. net.*

Aldis (Janet). MADAME GEOFFRIN, HER SALON, AND HER TIMES. With many Portraits and Illustrations. *Second Edition. Demy 8vo. 10s. 6d. net.*
A Colonial Edition is also published.

Alexander (William), D.D., Archbishop of Armagh. THOUGHTS AND COUNSELS OF MANY YEARS. *Demy 16mo. 2s. 6d.*

Alken (Henry). THE NATIONAL SPORTS OF GREAT BRITAIN. With descriptions in English and French. With 51 Coloured Plates. *Royal Folio. Five Guineas net.* The Plates can be had separately in a Portfolio. *£3, 3s. net.*
See also I.P.L.

Allen (C. C.) See Textbooks of Technology.

Allen (Jessie). See Little Books on Art.

Allen (J. Romilly), F.S.A. See Antiquary's Books.

Almack (E.). See Little Books on Art.

Amherst (Lady). A SKETCH OF EGYPTIAN HISTORY FROM THE EARLIEST TIMES TO THE PRESENT DAY. With many Illustrations. *Demy 8vo. 7s. 6d. net.*

Anderson (F. M.). THE STORY OF THE BRITISH EMPIRE FOR CHILDREN. With many Illustrations. *Cr. 8vo. 2s.*

Anderson (J. G.), B.A., Examiner to London University, NOUVELLE GRAMMAIRE FRANÇAISE. *Cr. 8vo. 2s.*
EXERCICES DE GRAMMAIRE FRANÇAISE. *Cr. 8vo. 1s. 6d.*

Andrewes (Bishop). PRECES PRIVATAE. Edited, with Notes, by F. E. BRIGHTMAN, M.A., of Pusey House, Oxford. *Cr. 8vo. 6s.*

Anglo-Australian. AFTER-GLOW MEMORIES. *Cr. 8vo. 6s.*
A Colonial Edition is also published.

Anon. FELISSA; OR, THE LIFE AND OPINIONS OF A KITTEN OF SENTIMENT. With 12 Coloured Plates. *Post 16mo. 2s. 6d. net.*

Aristotle. THE NICOMACHEAN ETHICS. Edited, with an Introduction and Notes, by JOHN BURNET, M.A., Professor of Greek at St. Andrews. *Cheaper issue. Demy 8vo. 10s. 6d. net.*

Atkins (H. G.). See Oxford Biographies.

Atkinson (C. M.). JEREMY BENTHAM. *Demy 8vo. 5s. net.*

Atkinson (T. D.). A SHORT HISTORY OF ENGLISH ARCHITECTURE. With over 200 Illustrations. *Second Edition. Fcap. 8vo. 3s. 6d. net.*
A GLOSSARY OF TERMS USED IN ENGLISH ARCHITECTURE. Illustrated. *Second Ed. Fcap. 8vo. 3s. 6d. net.*

Auden (T.), M.A., F.S.A. See Ancient Cities.

Aurelius (Marcus) and Epictetus. WORDS OF THE ANCIENT WISE: Thoughts from. Edited by W. H. D. ROUSE, M.A., Litt.D. *Fcap. 8vo. 3s. 6d. net.* See also Standard Library.

Austen (Jane). See Little Library and Standard Library.

Bacon (Francis). See Little Library and Standard Library.

Baden-Powell (R. S. S.), Major-General. THE DOWNFALL OF, PREMPEH. A Diary of Life in Ashanti 1895. Illustrated. *Third Edition. Large Cr. 8vo. 6s.*
A Colonial Edition is also published.

THE MATABELE CAMPAIGN, 1896. With nearly 100 Illustrations. *Fourth Edition. Large Cr. 8vo. 6s.*
A Colonial Edition is also published.

Bailey (J. C.), M.A. See Cowper.

Baker (W. G.), M.A. See Junior Examination Series.

Baker (Julian L.), F.I.C., F.C.S. See Books on Business.

Balfour (Graham). THE LIFE OF ROBERT LOUIS STEVENSON. *Third and Cheaper Edition, Revised. Cr. 8vo. 6s.*
A Colonial Edition is also published.

Ballard (A.), B.A., LL.B. See Antiquary's Books.

Bally (S. E.). See Commercial Series.

Banks (Elizabeth L.). THE AUTO-BIOGRAPHY OF A 'NEWSPAPER GIRL.' *Second Edition. Cr. 8vo. 6s.*
A Colonial Edition is also published.

Barham (R. H.). See Little Library.

Baring (The Hon. Maurice). WITH THE RUSSIANS IN MANCHURIA. *Third Edition. Demy 8vo. 7s. 6d. net.*
A Colonial Edition is also published.

A YEAR IN RUSSIA. *Second Edition. Demy 8vo. 7s. 6d.*

Baring=Gould (S.). THE LIFE OF NAPOLEON BONAPARTE. With over 450 Illustrations in the Text, and 12 Photogravure Plates. *Gilt top. Large quarto. 36s.*

THE TRAGEDY OF THE CÆSARS. With numerous Illustrations from Busts, Gems, Cameos, etc. *Sixth Edition. Royal 8vo. 10s. 6d. net.*

A BOOK OF FAIRY TALES. With numerous Illustrations by A. J. GASKIN. *Third Edition. Cr. 8vo. Buckram. 6s.*

OLD ENGLISH FAIRY TALES. With numerous Illustrations by F. D. BEDFORD. *Third Edition. Cr. 8vo. Buckram. 6s.*

THE VICAR OF MORWENSTOW. Revised Edition. With a Portrait. *Third Edition. Cr. 8vo. 3s. 6d.*

A BOOK OF DARTMOOR: A Descriptive and Historical Sketch. With Plans and numerous Illustrations. *Second Edition. Cr. 8vo. 6s.*

A BOOK OF DEVON. Illustrated. *Second Edition. Cr. 8vo. 6s.*

A BOOK OF CORNWALL. Illustrated. *Second Edition. Cr. 8vo. 6s.*

A BOOK OF NORTH WALES. Illustrated. *Cr. 8vo. 6s.*

A BOOK OF SOUTH WALES. Illustrated. *Cr. 8vo. 6s.*

A BOOK OF BRITTANY. Illustrated. *Cr. 8vo. 6s.*

A BOOK OF THE RIVIERA. Illustrated. *Cr. 8vo. 6s.*
A Colonial Edition is also published.

A BOOK OF THE RHINE: From Cleve to Mainz. Illustrated. *Second Edition. Crown 8vo. 6s.*
A Colonial Edition is also published.

A BOOK OF THE PYRENEES. With 24 Illustrations. *Crown 8vo. 6s.*
A Colonial Edition is also published.

A BOOK OF GHOSTS. With 8 Illustrations by D. MURRAY SMITH. *Second Edition. Cr. 8vo. 6s.*

OLD COUNTRY LIFE. With 67 Illustrations. *Fifth Edition. Large Cr. 8vo. 6s.*

A GARLAND OF COUNTRY SONG: English Folk Songs with their Traditional Melodies. Collected and arranged by S. BARING-GOULD and H. F. SHEPPARD. *Demy 4to. 6s.*

SONGS OF THE WEST: Folk Songs of Devon and Cornwall. Collected from the Mouths of the People. By S. BARING-GOULD, M.A., and H. FLEETWOOD SHEPPARD, M.A. New and Revised Edition, under the musical editorship of CECIL J. SHARP, Principal of the Hampstead Conservatoire. *Large Imperial 8vo. 5s. net.*

A BOOK OF NURSERY SONGS AND RHYMES. Edited by S. BARING-GOULD, and Illustrated by the Birmigham Art School. *A New Edition. Long Cr. 8vo. 2s. 6d. net.*

STRANGE SURVIVALS AND SUPER-STITIONS. *Third Edition. Cr. 8vo. 2s. 6d. net.*

YORKSHIRE ODDITIES AND STRANGE EVENTS. *New and Revised Edition. Cr. 8vo. 2s. 6d. net.*
See also Little Guides.

Barker (Aldred F.). See Textbooks of Technology.

Barker (E.), M.A. (Late) Fellow of Merton College, Oxford. THE POLITICAL THOUGHT OF PLATO AND ARISTOTLE. *Demy 8vo. 10s. 6d. net.*

Barnes (W. E.), D.D. See Churchman's Bible.

Barnett (Mrs. P. A.). See Little Library.

Baron (R. R. N.), M.A. FRENCH PROSE COMPOSITION. *Second Edition. Cr. 8vo. 2s. 6d. Key, 3s. net.*
See also Junior School Books.

Barron (H. M.), M.A., Wadham College, Oxford. TEXTS FOR SERMONS. With a Preface by Canon SCOTT HOLLAND. *Cr. 8vo. 3s. 6d.*

Bartholomew (J. G.), F.R.S.E. See C. G. Robertson.

Bastable (C. F.), M.A. THE COMMERCE OF NATIONS. *Fourth Ed. Cr. 8vo. 2s. 6d.*

Bastian (H. Charlton), M.D., F.R.S. THE EVOLUTION OF LIFE. Illustrated. *Demy 8vo. 7s. 6d. net.*

Batson (Mrs. Stephen). A CONCISE HANDBOOK OF GARDEN FLOWERS. *Fcap. 8vo. 3s. 6d.*

Batten (Loring W.), Ph.D., S.T.D. THE HEBREW PROPHET. *Cr. 8vo. 3s. 6d. net.*

Bayley (R. Child). THE COMPLETE PHOTOGRAPHER. With over 100 Illustrations. *Second Edition. Demy 8vo. 10s. 6d. net.*

Beard (W. S.). EASY EXERCISES IN ALGEBRA. *Cr. 8vo. 1s. 6d.* See Junior Examination Series and Beginner's Books.

Beckford (Peter). THOUGHTS ON HUNTING. Edited by J. OTHO PAGET, and Illustrated by G. H. JALLAND. *Second Edition. Demy 8vo.* 6s.

Beckford (William). See Little Library.

Beeching (H. C.), M.A., Canon of Westminster. See Library of Devotion.

Begbie (Harold). MASTER WORKERS. Illustrated. *Demy 8vo.* 7s. 6d. net.

Behmen (Jacob). DIALOGUES ON THE SUPERSENSUAL LIFE. Edited by BERNARD HOLLAND. *Fcap. 8vo.* 3s. 6d.

Belloc (Hilaire), M.P. PARIS. With Maps and Illustrations. *Second Edition, Revised. Cr. 8vo.* 6s.
HILLS AND THE SEA. *Second Edition. Crown 8vo.* 6s.

Bellot (H. H. L.), M.A. THE INNER AND MIDDLE TEMPLE. With numerous Illustrations. *Crown 8vo.* 6s. net.

Bennett (W. H.), M.A. A PRIMER OF THE BIBLE. *Fourth Edition. Cr. 8vo.* 2s. 6d.

Bennett (W. H.) and Adeney (W. F.). A BIBLICAL INTRODUCTION. *Fourth Edition. Cr. 8vo.* 7s. 6d.

Benson (Archbishop) GOD'S BOARD: Communion Addresses. *Fcap. 8vo.* 3s. 6d. net.

Benson (A. C.), M.A. See Oxford Biographies.

Benson (R. M.). THE WAY OF HOLINESS: a Devotional Commentary on the 119th Psalm. *Cr. 8vo.* 5s.

Bernard (E. R.), M.A., Canon of Salisbury. THE ENGLISH SUNDAY. *Fcap. 8vo.* 1s. 6d.

Bertouch (Baroness de). THE LIFE OF FATHER IGNATIUS. Illustrated. *Demy 8vo.* 10s. 6d. net.

Beruete (A. de). See Classics of Art.

Betham-Edwards (M.). HOME LIFE IN FRANCE. Illustrated. *Fourth and Cheaper Edition. Crown 8vo.* 6s.
A Colonial Edition is also published.

Bethune-Baker (J. F.), M.A. See Handbooks of Theology.

Bidez (M.). See Byzantine Texts.

Biggs (C. R. D.), D.D. See Churchman's Bible.

Bindley (T. Herbert), B.D. THE OECUMENICAL DOCUMENTS OF THE FAITH. With Introductions and Notes. *Second Edition. Cr. 8vo.* 6s. net.

Binns (H. B.). THE LIFE OF WALT WHITMAN. Illustrated. *Demy 8vo.* 10s. 6d. net.
A Colonial Edition is also published.

Binyon (Lawrence). THE DEATH OF ADAM, AND OTHER POEMS. *Cr. 8vo.* 3s. 6d. net.
See also W. Blake.

Birnstingl (Ethel). See Little Books on Art.

Blair (Robert). See I.P.L.

Blake (William). THE LETTERS OF WILLIAM BLAKE, TOGETHER WITH A LIFE BY FREDERICK TATHAM. Edited from the Original Manuscripts, with an Introduction and Notes, by ARCHIBALD G. B. RUSSELL. With 12 Illustrations. *Demy 8vo.* 7s. 6d. net.
ILLUSTRATIONS OF THE BOOK OF JOB. With a General Introduction by LAWRENCE BINYON. *Quarto.* 21s. net.
See also I.P.L. and Little Library.

Blaxland (B.), M.A. See Library of Devotion.

Bloom (J. Harvey), M.A. SHAKESPEARE'S GARDEN. Illustrated. *Fcap. 8vo.* 3s. 6d.; *leather,* 4s. 6d. net.
See also Antiquary's Books

Blouet (Henri). See Beginner's Books.

Boardman (T. H.), M.A. See Textbooks of Science.

Bodley (J. E. C.), Author of 'France.' THE CORONATION OF EDWARD VII. *Demy 8vo.* 21s. net. By Command of the King.

Body (George), D.D. THE SOUL'S PILGRIMAGE: Devotional Readings from his writings. Selected by J. H. BURN, B.D., F.R.S.E. *Demy 16mo.* 2s. 6d.

Bona (Cardinal). See Library of Devotion.

Boon (F. C.). See Commercial Series.

Borrow (George). See Little Library.

Bos (J. Ritzema). AGRICULTURAL ZOOLOGY. Translated by J. R. AINSWORTH DAVIS, M.A. With 155 Illustrations. *Cr. 8vo. Third Edition.* 3s. 6d.

Botting (C. G.), B.A. EASY GREEK EXERCISES. *Cr. 8vo.* 2s. See also Junior Examination Series.

Boulting (W.). TASSO AND HIS TIMES. With 24 Illustrations. *Demy 8vo.* 10s. 6d. net.

Boulton (E. S.), M.A. GEOMETRY ON MODERN LINES. *Cr. 8vo.* 2s.

Boulton (William B.). THOMAS GAINSBOROUGH. With 40 Illustrations. *Demy 8vo.* 7s. 6d. net.
SIR JOSHUA REYNOLDS, P.R.A. With 49 Illustrations. *Demy 8vo.* 7s. 6d. net.

Bowden (E. M.). THE IMITATION OF BUDDHA: Being Quotations from Buddhist Literature for each Day in the Year. *Fifth Edition. Cr. 16mo.* 2s. 6d.

Boyd-Carpenter (Margaret). THE CHILD IN ART. Illustrated. *Second Edition. Large Crown 8vo.* 6s.

Boyle (W.). CHRISTMAS AT THE ZOO. With Verses by W. BOYLE and 24 Coloured Pictures by H. B. NEILSON. *Super Royal 16mo.* 2s.

Brabant (F. G.), M.A. See Little Guides.

Bradley (A. G.) ROUND ABOUT WILTSHIRE. With 30 Illustrations of which 14 are in colour by T. C. GOTCH. *Second Ed. Cr. 8vo.* 6s.

Bradley (J. W.). See Little Books on Art.

Braid (James) and Others. GREAT GOLFERS IN THE MAKING. By Thirty-Four Famous Players. Edited, with an Introduction, by HENRY LEACH. With 34 Portraits. *Demy 8vo.* 7s. 6d. net.
A Colonial Edition is also published.

Brailsford (H. N.). MACEDONIA: ITS RACES AND ITS FUTURE. Illustrated. *Demy 8vo.* 12s. 6d. net.

Brodrick (Mary) and **Morton (Anderson).** A CONCISE HANDBOOK OF EGYPTIAN ARCHÆOLOGY. Illustrated. *Cr. 8vo.* 3s. 6d.

Brooks (E. E.), B.Sc. See Textbooks of Technology.

Brooks (E. W.). See Byzantine Texts.

Brown (P. H.), LL.D., Fraser Professor of Ancient (Scottish) History at the University of Edinburgh. SCOTLAND IN THE TIME OF QUEEN MARY. *Demy 8vo.* 7s. 6d. net.

Brown (S. E.), M.A., Camb., B.A., B.Sc., London; Senior Science Master at Uppingham School. A PRACTICAL CHEMISTRY NOTE-BOOK FOR MATRICULATION AND ARMY CANDIDATES: EASIER EXPERIMENTS ON THE COMMONER SUBSTANCES. *Cr. 4to.* 1s. 6d. net.

Browne (Sir Thomas). See Standard Library.

Brownell (C. L.). THE HEART OF JAPAN. Illustrated. *Third Edition. Cr. 8vo.* 6s.; also *Demy 8vo.* 6d.

Browning (Robert). See Little Library.

Buckland (Francis T.). CURIOSITIES OF NATURAL HISTORY. Illustrated by H. B. NEILSON. *Cr. 8vo.* 3s. 6d.

Buckton (A. M.) THE BURDEN OF ENGELA: a Ballad-Epic. *Second Edition. Cr. 8vo.* 3s. 6d. net.

KINGS IN BABYLON. A Drama. *Crown 8vo.* 1s. net.

EAGER HEART: A Mystery Play. *Fifth Edition. Cr. 8vo.* 1s. net.

Budge (E. A. Wallis). THE GODS OF THE EGYPTIANS. With over 100 Coloured Plates and many Illustrations. *Two Volumes. Royal 8vo.* £3, 3s. net.

Buist (H. Massac). THE MOTOR YEAR BOOK AND AUTOMOBILISTS' ANNUAL FOR 1906. *Demy 8vo.* 7s. 6d. net.

Bull (Paul), Army Chaplain. GOD AND OUR SOLDIERS. *Second Edition. Cr. 8vo.* 6s.

Bulley (Miss). See Lady Dilke.

Bunyan (John). THE PILGRIM'S PROGRESS. Edited, with an Introduction, by C. H. FIRTH, M.A. With 39 Illustrations by R. ANNING BELL. *Cr. 8vo.* 6s. See also Library of Devotion and Standard Library.

Burch (G. J.), M.A., F.R.S. A MANUAL OF ELECTRICAL SCIENCE. Illustrated. *Cr. 8vo.* 3s.

Burgess (Gelett). GOOPS AND HOW TO BE THEM. Illustrated. *Small 4to.* 6s.

Burke (Edmund). See Standard Library.

Burn (A. E.), D.D., Rector of Handsworth and Prebendary of Lichfield.
See Handbooks of Theology.

Burn (J. H.), B.D. THE CHURCHMAN'S TREASURY OF SONG. Selected and Edited by. *Fcap 8vo.* 3s. 6d. net. See also Library of Devotion.

Burnand (Sir F. C.). RECORDS AND REMINISCENCES. With a Portrait by H. v. HERKOMER. *Cr. 8vo. Fourth and Cheaper Edition.* 6s.
A Colonial Edition is also published.

Burns (Robert), THE POEMS OF. Edited by ANDREW LANG and W. A. CRAIGIE. With Portrait. *Third Edition. Demy 8vo, gilt top.* 6s.

Burnside (W. F.), M.A. OLD TESTAMENT HISTORY FOR USE IN SCHOOLS. *Second Edition. Cr. 8vo.* 3s. 6d.

Burton (Alfred). See I.P.L.

Bussell (F. W.), D.D., Fellow and Vice Principal of Brasenose College, Oxford. CHRISTIAN THEOLOGY AND SOCIAL PROGRESS: The Bampton Lectures for 1905. *Demy 8vo.* 10s. 6d. net.

Butler (Joseph). See Standard Library.

Caldecott (Alfred), D.D. See Handbooks of Theology.

Calderwood (D. S.), Headmaster of the Normal School, Edinburgh. TEST CARDS IN EUCLID AND ALGEBRA. In three packets of 40, with Answers. 1s. each. Or in three Books, price 2d., 2d., and 3d.

Cambridge (Ada) [Mrs. Cross]. THIRTY YEARS IN AUSTRALIA. *Demy 8vo.* 7s. 6d.

Canning (George). See Little Library.

Capey (E. F. H.). See Oxford Biographies.

Careless (John). See I.P.L.

Carlyle (Thomas). THE FRENCH REVOLUTION. Edited by C. R. L. FLETCHER, Fellow of Magdalen College, Oxford. *Three Volumes. Cr. 8vo.* 18s.

THE LIFE AND LETTERS OF OLIVER CROMWELL. With an Introduction by C. H. FIRTH, M.A., and Notes and Appendices by Mrs. S. C. LOMAS. *Three Volumes. Demy 8vo.* 18s. net.

Carlyle (R. M. and A. J.), M.A. See Leaders of Religion.

Channer (C. C.) and Roberts (M. E.). LACEMAKING IN THE MIDLANDS, PAST AND PRESENT. With 16 full-page Illustrations. *Cr. 8vo.* 2s. 6d.

Chapman (S. J.). See Books on Business.

Chatterton (Thomas). See Standard Library.

Chesterfield (Lord), THE LETTERS OF, TO HIS SON. Edited, with an Introduction by C. STRACHEY, and Notes by A. CALTHROP. *Two Volumes. Cr. 8vo.* 12s.

Chesterton (G. K.). CHARLES DICKENS. With two Portraits in photogravure. *Fourth Edition. Demy 8vo.* 7s. 6d. net.
A Colonial Edition is also published.

Childe (Charles P.), B.A., F.R.C.S. THE CONTROL OF A SCOURGE: OR, How CANCER IS CURABLE. *Demy 8vo.* 7s. 6d. net.

Christian (F. W.). THE CAROLINE ISLANDS. With many Illustrations and Maps. *Demy 8vo.* 12s. 6d. net.

Cicero. See Classical Translations.

Clarke (F. A.), M.A. See Leaders of Religion.

Clausen (George), A.R.A., R.W.S. AIMS AND IDEALS IN ART : Eight Lectures delivered to the Students of the Royal Academy of Arts. With 32 Illustrations. *Second Edition. Large Post 8vo.* 5s. net.
SIX LECTURES ON PAINTING. *First Series.* With 19 Illustrations. *Third Edition, Large Post 8vo.* 3s. 6d. net.

Cleather (A. L.). See Wagner.

Clinch (G.). See Little Guides.

Clough (W. T.). See Junior School Books and Textbooks of Science.

Clouston (T. S.), M.D., C.C.D., F.R.S.E., Lecturer on Mental Diseases in the University of Edinburgh. THE HYGIENE OF MIND. With 10 Illustrations. *Fourth Edition. Demy 8vo.* 7s. 6d. net.

Coast (W. G.), B.A. EXAMINATION PAPERS IN VERGIL. *Cr. 8vo.* 2s.

Cobb (W. F.), M.A. THE BOOK OF PSALMS : with a Commentary. *Demy 8vo.* 10s. 6d. net.

Coleridge (S. T.). POEMS OF. Selected and Arranged by ARTHUR SYMONS. With a photogravure Frontispiece. *Fcap. 8vo.* 2s. 6d. net.

Collingwood (W. G.), M.A. THE LIFE OF JOHN RUSKIN. With Portraits. *Sixth Edition. Cr. 8vo.* 2s. 6d. net.

Collins (W. E.), M.A. See Churchman's Library.

Colonna. HYPNEROTOMACHIA POLIPHILI UBI HUMANA OMNIA NON NISI SOMNIUM ESSE DOCET ATQUE OBITER PLURIMA SCITU SANE QUAM DIGNA COMMEMORAT. An edition limited to 350 copies on handmade paper. *Folio.* £3, 3s. net.

Combe (William). See I.P.L.

Conrad (Joseph). THE MIRROR OF THE SEA : Memories and Impressions. *Third Edition. Cr. 8vo.* 6s.

Cook (A. M.), M.A., and **Marchant (C. E.),** M.A. PASSAGES FOR UNSEEN TRANSLATION. Selected from Greek and Latin Literature. *Third Edition. Cr. 8vo.* 3s. 6d.
LATIN PASSAGES FOR UNSEEN TRANSLATION. *Third Edition. Cr. 8vo.* 1s. 6d.

Cooke-Taylor (R. W.). THE FACTORY SYSTEM. *Cr. 8vo.* 2s. 6d.

Corelli (Marie). THE PASSING OF THE GREAT QUEEN. *Second Ed. Fcap. 4to.* 1s.
A CHRISTMAS GREETING. *Cr. 4to.* 1s.

Corkran (Alice). See Little Books on Art.

Cotes (Everard). SIGNS AND PORTENTS IN THE FAR EAST. With 24 Illustrations. *Second Edition. Demy 8vo.* 7s. 6d. net.

Cotes (Rosemary). DANTE'S GARDEN. With a Frontispiece. *Second Edition. Fcap. 8vo.* 2s. 6d.; *leather,* 3s. 6d. net.

BIBLE FLOWERS. With a Frontispiece and Plan. *Fcap. 8vo.* 2s. 6d. net.

Cowley (Abraham). See Little Library.

Cowper (William), THE POEMS OF. Edited with an Introduction and Notes by J. C. BAILEY, M.A. Illustrated, including two unpublished designs by WILLIAM BLAKE. *Demy 8vo.* 10s. 6d. net.

Cox (J. Charles), LL.D., F.S.A. See Little Guides, The Antiquary's Books, and Ancient Cities.

Cox (Harold), B.A., M.P. LAND NATIONALISATION AND LAND TAXATION. *Second Edition revised. Cr. 8vo.* 3s. 6d. net.

Crabbe (George). See Little Library.

Craigie (W. A.). A PRIMER OF BURNS. *Cr. 8vo.* 2s. 6d.

Craik (Mrs.). See Little Library.

Crane (Capt. C. P.). See Little Guides.

Crashaw (Richard). See Little Library.

Crawford (F. G.). See Mary C. Danson.

Crofts (T. R. N.), M.A. See Simplified French Texts.

Cross (J. A.), M.A. THE FAITH OF THE BIBLE. *Fcap. 8vo.* 2s. 6d. net.

Cruikshank (G.). THE LOVING BALLAD OF LORD BATEMAN. With 11 Plates. *Cr. 16mo.* 1s. 6d. net.

Crump (B.). See Wagner.

Cunliffe (Sir F. H. E.), Fellow of All Souls' College, Oxford. THE HISTORY OF THE BOER WAR. With many Illustrations, Plans, and Portraits. *In 2 vols. Quarto.* 15s. each.

Cunynghame (H. H.), C.B. See Connoisseur's Library.

Cutts (E. L.), D.D. See Leaders of Religion.

Daniell (G. W.), M.A. See Leaders of Religion.

Danson (Mary C.) and Crawford (F. G.). FATHERS IN THE FAITH. *Fcap. 8vo.* 1s. 6d.

Dante. LA COMMEDIA DI DANTE. The Italian Text edited by PAGET TOYNBEE, M.A., D.Litt. *Cr. 8vo.* 6s.
THE PURGATORIO OF DANTE. Translated into Spenserian Prose by C. GORDON WRIGHT. With the Italian text. *Fcap. 8vo.* 2s. 6d. net.
See also Paget Toynbee, Little Library, Standard Library, and Warren-Vernon.

Darley (George). See Little Library.

D'Arcy (R. F.), M.A. A NEW TRIGONOMETRY FOR BEGINNERS. With numerous diagrams. *Cr. 8vo.* 2s. 6d.

Davenport (Cyril). See Connoisseur's Library and Little Books on Art.

Davey (Richard). THE PAGEANT OF LONDON. With 40 Illustrations in Colour by JOHN FULLEYLOVE, R.I. *In Two Volumes. Demy 8vo.* 15s. net.

Davis (H. W. C.), M.A., Fellow and Tutor of Balliol College, Author of 'Charlemagne.' ENGLAND UNDER THE NORMANS AND ANGEVINS : 1066-1272. With Maps and Illustrations. *Demy 8vo.* 10s. 6d. net.

Dawson (Nelson). See Connoisseur's Library.

Dawson (Mrs. N.). See Little Books on Art.

Deane (A. C.). See Little Library.

Dearmer (Mabel). A CHILD'S LIFE OF CHRIST. With 8 Illustrations in Colour by E. FORTESCUE-BRICKDALE. *Large Cr. 8vo. 6s.*

Delbos (Leon). THE METRIC SYSTEM. *Cr. 8vo. 2s.*

Demosthenes. AGAINST CONON AND CALLICLES. Edited by F. DARWIN SWIFT, M.A. *Second Edition. Fcap. 8vo. 2s.*

Dickens (Charles). See Little Library, I.P.L., and Chesterton.

Dickinson (Emily). POEMS. *Cr. 8vo. 4s. 6d. net.*

Dickinson (G. L.), M.A., Fellow of King's College, Cambridge. THE GREEK VIEW OF LIFE. *Sixth Edition. Cr. 8vo. 2s. 6d.*

Dilke (Lady), Bulley (Miss), and **Whitley (Miss).** WOMEN'S WORK. *Cr. 8vo. 2s. 6d.*

Dillon (Edward). See Connoisseur's Library and Little Books on Art.

Ditchfield (P. H.), M.A., F.S.A. THE STORY OF OUR ENGLISH TOWNS. With an Introduction by AUGUSTUS JESSOPP, D.D. *Second Edition. Cr. 8vo. 6s.*
OLD ENGLISH CUSTOMS: Extant at the Present Time. *Cr. 8vo. 6s.*
ENGLISH VILLAGES. Illustrated. *Second Edition. Cr. 8vo. 2s. 6d. net.*
THE PARISH CLERK. With 31 Illustrations. *Third Edition. Demy 8vo. 7s. 6d. net.*

Dixon (W. M.), M.A. A PRIMER OF TENNYSON. *Second Edition. Cr. 8vo. 2s. 6d.*
ENGLISH POETRY FROM BLAKE TO BROWNING. *Second Edition. Cr. 8vo. 2s. 6d*

Doney (May). SONGS OF THE REAL. *Cr. 8vo. 3s. 6d. net.*
A volume of poems.

Douglas (James). THE MAN IN THE PULPIT. *Cr. 8vo. 2s. 6d. net.*

Dowden (J.), D.D., Lord Bishop of Edinburgh. See Churchman's Library.

Drage (G.). See Books on Business.

Driver (S. R.), D.D., D.C.L., Canon of Christ Church, Regius Professor of Hebrew in the University of Oxford. SERMONS ON SUBJECTS CONNECTED WITH THE OLD TESTAMENT. *Cr. 8vo. 6s.*
See also Westminster Commentaries.

Dry (Wakeling). See Little Guides.

Dryhurst (A. R.). See Little Books on Art.

Du Buisson (J. C.), M.A. See Churchman's Bible.

Duguid (Charles). See Books on Business.

Dumas (Alexander). MY MEMOIRS. Translated by E. M. WALLER. With Portraits. *In Six Volumes. Cr. 8vo. 6s. each.*
Volume I.

Dunn (J. T)., D.Sc., **and Mundella (V. A.).** GENERAL ELEMENTARY SCIENCE. With 114 Illustrations. *Second Edition. Cr. 8vo. 3s. 6d.*

Dunstan (A. E.), B.Sc. See Junior School Books and Textbooks of Science.

Durham (The Earl of). A REPORT ON CANADA. With an Introductory Note. *Demy 8vo. 4s. 6d. net.*

Dutt (W. A.). THE NORFOLK BROADS. With coloured Illustrations by FRANK SOUTHGATE. *Cr. 8vo. 6s.*
WILD LIFE IN EAST ANGLIA. With 16 Illustrations in colour by FRANK SOUTHGATE, R.B.A. *Second Edition. Demy 8vo. 7s. 6d. net.*
See also Little Guides.

Earle (John), Bishop of Salisbury. MICRO-COSMOGRAPHIE, OR A PIECE OF THE WORLD DISCOVERED. *Post 16mo. 2s net.*

Edmonds (Major J. E.). See W. B. Wood.

Edwards (Clement), M.P. RAILWAY NATIONALIZATION. *Second Edition Revised. Crown 8vo. 2s. 6d. net.*

Edwards (W. Douglas). See Commercial Series.

Egan (Pierce). See I.P.L.

Egerton (H. E.), M.A. A HISTORY OF BRITISH COLONIAL POLICY. New and Cheaper Issue. *Demy 8vo. 7s. 6d. net.*
A Colonial Edition is also published.

Ellaby (C. G.). See Little Guides.

Ellerton (F. G.). See S. J. Stone.

Ellwood (Thomas), THE HISTORY OF THE LIFE OF. Edited by C. G. CRUMP, M.A. *Cr. 8vo. 6s.*

Epictetus. See Aurelius.

Erasmus. A Book called in Latin EN-CHIRIDION MILITIS CHRISTIANI, and in English the Manual of the Christian Knight.
From the edition printed by Wynken de Worde, 1533. *Fcap. 8vo. 3s. 6d. net.*

Fairbrother (W. H.), M.A. THE PHILO-SOPHY OF T. H. GREEN. *Second Edition. Cr. 8vo. 3s. 6d.*

Farrer (Reginald). THE GARDEN OF ASIA. *Second Edition. Cr. 8vo. 6s.*

Fea (Allan). SOME BEAUTIES OF THE SEVENTEENTH CENTURY. With 82 Illustrations. *Second Edition. Demy 8vo. 12s. 6d. net.*

Ferrier (Susan). See Little Library.

Fidler (T. Claxton), M.Inst. C.E. See Books on Business.

Fielding (Henry). See Standard Library.

Finn (S. W.), M.A. See Junior Examination Series.

Firth (J. B.). See Little Guides.

Firth (C. H.), M.A. CROMWELL'S ARMY: A History of the English Soldier during the Civil Wars, the Commonwealth, and the Protectorate. *Cr. 8vo. 6s.*

Fisher (G. W.), M.A. ANNALS OF SHREWSBURY SCHOOL. Illustrated. *Demy 8vo.* 10s. 6d.

FitzGerald (Edward). THE RUBÁIYÁT OF OMAR KHAYYÁM. Printed from the Fifth and last Edition. With a Commentary by Mrs. Stephen Batson, and a Biography of Omar by E. D. Ross. *Cr. 8vo.* 6s. See also Miniature Library.

FitzGerald (H. P.). A CONCISE HANDBOOK OF CLIMBERS, TWINERS, AND WALL SHRUBS. Illustrated. *Fcap. 8vo.* 3s. 6d. net.

Fitzpatrick (S. A. O.). See Ancient Cities.

Flecker (W. H.), M.A., D.C.L., Headmaster of the Dean Close School, Cheltenham. THE STUDENT'S PRAYER BOOK. The Text of Morning and Evening Prayer and Litany. With an Introduction and Notes. *Cr. 8vo.* 2s. 6d.

Flux (A. W.), M.A., William Dow Professor of Political Economy in M'Gill University, Montreal. ECONOMIC PRINCIPLES. *Demy 8vo.* 7s. 6d. net.

Fortescue (Mrs. G.). See Little Books on Art.

Fraser (David). A MODERN CAMPAIGN; OR, WAR AND WIRELESS TELEGRAPHY IN THE FAR EAST. Illustrated. *Cr. 8vo.* 6s.
     A Colonial Edition is also published.

Fraser (J. F.). ROUND THE WORLD ON A WHEEL. With 100 Illustrations. *Fifth Edition Cr. 8vo.* 6s.

French (W.), M.A. See Textbooks of Science.

Freudenreich (Ed. von). DAIRY BACTERIOLOGY. A Short Manual for the Use of Students. Translated by J. R. Ainsworth Davis, M.A. *Second Edition.* Revised. *Cr. 8vo.* 2s. 6d.

Fulford (H. W.), M.A. See Churchman's Bible.

Gallaher (D.) and Stead (W. J.). THE COMPLETE RUGBY FOOTBALLER, ON THE NEW ZEALAND SYSTEM. With an Account of the Tour of the New Zealanders in England. With 35 Illustrations. *Demy 8vo.* 10s. 6d. net.

Gallichan (W. M.). See Little Guides.

Gambado (Geoffrey, Esq.). See I.P.L.

Gaskell (Mrs.). See Little Library and Standard Library.

Gasquet, the Right Rev. Abbot, O.S.B. See Antiquary's Books.

George (H. B.), M.A., Fellow of New College, Oxford. BATTLES OF ENGLISH HISTORY. With numerous Plans. *Fourth Edition.* Revised, with a new Chapter including the South African War. *Cr. 8vo.* 3s. 6d.

A HISTORICAL GEOGRAPHY OF THE BRITISH EMPIRE. *Second Edition. Cr. 8vo.* 3s. 6d.

Gibbins (H. de B.), Litt.D., M.A. INDUSTRY IN ENGLAND: HISTORICAL OUTLINES. With 5 Maps. *Fourth Edition. Demy 8vo.* 10s. 6d.

THE INDUSTRIAL HISTORY OF ENGLAND. *Thirteenth Edition.* Revised. With Maps and Plans. *Cr. 8vo.* 3s.

ENGLISH SOCIAL REFORMERS. *Second Edition. Cr. 8vo.* 2s. 6d.
     See also Commercial Series and R. A. Hadfield.

Gibbon (Edward). THE DECLINE AND FALL OF THE ROMAN EMPIRE. Edited with Notes, Appendices, and Maps, by J. B. Bury, M.A., Litt.D., Regius Professor of Greek at Cambridge. *In Seven Volumes. Demy 8vo. Gilt top, 8s. 6d. each. Also, Cr. 8vo.* 6s. *each.*

MEMOIRS OF MY LIFE AND WRITINGS. Edited by G. Birkbeck Hill, LL.D *Cr. 8vo.* 6s.
     See also Standard Library.

Gibson (E. C. S.), D.D., Lord Bishop of Gloucester. See Westminster Commentaries, Handbooks of Theology, and Oxford Biographies.

Gilbert (A. R.). See Little Books on Art.

Gloag (M. R.) and Wyatt (Kate M.). A BOOK OF ENGLISH GARDENS. With 24 Illustrations in Colour. *Demy 8vo.* 10s. 6d. net.

Godfrey (Elizabeth). A BOOK OF REMEMBRANCE. Edited by. *Fcap. 8vo.* 2s. 6d. net.

Godley (A. D.), M.A., Fellow of Magdalen College, Oxford. LYRA FRIVOLA. *Third Edition. Fcap. 8vo.* 2s. 6d.

VERSES TO ORDER. *Second Edition. Fcap. 8vo.* 2s. 6d.

SECOND STRINGS. *Fcap. 8vo.* 2s. 6d.

Goldsmith (Oliver). THE VICAR OF WAKEFIELD. *Fcap. 32mo.* With 10 Plates in Photogravure by Tony Johannot. *Leather,* 2s. 6d. *net.*
     See also I.P.L. and Standard Library.

Goodrich-Freer (A.). IN A SYRIAN SADDLE. *Demy 8vo.* 7s. 6d. net.
     A Colonial Edition is also published.

Gorst (Rt. Hon. Sir John). THE CHILDREN OF THE NATION. *Second Edition. Demy 8vo.* 7s. 6d. net.

Goudge (H. L.), M.A., Principal of Wells Theological College. See Westminster Commentaries.

Graham (P. Anderson). THE RURAL EXODUS. *Cr. 8vo.* 2s. 6d.

Granger (F. S.), M.A., Litt.D. PSYCHOLOGY. *Third Edition. Cr. 8vo.* 2s. 6d.

THE SOUL OF A CHRISTIAN. *Cr. 8vo.* 6s.

Gray (E. M'Queen). GERMAN PASSAGES FOR UNSEEN TRANSLATION. *Cr. 8vo.* 2s. 6d.

Gray (P. L.), B.Sc. THE PRINCIPLES OF MAGNETISM AND ELECTRICITY: an Elementary Text-Book. With 181 Diagrams. *Cr. 8vo.* 3s. 6d.

Green (G. Buckland), M.A., late Fellow of St. John's College, Oxon. NOTES ON GREEK AND LATIN SYNTAX. *Second Edition. Crown 8vo.* 3s. 6d.

Green (E. T.), M.A. See Churchman's Library.

Greenidge (A. H. J.), M.A. A HISTORY OF ROME: From 133-104 B.C. *Demy 8vo.* 10s. 6d. net.

Greenwell (Dora). See Miniature Library.

Gregory (R. A.). THE VAULT OF HEAVEN. A Popular Introduction to Astronomy. Illustrated. *Cr. 8vo.* 2s. 6d.

Gregory (Miss E. C.). See Library of Devotion.

Grubb (H. C.). See Textbooks of Technology.

Gwynn (M. L.). A BIRTHDAY BOOK. New and cheaper issue. *Royal 8vo.* 5s. net.

Haddon (A. C.), Sc.D., F.R.S. HEAD-HUNTERS BLACK, WHITE, AND BROWN. With many Illustrations and a Map. *Demy 8vo.* 15s.

Hadfield (R. A.) and Gibbins (H. de B.). A SHORTER WORKING DAY. *Cr. 8vo.* 2s. 6d.

Hall (R. N.) and Neal (W. G.). THE ANCIENT RUINS OF RHODESIA. Illustrated. *Second Edition, revised. Demy 8vo.* 10s. 6d. net.

Hall (R. N.). GREAT ZIMBABWE. With numerous Plans and Illustrations. *Second Edition. Royal 8vo.* 10s. 6d. net.

Hamilton (F. J.), D.D. See Byzantine Texts.

Hammond (J. L.). CHARLES JAMES FOX. *Demy 8vo.* 10s. 6d.

Hannay (D.). A SHORT HISTORY OF THE ROYAL NAVY, 1200-1688. Illustrated. *Demy 8vo.* 7s. 6d. each.

Hannay (James O.), M.A. THE SPIRIT AND ORIGIN OF CHRISTIAN MONASTICISM. *Cr. 8vo.* 6s.
THE WISDOM OF THE DESERT. *Fcap. 8vo.* 3s. 6d. net.

Hardie (Martin). See Connoisseur's Library.

Hare (A. T.), M.A. THE CONSTRUCTION OF LARGE INDUCTION COILS. With numerous Diagrams. *Demy 8vo.* 6s.

Harrison (Clifford). READING AND READERS. *Fcap. 8vo.* 2s. 6d.

Harvey (Alfred), M.B. See Ancient Cities.

Hawthorne (Nathaniel). See Little Library.
HEALTH, WEALTH AND WISDOM. *Cr. 8vo.* 1s. net.

Heath (Frank R.). See Little Guides.

Heath (Dudley). See Connoisseur's Library.

Hello (Ernest). STUDIES IN SAINT-SHIP. Translated from the French by V. M. CRAWFORD. *Fcap 8vo.* 3s. 6d.

Henderson (B. W.), Fellow of Exeter College, Oxford. THE LIFE AND PRINCIPATE OF THE EMPEROR NERO. Illustrated. *New and cheaper issue. Demy 8vo.* 7s. 6d. net.
AT INTERVALS. *Fcap 8vo.* 2s. 6d. net.

Henderson (T. F.). See Little Library and Oxford Biographies.

Henley (W. E.). ENGLISH LYRICS. *Second Edition. Cr. 8vo.* 2s. 6d. net.

Henley (W. E.) and Whibley (C.). A BOOK OF ENGLISH PROSE. *Cr. 8vo.* 2s. 6d. net.

Henson (H. H.), B.D., Canon of Westminster. APOSTOLIC CHRISTIANITY: As Illustrated by the Epistles of St. Paul to the Corinthians. *Cr. 8vo.* 6s.
LIGHT AND LEAVEN : HISTORICAL AND SOCIAL SERMONS. *Cr. 8vo.* 6s.

Herbert (George). See Library of Devotion.

Herbert of Cherbury (Lord). See Miniature Library.

Hewins (W. A. S.), B.A. ENGLISH TRADE AND FINANCE IN THE SEVENTEENTH CENTURY. *Cr. 8vo.* 2s. 6d.

Hewitt (Ethel M.) A GOLDEN DIAL. A Day Book of Prose and Verse. *Fcap. 8vo.* 2s. 6d. net.

Heywood (W.). PALIO AND PONTE : A Book of Tuscan Games. Illustrated. *Royal 8vo.* 21s net.
See also St. Francis of Assisi.

Hill (Clare). See Textbooks of Technology.

Hill (Henry), B.A., Headmaster of the Boy's High School, Worcester, Cape Colony. A SOUTH AFRICAN ARITHMETIC. *Cr. 8vo.* 3s. 6d.

Hind (C. Lewis). DAYS IN CORNWALL. With 16 Illustrations in Colour by WILLIAM PASCOE, and 20 Photographs. *Cr. 8vo.* 6s.
A Colonial Edition is also published.

Hirst (F. W.) See Books on Business.

Hoare (J. Douglas). ARCTIC EXPLORATION. With 18 Illustrations and Maps. *Demy 8vo.* 7s. 6d. net.

Hobhouse (L. T.), Fellow of C.C.C., Oxford. THE THEORY OF KNOWLEDGE. *Demy 8vo.* 10s. 6d. net.

Hobson (J. A.), M.A. INTERNATIONAL TRADE : A Study of Economic Principles. *Cr. 8vo.* 2s. 6d. net.
PROBLEMS OF POVERTY. *Sixth Edition. Cr. 8vo.* 2s. 6d.
THE PROBLEM OF THE UNEMPLOYED. *Third Edition. Cr. 8vo.* 2s. 6d.

Hodgkin (T.), D.C.L. See Leaders of Religion.

Hodgson (Mrs. W.) HOW TO IDENTIFY OLD CHINESE PORCELAIN. *Second Edition. Post 8vo.* 6s.

Hogg (Thomas Jefferson). SHELLEY AT OXFORD. With an Introduction by R. A. STREATFEILD. *Fcap. 8vo.* 2s. net.

Holden-Stone (G. de). See Books on Business.

Holdich (Sir T. H.), K.C.I.E. THE INDIAN BORDERLAND : being a Personal Record of Twenty Years. Illustrated. *Demy 8vo.* 10s. 6d. net.
A Colonial Edition is also published.

Holdsworth (W. S.), M.A. A HISTORY OF ENGLISH LAW. *In Two Volumes. Vol. I. Demy 8vo.* 10s. 6d. net.

Holland (H. Scott), Canon of St. Paul's See Library of Devotion.

Holt (Emily). THE SECRET OF POPU-LARITY: How to Achieve Social Success. *Cr. 8vo.* 3s. 6d. net.
A Colonial Edition is also published.

Holyoake (G. J.). THE CO-OPERATIVE MOVEMENT TO-DAY. *Fourth Edition. Cr. 8vo.* 2s. 6d.

Hone (Nathaniel J.). See Antiquary's Books.

Hoppner. See Little Galleries.

Horace. See Classical Translations.

Horsburgh (E. L. S.), M.A. WATERLOO: A Narrative and Criticism. With Plans. *Second Edition. Cr. 8vo.* 5s.
See also Oxford Biographies.

Horth (A. C.). See Textbooks of Technology.

Horton (R. F.), D.D. See Leaders of Religion.

Hosie (Alexander). MANCHURIA. With Illustrations and a Map. *Second Edition. Demy 8vo.* 7s. 6d. net.
A Colonial Edition is also published.

How (F. D.). SIX GREAT SCHOOL-MASTERS. With Portraits and Illustrations. *Second Edition. Demy 8vo.* 7s. 6d.

Howell (A. G. Ferrers). FRANCISCAN DAYS. Translated and arranged by. *Cr. 8vo.* 3s. 6d. net.

Howell (G.). TRADE UNIONISM—NEW AND OLD. *Fourth Edition. Cr. 8vo.* 2s. 6d.

Hudson (Robert). MEMORIALS OF A WARWICKSHIRE PARISH. Illustrated. *Demy 8vo.* 15s. net.

Huggins (Sir William), K.C.B., O.M., D.C.L., F.R.S. THE ROYAL SOCIETY; OR, SCIENCE IN THE STATE AND IN THE SCHOOLS. With 25 Illustrations. *Wide Royal 8vo.* 4s. 6d. net.

Hughes (C. E.). THE PRAISE OF SHAKESPEARE. An English Anthology. With a Preface by SIDNEY LEE. *Demy 8vo.* 3s. 6d. net.

Hughes (Thomas). TOM BROWN'S SCHOOLDAYS. With an Introduction and Notes by VERNON RENDALL. *Leather. Royal 32mo.* 2s. 6d. net.

Hutchinson (Horace G.) THE NEW FOREST. Illustrated in colour with 50 Pictures by WALTER TYNDALE and 4 by LUCY KEMP-WELCH. *Third Edition. Cr. 8vo.* 6s.

Hutton (A. W.), M.A. See Leaders of Religion and Library of Devotion.

Hutton (Edward). THE CITIES OF UMBRIA. With many Illustrations, of which 20 are in Colour, by A. PISA. *Second Edition. Cr. 8vo.* 6s.
A Colonial Edition is also published.

THE CITIES OF SPAIN. *Second Edition.* With many Illustrations, of which 24 are in Colour, by A. W. RIMINGTON. *Demy 8vo.* 7s. 6d. net.

FLORENCE AND NORTHERN TUS-CANY. With Coloured Illustrations by WILLIAM PARKINSON. *Cr. 8vo.* 6s.
A Colonial Edition is also published.

ENGLISH LOVE POEMS. Edited with an Introduction. *Fcap. 8vo.* 3s. 6d. net.

Hutton (R. H.). See Leaders of Religion.

Hutton (W. H.), M.A. THE LIFE OF SIR THOMAS MORE. With Portraits. *Second Edition. Cr. 8vo.* 5s.
See also Leaders of Religion.

Hyde (A. G.) GEORGE HERBERT AND HIS TIMES. With 32 Illustrations. *Demy 8vo.* 10s. 6d. net.

Hyett (F. A.). A SHORT HISTORY OF FLORENCE. *Demy 8vo.* 7s. 6d. net.

Ibsen (Henrik). BRAND. A Drama. Translated by WILLIAM WILSON. *Third Edition. Cr. 8vo.* 3s. 6d.

Inge (W. R.), M.A., Fellow and Tutor of Hertford College, Oxford. CHRISTIAN MYSTICISM. The Bampton Lectures for 1899. *Demy 8vo.* 12s. 6d. net. See also Library of Devotion.

Innes (A. D.), M.A. A HISTORY OF THE BRITISH IN INDIA. With Maps and Plans. *Cr. 8vo.* 6s.

ENGLAND UNDER THE TUDORS. With Maps. *Demy 8vo.* 10s. 6d. net.

Jackson (C. E.), B.A. See Textbooks of Science.

Jackson (S.), M.A. See Commercial Series.

Jackson (F. Hamilton). See Little Guides.

Jacob (F.), M.A. See Junior Examination Series.

James (W. H. N.), A.R.C.S., A.I.E.E. See Textbooks of Technology.

Jeans (J. Stephen). TRUSTS, POOLS, AND CORNERS. *Cr. 8vo.* 2s. 6d.
See also Books on Business.

Jeffreys (D. Gwyn). DOLLY'S THEATRI-CALS. Described and Illustrated with 24 Coloured Pictures. *Super Royal 16mo.* 2s.6d.

Jenks (E.), M.A., Reader of Law in the University of Oxford. ENGLISH LOCAL GOVERNMENT. *Second Edition. Cr. 8vo.* 2s. 6d.

Jenner (Mrs. H.). See Little Books on Art.

Jennings (Oscar), M.D., Member of the Bibliographical Society. EARLY WOOD-CUT INITIALS, containing over thirteen hundred Reproductions of Pictorial Letters of the Fifteenth and Sixteenth Centuries. *Demy 4to.* 21s. net.

Jessopp (Augustus), D.D. See Leaders of Religion.

Jevons (F. B.), M.A., Litt.D., Principal of Bishop Hatfield's Hall, Durham. RE-LIGION IN EVOLUTION. *Cr. 8vo.* 3s. 6d. net.
See also Churchman's Library and Hand-books of Theology.

Johnson (Mrs. Barham). WILLIAM BOD-HAM DONNE AND HIS FRIENDS. Illustrated. *Demy 8vo.* 10s. 6d. net.

Johnston (Sir H. H.), K.C.B. BRITISH CENTRAL AFRICA. With nearly 200 Illustrations and Six Maps. *Third Edition. Cr. 4to. 18s. net.*
A Colonial Edition is also published.

Jones (R. Crompton), M.A. POEMS OF THE INNER LIFE. Selected by. *Thirteenth Edition. Fcap. 8vo. 2s. 6d. net.*

Jones (H.). See Commercial Series.

Jones (H. F.). See Textbooks of Science.

Jones (L. A. Atherley), K.C., M.P. THE MINERS' GUIDE TO THE COAL MINES REGULATION ACTS. *Cr. 8vo. 2s. 6d. net.*
COMMERCE IN WAR. *Royal 8vo. 21s. net.*

Jonson (Ben). See Standard Library.

Juliana (Lady) of Norwich. REVELATIONS OF DIVINE LOVE. Ed. by GRACE WARRACK. *Second Edit. Cr. 8vo. 3s. 6d.*

Juvenal. See Classical Translations.

'Kappa.' LET YOUTH BUT KNOW: A Plea for Reason in Education. *Cr. 8vo. 3s. 6d. net.*

Kaufmann (M.). SOCIALISM AND MODERN THOUGHT. *Second Edition. Cr. 8vo. 2s. 6d. net.*

Keating (J. F.), D.D. THE AGAPE AND THE EUCHARIST. *Cr. 8vo. 3s. 6d.*

Keats (John). THE POEMS OF. Edited with Introduction and Notes by E. de Selincourt, M.A. *Second Edition. Demy 8vo. 7s. 6d. net.*
REALMS OF GOLD. Selections from the Works of. *Fcap. 8vo. 3s. 6d. net.*
See also Little Library and Standard Library.

Keble (John). THE CHRISTIAN YEAR. With an Introduction and Notes by W. LOCK, D.D., Warden of Keble College. Illustrated by R. ANNING BELL. *Third Edition. Fcap. 8vo. 3s. 6d. ; padded morocco, 5s.*
See also Library of Devotion.

Kelynack (T. N.), M.D., M.R.C.P., Hon. Secretary of the Society for the Study of Inebriety. THE DRINK PROBLEM IN ITS MEDICO-SOCIOLOGICAL ASPECT. Edited by. With 2 Diagrams. *Demy 8vo. 7s. 6d. net.*

Kempis (Thomas à). THE IMITATION OF CHRIST. With an Introduction by DEAN FARRAR. Illustrated by C. M. GERE. *Third Edition. Fcap. 8vo. 3s. 6d.; padded morocco. 5s.*
Also Translated by C. BIGG, D.D. *Cr. 8vo. 3s. 6d.* See also Library of Devotion and Standard Library.

Kennedy (Bart.). THE GREEN SPHINX. *Cr. 8vo. 3s. 6d. net.*
A Colonial Edition is also published.

Kennedy (James Houghton), D.D., Assistant Lecturer in Divinity in the University of Dublin. ST. PAUL'S SECOND AND THIRD EPISTLES TO THE CORINTHIANS. With Introduction, Dissertations and Notes. *Cr. 8vo. 6s.*

Kimmins (C. W.), M.A. THE CHEMISTRY OF LIFE AND HEALTH. Illustrated. *Cr. 8vo. 2s. 6d.*

Kinglake (A. W.). See Little Library.

Kipling (Rudyard). BARRACK-ROOM BALLADS. *80th Thousand. Twenty-second Edition. Cr. 8vo. 6s.*
A Colonial Edition is also published.
THE SEVEN SEAS. *63rd Thousand. Eleventh Edition. Cr. 8vo. 6s.*
A Colonial Edition is also published.
THE FIVE NATIONS. *41st Thousand. Second Edition. Cr. 8vo. 6s.*
A Colonial Edition is also published.
DEPARTMENTAL DITTIES. *Sixteenth Edition. Cr. 8vo. 6s.*
A Colonial Edition is also published.

Knight (Albert E.). THE COMPLETE CRICKETER. Illus. *Demy 8vo. 7s. 6d. net.*
A Colonial Edition is also published.

Knight (H. J. C.), M.A. See Churchman's Bible.

Knowling (R. J.), M.A., Professor of New Testament Exegesis at King's College, London. See Westminster Commentaries.

Lamb (Charles and Mary), THE WORKS OF. Edited by E. V. LUCAS. Illustrated *In Seven Volumes. Demy 8vo. 7s. 6d. each.*
See also Little Library and E. V. Lucas.

Lambert (F. A. H.). See Little Guides.

Lambros (Professor). See Byzantine Texts.

Lane-Poole (Stanley). A HISTORY OF EGYPT IN THE MIDDLE AGES. Fully Illustrated. *Cr. 8vo. 6s.*

Langbridge (F.), M.A. BALLADS OF THE BRAVE: Poems of Chivalry, Enterprise, Courage, and Constancy. *Third Edition. Cr. 8vo. 2s. 6d.*

Law (William). See Library of Devotion and Standard Library.

Leach (Henry). THE DUKE OF DEVONSHIRE. A Biography. With 12 Illustrations. *Demy 8vo. 12s. 6d. net.*
See also James Braid.
GREAT GOLFERS IN THE MAKING. With 34 Portraits. *Demy 8vo. 7s. 6d. net.*

Le Braz (Anatole). THE LAND OF PARDONS. Translated by FRANCES M. GOSTLING. Illustrated in colour. *Second Edition. Demy 8vo. 7s. 6d. net.*

Lee (Captain L. Melville). A HISTORY OF POLICE IN ENGLAND. *Cr. 8vo. 3s. 6d. net.*

Leigh (Percival). THE COMIC ENGLISH GRAMMAR. Embellished with upwards of 50 characteristic Illustrations by JOHN LEECH. *Post 16mo. 2s. 6d. net.*

Lewes (V. B.), M.A. AIR AND WATER. Illustrated. *Cr. 8vo. 2s. 6d.*

Lewis (Mrs. Gwyn). A CONCISE HANDBOOK OF GARDEN SHRUBS. Illustrated. *Fcap. 8vo. 3s. 6d. net.*

Lisle (Fortunée de). See Little Books on Art.

Littlehales (H.). See Antiquary's Books.

Lock (Walter), D.D., Warden of Keble College. ST. PAUL, THE MASTER-BUILDER. *Second Ed. Cr. 8vo. 3s. 6d.*
THE BIBLE AND CHRISTIAN LIFE. *Cr. 8vo. 6s.*
See also Leaders of Religion and Library of Devotion.

Locker (F.). See Little Library.

Lodge (Sir Oliver), F.R.S. THE SUBSTANCE OF FAITH ALLIED WITH SCIENCE: A Catechism for Parents and Teachers. *Seventh Ed. Cr. 8vo. 2s. net.*

Lofthouse (W. F.), M.A. ETHICS AND ATONEMENT. With a Frontispiece. *Demy 8vo. 5s. net.*

Longfellow (H. W.). See Little Library.

Lorimer (George Horace). LETTERS FROM A SELF-MADE MERCHANT TO HIS SON. *Sixteenth Edition. Cr. 8vo. 3s. 6d.*
A Colonial Edition is also published.

OLD GORGON GRAHAM. *Second Edition. Cr. 8vo. 6s.*
A Colonial Edition is also published.

Lover (Samuel). See I. P. L.

E. V. L. and C. L. G. ENGLAND DAY BY DAY : Or, The Englishman's Handbook to Efficiency. Illustrated by GEORGE MORROW. *Fourth Edition. Fcap. 4to. 1s. net.*

Lucas (E. V.). THE LIFE OF CHARLES LAMB. With 25 Illustrations. *Third Edition. Demy 8vo. 7s. 6d. net.*
A Colonial Edition is also published.

A WANDERER IN HOLLAND. With many Illustrations, of which 20 are in Colour by HERBERT MARSHALL. *Seventh Edition. Cr. 8vo. 6s.*
A Colonial Edition is also published.

A WANDERER IN LONDON. With 16 Illustrations in Colour by NELSON DAWSON, and 36 other Illustrations. *Fifth Edition. Cr. 8vo. 6s.*
A Colonial Edition is also published.

FIRESIDE AND SUNSHINE. *Third Edition. Fcap. 8vo. 5s.*

THE OPEN ROAD : a Little Book for Wayfarers. *Eleventh Edition. Fcap. 8vo. 5s. ; India Paper, 7s. 6d.*

THE FRIENDLY TOWN : a Little Book for the Urbane. *Third Edition. Fcap. 8vo. 5s. ; India Paper, 7s. 6d.*

Lucian. See Classical Translations.

Lyde (L. W.), M.A. See Commercial Series.

Lydon (Noel S.). See Junior School Books .

Lyttelton (Hon. Mrs. A.). WOMEN AND THEIR WORK. *Cr. 8vo. 2s. 6d.*

Macaulay (Lord). CRITICAL AND HISTORICAL ESSAYS. Edited by F. C. MONTAGUE, M.A. *Three Volumes. Cr. 8vo. 18s.*
The only edition of this book completely annotated.

M'Allen (J. E B.), M.A. See Commercial Series.

MacCulloch (J. A.). See Churchman's Library.

MacCunn (Florence A.). MARY STUART. With over 60 Illustrations, including a Frontispiece in Photogravure. *Second and Cheaper Edition. Cr. 8vo. 6s.*
See also Leaders of Religion.

McDermott (E. R.). See Books on Business.

M'Dowall (A. S.). See Oxford Biographies.

Mackay (A. M.). See Churchman's Library.

Macklin (Herbert W.), M.A. See Antiquary's Books.

Mackenzie (W. Leslie), M.A., M.D., D.P.H., etc. THE HEALTH OF THE SCHOOL CHILD. *Cr. 8vo. 2s. 6d.*

Mdlle Mori (Author of). ST. CATHERINE OF SIENA AND HER TIMES. With 28 Illustrations. *Demy 8vo. 7s. 6d. net.*

Magnus (Laurie), M.A. A PRIMER OF WORDSWORTH. *Cr. 8vo. 2s. 6d.*

Mahaffy (J. P.), Litt.D. A HISTORY OF THE EGYPT OF THE PTOLEMIES. Fully Illustrated. *Cr. 8vo. 6s.*

Maitland (F. W.), LL.D., Downing Professor of the Laws of England in the University of Cambridge. CANON LAW IN ENGLAND. *Royal 8vo. 7s. 6d.*

Malden (H. E.), M.A. ENGLISH RECORDS. A Companion to the History of England. *Cr. 8vo. 3s. 6d.*

THE ENGLISH CITIZEN : HIS RIGHTS AND DUTIES. *Seventh Edition. Cr. 8vo. 1s. 6d.*
See also School Histories.

Marchant (E. C.), M.A., Fellow of Peterhouse, Cambridge. A GREEK ANTHOLOGY *Second Edition. Cr. 8vo. 3s. 6d.*
See also A. M. Cook.

Marr (J. E.), F.R.S., Fellow of St John's College, Cambridge. THE SCIENTIFIC STUDY OF SCENERY. *Second Edition. Illustrated. Cr. 8vo. 6s.*

AGRICULTURAL GEOLOGY. Illustrated. *Cr. 8vo. 6s.*

Marriott (J. A. R.). FALKLAND AND HIS TIMES. With 20 Illustrations. *Second Ed. Demy 8vo. 7s. 6d. net.*
A Colonial Edition is also published.

Marvell (Andrew). See Little Library.

Masefield (John). SEA LIFE IN NELSON'S TIME. Illustrated. *Cr. 8vo. 3s. 6d. net.*

ON THE SPANISH MAIN. With 22 Illustrations and a Map. *Demy 8vo. 10s. 6d. net.*

A SAILOR'S GARLAND. Edited and Selected by. *Cr. 8vo. 3s. 6d. net.*

Maskell (A.). See Connoisseur's Library.

Mason (A. J.), D.D. See Leaders of Religion.

Massee (George). THE EVOLUTION OF PLANT LIFE : Lower Forms. Illustrated. *Cr. 8vo. 2s. 6d.*

Masterman (C. F. G.), M.A., M.P. TENNYSON AS A RELIGIOUS TEACHER. *Cr. 8vo. 6s.*

Matheson (Mrs. E. F.). COUNSELS OF LIFE. *Fcap. 8vo. 2s. 6d. net.*

May (Phil). THE PHIL MAY ALBUM. *Second Edition. 4to. 1s. net.*

Mellows (Emma S.). A SHORT STORY OF ENGLISH LITERATURE. *Cr. 8vo. 3s. 6d.*

Methuen (A. M. S.). THE TRAGEDY OF SOUTH AFRICA. *Cr. 8vo. 2s. net. Also Cr. 8vo. 3d. net.*
A revised and enlarged edition of the author's 'Peace or War in South Africa.'

ENGLAND'S RUIN : DISCUSSED IN SIX-
TEEN LETTERS TO THE RIGHT HON.
JOSEPH CHAMBERLAIN, M.P. *Seventh Edi-
tion. Cr. 8vo. 3d. net.*

Miles (Eustace), M.A. LIFE AFTER
LIFE, OR, THE THEORY OF REIN-
CARNATION. *Cr. 8vo. 2s. 6d. net.*

Millais (J. G.). THE LIFE AND LET-
TERS OF SIR JOHN EVERETT
MILLAIS, President of the Royal Academy.
With many Illustrations, of which 2 are in
Photogravure. *New Edition. Demy 8vo.
7s. 6d. net.*
  See also Little Galleries.

Millin (G. F.). PICTORIAL GARDEN-
ING. Illustrated. *Cr. 8vo. 3s. 6d. net.*

Millis (C. T.), M.I.M.E. See Textbooks of
Technology.

Milne (J. G.), M.A. A HISTORY OF
ROMAN EGYPT. Fully Illus. *Cr. 8vo. 6s.*

Milton (John). A DAY BOOK OF.
Edited by R. F. Towndrow. *Fcap. 8vo.
3s. 6d. net.*
  See also Little Library and Standard
Library.

Minchin (H. C.), M.A. See R. Peel.

Mitchell (P. Chalmers), M.A. OUTLINES
OF BIOLOGY. Illustrated. *Second Edition. Cr. 8vo. 6s.*

Mitton (G. E.). JANE AUSTEN AND
HER TIMES. With many Portraits and
Illustrations. *Second and Cheaper Edition.
Cr. 8vo. 6s.*
  A Colonial Edition is also published.

Moffat (Mary M.). QUEEN LOUISA OF
PRUSSIA. With 20 Illustrations. *Fourth
Edition. Demy 8vo. 7s. 6d. net.*

' Moil (A.).' See Books on Business.

Moir (D. M.). See Little Library.

Molinos (Dr. Michael de). See Library of
Devotion.

Money (L. G. Chiozza), M.P. RICHES
AND POVERTY. *Third Edition. Demy
8vo. 5s. net.*

Montagu (Henry), Earl of Manchester. See
Library of Devotion.

Montaigne. A DAY BOOK OF. Edited
by C. F. Pond. *Fcap. 8vo. 3s. 6d. net.*

Montmorency (J. E. G. de), B.A., LL.B.
THOMAS À KEMPIS, HIS AGE AND
BOOK. With 22 Illustrations. *Second
Edition. Demy 8vo. 7s. 6d. net.*

Moore (H. E.). BACK TO THE LAND.
An Inquiry into Rural Depopulation. *Cr.
8vo. 2s. 6d.*

Moorhouse (E. Hallam). NELSON'S
LADY HAMILTON. With 51 Portraits.
Second Edition. Demy 8vo. 7s. 6d. net.
  A Colonial Edition is also published.

Moran (Clarence G.). See Books on Business.

More (Sir Thomas). See Standard Library.

Morfill (W. R.), Oriel College, Oxford. A
HISTORY OF RUSSIA FROM PETER
THE GREAT TO ALEXANDER II.
With Maps and Plans. *Cr. 8vo. 3s. 6d.*

Morich (R. J.), late of Clifton College. See
School Examination Series.

Morris (J.). THE MAKERS OF JAPAN.
With 24 Illustrations. *Demy 8vo. 12s. 6d.
net.*
  A Colonial Edition is also published.

Morris (J. E.). See Little Guides.

Morton (Miss Anderson). See Miss Brodrick.

Moule (H. C. G.), D.D., Lord Bishop of Durham. See Leaders of Religion.

Muir (M. M. Pattison), M.A. THE
CHEMISTRY OF FIRE. Illustrated.
Cr. 8vo. 2s. 6d.

Mundella (V. A.), M.A. See J. T. Dunn.

Munro (R.), LL.D. See Antiquary's Books.

Naval Officer (A). See I. P. L.

Neal (W. G.). See R. N. Hall.

Newman (Ernest). HUGO WOLF.
Demy 8vo. 6s.

Newman (George), M.D., D.P.H., F.R.S.E.,
Lecturer on Public Health at St. Bartholo-
mew's Hospital, and Medical Officer of
Health of the Metropolitan Borough of
Finsbury. INFANT MORTALITY, A
SOCIAL PROBLEM. With 16 Diagrams.
Demy 8vo. 7s. 6d. net.

Newman (J. H.) and others. See Library
of Devotion.

Nichols (J. B. B.). See Little Library.

Nicklin (T.), M.A. EXAMINATION
PAPERS IN THUCYDIDES. *Cr. 8vo. 2s.*

Nimrod. See I. P. L.

Norgate (G. Le Grys). THE LIFE OF
SIR WALTER SCOTT. Illustrated.
Demy 8vo. 7s. 6d. net.

Norregaard (B. W.). THE GREAT
SIEGE : The Investment and Fall of Port
Arthur. Illustrated. *Demy 8vo. 10s. 6d. net.*

Norway (A. H.). NAPLES. With 25 Coloured Illustrations by MAURICE GREIFFEN-
HAGEN. *Second Edition. Cr. 8vo. 6s.*

Novalis. THE DISCIPLES AT SAÏS AND
OTHER FRAGMENTS. Edited by Miss
UNA BIRCH. *Fcap. 8vo. 3s. 6d.*

Oldfield (W. J.), M.A., Prebendary of
Lincoln. A PRIMER OF RELIGION.
BASED ON THE CATECHISM OF THE CHURCH
OF ENGLAND. *Fcap. 8vo. 2s. 6d.*

Oldham (F. M.), B.A. See Textbooks of
Science.

Oliphant (Mrs.). See Leaders of Religion.

Oman (C. W. C.), M.A., Fellow of All Souls',
Oxford. A HISTORY OF THE ART
OF WAR. The Middle Ages, from the
Fourth to the Fourteenth Century. Illus-
trated. *Demy 8vo. 10s. 6d. net.*

Ottley (R. L.), D.D. See Handbooks of
Theology and Leaders of Religion.

Overton (J. H.). See Leaders of Religion.

Owen (Douglas). See Books on Business.

Oxford (M. N.), of Guy's Hospital. A HAND-
BOOK OF NURSING. *Fourth Edition.
Cr. 8vo. 3s. 6d.*

Pakes (W. C. C.). THE SCIENCE OF
HYGIENE. Illustrated. *Demy 8vo. 15s.*

Palmer (Frederick). WITH KUROKI IN
MANCHURIA. Illustrated. *Third
Edition. Demy 8vo. 7s. 6d. net.*

Parker (Gilbert). A LOVER'S DIARY. *Fcap. 8vo.* 5s.

Parkes (A. K.). SMALL LESSONS ON GREAT TRUTHS. *Fcap. 8vo.* 1s. 6d.

Parkinson (John). PARADISI IN SOLE PARADISUS TERRESTRIS, OR A GARDEN OF ALL SORTS OF PLEASANT FLOWERS. *Folio.* £3, 3s. *net.*

Parmenter (John). HELIO-TROPES, OR NEW POSIES FOR SUNDIALS, 1625. Edited by PERCIVAL LANDON. *Quarto.* 3s. 6d. *net.*

Parmentier (Prof. Leon). See Byzantine Texts.

Parsons (Mrs. Clement). GARRICK AND HIS CIRCLE. With 36 Illustrations. *Second Edition. Demy 8vo.* 12s. 6d. *net.*
    A Colonial Edition is also published.

Pascal. See Library of Devotion.

Paston (George). SOCIAL CARICATURE IN THE EIGHTEENTH CENTURY. With over 200 Illustrations. *Imperial Quarto.* £2, 12s. 6d. *net.*
    See also Little Books on Art and I.P.L.

LADY MARY WORTLEY MONTAGU. With 24 Portraits and Illustrations. *Second Edition. Demy 8vo.* 15s. *net.*
    A Colonial Edition is also published.

Paterson (W. R.) (Benjamin Swift). LIFE'S QUESTIONINGS. *Cr. 8vo.* 3s. 6d. *net.*

Patterson (A. H.). NOTES OF AN EAST COAST NATURALIST. Illustrated in Colour by F. SOUTHGATE. *Second Edition. Cr. 8vo.* 6s.

NATURE IN EASTERN NORFOLK. A series of observations on the Birds, Fishes, Mammals, Reptiles, and Stalk-eyed Crustaceans found in that neighbourhood, with a list of the species. With 12 Illustrations in colour, by FRANK SOUTHGATE. *Second Edition. Cr. 8vo.* 6s.

Peacock (N.). See Little Books on Art.

Peake (C. M. A.), F.R.H.S. A CONCISE HANDBOOK OF GARDEN ANNUAL AND BIENNIAL PLANTS. With 24 Illustrations. *Fcap. 8vo.* 3s. 6d. *net.*

Pe██ (Robert), and **Minchin (H. C.),** M.A. OXFORD. With 100 Illustrations in Colour. *Cr. 8vo.* 6s.

Peel (Sidney), late Fellow of Trinity College, Oxford, and Secretary to the Royal Commission on the Licensing Laws. PRACTICAL LICENSING REFORM. *Second Edition. Cr. 8vo.* 1s. 6d.

Petrie (W. M. Flinders), D.C.L., LL.D., Professor of Egyptology at University College. A HISTORY OF EGYPT, FROM THE EARLIEST TIMES TO THE PRESENT DAY. Fully Illustrated. *In six volumes. Cr. 8vo.* 6s. each.

VOL. I. PREHISTORIC TIMES TO XVITH DYNASTY. *Sixth Edition.*

VOL. II. THE XVIITH AND XVIIITH DYNASTIES. *Fourth Edition.*

VOL. III. XIXTH TO XXXTH DYNASTIES.

VOL. IV. THE EGYPT OF THE PTOLEMIES. J. P. MAHAFFY, Litt. D.

VOL. V. ROMAN EGYPT. J. G. MILNE, M.A.

VOL. VI. EGYPT IN THE MIDDLE AGES. STANLEY LANE-POOLE, M.A.

RELIGION AND CONSCIENCE IN ANCIENT EGYPT. Illustrated. *Cr. 8vo.* 2s. 6d.

SYRIA AND EGYPT, FROM THE TELL EL AMARNA TABLETS. *Cr. 8vo.* 2s. 6d.

EGYPTIAN TALES. Illustrated by TRISTRAM ELLIS. *In Two Volumes. Cr. 8vo.* 3s. 6d. each.

EGYPTIAN DECORATIVE ART. With 120 Illustrations. *Cr. 8vo.* 3s. 6d.

Phillips (W. A.). See Oxford Biographies.

Phillpotts (Eden). MY DEVON YEAR. With 38 Illustrations by J. LEY PETHYBRIDGE. *Second and Cheaper Edition. Large Cr. 8vo.* 6s.

UP ALONG AND DOWN ALONG. Illustrated by CLAUDE SHEPPERSON. *Cr. 4to.* 5s. *net.*
    A volume of poems.

Plarr (Victor G.). See School Histories.

Plato. See Standard Library.

Plautus. THE CAPTIVI. Edited, with an Introduction, Textual Notes, and a Commentary, by W. M. LINDSAY, Fellow of Jesus College, Oxford. *Demy 8vo.* 10s. 6d. *net.*

Plowden-Wardlaw (J. T.), B.A., King's College, Cambridge. See School Examination Series.

Podmore (Frank). MODERN SPIRITUALISM. *Two Volumes. Demy 8vo.* 21s. *net.*
    A History and a Criticism.

Poer (J. Patrick Le). A MODERN LEGIONARY. *Cr. 8vo.* 6s.

Pollard (Alice). See Little Books on Art.

Pollard (A. W.). OLD PICTURE BOOKS. Illustrated. *Demy 8vo.* 7s. 6d. *net.*

Pollard (Eliza F.). See Little Books on Art.

Pollock (David), M.I.N.A. See Books on Business.

Potter (M. C.), M.A., F.L.S. A TEXT-BOOK OF AGRICULTURAL BOTANY. Illustrated. *Second Edition. Cr. 8vo.* 4s. 6d.

Power (J. O'Connor). THE MAKING OF AN ORATOR. *Cr. 8vo.* 6s.

Prance (G.). See R. Wyon.

Prescott (O. L.). ABOUT MUSIC, AND WHAT IT IS MADE OF. *Cr. 8vo.* 3s. 6d. *net.*

Price (L. L.), M.A., Fellow of Oriel College, Oxon. A HISTORY OF ENGLISH POLITICAL ECONOMY. *Fourth Edition. Cr. 8vo.* 2s. 6d.

Primrose (Deborah). A MODERN BŒOTIA. *Cr. 8vo.* 6s.

Protheroe (Ernest). THE DOMINION OF MAN. GEOGRAPHY IN ITS HUMAN ASPECT. With 32 full-page Illustrations. *Cr. 8vo.* 2s.

Pugin and **Rowlandson.** THE MICRO-COSM OF LONDON, OR LONDON IN MINIATURE. With 104 Illustrations in colour. *In Three Volumes. Small 4to.* £3, 3s. net.

'Q' (A. T. Quiller Couch). THE GOLDEN POMP. A PROCESSION OF ENGLISH LYRICS. *Second Edition. Cr. 8vo.* 2s. 6d. net.

Quevedo Villegas. See Miniature Library.

G.R. and **E.S.** THE WOODHOUSE CORRESPONDENCE. *Cr. 8vo.* 6s.
A Colonial Edition is also published.

Rackham (R. B.), M.A. See Westminster Commentaries.

Ragg (Laura M.). THE WOMEN-ARTISTS OF BOLOGNA. With 20 Illustrations. *Demy 8vo.* 7s. 6d. net.

Ragg (Lonsdale). B.D., Oxon. DANTE AND HIS ITALY. With 32 Illustrations largely from contemporary Frescoes and Documents. *Demy 8vo.* 12s. 6d. net.

Rahtz (F. J.), M.A., B.Sc., Lecturer in English at Merchant Venturers' Technical College, Bristol. HIGHER ENGLISH. *Cr. 8vo.* 3s. 6d.

Randolph (B. W.), D.D. See Library of Devotion.

Rannie (D. W.), M.A. A STUDENT'S HISTORY OF SCOTLAND. *Cr. 8vo.* 3s. 6d.

Rashdall (Hastings), M.A., Fellow and Tutor of New College, Oxford. DOCTRINE AND DEVELOPMENT. *Cr. 8vo.* 6s.

Raven (J. J.), D.D. See Antiquary's Books.

Rawstorne (Lawrence, Esq.). See I.P.L.

Raymond (Walter). See School Histories.

A Real Paddy. See I.P.L.

Reason (W.), M.A. UNIVERSITY AND SOCIAL SETTLEMENTS. *Cr. 8vo.* 2s. 6d.

Redpath (H. A.), M.A. See Westminster Commentaries.

Reynolds. See Little Galleries.

Rhoades (J.F.). See Simplified French Texts.

Rhodes (W. E.). See School Histories.

Rieu (H.), M.A. See Simplified French Texts.

Roberts (M. E.). See C. C. Channer.

Robertson (A.), D.D., Lord Bishop of Exeter. REGNUM DEI. The Bampton Lectures of 1901. *Demy 8vo.* 7s. 6d. net.

Robertson (C. Grant). M.A., Fellow of All Souls' College, Oxford, Examiner in the Honours School of Modern History, Oxford, 1901-1904. SELECT STATUTES, CASES, AND CONSTITUTIONAL DOCUMENTS, 1660-1832. *Demy 8vo.* 10s. 6d. net.

Robertson (C. Grant) and **Bartholomew (J. G.),** F.R.S.E., F.R.G.S. A HISTORICAL AND MODERN ATLAS OF THE BRITISH EMPIRE. *Demy Quarto.* 4s. 6d. net.

Robertson (Sir G. S.), K.C.S.I. CHITRAL: THE STORY OF A MINOR SIEGE. *Third Edition.* Illustrated. *Cr. 8vo.* 2s. 6d. net.

Robinson (A. W.), M.A. See Churchman's Bible.

Robinson (Cecilia). THE MINISTRY OF DEACONESSES. With an Introduction by the late Archbishop of Canterbury. *Cr. 8vo.* 3s. 6d.

Robinson (F. S.). See Connoisseur's Library.

Rochefoucauld (La). See Little Library.

Rodwell (G.), B.A. NEW TESTAMENT GREEK. A Course for Beginners. With a Preface by WALTER LOCK, D.D., Warden of Keble College. *Fcap. 8vo.* 3s. 6d.

Roe (Fred). OLD OAK FURNITURE. With many Illustrations by the Author, including a frontispiece in colour. *Demy 8vo.* 10s. 6d. net.

Rogers (A. G. L.), M.A. See Books on Business.

Romney. See Little Galleries.

Roscoe (E. S.). See Little Guides.

Rose (Edward). THE ROSE READER. Illustrated. *Cr. 8vo.* 2s. 6d. Also in 4 Parts. *Parts I. and II.* 6d. each; *Part III.* 8d.; *Part IV.* 10d.

Rowntree (Joshua). THE IMPERIAL DRUG TRADE. A RE-STATEMENT OF THE OPIUM QUESTION. *Second and Cheaper Edition. Cr. 8vo.* 2s. net.

Royde-Smith (N. G.). THE PILLOW BOOK: A GARNER OF MANY MOODS. *Second Edition. Cr. 8vo.* 4s. 6d. net.

Rubie (A. E.), D.D. See Junior School Books.

Russell (W. Clark). THE LIFE OF ADMIRAL LORD COLLINGWOOD. With Illustrations by F. BRANGWYN. *Fourth Edition. Cr. 8vo.* 6s.

Sainsbury (Harrington), M.D., F.R.C.P. PRINCIPIA THERAPEUTICA. *Demy 8vo.* 7s. 6d. net.

St. Anselm. See Library of Devotion.

St. Augustine. See Library of Devotion.

St. Bernard. See Library of Devotion.

Sales (St. Francis de). See Library of Devotion.

St. Cyres (Viscount). See Oxford Biographies.

St. Francis of Assisi. THE LITTLE FLOWERS OF THE GLORIOUS MESSER ST. FRANCIS AND HIS FRIARS. Newly translated by WILLIAM HEYWOOD. With an Introduction by A. G. F. HOWELL, and 40 Illustrations from Italian Painters. *Demy 8vo.* 5s. net.
See also Standard Library and Library of Devotion.

'Saki' (H. Munro). REGINALD. *Second Edition. Fcap. 8vo.* 2s. 6d. net.

Salmon (A. L.). See Little Guides.

Sargeaunt (J.), M.A. ANNALS OF WESTMINSTER SCHOOL. Illustrated. *Demy 8vo.* 7s. 6d.

Sathas (C.). See Byzantine Texts.

Schmitt (John). See Byzantine Texts.

Scott (A. M.). WINSTON SPENCER CHURCHILL. With Portraits and Illustrations. *Cr. 8vo.* 3s. 6d.

Scudamore (Cyril). See Little Guides.

Sells (V. P.), M.A. THE MECHANICS OF DAILY LIFE. Illustrated. *Cr. 8vo.* *2s. 6d.*

Selous (Edmund). TOMMY SMITH'S ANIMALS. Illustrated by G. W. ORD. *Eighth Edition. Fcap. 8vo. 2s. 6d.*
School Edition, 1s. 6d.
TOMMY SMITH'S OTHER ANIMALS. With 12 Illustrations by AUGUSTA GUEST. *Second Edition. Fcap. 8vo. 2s. 6d.*

Settle (J. H.). ANECDOTES OF SOLDIERS. *Cr. 8vo. 3s. 6d. net.*

Shakespeare (William).
THE FOUR FOLIOS, 1623; 1632; 1664; 1685. Each £4, 4s. *net*, or a complete set, £12, 12s. *net*.
Folios 3 and 4 are ready.
Folio 2 is nearly ready.
See also Arden, Standard Library and Little Quarto Shakespeare.

Sharp (A.). VICTORIAN POETS. *Cr. 8vo. 2s. 6d.*

Sharp (Cecil). See S. Baring-Gould.

Sharp (Mrs. E. A.). See Little Books on Art.

Shedlock (J. S.) THE PIANOFORTE SONATA. *Cr. 8vo. 5s.*

Shelley (Percy B.). ADONAIS; an Elegy on the death of John Keats, Author of 'Endymion,' etc. Pisa. From the types of Didot, 1821. *2s. net.*

Sheppard (H. F.), M.A. See S. Baring-Gould.

Sherwell (Arthur), M A. LIFE IN WEST LONDON. *Third Edition. Cr. 8vo. 2s. 6d.*

Shipley (Mary E.). AN ENGLISH CHURCH HISTORY FOR CHILDREN. A.D. 597-1066. With a Preface by the Bishop of Gibraltar. With Maps and Illustrations. *Cr. 8vo. 2s. 6d. net.*

Sime (J.). See Little Books on Art.

Simonson (G. A.). FRANCESCO GUARDI. With 41 Plates. *Imperial 4to. £2, 2s. net.*

Sketchley (R. E. D.). See Little Books on Art.

Skipton (H. P. K.). See Little Books on Art.

Sladen (Douglas). SICILY: The New Winter Resort. With over 200 Illustrations. *Second Edition. Cr. 8vo. 5s. net.*

Small (Evan), M.A. THE EARTH. An Introduction to Physiography. Illustrated. *Cr. 8vo. 2s. 6d.*

Smallwood (M. G.). See Little Books on Art.

Smedley (F. E.). See I.P.L.

Smith (Adam). THE WEALTH OF NATIONS. Edited with an Introduction and numerous Notes by EDWIN CANNAN, M.A. *Two volumes. Demy 8vo. 21s. net.*

Smith (Horace and James). See Little Library.

Smith (H. Bompas), M.A. A NEW JUNIOR ARITHMETIC. *Crown 8vo. 2s.* With Answers, 2s. 6d.

Smith (R. Mudie). THOUGHTS FOR THE DAY. Edited by. *Fcap. 8vo. 3s. 6d. net.*

Smith (Nowell C.). See W. Wordsworth.

Smith (John Thomas). A BOOK FOR A RAINY DAY: Or, Recollections of the Events of the Years 1766-1833. Edited by WILFRED WHITTEN. Illustrated. *Wide Demy 8vo. 12s. 6d. net.*

Snell (F. J.). A BOOK OF EXMOOR. Illustrated. *Cr. 8vo. 6s.*

Snowden (C. E.). A HANDY DIGEST OF BRITISH HISTORY. *Demy 8vo. 4s. 6d.*

Sophocles. See Classical Translations.

Sornet (L. A.). See Junior School Books.

South (E. Wilton), M.A. See Junior School Books.

Southey (R.). ENGLISH SEAMEN. Edited by DAVID HANNAY.
Vol. I. (Howard, Clifford, Hawkins, Drake, Cavendish). *Second Edition. Cr. 8vo. 6s.*
Vol. II. (Richard Hawkins, Grenville, Essex, and Raleigh). *Cr. 8vo. 6s.*
See also Standard Library.

Spence (C. H.), M.A. See School Examination Series.

Spicer (A. D.). THE PAPER TRADE. With Maps and Diagrams. *Demy 8vo. 12s. 6d. net.*

Spooner (W. A.), M.A. See Leaders of Religion.

Staley (Edgcumbe). THE GUILDS OF FLORENCE. Illustrated. *Second Edition. Royal 8vo. 16s. net.*

Stanbridge (J. W.), B.D. See Library of Devotion.

'Stancliffe.' GOLF DO'S AND DONT'S. *Second Edition. Fcap. 8vo. 1s.*

Stead (W. J.). See D. Gallaher.

Stedman (A. M. M.), M.A.
INITIA LATINA: Easy Lessons on Elementary Accidence. *Ninth Edition. Fcap. 8vo. 1s.*
FIRST LATIN LESSONS. *Tenth Edition. Cr. 8vo. 2s.*
FIRST LATIN READER. With Notes adapted to the Shorter Latin Primer and Vocabulary. *Seventh Ed. revised. 18mo. 1s. 6d.*
EASY SELECTIONS FROM CÆSAR. The Helvetian War. *Third Edition. 18mo. 1s.*
EASY SELECTIONS FROM LIVY. The Kings of Rome. *18mo. Third Edition. 1s. 6d.*
EASY LATIN PASSAGES FOR UNSEEN TRANSLATION. *Eleventh Ed. Fcap. 8vo. 1s. 6d.*
EXEMPLA LATINA. First Exercises in Latin Accidence. With Vocabulary. *Third Edition. Cr. 8vo. 1s.*

EASY LATIN EXERCISES ON THE SYNTAX OF THE SHORTER AND REVISED LATIN PRIMER. With Vocabulary. *Eleventh and Cheaper Edition, re-written. Cr. 8vo. 1s. 6d. Original Edition. 2s. 6d.* KEY, 3s. *net.*

THE LATIN COMPOUND SENTENCE : Rules and Exercises. *Second Edition. Cr. 8vo. 1s. 6d.* With Vocabulary. *2s.*

NOTANDA QUAEDAM : Miscellaneous Latin Exercises on Common Rules and Idioms. *Fourth Edition. Fcap. 8vo. 1s. 6d.* With Vocabulary. *2s.* Key, *2s. net.*

LATIN VOCABULARIES FOR REPETITION : Arranged according to Subjects. *Fourteenth Edition. Fcap. 8vo. 1s. 6d.*

A VOCABULARY OF LATIN IDIOMS. *18mo. Fourth Edition. 1s.*

STEPS TO GREEK. *Third Edition, revised. 18mo. 1s.*

A SHORTER GREEK PRIMER. *Second Edition. Cr. 8vo. 1s. 6d.*

EASY GREEK PASSAGES FOR UNSEEN TRANSLATION. *Fourth Edition, revised. Fcap. 8vo. 1s. 6d.*

GREEK VOCABULARIES FOR REPETITION. Arranged according to Subjects. *Fourth Edition. Fcap. 8vo. 1s 6d.*

GREEK TESTAMENT SELECTIONS. For the use of Schools. With Introduction, Notes, and Vocabulary. *Fourth Edition. Fcap. 8vo. 2s. 6d.*

STEPS TO FRENCH. *Eighth Edition. 18mo. 8d.*

FIRST FRENCH LESSONS. *Seventh Edition, revised. Cr. 8vo. 1s.*

EASY FRENCH PASSAGES FOR UNSEEN TRANSLATION. *Fifth Edition, revised. Fcap. 8vo. 1s. 6d.*

EASY FRENCH EXERCISES ON ELEMENTARY SYNTAX. With Vocabulary. *Fourth Edition. Cr. 8vo. 2s. 6d.* KEY. *3s. net.*

FRENCH VOCABULARIES FOR REPETITION : Arranged according to Subjects. *Thirteenth Edition. Fcap. 8vo. 1s.* See also School Examination Series.

Steel (R. Elliott), M.A., F.C.S. THE WORLD OF SCIENCE. With 147 Illustrations. *Second Edition. Cr. 8vo. 2s. 6d.* See also School Examination Series.

Stephenson (C.), of the Technical College, Bradford, and **Suddards (F.)** of the Yorkshire College, Leeds. ORNAMENTAL DESIGN FOR WOVEN FABRICS. Illustrated. *Demy 8vo. Third Edition. 7s. 6d.*

Stephenson (J.), M.A. THE CHIEF TRUTHS OF THE CHRISTIAN FAITH. *Cr. 8vo. 3s. 6d.*

Sterne (Laurence). See Little Library.

Sterry (W.). M.A. ANNALS OF ETON COLLEGE. Illustrated. *Demy 8vo. 7s. 6d.*

Steuart (Katherine). BY ALLAN WATER. *Second Edition. Cr. 8vo. 6s*

Stevenson (R. L.) THE LETTERS OF ROBERT LOUIS STEVENSON TO HIS FAMILY AND FRIENDS. Selected and Edited by SIDNEY COLVIN. *Third Edition. Cr. 8vo. 12s.*

LIBRARY EDITION. *Demy 8vo. 2 vols. 25s. net.* A Colonial Edition is also published.

VAILIMA LETTERS. With an Etched Portrait by WILLIAM STRANG. *Fifth Edition. Cr. 8vo. Buckram. 6s.* A Colonial Edition is also published.

THE LIFE OF R. L. STEVENSON. See G. Balfour.

Stevenson (M. I.). FROM SARANAC TO THE MARQUESAS. Being Letters written by Mrs. M. I. STEVENSON during 1887-8. *Cr. 8vo. 6s. net.*

LETTERS FROM SAMOA, 1891-95. Edited and arranged by M. C. BALFOUR. With many Illustrations. *Second Edition Cr. 8vo. 6s. net.*

Stoddart (Anna M.). See Oxford Biographies.

Stokes (F. G.), B.A. HOURS WITH RABELAIS. From the translation of SIR T. URQUHART and P. A. MOTTEUX. With a Portrait in Photogravure. *Cr. 8vo. 3s. 6d. net.*

Stone (S. J.). POEMS AND HYMNS. With a Memoir by F. G. ELLERTON, M.A. With Portrait. *Cr. 8vo. 6s.*

Storr (Vernon F.), M.A., Lecturer in the Philosophy of Religion in Cambridge University ; Examining Chaplain to the Archbishop of Canterbury; formerly Fellow of University College, Oxford. DEVELOPMENT AND DIVINE PURPOSE *Cr. 8vo. 5s. net.*

Straker (F.). See Books on Business.

Streane (A. W.), D.D. See Churchman's Bible.

Streatfeild (R. A.). MODERN MUSIC AND MUSICIANS. With 24 Illustrations. *Second Edition. Demy 8vo. 7s. 6d. net.*

Stroud (H.), D.Sc., M.A. PRACTICAL PHYSICS. With many Diagrams. *Second Edition. 3s. net.*

Strutt (Joseph). THE SPORTS AND PASTIMES OF THE PEOPLE OF ENGLAND. Illustrated by many Engravings. Revised by J. CHARLES COX, LL.D., F.S.A. *Quarto. 21s. net.*

Stuart (Capt. Donald). THE STRUGGLE FOR PERSIA. With a Map. *Cr. 8vo. 6s.*

Sturch (F.)., Staff Instructor to the Surrey County Council. MANUAL TRAINING DRAWING (WOODWORK). Its Principles and Application, with Solutions to Examination Questions, 1892-1905, Orthographic, Isometric and Oblique Projection. With 50 Plates and 140 Figures. *Foolscap. 5s. net.*

Suddards (F.). See C. Stephenson.

Surtees (R. S.). See I.P.L.

Symes (J. E.), M.A. THE FRENCH REVOLUTION. *Second Edition. Cr. 8vo. 2s. 6d.*

A 3

Sympson (E. M.), M.A., M.D. See Ancient Cities.

Tacitus. AGRICOLA. With Introduction Notes, Map, etc., by R. F. DAVIS, M.A., *Fcap. 8vo.* 2s.

GERMANIA. By the same Editor. *Fcap. 8vo.* 2s. See also Classical Translations.

Tallack (W.). HOWARD LETTERS AND MEMORIES. *Demy 8vo.* 10s. 6d. net.

Tauler (J.). See Library of Devotion.

Taylor (A. E.). THE ELEMENTS OF METAPHYSICS. *Demy 8vo.* 10s. 6d. net.

Taylor (F. G.), M.A. See Commercial Series.

Taylor (I. A.). See Oxford Biographies.

Taylor (John W.). THE COMING OF THE SAINTS : Imagination and Studies in Early Church History and Tradition. With 26 Illustrations. *Demy 8vo.* 7s. 6d. net.

Taylor (T. M.), M.A., Fellow of Gonville and Caius College, Cambridge. A CONSTITUTIONAL AND POLITICAL HISTORY OF ROME. *Cr. 8vo.* 7s. 6d.

Tennyson (Alfred, Lord). THE EARLY POEMS OF. Edited, with Notes and an Introduction, by J. CHURTON COLLINS, M.A. *Cr. 8vo.* 6s.

IN MEMORIAM, MAUD, AND THE PRINCESS. Edited by J. CHURTON COLLINS, M.A. *Cr. 8vo.* 6s. See also Little Library.

Terry (C. S.). See Oxford Biographies.

Thackeray (W. M.). See Little Library.

Theobald (F. V.), M.A. INSECT LIFE. Illustrated. *Second Edition Revised. Cr. 8vo.* 2s. 6d.

Thompson (A. H.). See Little Guides.

Tileston (Mary W.). DAILY STRENGTH FOR DAILY NEEDS. *Thirteenth Edition. Medium 16mo.* 2s. 6d. net. Also an edition in superior binding, 6s.

Tompkins (H. W.), F.R.H.S. See Little Guides.

Townley (Lady Susan). MY CHINESE NOTE-BOOK With 16 Illustrations and 2 Maps. *Third Edition. Demy 8vo.* 10s. 6d. net.

Toynbee (Paget), M.A., D.Litt. See Oxford Biographies.

Trench (Herbert). DEIRDRE WEDDED AND OTHER POEMS. *Cr. 8vo.* 5s.

An episode of Thirty hours delivered by the three voices. It deals with the love of Deirdre for Naris and is founded on a Gaelic Version of the Tragical Tale of the Sons of Usnach.

Trevelyan (G. M.), Fellow of Trinity College, Cambridge. ENGLAND UNDER THE STUARTS. With Maps and Plans. *Second Edition. Demy 8vo.* 10s. 6d. net.

Troutbeck (G. E.). See Little Guides.

Tyler (E. A.), B.A., F.C.S. See Junior School Books.

Tyrrell-Gill (Frances). See Little Books on Art.

Vardon (Harry). THE COMPLETE GOLFER. Illustrated. *Eighth Edition. Demy 8vo.* 10s. 6d. net.

A Colonial Edition is also published.

Vaughan (Henry). See Little Library.

Vaughan (Herbert M.), B.A. (Oxon.). THE LAST OF THE ROYAL STUARTS, HENRY STUART, CARDINAL, DUKE OF YORK. With 20 Illustrations. *Second Edition. Demy 8vo.* 10s. 6d. net.

THE NAPLES RIVERIA. With 25 Illustrations in Colour by MAURICE GREIFFENHAGEN. *Cr. 8vo.* 6s.

A Colonial Edition is also published.

Voegelin (A.), M.A. See Junior Examination Series.

Waddell (Col. L. A.), LL.D., C.B. LHASA AND ITS MYSTERIES. With a Record of the Expedition of 1903-1904. With 155 Illustrations and Maps. *Third and Cheaper Edition. Demy 8vo.* 7s. 6d. net.

Wade (G. W.), D.D. OLD TESTAMENT HISTORY. With Maps. *Fourth Edition. Cr. 8vo.* 6s.

Wagner (Richard). MUSIC DRAMAS : Interpretations, embodying Wagner's own explanations. By A. L. CLEATHER and B. CRUMP. *In Four Volumes. Fcap 8vo.* 2s. 6d. each.

   VOL. I.—THE RING OF THE NIBELUNG. *Third Edition.*

   VOL. II.—PARSIFAL, LOHENGRIN, and THE HOLY GRAIL.

   VOL. III.—TRISTAN AND ISOLDE.

Wall (J. C.). DEVILS. Illustrated by the Author and from photographs. *Demy 8vo.* 4s. 6d. net. See also Antiquary's Books.

Walters (H. B.). See Little Books on Art and Classics of Art.

Walton (F. W.). See School Histories.

Walton (Izaac) and **Cotton (Charles).** See I.P.L., Standard Library, and Little Library.

Warren-Vernon (Hon. William), M.A. READINGS ON THE INFERNO OF DANTE, based on the Commentary of BENVENUTO DA IMOLA and other authorities. With an Introduction by the Rev. Dr. MOORE. In Two Volumes. *Second Edition, entirely re-written. Cr. 8vo.* 15s. net.

Waterhouse (Mrs. Alfred). WITH THE SIMPLE-HEARTED : Little Homilies to Women in Country Places. *Second Edition. Small Pott 8vo.* 2s. net.

See also Little Library.

Weatherhead (T. C.), M.A. EXAMINATION PAPERS IN HORACE. *Cr. 8vo.* 2s. See also Junior Examination Series.

Webber (F. C.). See Textbooks of Technology.

Weir (Archibald), M.A. AN INTRODUCTION TO THE HISTORY OF MODERN EUROPE. *Cr. 8vo.* 6s.

Wells (Sidney H.) See Textbooks of Science.

Wells (J.), M.A., Fellow and Tutor of Wadham College. OXFORD AND OXFORD LIFE. *Third Edition. Cr 8vo.* 3s. 6d.

A SHORT HISTORY OF ROME. *Seventh Edition.* With 3 Maps. *Cr. 8vo.* 3s. 6d.

See also Little Guides.

Wheldon (F. W.). A LITTLE BROTHER TO THE BIRDS. With 15 Illustrations,

7 of which are by A. H. BUCKLAND. *Large Cr. 8vo. 6s.*

Whibley (C). See W. E. Henley.

Whibley (L.), M.A., Fellow of Pembroke College, Cambridge. GREEK OLIGARCHIES: THEIR ORGANISATION AND CHARACTER. *Cr. 8vo. 6s.*

Whitaker (G. H.), M.A. See Churchman's Bible.

White (Gilbert). THE NATURAL HISTORY OF SELBORNE. Edited by L. C. MIALL, F.R.S., assisted by W. WARDE FOWLER, M.A. *Cr. 8vo. 6s.*
See also Standard Library.

Whitfield (E. E.). See Commercial Series.

Whitehead (A. W.). GASPARD DE COLIGNY. Illustrated. *Demy 8vo. 12s. 6d. net.*

Whiteley (R. Lloyd), F.I.C., Principal of the Municipal Science School, West Bromwich. AN ELEMENTARY TEXTBOOK OF INORGANIC CHEMISTRY. *Cr. 8vo. 2s. 6d.*

Whitley (Miss). See Lady Dilke.

Whitten (W.). See John Thomas Smith.

Whyte (A. G.), B.Sc. See Books on Business.

Wilberforce (Wilfrid). See Little Books on Art.

Wilde (Oscar). DE PROFUNDIS. *Ninth Edition. Cr. 8vo. 5s. net.*
A Colonial Edition is also published.

THE DUCHESS OF PADUA. *Demy 8vo. 12s. 6d. net.*

POEMS. *Demy 8vo. 12s. 6d. net.*

INTENTIONS. *Demy 8vo. 12s. 6d. net.*

SALOME, AND OTHER PLAYS. *Demy 8vo. 12s. 6d. net.*

LADY WINDERMERE'S FAN. *Demy 8vo. 12s. 6d. net.*

A WOMAN OF NO IMPORTANCE. *Demy 8vo. 12s. 6d. net.*

AN IDEAL HUSBAND. *Demy 8vo. 12s. 6d. net.*

THE IMPORTANCE OF BEING EARNEST. *Demy 8vo. 12s. 6d. net.*

A HOUSE OF POMEGRANATES and THE HAPPY PRINCE. *Demy 8vo. 12s. 6d. net.*

LORD ARTHUR SAVILE'S CRIME and OTHER PROSE PIECES. *Demy 8vo. 12s. 6d. net.*

Wilkins (W. H.), B.A. THE ALIEN INVASION. *Cr. 8vo. 2s. 6d.*

Williams (A.). PETROL PETER: or Pretty Stories and Funny Pictures. Illustrated in Colour by A. W. MILLS. *Demy 4to. 3s. 6d. net.*

Williamson (M. G.). See Ancient Cities.

Williamson (W.). THE BRITISH GARDENER. Illustrated. *Demy 8vo. 10s. 6d.*

Williamson (W.), B.A. See Junior Examination Series, Junior School Books, and Beginner's Books.

Willson (Beckles). LORD STRATHCONA: the Story of his Life. Illustrated. *Demy 8vo. 7s. 6d.*
A Colonial Edition is also published.

Wilmot=Buxton (E. M.). MAKERS OF EUROPE. *Cr. 8vo. Seventh Ed. 3s. 6d.*
A Text-book of European History for Middle Forms.

THE ANCIENT WORLD. With Maps and Illustrations. *Cr. 8vo. 3s. 6d.*
See also Beginner's Books.

Wilson (Bishop.). See Library of Devotion.

Wilson (A. J.). See Books on Business.

Wilson (H. A.). See Books on Business.

Wilson (J. A.). See Simplified French Texts.

Wilton (Richard), M.A. LYRA PASTORALIS: Songs of Nature, Church, and Home. *Pott 8vo. 2s. 6d.*

Winbolt (S. E.), M.A. EXERCISES IN LATIN ACCIDENCE. *Cr. 8vo. 1s. 6d.*

LATIN HEXAMETER VERSE: An Aid to Composition. *Cr. 8vo. 3s. 6d.* KEY, *5s. net.*

Windle (B. C. A.), F.R.S., F.S.A. See Antiquary's Books, Little Guides, Ancient Cities, and School Histories.

Winterbotham (Canon), M.A., B.Sc., LL.B. See Churchman's Library.

Wood (Sir Evelyn), F.M., V.C., G.C.B., G.C.M.G. FROM MIDSHIPMAN TO FIELD-MARSHAL. With 24 Illustrations and Maps. *Two Volumes. Fourth Edition. Demy 8vo. 25s. net.*
A Colonial Edition is also published.

Wood (J. A. E.). See Textbooks of Technology.

Wood (J. Hickory). DAN LENO. Illustrated. *Third Edition. Cr. 8vo. 6s.*
A Colonial Edition is also published.

Wood (W. Birkbeck), M.A., late Scholar of Worcester College, Oxford, and **Edmonds (Major J. E.),** R.E., D.A.Q.-M.G. A HISTORY OF THE CIVIL WAR IN THE UNITED STATES. With an Introduction by H. SPENSER WILKINSON. With 24 Maps and Plans. *Demy 8vo. 12s. 6d. net.*

Wordsworth (Christopher). See Antiquary's Books.

Wordsworth (W.). POEMS BY. Selected by STOPFORD A. BROOKE. With 40 Illustrations by EDMUND H. NEW. With a Frontispiece in Photogravure. *Demy 8vo. 7s. 6d. net.*
A Colonial Edition is also published.

Wordsworth (W.) and Coleridge (S. T.). See Little Library.

Wright (Arthur), D.D., Fellow of Queen's College, Cambridge. See Churchman's Library.

Wright (C. Gordon). See Dante.

Wright (J. C.). TO-DAY. *Demy 16mo. 1s. 6d. net.*

Wright (Sophie). GERMAN VOCABULARIES FOR REPETITION. *Fcap. 8vo. 1s. 6d.*

Wrong (George M.), Professor of History in the University of Toronto. THE EARL OF ELGIN. Illustrated. *Demy 8vo. 7s. 6d. net.*
A Colonial Edition is also published.

Wyatt (Kate M.). See M. R. Gloag.

Wylde (A. B.). MODERN ABYSSINIA. With a Map and a Portrait. *Demy 8vo.* 15s. net.
A Colonial Edition is also published.

Wyndham (Rt. Hon. George). M.P. THE POEMS OF WILLIAM SHAKE-SPEARE. With an Introduction and Notes. *Demy 8vo. Buckram, gilt top.* 10s. 6d.

Wyon (R.) and **Prance (G.).** THE LAND OF THE BLACK MOUNTAIN. Being a Description of Montenegro. With 40 Illustrations. *Cr. 8vo.* 2s. 6d. net.

Yeats (W. B.). A BOOK OF IRISH VERSE. Selected from Modern Writers.

Revised and Enlarged Edition. Cr. 8vo. 3s. 6d.

Young (Filson). THE COMPLETE MOTORIST. With 138 Illustrations. *Sixth Edition. Demy 8vo.* 12s. 6d. net.
A Colonial Edition is also published.

THE JOY OF THE ROAD: An Appreciation of the Motor Car. *Small Demy 8vo.* 5s. net.

Young (T. M.). THE AMERICAN COTTON INDUSTRY: A Study of Work and Workers. *Cr. 8vo. Cloth,* 2s. 6d.; *paper boards,* 1s. 6d.

Zimmern (Antonia). WHAT DO WE KNOW CONCERNING ELECTRICITY? *Fcap. 8vo.* 1s. 6d. net.

Ancient Cities

General Editor, B. C. A. WINDLE, D.Sc., F.R.S.

Cr. 8vo.   4s. 6d. net.

CHESTER. By B. C. A. Windle, D.Sc. F.R.S. Illustrated by E. H. New.

SHREWSBURY. By T. Auden, M.A., F.S.A. Illustrated.

CANTERBURY. By J. C. Cox, LL.D., F.S.A. Illustrated.

EDINBURGH. By M. G. Williamson, M.A. Illustrated by Herbert Railton.

LINCOLN. By E. Mansel Sympson, M.A., M.D. Illustrated by E. H. New.

BRISTOL. By Alfred Harvey. Illustrated by E. H. New.

DUBLIN. By S. A. O. Fitzpatrick. Illustrated by W. C. Green.

The Antiquary's Books

General Editor, J. CHARLES COX, LL.D., F.S.A.

Demy 8vo.   7s. 6d. net.

ENGLISH MONASTIC LIFE. By the Right Rev. Abbot Gasquet, O.S.B. Illustrated. *Third Edition.*

REMAINS OF THE PREHISTORIC AGE IN ENGLAND. By B. C. A. Windle, D.Sc., F.R.S. With numerous Illustrations and Plans.

OLD SERVICE BOOKS OF THE ENGLISH CHURCH. By Christopher Wordsworth, M.A., and Henry Littlehales. With Coloured and other Illustrations.

CELTIC ART. By J. Romilly Allen, F.S.A. With numerous Illustrations and Plans.

ARCHÆOLOGY AND FALSE ANTIQUITIES. By R. Munro, LL.D. Illustrated.

SHRINES OF BRITISH SAINTS. By J. C. Wall. With numerous Illustrations and Plans.

THE ROYAL FORESTS OF ENGLAND. By J. C. Cox, LL.D., F.S.A. Illustrated.

THE MANOR AND MANORIAL RECORDS. By Nathaniel J. Hone. Illustrated.

ENGLISH SEALS. By J. Harvey Bloom. Illustrated.

THE DOMESDAY INQUEST. By Adolphus Ballard, B.A., LL.B. With 27 Illustrations.

THE BRASSES OF ENGLAND. By Herbert W. Macklin, M.A. With many Illustrations. *Second Edition.*

PARISH LIFE IN MEDIÆVAL ENGLAND. By the Right Rev. Abbott Gasquet, O.S.B. With many Illustrations. *Second Edition.*

THE BELLS OF ENGLAND. By Canon J. J. Raven, D.D., F.S.A. With Illustrations. *Second Edition.*

The Arden Shakespeare

Demy 8vo.   2s. 6d. net each volume.

General Editor, W. J. CRAIG.

An edition of Shakespeare in single Plays. Edited with a full Introduction, Textual Notes, and a Commentary at the foot of the page.

HAMLET. Edited by Edward Dowden.

ROMEO AND JULIET. Edited by Edward Dowden.

KING LEAR. Edited by W. J. Craig.

JULIUS CAESAR. Edited by M. Macmillan.

THE TEMPEST. Edited by Moreton Luce.

[Continued

ARDEN SHAKESPEARE—*continued*.

OTHELLO. Edited by H. C. Hart.

TITUS ANDRONICUS. Edited by H. B. Baildon.

CYMBELINE. Edited by Edward Dowden.

THE MERRY WIVES OF WINDSOR. Edited by H. C. Hart.

A MIDSUMMER NIGHT'S DREAM. Edited by H. Cuningham.

KING HENRY V. Edited by H. A. Evans.

ALL'S WELL THAT ENDS WELL. Edited by W. O. Brigstocke.

THE TAMING OF THE SHREW. Edited by R. Warwick Bond.

TIMON OF ATHENS. Edited by K. Deighton.

MEASURE FOR MEASURE. Edited by H. C. Hart.

TWELFTH NIGHT. Edited by Moreton Luce.

THE MERCHANT OF VENICE. Edited by C. Knox Pooler.

TROILUS AND CRESSIDA. Edited by K. Deighton.

ANTONY AND CLEOPATRA. Edited by R. H. Case.

LOVE'S LABOUR'S LOST. Edited by H. C. Hart.

THE TWO GENTLEMAN OF VERONA. R, Warwick Bond.

PERICLES. Edited by K. Deighton.

THE COMEDY OF ERRORS. Edited by H. Cuningham.

KING RICHARD III. Edited by A. H. Thompson.

KING JOHN. Edited by Ivor B. John.

The Beginner's Books
Edited by W. WILLIAMSON, B.A.

EASY FRENCH RHYMES. By Henri Blouet. *Second Edition.* Illustrated. *Fcap. 8vo.* 1s.

EASY STORIES FROM ENGLISH HISTORY. By E. M. Wilmot-Buxton, Author of 'Makers of Europe.' *Third Edition. Cr. 8vo.* 1s.

EASY EXERCISES IN ARITHMETIC. Arranged by W. S. Beard. *Second Edition. Fcap.*

8vo. Without Answers, 1s. With Answers. 1s. 3d.

EASY DICTATION AND SPELLING. By W. Williamson, B.A. *Fifth Ed. Fcap. 8vo.* 1s.

AN EASY POETRY BOOK. Selected and arranged by W. Williamson, B.A., Author of 'Dictation Passages.' *Second Edition. Cr. 8vo.* 1s.

Books on Business
Cr. 8vo. 2s. 6d. *net.*

PORTS AND DOCKS. By Douglas Owen.

RAILWAYS. By E. R. McDermott.

THE STOCK EXCHANGE. By Chas. Duguid. *Second Edition.*

THE BUSINESS OF INSURANCE. By A. J. Wilson.

THE ELECTRICAL INDUSTRY : LIGHTING, TRACTION, AND POWER. By A. G. Whyte, B.Sc.

THE SHIPBUILDING INDUSTRY : Its History, Science, Practice, and Finance. By David Pollock, M.I.N.A.

THE MONEY MARKET. By F. Straker.

THE BUSINESS SIDE OF AGRICULTURE. By A. G. L. Rogers, M.A.

LAW IN BUSINESS. By H. A. Wilson.

THE BREWING INDUSTRY. By Julian L. Baker, F.I.C., F.C.S.

THE AUTOMOBILE INDUSTRY. By G. de H. Stone.

MINING AND MINING INVESTMENTS. By 'A. Moil.'

THE BUSINESS OF ADVERTISING. By Clarence G. Moran, Barrister-at-Law. Illustrated.

TRADE UNIONS. By G. Drage.

CIVIL ENGINEERING. By T. Claxton Fidler, M.Inst. C.E. Illustrated.

THE IRON TRADE OF GREAT BRITAIN. By J. Stephen Jeans. Illustrated.

MONOPOLIES, TRUSTS, AND KARTELLS. By F. W. Hirst.

THE COTTON INDUSTRY AND TRADE. By Prof. S. J. Chapman, Dean of the Faculty of Commerce in the University of Manchester. Illustrated.

Byzantine Texts
Edited by J. B. BURY, M.A., Litt.D.

A series of texts of Byzantine Historians, edited by English and foreign scholars.

ZACHARIAH OF MITYLENE. Translated by F. J. Hamilton, D.D., and E. W. Brooks. *Demy 8vo.* 12s. 6d. *net.*

EVAGRIUS. Edited by Léon Parmentier and M. Bidez. *Demy 8vo.* 10s. 6d. *net.*

THE HISTORY OF PSELLUS. Edited by C. Sathas. *Demy 8vo.* 15s. *net.*

ECTHESIS CHRONICA. Edited by Professor Lambros. *Demy 8vo.* 7s. 6d. *net.*

THE CHRONICLE OF MOREA. Edited by John Schmitt. *Demy 8vo.* 15s. *net.*

The Churchman's Bible

General Editor, J. H. BURN, B.D., F.R.S.E.

Fcap. 8vo.   1s. 6d. net each.

A series of Expositions on the Books of the Bible, which will be of service to the general reader in the practical and devotional study of the Sacred Text.

Each Book is provided with a full and clear Introductory Section, in which is stated what is known or conjectured respecting the date and occasion of the composition of the Book, and any other particulars that may help to elucidate its meaning as a whole.   The Exposition is divided into sections of a convenient length, corresponding as far as possible with the divisions of the Church Lectionary.   The Translation of the Authorised Version is printed in full, such corrections as are deemed necessary being placed in footnotes.

THE EPISTLE OF ST. PAUL THE APOSTLE TO THE GALATIANS. Edited by A. W. Robinson, M.A.   *Second Edition.*

ECCLESIASTES.   Edited by A. W. Streane, D.D.

THE EPISTLE OF ST. PAUL THE APOSTLE TO THE PHILIPPIANS.   Edited by C. R. D. Biggs, D.D.   *Second Edition.*

THE EPISTLE OF ST. JAMES.   Edited by H. W. Fulford M.A.

ISAIAH.   Edited by W. E. Barnes, D.D.   *Two Volumes.*   With Map.   *2s. net each.*

THE EPISTLE OF ST. PAUL THE APOSTLE TO THE EPHESIANS. Edited by G. H. Whitaker, M.A.

THE GOSPEL ACCORDING TO ST. MARK. Edited by J. C. Du Buisson, M.A.   *2s. 6d. net.*

ST. PAUL'S EPISTLES TO THE COLOSSIANS AND PHILEMON. Edited by H. J. C. Knight, M.A.   *2s. net.*

The Churchman's Library

General Editor, J. H. BURN, B.D., F.R.S.E.

Crown 8vo.   3s. 6d. each.

THE BEGINNINGS OF ENGLISH CHRISTIANITY. By W. E. Collins, M.A.   With Map.

THE KINGDOM OF HEAVEN HERE AND HEREAFTER.   By Canon Winterbotham, M.A., B.Sc., LL.B.

THE WORKMANSHIP OF THE PRAYER BOOK: Its Literary and Liturgical Aspects.   By J. Dowden, D.D.   *Second Edition.*

EVOLUTION.   By F. B. Jevons, M.A., Litt.D.

SOME NEW TESTAMENT PROBLEMS.   By Arthur Wright, D.D.   6s.

THE CHURCHMAN'S INTRODUCTION TO THE OLD TESTAMENT.   By A. M. Mackay, B.A.

THE CHURCH OF CHRIST.   By E. T. Green, M.A.   6s.

COMPARATIVE THEOLOGY.   By J. A. MacCulloch.   6s.

Classical Translations

Edited by H. F. FOX, M.A., Fellow and Tutor of Brasenose College, Oxford.

Crown 8vo.

A series of Translations from the Greek and Latin Classics, distinguished by literary excellence as well as by scholarly accuracy.

ÆSCHYLUS—Agamemnon Choephoroe, Eumenides.   Translated by Lewis Campbell, LL.D.   5s.

CICERO—De Oratore I.   Translated by E. N. P. Moor, M.A.   3s. 6d.

CICERO—Select Orations (Pro Milone, Pro Mureno, Philippic II., in Catilinam). Translated by H. E. D. Blakiston, M.A.   5s.

CICERO—De Natura Deorum.   Translated by F. Brooks, M.A.   3s. 6d.

CICERO—De Officiis.   Translated by G. B. Gardiner, M.A.   2s. 6d.

HORACE—The Odes and Epodes.   Translated by A. D. Godley, M.A.   2s.

LUCIAN—Six Dialogues (Nigrinus, Icaro-Menippus, The Cock, The Ship, The Parasite, The Lover of Falsehood)   Translated by S. T. Irwin, M.A.   3s. 6d.

SOPHOCLES—Electra and Ajax.   Translated by E. D. A. Morshead, M.A.   2s. 6d.

TACITUS—Agricola and Germania.   Translated by R. B. Townshend.   2s. 6d.

THE SATIRES OF JUVENAL.   Translated by S. G. Owen.   2s. 6d.

Classics of Art

Edited by DR. J. H. W. LAING

THE ART OF THE GREEKS. By H. B. Walters. With 112 Plates and 18 Illustrations in the Text. *Wide Royal 8vo. 12s. 6d. net.*

VELAZQUEZ. By A. de Beruete. With 94 Plates. *Wide Royal 8vo. 10s. 6d. net.*

Commercial Series

Edited by H. DE B. GIBBINS, Litt.D., M.A.

Crown 8vo.

COMMERCIAL EDUCATION IN THEORY AND PRACTICE. By E. E. Whitfield, M.A. 5s.
An introduction to Methuen's Commercial Series treating the question of Commercial Education fully from both the point of view of the teacher and of the parent.

BRITISH COMMERCE AND COLONIES FROM ELIZABETH TO VICTORIA. By H. de B. Gibbins, Litt.D., M.A. *Third Edition.* 2s.

COMMERCIAL EXAMINATION PAPERS. By H. de B. Gibbins, Litt.D., M.A. 1s. 6d.

THE ECONOMICS OF COMMERCE. By H. de B. Gibbins, Litt.D., M.A. *Second Edition.* 1s. 6d.

A GERMAN COMMERCIAL READER. By S. E. Bally. With Vocabulary. 2s.

A COMMERCIAL GEOGRAPHY OF THE BRITISH EMPIRE. By L. W. Lyde, M.A. *Sixth Edition.* 2s.

A COMMERCIAL GEOGRAPHY OF FOREIGN NATIONS. By F. C. Boon, B.A. 2s.

A PRIMER OF BUSINESS. By S. Jackson, M.A. *Third Edition.* 1s. 6d.

COMMERCIAL ARITHMETIC. By F. G. Taylor, M.A. *Fourth Edition.* 1s. 6d.

FRENCH COMMERCIAL CORRESPONDENCE. By S. E. Bally. With Vocabulary. *Third Edition.* 2s.

GERMAN COMMERCIAL CORRESPONDENCE. By S. E. Bally. With Vocabulary. *Second Edition.* 2s. 6d.

A FRENCH COMMERCIAL READER. By S. E. Bally. With Vocabulary. *Second Edition.* 2s.

PRECIS WRITING AND OFFICE CORRESPONDENCE. By E. E. Whitfield, M.A. *Second Edition.* 2s.

A GUIDE TO PROFESSIONS AND BUSINESS. By H. Jones. 1s. 6d.

THE PRINCIPLES OF BOOK-KEEPING BY DOUBLE ENTRY. By J. E. B. M'Allen, M.A. 2s.

COMMERCIAL LAW. By W. Douglas Edwards. *Second Edition.* 2s.

The Connoisseur's Library

Wide Royal 8vo. 25s. net.

A sumptuous series of 20 books on art, written by experts for collectors, superbly illustrated in photogravure, collotype, and colour. The technical side of the art is duly treated. The first volumes are—

MEZZOTINTS. By Cyril Davenport. With 40 Plates in Photogravure.

PORCELAIN. By Edward Dillon. With 19 Plates in Colour, 20 in Collotype, and 5 in Photogravure.

MINIATURES. By Dudley Heath. With 9 Plates in Colour, 15 in Collotype, and 15 in Photogravure.

IVORIES. By A. Maskell. With 80 Plates in Collotype and Photogravure.

ENGLISH FURNITURE. By F. S. Robinson. With 160 Plates in Collotype and one in Photogravure. *Second Edition.*

EUROPEAN ENAMELS. By Henry H. Cunynghame, C.B. With 54 Plates in Collotype and Half-tone and 4 Plates in Colour.

GOLDSMITHS' AND SILVERSMITHS' WORK. By Nelson Dawson. With many Plates in Collotype and a Frontispiece in Photogravure.

ENGLISH COLOURED BOOKS. By Martin Hardie. With 28 Illustrations in Colour and Collotype.

GLASS. By Edward Dillon. With 37 Illustrations in Collotype and 12 in Colour.

The Library of Devotion

With Introductions and (where necessary) Notes.

Small Pott 8vo, cloth, 2s. ; leather, 2s. 6d. net.

THE CONFESSIONS OF ST. AUGUSTINE. Edited by C. Bigg, D.D. *Fifth Edition.*

THE CHRISTIAN YEAR. Edited by Walter Lock, D.D. *Third Edition.*

THE IMITATION OF CHRIST. Edited by C. Bigg, D.D. *Fourth Edition.*

A BOOK OF DEVOTIONS. Edited by J. W. Stanbridge. B.D. *Second Edition.*

[*Continued.*

THE LIBRARY OF DEVOTION—*continued.*

LYRA INNOCENTIUM. Edited by Walter Lock, D.D.

A SERIOUS CALL TO A DEVOUT AND HOLY LIFE. Edited by C. BIGG, D.D. *Fourth Edition.*

THE TEMPLE. Edited by E. C. S. Gibson, D.D. *Second Edition.*

A GUIDE TO ETERNITY. Edited by J. W. Stanbridge, B.D.

THE PSALMS OF DAVID. Edited by B. W. Randolph, D.D.

LYRA APOSTOLICA. By Cardinal Newman and others. Edited by Canon Scott Holland and Canon H. C. Beeching, M.A.

THE INNER WAY. By J. Tauler. Edited by A. W. Hutton, M.A.

THE THOUGHTS OF PASCAL. Edited by C. S. Jerram, M.A.

ON THE LOVE OF GOD. By St. Francis de Sales. Edited by W. J. Knox-Little, M.A.

A MANUAL OF CONSOLATION FROM THE SAINTS AND FATHERS. Edited by J. H. Burn, B.D.

THE SONG OF SONGS. Edited by B. Blaxland, M.A.

THE DEVOTIONS OF ST. ANSELM. Edited by C. C. J. Webb, M.A.

GRACE ABOUNDING. By John Bunyan. Edited by S. C. Freer, M.A.

BISHOP WILSON'S SACRA PRIVATA. Edited by A. E. Burn, B.D.

LYRA SACRA : A Book of Sacred Verse. Edited by H. C. Beeching, M.A., Canon of Westminster.

A DAY BOOK FROM THE SAINTS AND FATHERS. Edited by J. H. Burn, B.D.

HEAVENLY WISDOM. A Selection from the English Mystics. Edited by E C. Gregory.

LIGHT, LIFE, and LOVE. A Selection from the German Mystics. Edited by R. Inge, M.A.

AN INTRODUCTION TO THE DEVOUT LIFE. By St. Francis de Sales. Translated and Edited by T. Barns, M.A.

MANCHESTER AL MONDO : a Contemplation of Death and Immortality. By Henry Montagu, Earl of Manchester. With an Introduction by Elizabeth Waterhouse, Editor of 'A Little Book of Life and Death.'

THE LITTLE FLOWERS OF THE GLORIOUS MESSER ST. FRANCIS AND OF HIS FRIARS. Done into English by W. Heywood. With an Introduction by A. G. Ferrers Howell.

THE SPIRITUAL GUIDE, which Disentangles the Soul and brings it by the Inward Way to the Fruition of Perfect Contemplation, and the Rich Treasure of Internal Peace. Written by Dr. Michael de Molinos, Priest. Translated from the Italian copy, printed at Venice, 1685. Edited with an Introduction by Kathleen Lyttelton. With a Preface by Canon Scott Holland.

The Illustrated Pocket Library of Plain and Coloured Books

Fcap 8vo. 3s. 6d. net each volume.

A series, in small form, of some of the famous illustrated books of fiction and general literature. These are faithfully reprinted from the first or best editions without introduction or notes. The Illustrations are chiefly in colour.

COLOURED BOOKS

OLD COLOURED BOOKS. By George Paston. With 16 Coloured Plates. *Fcap. 8vo. 2s. net.*

THE LIFE AND DEATH OF JOHN MYTTON, ESQ. By Nimrod. With 18 Coloured Plates by Henry Alken and T. J. Rawlins. *Fourth Edition.*

THE LIFE OF A SPORTSMAN. By Nimrod. With 35 Coloured Plates by Henry Alken.

HANDLEY CROSS. By R. S. Surtees. With 17 Coloured Plates and 100 Woodcuts in the Text by John Leech. *Second Edition.*

MR. SPONGE'S SPORTING TOUR. By R. S. Surtees. With 13 Coloured Plates and 90 Woodcuts in the Text by John Leech.

JORROCKS' JAUNTS AND JOLLITIES. By R. S. Surtees. With 15 Coloured Plates by H. Alken. *Second Edition.*

This volume is reprinted from the extremely rare and costly edition of 1843, which contains Alken's very fine illustrations instead of the usual ones by Phiz.

ASK MAMMA. By R. S. Surtees. With 13 Coloured Plates and 70 Woodcuts in the Text by John Leech.

THE ANALYSIS OF THE HUNTING FIELD. By R. S. Surtees. With 7 Coloured Plates by Henry Alken, and 43 Illustrations on Wood.

THE TOUR OF DR. SYNTAX IN SEARCH OF THE PICTURESQUE. By William Combe. With 30 Coloured Plates by T. Rowlandson.

THE TOUR OF DOCTOR SYNTAX IN SEARCH OF CONSOLATION. By William Combe. With 24 Coloured Plates by T. Rowlandson.

THE THIRD TOUR OF DOCTOR SYNTAX IN SEARCH OF A WIFE. By William Combe. With 24 Coloured Plates by T. Rowlandson.

THE HISTORY OF JOHNNY QUAE GENUS : the Little Foundling of the late Dr. Syntax. By the Author of 'The Three Tours.' With 24 Coloured Plates by Rowlandson.

THE ENGLISH DANCE OF DEATH, from the Designs of T. Rowlandson, with Metrical Illustrations by the Author of 'Doctor Syntax.' *Two Volumes.*

This book contains 76 Coloured Plates.

THE DANCE OF LIFE : A Poem. By the Author of 'Doctor Syntax.' Illustrated with 26 Coloured Engravings by T. Rowlandson.

[*Continued.*

LIFE IN LONDON: or, the Day and Night Scenes of Jerry Hawthorn, Esq., and his Elegant Friend, Corinthian Tom. By Pierce Egan. With 36 Coloured Plates by I. R. and G. Cruikshank. With numerous Designs on Wood.

REAL LIFE IN LONDON: or, the Rambles and Adventures of Bob Tallyho, Esq., and his Cousin, The Hon. Tom Dashall. By an Amateur (Pierce Egan). With 31 Coloured Plates by Alken and Rowlandson, etc. *Two Volumes.*

THE LIFE OF AN ACTOR. By Pierce Egan. With 27 Coloured Plates by Theodore Lane, and several Designs on Wood.

THE VICAR OF WAKEFIELD. By Oliver Goldsmith. With 24 Coloured Plates by T. Rowlandson.

THE MILITARY ADVENTURES OF JOHNNY NEWCOME. By an Officer. With 15 Coloured Plates by T. Rowlandson.

THE NATIONAL SPORTS OF GREAT BRITAIN. With Descriptions and 51 Coloured Plates by Henry Alken.

This book is completely different from the large folio edition of 'National Sports' by the same artist, and none of the plates are similar.

THE ADVENTURES OF A POST CAPTAIN. By A Naval Officer. With 24 Coloured Plates by Mr. Williams.

GAMONIA: or, the Art of Preserving Game; and an Improved Method of making Plantations and Covers, explained and illustrated by Lawrence Rawstorne, Esq. With 15 Coloured Plates by T. Rawlins.

AN ACADEMY FOR GROWN HORSEMEN: Containing the completest Instructions for Walking, Trotting, Cantering, Galloping, Stumbling, and Tumbling. Illustrated with 27 Coloured Plates, and adorned with a Portrait of the Author. By Geoffrey Gambado, Esq.

REAL LIFE IN IRELAND, or, the Day and Night Scenes of Brian Boru, Esq., and his Elegant Friend, Sir Shawn O'Dogherty. By a Real Paddy. With 19 Coloured Plates by Heath, Marks, etc.

THE ADVENTURES OF JOHNNY NEWCOME IN THE NAVY. By Alfred Burton. With 16 Coloured Plates by T. Rowlandson.

THE OLD ENGLISH SQUIRE: A Poem. By John Careless, Esq. With 20 Coloured Plates after the style of T. Rowlandson.

PLAIN BOOKS

THE GRAVE: A Poem. By Robert Blair. Illustrated by 12 Etchings executed by Louis Schiavonetti from the original Inventions of William Blake. With an Engraved Title Page and a Portrait of Blake by T. Phillips, R.A.

The illustrations are reproduced in photogravure.

ILLUSTRATIONS OF THE BOOK OF JOB. Invented and engraved by William Blake.

These famous Illustrations—21 in number—are reproduced in photogravure.

ÆSOP'S FABLES. With 380 Woodcuts by Thomas Bewick.

WINDSOR CASTLE. By W. Harrison Ainsworth. With 22 Plates and 87 Woodcuts in the Text by George Cruikshank.

THE TOWER OF LONDON. By W. Harrison Ainsworth. With 40 Plates and 58 Woodcuts in the Text by George Cruikshank.

FRANK FAIRLEGH. By F. E. Smedley. With 30 Plates by George Cruikshank.

HANDY ANDY. By Samuel Lover. With 24 Illustrations by the Author.

THE COMPLEAT ANGLER. By Izaak Walton and Charles Cotton. With 14 Plates and 77 Woodcuts in the Text.

This volume is reproduced from the beautiful edition of John Major of 1824.

THE PICKWICK PAPERS. By Charles Dickens. With the 43 Illustrations by Seymour and Phiz, the two Buss Plates, and the 32 Contemporary Onwhyn Plates.

Junior Examination Series

Edited by A. M. M. STEDMAN, M.A. *Fcap. 8vo.* 1s.

JUNIOR FRENCH EXAMINATION PAPERS. By F. Jacob, M.A. *Second Edition.*

JUNIOR LATIN EXAMINATION PAPERS. By C. G. Botting, B.A. *Fourth Edition.*

JUNIOR ENGLISH EXAMINATION PAPERS. By W. Williamson, B.A.

JUNIOR ARITHMETIC EXAMINATION PAPERS. By W. S. Beard. *Third Edition.*

JUNIOR ALGEBRA EXAMINATION PAPERS. By S. W. Finn, M.A.

JUNIOR GREEK EXAMINATION PAPERS. By T. C. Weatherhead, M.A.

JUNIOR GENERAL INFORMATION EXAMINATION PAPERS. By W. S. Beard.

A KEY TO THE ABOVE. 3s. 6d. *net.*

JUNIOR GEOGRAPHY EXAMINATION PAPERS. By W. G. Baker, M.A.

JUNIOR GERMAN EXAMINATION PAPERS. By A. Voegelin, M.A.

Junior School-Books

Edited by O. D. INSKIP, LL.D., and W. WILLIAMSON, B.A.

A CLASS-BOOK OF DICTATION PASSAGES. By W. Williamson, B.A. *Twelfth Edition.* *Cr. 8vo.* 1s. 6d.

THE GOSPEL ACCORDING TO ST. MATTHEW. Edited by E. Wilton South, M.A. With Three Maps. *Cr. 8vo.* 1s. 6d.

THE GOSPEL ACCORDING TO ST. MARK. Edited by A. E. Rubie, D.D. With Three Maps. *Cr. 8vo.* 1s. 6d.

A JUNIOR ENGLISH GRAMMAR. By W. Williamson, B.A. With numerous passages for parsing and analysis, and a chapter on Essay Writing. *Third Edition.* *Cr. 8vo.* 2s.

A JUNIOR CHEMISTRY. By E. A. Tyler, B.A., F.C.S. With 78 Illustrations. *Third Edition.* *Cr. 8vo.* 2s. 6d.

THE ACTS OF THE APOSTLES. Edited by A. E. Rubie, D.D. *Cr. 8vo.* 2s.

A JUNIOR FRENCH GRAMMAR. By L. A. Sornet and M. J. Acatos. *Cr. 8vo.* 2s.

ELEMENTARY EXPERIMENTAL SCIENCE. PHYSICS by W. T. Clough, A.R.C.S. CHEMISTRY by A. E. Dunstan, B.Sc. With 2 Plates and 154 Diagrams. *Fourth Edition.* *Cr. 8vo.* 2s. 6d.

A JUNIOR GEOMETRY. By Noel S. Lydon. With 276 Diagrams. *Fourth Edition.* *Cr. 8vo.* 2s.

ELEMENTARY EXPERIMENTAL CHEMISTRY. By A. E. Dunstan, B.Sc. With 4 Plates and 109 Diagrams. *Second Edition.* *Cr. 8vo.* 2s.

A JUNIOR FRENCH PROSE. By R. R. N. Baron, M.A. *Second Edition.* *Cr. 8vo.* 2s.

THE GOSPEL ACCORDING TO ST. LUKE. With an Introduction and Notes by William Williamson, B.A. With Three Maps. *Cr. 8vo.* 2s.

THE FIRST BOOK OF KINGS. Edited by A. E. RUBIE, D.D. With Maps. *Cr. 8vo.* 2s.

Leaders of Religion

Edited by H. C. BEECHING, M.A., Canon of Westminster. *With Portraits.*

Cr. 8vo. 2s. net.

CARDINAL NEWMAN. By R. H. Hutton.

JOHN WESLEY. By J. H. Overton, M.A.

BISHOP WILBERFORCE. By G. W. Daniell, M.A.

CARDINAL MANNING. By A. W. Hutton, M.A.

CHARLES SIMEON. By H. C. G. Moule, D.D.

JOHN KEBLE. By Walter Lock, D.D.

THOMAS CHALMERS. By Mrs. Oliphant.

LANCELOT ANDREWES. By R. L. Ottley, D.D. *Second Edition.*

AUGUSTINE OF CANTERBURY. By E. L. Cutts, D.D.

WILLIAM LAUD. By W. H. Hutton, M.A. *Third Edition.*

JOHN KNOX. By F. MacCunn. *Second Edition.*

JOHN HOWE. By R. F. Horton, D.D.

BISHOP KEN. By F. A. Clarke, M.A.

GEORGE FOX, THE QUAKER. By T. Hodgkin, D.C.L. *Third Edition.*

JOHN DONNE. By Augustus Jessopp, D.D.

THOMAS CRANMER. By A. J. Mason, D.D.

BISHOP LATIMER. By R. M. Carlyle and A. J. Carlyle, M.A.

BISHOP BUTLER. By W. A. Spooner, M.A.

Little Books on Art

With many Illustrations. Demy 16mo. 2s. 6d. net.

A series of monographs in miniature, containing the complete outline of the subject under treatment and rejecting minute details. These books are produced with the greatest care. Each volume consists of about 200 pages, and contains from 30 to 40 illustrations, including a frontispiece in photogravure.

GREEK ART. H. B. Walters. *Third Edition.*

BOOKPLATES. E. Almack.

REYNOLDS. J. Sime. *Second Edition.*

ROMNEY. George Paston.

GREUZE AND BOUCHER. Eliza F. Pollard.

VANDYCK. M. G. Smallwood.

TURNER. Frances Tyrrell-Gill.

DÜRER. Jessie Allen.

HOPPNER. H. P. K. Skipton.

HOLBEIN. Mrs. G. Fortescue.

WATTS. R. E. D. Sketchley.

LEIGHTON. Alice Corkran.

VELASQUEZ. Wilfrid Wilberforce and A. R. Gilbert.

COROT. Alice Pollard and Ethel Birnstingl.

RAPHAEL. A. R. Dryhurst.

MILLET. Netta Peacock.

ILLUMINATED MSS. J. W. Bradley.

CHRIST IN ART. Mrs. Henry Jenner.

JEWELLERY. Cyril Davenport.

[Continued.

LITTLE BOOKS ON ART—*continued.*

BURNE-JONES. Fortunée de Lisle. *Second Edition.*
REMBRANDT. Mrs. E. A. Sharp.

CLAUDE. Edward Dillon.
THE ARTS OF JAPAN. Edward Dillon.
ENAMELS. Mrs. Nelson Dawson.

The Little Galleries

Demy 16mo. 2s. 6d. net.

A series of little books containing examples of the best work of the great painters. Each volume contains 20 plates in photogravure, together with a short outline of the life and work of the master to whom the book is devoted.

A LITTLE GALLERY OF REYNOLDS.
A LITTLE GALLERY OF ROMNEY.
A LITTLE GALLERY OF HOPPNER.

A LITTLE GALLERY OF MILLAIS.
A LITTLE GALLERY OF ENGLISH POETS.

The Little Guides

With many Illustrations by E. H. NEW and other artists, and from photographs.

Small Pott 8vo, cloth, 2s. 6d. net.; leather, 3s. 6d. net.

Messrs. METHUEN are publishing a small series of books under the general title of THE LITTLE GUIDES. The main features of these books are (1) a handy and charming form, (2) artistic Illustrations by E. H. NEW and others, (3) good plans and maps, (4) an adequate but compact presentation of everything that is interesting in the natural features, history, archæology, and architecture of the town or district treated.

CAMBRIDGE AND ITS COLLEGES. By A. Hamilton Thompson. *Second Edition.*
OXFORD AND ITS COLLEGES. By J. Wells, M.A. *Seventh Edition.*
ST. PAUL'S CATHEDRAL. By George Clinch.
WESTMINSTER ABBEY. By G. E. Troutbeck.

THE ENGLISH LAKES. By F. G. Brabant, M.A.
THE MALVERN COUNTRY. By B. C. A. Windle, D.Sc., F.R.S.
SHAKESPEARE'S COUNTRY. By B. C. A. Windle, D.Sc., F.R.S. *Second Edition.*

BUCKINGHAMSHIRE. By E. S. Roscoe.
CHESHIRE. By W. M. Gallichan.
CORNWALL. By A. L. Salmon.
DERBYSHIRE. By J. Charles Cox, LL.D., F.S.A.
DEVON. By S. Baring-Gould.
DORSET. By Frank R. Heath.
HAMPSHIRE. By J. Charles Cox, LL.D., F.S.A.

HERTFORDSHIRE. By H. W. Tompkins, F.R.H.S.
THE ISLE OF WIGHT. By G. Clinch.
KENT. By G. Clinch.
KERRY. By C. P. Crane.
MIDDLESEX. By John B. Firth.
NORTHAMPTONSHIRE. By Wakeling Dry.
NORFOLK. By W. A. Dutt.
OXFORDSHIRE. By F. G. Brabant, M.A.
SUFFOLK. By W. A. Dutt.
SURREY. By F. A. H. Lambert.
SUSSEX. By F. G. Brabant, M.A. *Second Edition.*
THE EAST RIDING OF YORKSHIRE. By J. E. Morris.
THE NORTH RIDING OF YORKSHIRE. By J. E. Morris.

BRITTANY. By S. Baring-Gould.
NORMANDY. By C. Scudamore.
ROME By C. G. Ellaby.
SICILY. By F. Hamilton Jackson.

The Little Library

With Introductions, Notes, and Photogravure Frontispieces.

Small Pott 8vo. Each Volume, cloth, 1s. 6d. net ; leather, 2s. 6d. net.

Anon. ENGLISH LYRICS, A LITTLE BOOK OF.
Austen (Jane). PRIDE AND PREJUDICE. Edited by E. V. Lucas. *Two Vols.*

NORTHANGER ABBEY. Edited by E. V. Lucas.
Bacon (Francis). THE ESSAYS OF LORD BACON. Edited by EDWARD WRIGHT.

[*Continued.*

THE LITTLE LIBRARY—*continued.*

Barham (R. H.). THE INGOLDSBY LEGENDS. Edited by J. B. ATLAY. *Two Volumes.*

Barnett (Mrs. P. A.). A LITTLE BOOK OF ENGLISH PROSE.

Beckford (William). THE HISTORY OF THE CALIPH VATHEK. Edited by E. DENISON ROSS.

Blake (William). SELECTIONS FROM WILLIAM BLAKE. Edited by M. PERUGINI.

Borrow (George). LAVENGRO. Edited by F. HINDES GROOME. *Two Volumes.*

THE ROMANY RYE. Edited by JOHN SAMPSON.

Browning (Robert). SELECTIONS FROM THE EARLY POEMS OF ROBERT BROWNING. Edited by W. HALL GRIFFIN, M.A.

Canning (George). SELECTIONS FROM THE ANTI-JACOBIN : with GEORGE CANNING's additional Poems. Edited by LLOYD SANDERS.

Cowley (Abraham). THE ESSAYS OF ABRAHAM COWLEY. Edited by H. C. MINCHIN.

Crabbe (George). SELECTIONS FROM GEORGE CRABBE. Edited by A. C. DEANE.

Craik (Mrs.). JOHN HALIFAX, GENTLEMAN. Edited by ANNE MATHESON. *Two Volumes.*

Crashaw (Richard). THE ENGLISH POEMS OF RICHARD CRASHAW. Edited by EDWARD HUTTON.

Dante (Alighieri). THE INFERNO OF DANTE. Translated by H. F. CARY. Edited by PAGET TOYNBEE, M.A., D.Litt.

THE PURGATORIO OF DANTE. Translated by H. F. CARY. Edited by PAGET TOYNBEE, M.A., D.Litt.

THE PARADISO OF DANTE. Translated by H. F. CARY. Edited by PAGET TOYNBEE, M.A., D.Litt.

Darley (George). SELECTIONS FROM THE POEMS OF GEORGE DARLEY. Edited by R. A. STREATFEILD.

Deane (A. C.). A LITTLE BOOK OF LIGHT VERSE.

Dickens (Charles). CHRISTMAS BOOKS. *Two Volumes.*

Ferrier (Susan). MARRIAGE. Edited by A. GOODRICH - FREER and LORD IDDESLEIGH. *Two Volumes.*

THE INHERITANCE. *Two Volumes.*

Gaskell (Mrs.). CRANFORD. Edited by E. V. LUCAS. *Second Edition.*

Hawthorne (Nathaniel). THE SCARLET LETTER. Edited by PERCY DEARMER.

Henderson (T. F.). A LITTLE BOOK OF SCOTTISH VERSE.

Keats (John). POEMS. With an Introduction by L. BINYON, and Notes by J. MASEFIELD.

Kinglake (A. W.). EOTHEN. With an Introduction and Notes. *Second Edition.*

Lamb (Charles). ELIA, AND THE LAST ESSAYS OF ELIA. dited by E. V. LUCAS.

Locker (F.). LONDON LYRICS. Edited by A. D. GODLEY, M.A. A reprint of the First Edition.

Longfellow (H. W.). SELECTIONS FROM LONGFELLOW. Edited by L. M. FAITHFULL.

Marvell (Andrew). THE POEMS OF ANDREW MARVELL. Edited by E. WRIGHT.

Milton (John). THE MINOR POEMS OF JOHN MILTON. Edited by H. C. BEECHING, M.A., Canon of Westminster.

Moir (D. M.). MANSIE WAUCH. Edited by T. F. HENDERSON.

Nichols (J. B. B.). A LITTLE BOOK OF ENGLISH SONNETS.

Rochefoucauld (La). THE MAXIMS OF LA ROCHEFOUCAULD. Translated by Dean STANHOPE. Edited by G. H. POWELL.

Smith (Horace and James). REJECTED ADDRESSES. Edited by A. D. GODLEY, M.A.

Sterne (Laurence). A SENTIMENTAL JOURNEY. Edited by H. W. PAUL.

Tennyson (Alfred, Lord). THE EARLY POEMS OF ALFRED, LORD TENNYSON. Edited by J. CHURTON COLLINS, M.A.

IN MEMORIAM. Edited by H. C. BEECHING, M.A.

THE PRINCESS. Edited by ELIZABETH WORDSWORTH.

MAUD. Edited by ELIZABETH WORDSWORTH.

Thackeray (W. M.). VANITY FAIR. Edited by S. GWYNN. *Three Volumes.*

PENDENNIS. Edited by S. GWYNN. *Three Volumes.*

ESMOND. Edited by S. GWYNN.

CHRISTMAS BOOKS. Edited by S. GWYNN.

Vaughan (Henry). THE POEMS OF HENRY VAUGHAN. Edited by EDWARD HUTTON.

Walton (Izaak). THE COMPLEAT ANGLER. Edited by J. BUCHAN.

Waterhouse (Mrs. Alfred). A LITTLE BOOK OF LIFE AND DEATH. Edited by. *Tenth Edition.*
  Also on Japanese Paper. *Leather.* 5s. net.

Wordsworth (W.). SELECTIONS FROM WORDSWORTH. Edited by NOWELL C. SMITH.

Wordsworth (W.) and Coleridge (S. T.). LYRICAL BALLADS. Edited by GEORGE SAMPSON.

The Little Quarto Shakespeare

Edited by W. J. CRAIG. With Introductions and Notes

Pott 16mo. *In* 40 *Volumes. Leather, price* 1s. *net each volume.*
Mahogany Revolving Book Case. 10s. *net.*

Miniature Library

Reprints in miniature of a few interesting books which have qualities of
humanity, devotion, or literary genius.

EUPHRANOR: A Dialogue on Youth. By Edward FitzGerald. From the edition published by W. Pickering in 1851. *Demy* 32mo. *Leather,* 2s. *net.*

POLONIUS: or Wise Saws and Modern Instances. By Edward FitzGerald. From the edition published by W. Pickering in 1852. *Demy* 32mo. *Leather,* 2s. *net.*

THE RUBÁIYÁT OF OMAR KHAYYÁM. By Edward FitzGerald. From the 1st edition of 1859, *Third Edition. Leather,* 1s. *net.*

THE LIFE OF EDWARD, LORD HERBERT OF CHERBURY. Written by himself. From the edition printed at Strawberry Hill in the year 1764. *Demy* 32mo. *Leather,* 2s. *net.*

THE VISIONS OF DOM FRANCISCO QUEVEDO VILLEGAS, Knight of the Order of St. James. Made English by R. L. From the edition printed for H. Herringman, 1668. *Leather.* 2s. *net.*

POEMS. By Dora Greenwell. From the edition of 1848. *Leather,* 2s. *net.*

Oxford Biographies

Fcap. 8vo. *Each volume, cloth,* 2s. 6d. *net ; leather,* 3s. 6d. *net.*

DANTE ALIGHIERI. By Paget Toynbee, M.A., D.Litt. With 12 Illustrations. *Second Edition.*

SAVONAROLA. By E. L. S. Horsburgh, M.A. With 12 Illustrations. *Second Edition.*

JOHN HOWARD. By E. C. S. Gibson, D.D., Bishop of Gloucester. With 12 Illustrations.

TENNYSON. By A. C. BENSON, M.A. With 9 Illustrations.

WALTER RALEIGH. By I. A. Taylor. With 12 Illustrations.

ERASMUS. By E. F. H. Capey. With 12 Illustrations.

THE YOUNG PRETENDER. By C. S. Terry. With 12 Illustrations.

ROBERT BURNS. By T. F. Henderson. With 12 Illustrations.

CHATHAM. By A. S. M'Dowall. With 12 Illustrations.

ST. FRANCIS OF ASSISI. By Anna M. Stoddart. With 16 Illustrations.

CANNING. By W. Alison Phillips. With 12 Illustrations.

BEACONSFIELD. By Walter Sichel. With 12 Illustrations.

GOETHE. By H. G. Atkins. With 12 Illustrations.

FENELON. By Viscount St Cyres. With 12 Illustrations.

School Examination Series

Edited by A. M. M. STEDMAN, M.A. *Cr.* 8vo. 2s. 6d.

FRENCH EXAMINATION PAPERS. By A. M. M. Stedman, M.A. *Fourteenth Edition.*
   A KEY, issued to Tutors and Private Students only to be had on application to the Publishers. *Fifth Edition. Crown* 8vo. 6s. *net.*

LATIN EXAMINATION PAPERS. By A. M. M. Stedman, M.A. *Thirteenth Edition.*
   KEY (*Sixth Edition*) issued as above. 6s. *net.*

GREEK EXAMINATION PAPERS. By A. M. M. Stedman, M.A. *Ninth Edition.*
   KEY (*Fourth Edition*) issued as above. 6s. *net.*

GERMAN EXAMINATION PAPERS. By R. J. Morich. *Sixth Edition.*

KEY (*Third Edition*) issued as above 6s. *net.*

HISTORY AND GEOGRAPHY EXAMINATION PAPERS. By C. H. Spence, M.A. *Third Edition.*

PHYSICS EXAMINATION PAPERS. By R. E. Steel, M.A., F.C.S.

GENERAL KNOWLEDGE EXAMINATION PAPERS. By A. M. M. Stedman, M.A. *Sixth Edition.*
   KEY (*Fourth Edition*) issued as above. 7s. *net.*

EXAMINATION PAPERS IN ENGLISH HISTORY. By J. Tait Plowden-Wardlaw, B.A.

School Histories

Illustrated.   Crown 8vo.   1s. 6d.

A SCHOOL HISTORY OF WARWICKSHIRE. By
B. C. A. Windle, D.Sc., F.R.S.

A SCHOOL HISTORY OF SOMERSET. By
Walter Raymond.

A SCHOOL HISTORY OF LANCASHIRE. by
W. E. Rhodes.

A SCHOOL HISTORY OF SURREY. By H. E.
Malden, M.A.

A SCHOOL HISTORY OF MIDDLESEX. By V.
G. Plarr and F. W. Walton.

Textbooks of Science

Edited by G. F. GOODCHILD, M.A., B.Sc., and G. R. MILLS, M.A.

PRACTICAL MECHANICS. By Sidney H. Wells.
Third Edition. Cr. 8vo.   3s. 6d.

PRACTICAL CHEMISTRY. Part I. By W.
French, M.A. *Cr. 8vo. Fourth Edition.*
1s. 6d. Part II. By W. French, M.A., and
T. H. Boardman, M.A. *Cr. 8vo.   1s. 6d.*

TECHNICAL ARITHMETIC AND GEOMETRY.
By C. T. Millis, M.I.M.E. *Cr. 8vo.*
3s. 6d.

EXAMPLES IN PHYSICS. By C. E. Jackson,
B.A. *Cr. 8vo.   2s. 6d.*

PLANT LIFE, Studies in Garden and School.
By Horace F. Jones, F.C.S. With 320
Diagrams. *Cr. 8vo.   3s. 6d.*

THE COMPLETE SCHOOL CHEMISTRY. By F.
M. Oldham, B.A. With 126 Illustrations.
Cr. 8vo.

AN ORGANIC CHEMISTRY FOR SCHOOLS AND
TECHNICAL INSTITUTES. By A. E. Dunstan,
B.Sc. (Lond.), F.C.S. Illustrated.
Cr. 8vo.

ELEMENTARY SCIENCE FOR PUPIL TEACHERS.
PHYSICS SECTION. By W. T. Clough,
A.R.C.S. (Lond.), F.C.S. CHEMISTRY
SECTION. By A. E. Dunstan, B.Sc. (Lond.),
F.C.S. With 2 Plates and 10 Diagrams.
Cr. 8vo.   2s.

Methuen's Simplified French Texts

Edited by T. R. N. CROFTS, M.A.

One Shilling each.

L'HISTOIRE D'UNE TULIPE. Adapted by T. R.
N. Crofts, M.A.

ABDALLAH. Adapted by J. A. Wilson.

LA CHANSON DE ROLAND. Adapted by H.
Rieu, M.A.

MÉMOIRES DE CADICHON. Adapted by J. F.
Rhoades.

Methuen's Standard Library

In Sixpenny Volumes.

THE STANDARD LIBRARY is a new series of volumes containing the great classics of the
world, and particularly the finest works of English literature. All the great masters will be
represented, either in complete works or in selections. It is the ambition of the publishers to
place the best books of the Anglo-Saxon race within the reach of every reader, so that the
series may represent something of the diversity and splendour of our English tongue. The
characteristics of THE STANDARD LIBRARY are four :—1. SOUNDNESS OF TEXT. 2. CHEAPNESS.
3. CLEARNESS OF TYPE. 4. SIMPLICITY. The books are well printed on good paper at a
price which on the whole is without parallel in the history of publishing. Each volume contains from 100 to 250 pages, and is issued in paper covers, Crown 8vo, at Sixpence net, or in
cloth gilt at One Shilling net. In a few cases long books are issued as Double Volumes
or as Treble Volumes.

THE MEDITATIONS OF MARCUS AURELIUS.
The translation is by R. Graves.

SENSE AND SENSIBILITY. By Jane Austen.

ESSAYS AND COUNSELS and THE NEW
ATLANTIS. By Francis Bacon, Lord
Verulam.

RELIGIO MEDICI and URN BURIAL. By
Sir Thomas Browne. The text has been
collated by A. R. Waller.

THE PILGRIM'S PROGRESS. By John Bunyan.

REFLECTIONS ON THE FRENCH REVOLUTION.
By Edmund Burke.

THE POEMS AND SONGS OF ROBERT BURNS.
Double Volume.

THE ANALOGY OF RELIGION, NATURAL AND
REVEALED. By Joseph Butler, D.D.

THE POEMS OF THOMAS CHATTERTON. In 2
volumes.
Vol. I.—Miscellaneous Poems.

[Continued.

METHUEN'S STANDARD LIBRARY—*continued*.

Vol. II.—The Rowley Poems.

THE NEW LIFE AND SONNETS. By Dante. Translated into English by D. G. Rossetti.

TOM JONES. By Henry Fielding. Treble Vol.

CRANFORD. By Mrs. Gaskell.

THE HISTORY OF THE DECLINE AND FALL OF THE ROMAN EMPIRE. By Edward Gibbon. In 7 double volumes.

The Text and Notes have been revised by J. B. Bury, Litt.D., but the Appendices of the more expensive edition are not given.

THE VICAR OF WAKEFIELD. By Oliver Goldsmith.

THE POEMS AND PLAYS OF OLIVER GOLDSMITH.

THE WORKS OF BEN JONSON.

Vol. I.—The Case is Altered. Every Man in His Humour. Every Man out of His Humour.

Vol. II.—Cynthia's Revels ; The Poetaster. The text has been collated by H. C. Hart.

THE POEMS OF JOHN KEATS. Double volume. The Text has been collated by E. de Selincourt.

ON THE IMITATION OF CHRIST. By Thomas à Kempis. The translation is by C. Bigg, DD., Canon of Christ Church.

A SERIOUS CALL TO A DEVOUT AND HOLY LIFE. By William Law.

PARADISE LOST. By John Milton.

EIKONOKLASTES AND THE TENURE OF KINGS AND MAGISTRATES. By John Milton.

UTOPIA AND POEMS. By Sir Thomas More.

THE REPUBLIC OF PLATO. Translated by Sydenham and Taylor. Double Volume. The translation has been revised by W. H. D. Rouse.

THE LITTLE FLOWERS OF ST. FRANCIS. Translated by W. Heywood.

THE WORKS OF WILLIAM SHAKESPEARE. In 10 volumes.

Vol. I.—The Tempest ; The Two Gentlemen of Verona ; The Merry Wives of Windsor ; Measure for Measure ; The Comedy of Errors.

Vol. II.—Much Ado About Nothing ; Love's Labour's Lost ; A Midsummer Night's Dream ; The Merchant of Venice ; As You Like It.

Vol. III.—The Taming of the Shrew ; All 's Well that Ends Well; Twelfth Night ; The Winter's Tale.

Vol. IV.—The Life and Death of King John ; The Tragedy of King Richard the Second ; The First Part of King Henry IV. ; The Second Part of King Henry IV.

Vol. V.—The Life of King Henry V. ; The First Part of King Henry VI. ; The Second Part of King Henry VI.

Vol. VI.—The Third Part of King Henry VI. ; The Tragedy of King Richard III. ; The Famous History of the Life of King Henry VIII.

THE POEMS OF PERCY BYSSHE SHELLEY. In 4 volumes.

Vol. I.—Alastor ; The Dæmon of the World ; The Revolt of Islam, etc. The Text has been revised by C. D. Locock.

THE LIFE OF NELSON. By Robert Southey.

THE NATURAL HISTORY AND ANTIQUITIES OF SELBORNE. By Gilbert White.

Textbooks of Technology

Edited by G. F. GOODCHILD, M.A., B.Sc., and G. R. MILLS, M.A.

Fully Illustrated.

HOW TO MAKE A DRESS. By J. A. E. Wood. *Fourth Edition. Cr. 8vo. 1s. 6d.*

CARPENTRY AND JOINERY. By F. C. Webber. *Fifth Edition. Cr. 8vo. 3s. 6d.*

MILLINERY, THEORETICAL AND PRACTICAL. By Clare Hill. *Third Edition. Cr. 8vo. 2s.*

AN INTRODUCTION TO THE STUDY OF TEXTILE DESIGN. By Aldred F. Barker. *Demy 8vo. 7s. 6d.*

BUILDERS' QUANTITIES. By H. C. Grubb. *Cr. 8vo. 4s. 6d.*

RÉPOUSSÉ METAL WORK. By A. C. Horth. *Cr. 8vo. 2s. 6d.*

ELECTRIC LIGHT AND POWER: An Introduction to the Study of Electrical Engineering. By E. E. Brooks, B.Sc. (Lond.) Second Master and Instructor of Physics and Electrical Engineering, Leicester Technical School, and W. H. N. James, A.R.C.S., A.I.E.E., Assistant Instructor of Electrical Engineering, Manchester Municipal Technical School. *Cr. 8vo. 4s. 6d.*

ENGINEERING WORKSHOP PRACTICE. By C. C. Allen, Lecturer on Engineering, Municipal Technical Institute, Coventry. With many Diagrams. *Cr. 8vo. 2s.*

Handbooks of Theology

Edited by R. L. OTTLEY, D.D., Professor of Pastoral Theology at Oxford, and Canon of Christ Church, Oxford.

The series is intended, in part, to furnish the clergy and teachers or students of Theology with trustworthy Textbooks, adequately representing the present position of the questions dealt with; in part, to make accessible to the reading public an accurate and concise statement of facts and principles in all questions bearing on Theology and Religion.

THE XXXIX. ARTICLES OF THE CHURCH OF ENGLAND. Edited by E. C. S. Gibson, D.D. *Fifth and Cheaper Edition in one Volume. Demy 8vo. 12s. 6d.*

AN INTRODUCTION TO THE HISTORY OF RELIGION. By F. B. Jevons. M.A., Litt.D. *Third Edition. Demy 8vo. 10s. 6d.*

THE DOCTRINE OF THE INCARNATION. By R. L. Ottley, D.D. *Second and Cheaper Edition. Demy 8vo. 12s. 6d.*

AN INTRODUCTION TO THE HISTORY OF THE CREEDS. By A. E. Burn, D.D. *Demy 8vo. 10s. 6d.*

THE PHILOSOPHY OF RELIGION IN ENGLAND AND AMERICA. By Alfred Caldecott, D.D. *Demy 8vo. 10s. 6d.*

A HISTORY OF EARLY CHRISTIAN DOCTRINE. By J. F. Bethune-Baker, M.A. *Demy 8vo. 10s. 6d.*

The Westminster Commentaries

General Editor, WALTER LOCK, D.D., Warden of Keble College, Dean Ireland's Professor of Exegesis in the University of Oxford.

The object of each commentary is primarily exegetical, to interpret the author's meaning to the present generation. The editors will not deal, except very subordinately, with questions of textual criticism or philology; but, taking the English text in the Revised Version as their basis, they will try to combine a hearty acceptance of critical principles with loyalty to the Catholic Faith.

THE BOOK OF GENESIS. Edited with Introduction and Notes by S. R. Driver, D.D. *Sixth Edition Demy 8vo. 10s. 6d.*

THE BOOK OF JOB. Edited by E. C. S. Gibson, D.D. *Second Edition. Demy 8vo. 6s.*

THE ACTS OF THE APOSTLES. Edited by R. B. Rackham, M.A. *Demy 8vo. Third Edition. 10s. 6d.*

THE FIRST EPISTLE OF PAUL THE APOSTLE TO THE CORINTHIANS. Edited by H. L. Goudge, M.A. *Demy 8vo. 6s.*

THE EPISTLE OF ST. JAMES. Edited with Introduction and Notes by R. J. Knowling, D.D. *Demy 8vo. 6s.*

THE BOOK OF EZEKIEL. Edited H. A. Redpath, M.A., D. Litt. *Demy 8vo. 10s. 6d.*

PART II.——FICTION

Adderley (Hon. and Rev. James), Author of 'Stephen Remarx.' BEHOLD THE DAYS COME. *Second Edition. Cr. 8vo. 3s. 6d.*

Albanesi (E. Maria). SUSANNAH AND ONE OTHER. *Fourth Edition. Cr. 8vo. 6s.*

THE BLUNDER OF AN INNOCENT. *Second Edition. Cr. 8vo. 6s.*

CAPRICIOUS CAROLINE. *Second Edition. Cr. 8vo. 6s.*

LOVE AND LOUISA. *Second Edition. Cr. 8vo. 6s.*

PETER, A PARASITE. *Cr. 8vo. 6s.*

THE BROWN EYES OF MARY. *Third Edition. Cr. 8vo. 6s.*

I KNOW A MAIDEN. *Third Edition. Cr. 8vo. 6s.*

Anstey (F.). Author of 'Vice Versâ.' A BAYARD FROM BENGAL. Illustrated by BERNARD PARTRIDGE. *Third Edition. Cr. 8vo. 3s. 6d.*

Bagot (Richard). A ROMAN MYSTERY. *Third Edition. Cr. 8vo. 6s.*

THE PASSPORT. *Fourth Edition. Cr. 8vo 6s.*

TEMPTATION. *Fourth Edition. Cr. 8vo. 6s.*

CASTING OF NETS. *Twelfth Edition. Cr. 8vo. 6s.*

DONNA DIANA. *A New Edition. Cr. 8vo. 6s.*

LOVE'S PROXY. *A New Edition. Cr. 8vo. 6s.*

Baring-Gould (S.). ARMINELL. *Fifth Edition. Cr. 8vo. 6s.*

URITH. *Fifth Edition. Cr. 8vo. 6s.*

IN THE ROAR OF THE SEA. *Seventh Edition. Cr. 8vo. 6s.*

CHEAP JACK ZITA. *Fourth Edition. Cr. 8vo. 6s.*

MARGERY OF QUETHER. *Third Edition. Cr. 8vo. 6s.*

THE QUEEN OF LOVE. *Fifth Edition. Cr. 8vo. 6s.*

JACQUETTA. *Third Edition. Cr. 8vo. 6s.*

KITTY ALONE. *Fifth Edition. Cr. 8vo. 6s.*

NOÉMI. Illustrated. *Fourth Edition. Cr. 8vo. 6s.*

THE BROOM-SQUIRE. Illustrated. *Fifth Edition. Cr. 8vo. 6s.*

DARTMOOR IDYLLS. *Cr. 8vo. 6s.*

THE PENNYCOMEQUICKS. *Third Edition. Cr. 8vo. 6s.*

GUAVAS THE TINNER. Illustrated. *Second Edition. Cr. 8vo. 6s.*

BLADYS OF THE STEWPONEY. Illustrated. *Second Edition. Cr. 8vo. 6s.*
PABO THE PRIEST. *Cr. 8vo. 6s.*
WINEFRED. Illustrated. *Second Edition. Cr. 8vo. 6s.*
ROYAL GEORGIE. Illustrated. *Cr. 8vo. 6s.*
MISS QUILLET. Illustrated. *Cr. 8vo. 6s.*
CHRIS OF ALL SORTS. *Cr. 8vo. 6s.*
IN DEWISLAND. *Second Edition. Cr. 8vo. 6s.*
LITTLE TU'PENNY. *A New Edition. 6d.*
See also Shilling Novels.
Barnett (Edith A.). A WILDERNESS WINNER. *Second Edition. Cr. 8vo. 6s.*
Barr (James). LAUGHING THROUGH A WILDERNESS. *Cr. 8vo. 6s.*
Barr (Robert). IN THE MIDST OF ALARMS. *Third Edition. Cr. 8vo. 6s.*
THE STRONG ARM. *Second Edition. Cr. 8vo. 6s.*
THE MUTABLE MANY. *Third Edition. Cr. 8vo. 6s.*
THE COUNTESS TEKLA. *Fourth Edition. Cr. 8vo. 6s.*
THE LADY ELECTRA. *Second Edition. Cr. 8vo. 6s.*
THE TEMPESTUOUS PETTICOAT. Illustrated. *Third Edition. Cr. 8vo. 6s.*
See also Shilling Novels and S. Crane.
Begbie (Harold). THE ADVENTURES OF SIR JOHN SPARROW. *Cr. 8vo. 6s.*
Belloc (Hilaire). EMMANUEL BURDEN, MERCHANT. With 36 Illustrations by G. K. CHESTERTON. *Second Edition. Cr. 8vo. 6s.*
Benson (E. F.) DODO. *Fifteenth Edition. Cr. 8vo. 6s.*
See also Shilling Novels.
THE CAPSINA. *Second Edit. Cr. 8vo. 6s.*
Benson (Margaret). SUBJECT TO VANITY. *Cr. 8vo. 3s. 6d.*
Bretherton (Ralph). THE MILL. *Cr. 8vo. 6s.*
Burton (J. Bloundelle). THE FATE OF VALSEC. *Cr. 8vo. 6s.*
See also Shilling Novels.
Capes (Bernard), Author of 'The Lake of Wine.' THE EXTRAORDINARY CONFESSIONS OF DIANA PLEASE. *Third Edition. Cr. 8vo. 6s.*
A JAY OF ITALY. *Fourth Ed. Cr. 8vo. 6s.*
LOAVES AND FISHES. *Second Edition. Cr. 8vo. 6s.*
A ROGUE'S TRAGEDY. *Second Edition. Cr. 8vo. 6s.*
THE GREAT SKENE MYSTERY. *Second Edition. Cr. 8vo. 6s.*
Charlton (Randall). MAVE. *Second Edition. Cr. 8vo. 6s.*
Chesney (Weatherby). THE TRAGEDY OF THE GREAT EMERALD. *Cr. 8vo. 6s.*
THE MYSTERY OF A BUNGALOW. *Second Edition. Cr. 8vo. 6s.*
See also Shilling Novels.
Corelli (Marie). A ROMANCE OF TWO WORLDS. *Twenty-Seventh Edition. Cr. 8vo. 6s.*

VENDETTA. *Twenty-Fifth Edition. Cr. 8vo. 6s.*
THELMA. *Thirty-Seventh Edition. Cr. 8vo. 6s.*
ARDATH: THE STORY OF A DEAD SELF. *Seventeenth Edition. Cr. 8vo. 6s.*
THE SOUL OF LILITH. *Fourteenth Edition. Cr. 8vo. 6s.*
WORMWOOD. *Fifteenth Ed. Cr. 8vo. 6s.*
BARABBAS: A DREAM OF THE WORLD'S TRAGEDY. *Forty-second Edition. Cr. 8vo. 6s.*
THE SORROWS OF SATAN. *Fifty-second Edition. Cr. 8vo. 6s.*
THE MASTER CHRISTIAN. *Tenth Edition. Cr. 8vo. 6s.*
TEMPORAL POWER: A STUDY IN SUPREMACY. *150th Thousand. Cr. 8vo. 6s.*
GOD'S GOOD MAN: A SIMPLE LOVE STORY. *Eleventh Edition. Cr. 8vo. 6s.*
THE MIGHTY ATOM. *Twenty-sixth Edition. Cr. 8vo. 6s.*
BOY: a Sketch. *Ninth Edition. Cr. 8vo. 6s.*
CAMEOS. *Twelfth Edition. Cr. 8vo. 6s.*
Cotes (Mrs. Everard). See Sara Jeannette Duncan.
Cotterell (Constance). THE VIRGIN AND THE SCALES. Illustrated. *Second Edition. Cr. 8vo. 6s.*
Crane (Stephen) and **Barr (Robert).** THE O'RUDDY. *Cr 8vo. 6s.*
Crockett (S. R.), Author of 'The Raiders,' etc. LOCHINVAR. Illustrated. *Third Edition. Cr. 8vo. 6s.*
THE STANDARD BEARER. *Cr. 8vo. 6s.*
Croker (B. M.). THE OLD CANTONMENT. *Cr. 8vo. 6s.*
JOHANNA. *Second Edition. Cr. 8vo. 6s.*
THE HAPPY VALLEY. *Third Edition. Cr. 8vo. 6s.*
A NINE DAYS' WONDER. *Third Edition. Cr. 8vo. 6s.*
PEGGY OF THE BARTONS. *Sixth Edition. Cr. 8vo. 6s.*
ANGEL. *Fourth Edition. Cr. 8vo. 6s.*
A STATE SECRET. *Third Edition. Cr. 8vo. 3s. 6d.*
Crosbie (Mary). DISCIPLES. *Second Ed. Cr. 8vo. 6s.*
Dawson (A. J.) DANIEL WHYTE. *Cr. 8vo. 3s. 6d.*
Deane (Mary). THE OTHER PAWN. *Cr. 8vo. 6s.*
Doyle (A. Conan), Author of 'Sherlock Holmes,' 'The White Company,' etc. ROUND THE RED LAMP. *Tenth Edition. Cr. 8vo. 6s.*
Duncan (Sara Jeannette) (Mrs. Everard Cotes). THOSE DELIGHTFUL AMERICANS. Illustrated. *Third Edition. Cr. 8vo. 6s.* See also Shilling Novels.
Findlater (J. H.). THE GREEN GRAVES OF BALGOWRIE. *Fifth Edition. Cr. 8vo. 6s.*
THE LADDER TO THE STARS. *Second Edition. Cr. 8vo. 6s.*
See also Shilling Novels.

Findlater (Mary). A NARROW WAY. *Third Edition. Cr. 8vo.. 6s.*

THE ROSE OF JOY. *Third Edition. Cr. 8vo. 6s.*

A BLIND BIRD'S NEST. With 8 Illustrations. *Second Edition. Cr. 8vo. 6s.*
　See also Shilling Novels.

Fitzpatrick (K.) THE WEANS AT ROWALLAN. Illustrated. *Second Edition. Cr. 8vo. 6s.*

Francis (M. E.). STEPPING WESTWARD. *Second Edition. Cr. 8vo. 6s.*

Fraser (Mrs. Hugh), Author of 'The Stolen Emperor.' THE SLAKING OF THE SWORD. *Cr. 8vo. 6s.*

IN THE SHADOW OF THE LORD. *Third Edition. Crown 8vo. 6s.*

Fuller=Maitland (Ella), Author of ' The Day Book of Bethia Hardacre.' BLANCHE ESMEAD. *Second Edition. Cr. 8vo. 6s.*

Gates (Eleanor), Author of ' The Biography of a Prairie Girl.' THE PLOW-WOMAN. *Cr. 8vo. 6s.*

Gerard (Dorothea), Author of ' Lady Baby.' HOLY MATRIMONY. *Second Edition. Cr. 8vo. 6s.*

MADE OF MONEY. *Cr. 8vo. 6s.*

THE BRIDGE OF LIFE. *Cr. 8vo. 6s.*

THE IMPROBABLE IDYL. *Third Edition. Cr. 8vo. 6s.*
　See also Shilling Novels.

Gissing (George), Author of 'Demos,' 'In the Year of Jubilee,' etc. THE TOWN TRAVELLER. *Second Ed. Cr. 8vo. 6s.*

THE CROWN OF LIFE. *Cr. 8vo. 6s.*

Gleig (Charles). BUNTER'S CRUISE. Illustrated. *Cr. 8vo. 3s. 6d.*

Hamilton (M.), Author of 'Cut Laurels.' THE FIRST CLAIM. *Second Edition. Cr. 8vo. 6s.*

Harraden (Beatrice). IN VARYING MOODS. *Fourteenth Edition. Cr. 8vo. 6s.*

HILDA STRAFFORD and THE REMITTANCE MAN. *Twelfth Edition. Cr. 8vo. 6s.*

THE SCHOLAR'S DAUGHTER. *Fourth Edition. Cr. 8vo. 6s.*

Harrod (F.) (Frances Forbes Robertson). THE TAMING OF THE BRUTE. *Cr. 8vo. 6s.*

Herbertson (Agnes G.). PATIENCE DEAN. *Cr. 8vo. 6s.*

Hichens (Robert). THE PROPHET OF BERKELEY SQUARE. *Second Edition. Cr. 8vo. 6s.*

TONGUES OF CONSCIENCE. *Third Edition. Cr. 8vo. 6s.*

FELIX. *Fifth Edition. Cr. 8vo. 6s.*

THE WOMAN WITH THE FAN. *Sixth Edition. Cr. 8vo. 6s.*

BYEWAYS. *Cr. 8vo. 6s.*

THE GARDEN OF ALLAH. *Fifteenth Edition. Cr. 8vo. 6s.*

THE BLACK SPANIEL. *Cr. 8vo. 6s.*

THE CALL OF THE BLOOD. *Seventh Edition. Cr. 8vo. 6s.*

Hope (Anthony). THE GOD IN THE CAR. *Tenth Edition. Cr. 8vo. 6s.*

A CHANGE OF AIR. *Sixth Edition. Cr. 8vo. 6s.*

A MAN OF MARK. *Fifth Ed. Cr. 8vo. 6s.*

THE CHRONICLES OF COUNT ANTONIO. *Sixth Edition. Cr. 8vo. 6s.*

PHROSO. Illustrated by H. R. MILLAR. *Sixth Edition. Cr. 8vo. 6s.*

SIMON DALE. Illustrated. *Seventh Edition. Cr. 8vo. 6s.*

THE KING'S MIRROR. *Fourth Edition. Cr. 8vo. 6s.*

QUISANTE. *Fourth Edition. Cr. 8vo. 6s.*

THE DOLLY DIALOGUES. *Cr. 8vo. 6s.*

A SERVANT OF THE PUBLIC. Illustrated. *Fourth Edition. Cr. 8vo. 6s.*

Hope (Graham), Author of ' A Cardinal and his Conscience,' etc., etc. THE LADY OF LYTE. *Second Edition. Cr. 8vo. 6s.*

Housman (Clemence). THE LIFE OF SIR AGLOVALE DE GALIS. *Cr. 8vo. 6s.*

Hyne (C. J. Cutcliffe), Author of 'Captain Kettle.' MR. HORROCKS, PURSER. *Fourth Edition. Cr. 8vo. 6s.*

PRINCE RUPERT, THE BUCCANEER. Illustrated. *Third Edition. Cr. 8vo. 6s.*

Jacobs (W. W.). MANY CARGOES. *Twenty-Ninth Edition. Cr. 8vo. 3s. 6d.*

SEA URCHINS. *Fourteenth Edition.. Cr. 8vo. 3s. 6d.*

A MASTER OF CRAFT. Illustrated. *Seventh Edition. Cr. 8vo. 3s. 6d.*

LIGHT FREIGHTS. Illustrated. *Sixth Edition. Cr. 8vo. 3s. 6d.*

THE SKIPPER'S WOOING. *Eighth Edition. Cr. 8vo. 3s. 6d.*

DIALSTONE LANE. Illustrated. *Seventh Edition. Cr. 8vo. 3s. 6d.*

ODD CRAFT. Illustrated. *Seventh Edition. Cr. 8vo. 3s. 6d.*

AT SUNWICH PORT. Illustrated. *Seventh Edition. Cr. 8vo. 3s. 6d.*

James (Henry). THE SOFT SIDE. *Second Edition. Cr. 8vo. 6s.*

THE BETTER SORT. *Cr. 8vo. 6s.*

THE AMBASSADORS. *Second Edition. Cr. 8vo. 6s.*

THE GOLDEN BOWL. *Third Edition. Cr. 8vo. 6s.*

Keays (H. A. Mitchell). HE THAT EATETH BREAD WITH ME. *Cr. 8vo. 6s.*

Kester (Vaughan). THE FORTUNES OF THE LANDRAYS. *Cr. 8vo. 6s.*

Lawless (Hon. Emily). WITH ESSEX IN IRELAND. *Cr. 8vo. 6s.*
　See also Shilling Novels.

Le Queux (W.). THE HUNCHBACK OF WESTMINSTER. *Third Edition. Cr. 8vo. 6s.*

THE CLOSED BOOK. *Third Edition. Cr. 8vo. 6s.*

THE VALLEY OF THE SHADOW. Illustrated. *Third Edition.* *Cr. 8vo.* *6s.*

BEHIND THE THRONE. *Third Edition.* *Cr. 8vo.* *6s.*

Levett-Yeats (S.). ORRAIN. *Second Edition.* *Cr. 8vo.* *6s.*

London (Jack), Author of 'The Call of the Wild,' 'The Sea Wolf,' etc. WHITE FANG. *Fourth Edition.* *Cr. 8vo.* *6s.*

Lucas (E. V.). LISTENER'S LURE: An Oblique Narration. *Crown 8vo.* *Fourth Edition.* *Cr. 8vo.* *6s.*

Lyall (Edna). DERRICK VAUGHAN, NOVELIST. 42*nd Thousand.* *Cr. 8vo.* 3*s.* 6*d.*

M'Carthy (Justin H.), Author of 'If I were King.' THE LADY OF LOYALTY HOUSE. Illustrated. *Third Edition.* *Cr. 8vo.* *6s.*

THE DRYAD. *Second Edition.* *Cr. 8vo.* *6s.*

Macdonald (Ronald). THE SEA MAID. *Second Edition.* *Cr. 8vo.* *6s.*

A HUMAN TRINITY. *Second Edition.* *Cr. 8vo.* *6s.*

Macnaughtan (S.). THE FORTUNE OF CHRISTINA MACNAB. *Fourth Edition.* *Cr. 8vo.* *6s.*

Malet (Lucas). COLONEL ENDERBY'S WIFE. *Fourth Edition.* *Cr. 8vo.* *6s.*

A COUNSEL OF PERFECTION. *New Edition.* *Cr. 8vo.* *6s.*

THE WAGES OF SIN. *Fifteenth Edition.* *Cr. 8vo.* *6s.*

THE CARISSIMA. *Fifth Edition.* *Cr. 8vo.* *6s.*

THE GATELESS BARRIER. *Fourth Edition.* *Cr. 8vo.* *6s.*

THE HISTORY OF SIR RICHARD CALMADY. *Seventh Edition.* *Cr. 8vo.* *6s.* See also Books for Boys and Girls.

Mann (Mrs. M. E.). OLIVIA'S SUMMER. *Second Edition.* *Cr. 8vo.* *6s.*

A LOST ESTATE. *A New Edition.* *Cr. 8vo.* *6s.*

THE PARISH OF HILBY. *A New Edition.* *Cr. 8vo.* *6s.*

THE PARISH NURSE. *Fourth Edition.* *Cr. 8vo.* *6s.*

GRAN'MA'S JANE. *Cr. 8vo.* *6s.*

MRS. PETER HOWARD. *Cr. 8vo.* *6s.*

A WINTER'S TALE. *A New Edition.* *Cr. 8vo.* *6s.*

ONE ANOTHER'S BURDENS. *A New Edition.* *Cr. 8vo.* *6s.*

ROSE AT HONEYPOT. *Third Ed.* *Cr. 8vo.* *6s.* See also Books for Boys and Girls.

THE MEMORIES OF RONALD LOVE. *Cr. 8vo.* *6s.*

THE EGLAMORE PORTRAITS. *Third Edition.* *Cr. 8vo.* *6s.*

Marriott (Charles), Author of 'The Column.' GENEVRA. *Second Edition.* *Cr. 8vo.* *6s.*

Marsh (Richard). THE TWICKENHAM PEERAGE. *Second Edition.* *Cr. 8vo.* *6s.*

THE MARQUIS OF PUTNEY. *Second Edition.* *Cr. 8vo.* *6s.*

A DUEL. *Cr 8vo.* *6s.*

IN THE SERVICE OF LOVE. *Third Edition.* *Cr. 8vo.* *6s.* See also Shilling Novels.

Mason (A. E. W.), Author of 'The Four Feathers,' etc. CLEMENTINA. Illustrated. *Second Edition.* *Cr. 8vo.* *6s.*

Mathers (Helen), Author of 'Comin' thro' the Rye.' HONEY. *Fourth Edition.* *Cr. 8vo.* *6s.*

GRIFF OF GRIFFITHSCOURT. *Cr. 8vo.* *6s.*

THE FERRYMAN. *Second Edition.* *Cr. 8vo.* *6s.*

TALLY-HO! *Fourth Edition.* *Cr. 8vo.* *6s.*

Maxwell (W. B.), Author of 'The Ragged Messenger.' VIVIEN. *Eighth Edition.* *Cr. 8vo.* *6s.*

THE RAGGED MESSENGER. *Third Edition.* *Cr. 8vo.* *6s.*

FABULOUS FANCIES. *Cr. 8vo.* *6s.*

THE GUARDED FLAME. *Seventh Edition.* *Cr. 8vo.* *6s.*

THE COUNTESS OF MAYBURY. *Fourth Edition.* *Cr. 8vo.* *6s.*

ODD LENGTHS. *Second Ed.* *Cr. 8vo.* *6s.*

Meade (L. T.). DRIFT. *Second Edition.* *Cr. 8vo.* *6s.*

RESURGAM. *Cr. 8vo.* *6s.*

VICTORY. *Cr. 8vo.* *6s.* See also Books for Boys and Girls.

Melton (R.). CÆSAR'S WIFE. *Second Edition.* *Cr. 8vo.* *6s.*

Meredith (Ellis). HEART OF MY HEART. *Cr. 8vo.* *6s.*

Miller (Esther). LIVING LIES. *Third Edition.* *Cr. 8vo.* *6s.*

'Miss Molly' (The Author of). THE GREAT RECONCILER. *Cr. 8vo.* *6s.*

Mitford (Bertram). THE SIGN OF THE SPIDER. Illustrated. *Sixth Edition.* *Cr. 8vo.* 3*s.* 6*d.*

IN THE WHIRL OF THE RISING. *Third Edition.* *Cr. 8vo.* *6s.*

THE RED DERELICT. *Second Edition.* *Cr. 8vo.* *6s.*

Montresor (F. F.), Author of 'Into the Highways and Hedges.' THE ALIEN. *Third Edition.* *Cr. 8vo.* *6s.*

Morrison (Arthur). TALES OF MEAN STREETS. *Seventh Edition.* *Cr. 8vo.* *6s.*

A CHILD OF THE JAGO. *Fifth Edition.* *Cr. 8vo.* *6s.*

TO LONDON TOWN. *Second Edition.* *Cr. 8vo.* *6s.*

CUNNING MURRELL. *Cr. 8vo.* *6s.*

THE HOLE IN THE WALL. *Fourth Edition.* *Cr. 8vo.* *6s.*

DIVERS VANITIES. *Cr. 8vo.* *6s.*

Nesbit (E.). (Mrs. E. Bland). THE RED HOUSE. Illustrated. *Fourth Edition.* *Cr. 8vo.* *6s.* See also Shilling Novels.

Norris (W. E.). HARRY AND URSULA. *Second Edition.* *Cr. 8vo.* *6s.*

Ollivant (Alfred). OWD BOB, THE GREY DOG OF KENMUIR. *Ninth Edition.* *Cr. 8vo.* *6s.*

Oppenheim (E. Phillips). MASTER OF MEN. *Fourth Edition. Cr. 8vo. 6s.*

Oxenham (John), Author of 'Barbe of Grand Bayou.' A WEAVER OF WEBS. *Second Edition. Cr. 8vo. 6s.*

THE GATE OF THE DESERT. *Fifth Edition. Cr. 8vo. 6s.*

PROFIT AND LOSS. With a Frontispiece in photogravure by HAROLD COPPING. *Fourth Edition. Cr. 8vo. 6s.*

THE LONG ROAD. With a Frontispiece by HAROLD COPPING. *Third Edition. Cr. 8vo. 6s.*

Pain (Barry). LINDLEY KAYS. *Third Edition. Cr. 8vo. 6s.*

Parker (Gilbert). PIERRE AND HIS PEOPLE. *Sixth Edition. Cr. 8vo. 6s.*

MRS. FALCHION. *Fifth Edition. Cr. 8vo. 6s.*

THE TRANSLATION OF A SAVAGE. *Third Edition. Cr. 8vo. 6s.*

THE TRAIL OF THE SWORD. Illustrated. *Ninth Edition. Cr. 8vo. 6s.*

WHEN VALMOND CAME TO PONTIAC: The Story of a Lost Napoleon. *Sixth Edition. Cr. 8vo. 6s.*

AN ADVENTURER OF THE NORTH. The Last Adventures of 'Pretty Pierre.' *Third Edition. Cr. 8vo. 6s.*

THE SEATS OF THE MIGHTY. Illustrated. *Fifteenth Edition. Cr. 8vo. 6s.*

THE BATTLE OF THE STRONG: a Romance of Two Kingdoms. Illustrated. *Fifth Edition. Cr. 8vo. 6s.*

THE POMP OF THE LAVILETTES. *Second Edition. Cr. 8vo. 3s. 6d.*

Pemberton (Max). THE FOOTSTEPS OF A THRONE. Illustrated. *Third Edition. Cr. 8vo. 6s.*

I CROWN THEE KING. With Illustrations by Frank Dadd and A. Forrestier. *Cr. 8vo. 6s.*

Phillpotts (Eden). LYING PROPHETS. *Third Edition. Cr. 8vo. 6s.*

CHILDREN OF THE MIST. *Fifth Edition. Cr. 8vo. 6s.*

THE HUMAN BOY. With a Frontispiece. *Fourth Edition. Cr. 8vo. 6s.*

SONS OF THE MORNING. *Second Edition. Cr. 8vo. 6s.*

THE RIVER. *Third Edition. Cr. 8vo. 6s.*

THE AMERICAN PRISONER. *Fourth Edition. Cr. 8vo. 6s.*

THE SECRET WOMAN. *Fourth Edition. Cr. 8vo. 6s.*

KNOCK AT A VENTURE. With a Frontispiece. *Third Edition. Cr. 8vo. 6s.*

THE PORTREEVE. *Fourth Edition. Cr. 8vo. 6s.*

THE POACHER'S WIFE. *Second Edition. Cr. 8vo. 6s.*

See also Shilling Novels.

Pickthall (Marmaduke). SAÏD THE FISHERMAN. *Sixth Edition. Cr. 8vo. 6s.*

BRENDLE. *Second Edition. Cr. 8vo. 6s.*

THE HOUSE OF ISLAM. *Third Edition. Cr. 8vo. 6s.*

'Q,' Author of 'Dead Man's Rock.' THE WHITE WOLF. *Second Edition. Cr. 8vo. 6s,*

THE MAYOR OF TROY. *Fourth Edition. Cr. 8vo. 6s.*

MERRY GARDEN AND OTHER STORIES. *Cr. 8vo. 6s.*

Rawson (Maud Stepney), Author of 'A Lady of the Regency.' 'The Labourer's Comedy,' etc. THE ENCHANTED GARDEN. *Cr. 8vo. 6s.*

Rhys (Grace). THE WOOING OF SHEILA. *Second Edition. Cr. 8vo. 6s.*

Ridge (W. Pett). LOST PROPERTY. *Second Edition. Cr. 8vo. 6s.*

ERB. *Second Edition. Cr. 8vo. 6s.*

A SON OF THE STATE. *Second Edition. Cr. 8vo. 3s. 6d.*

A BREAKER OF LAWS. *A New Edition. Cr. 8vo. 3s. 6d.*

MRS. GALER'S BUSINESS. Illustrated. *Second Edition. Cr. 8vo. 6s.*

SECRETARY TO BAYNE, M.P. *Cr. 8vo. 3s. 6d.*

THE WICKHAMSES. *Fourth Edition. Cr. 8vo. 6s.*

Roberts (C. G. D.). THE HEART OF THE ANCIENT WOOD. *Cr. 8vo. 3s. 6d.*

Russell (W. Clark). MY DANISH SWEETHEART. Illustrated. *Fifth Edition. Cr. 8vo. 6s.*

HIS ISLAND PRINCESS. Illustrated. *Second Edition. Cr. 6vo. 6s.*

ABANDONED. *Second Edition. Cr. 8vo. 6s.* See also Books for Boys and Girls.

Sergeant (Adeline). BARBARA'S MONEY. *Cr. 8vo. 6s.*

THE PROGRESS OF RACHAEL. *Cr. 8vo. 6s.*

THE MYSTERY OF THE MOAT. *Second Edition. Cr. 8vo. 6s.*

THE COMING OF THE RANDOLPHS. *Cr. 8vo. 6s.*

See also Shilling Novels.

Shannon. (W.F. THE MESS DECK. *Cr. 8vo. 3s. 6d.*

See also Shilling Novels.

Shelley (Bertha). ENDERBY. *Third Ed. Cr. 8vo. 6s.*

Sidgwick (Mrs. Alfred), Author of 'Cynthia's Way.' THE KINSMAN. With 8 Illustrations by C. E. BROCK. *Third Ed. Cr. 8vo. 6s.*

Sonnichsen (Albert). DEEP-SEA VAGABONDS. *Cr. 8vo. 6s.*

Sunbury (George). THE HA'PENNY MILLIONAIRE. *Cr. 8vo. 3s. 6d.*

Urquhart (M.), A TRAGEDY IN COMMONPLACE. *Second Ed. Cr. 8vo. 6s.*

Waineman (Paul). THE SONG OF THE FOREST. *Cr. 8vo. 6s.*

See also Shilling Novels.

Waltz (E. C.). THE ANCIENT LANDMARK: A Kentucky Romance. *Cr. 8vo. 6s.*

Watson (H. B. Marriott). ALARUMS AND EXCURSIONS. *Cr. 8vo. 6s.*
CAPTAIN FORTUNE. *Third Edition. Cr. 8vo. 6s.*
TWISTED EGLANTINE. With 8 Illustrations by FRANK CRAIG. *Third Edition. Cr. 8vo. 6s.*
THE HIGH TOBY. With a Frontispiece. *Third Edition. Cr. 8vo. 6s.*
A MIDSUMMER DAY'S DREAM. *Third Edition. Crown 8vo. 6s.*
See also Shilling Novels.

Wells (H. G.). THE SEA LADY. *Cr. 8vo. 6s.*

Weyman (Stanley), Author of 'A Gentleman of France.' UNDER THE RED ROBE. With Illustrations by R. C. WOODVILLE. *Twentieth Edition. Cr. 8vo. 6s.*

White (Stewart E.), Author of 'The Blazed Trail.' CONJUROR'S HOUSE. A Romance of the Free Trail. *Second Edition. Cr. 8vo. 6s.*

White (Percy). THE SYSTEM. *Third Edition. Cr. 8vo. 6s.*
THE PATIENT MAN. *Second Edition. Cr. 8vo. 6s.*

Williams (Margery). THE BAR. *Cr. 8vo. 6s.*

Williamson (Mrs. C. N.), Author of 'The Barnstormers.' THE ADVENTURE OF PRINCESS SYLVIA. *Second Edition. Cr. 8vo. 6s.*
THE WOMAN WHO DARED. *Cr. 8vo. 6s.*
THE SEA COULD TELL. *Second Edition. Cr. 8vo. 6s.*
THE CASTLE OF THE SHADOWS. *Third Edition. Cr. 8vo. 6s.*
PAPA. *Cr. 8vo. 6s.*

Williamson (C. N. and A. M.). THE LIGHTNING CONDUCTOR : Being the Romance of a Motor Car. Illustrated. *Sixteenth Edition. Cr. 8vo. 6s.*
THE PRINCESS PASSES. Illustrated. *Eighth Edition. Cr. 8vo. 6s.*
MY FRIEND THE CHAUFFEUR. With 16 Illustrations. *Eighth Edit. Cr. 8vo. 6s.*
THE CAR OF DESTINY AND ITS ERRAND IN SPAIN. *Fourth Edition.* Illustrated.
LADY BETTY ACROSS THE WATER. *Ninth Edition. Cr. 8vo. 6s.*
THE BOTOR CHAPERON. *Third Ed. Cr. 8vo. 6s.*

Wyllarde (Dolf), Author of 'Uriah the Hittite.' THE PATHWAY OF THE PIONEER (Nous Autres). *Fourth Edition. Cr. 8vo. 6s.*

Methuen's Shilling Novels

Cr. 8vo. Cloth, 1s. net.

Author of 'Miss Molly.' THE GREAT RECONCILER.

Balfour (Andrew). VENGEANCE IS MINE.
TO ARMS.

Baring=Gould (S.). MRS. CURGENVEN OF CURGENVEN.
DOMITIA.
THE FROBISHERS.
CHRIS OF ALL SORTS.
DARTMOOR IDYLLS.

Barlow (Jane), Author of 'Irish Idylls.' FROM THE EAST UNTO THE WEST.
A CREEL OF IRISH STORIES.
THE FOUNDING OF FORTUNES.
THE LAND OF THE SHAMROCK.

Barr (Robert). THE VICTORS.

Bartram (George). THIRTEEN EVENINGS.

Benson (E. F.), Author of 'Dodo.' THE CAPSINA.

Bowles (G. Stewart). A STRETCH OFF THE LAND.

Brooke (Emma). THE POET'S CHILD.

Bullock (Shan F.). THE BARRYS.
THE CHARMER.
THE SQUIREEN.
THE RED LEAGUERS.

Burton (J. Bloundelle). THE CLASH OF ARMS.
DENOUNCED.
FORTUNE'S MY FOE.
A BRANDED NAME.

Capes (Bernard). AT A WINTER'S FIRE.

Chesney (Weatherby). THE BAPTIST RING.
THE BRANDED PRINCE.
THE FOUNDERED GALLEON.
JOHN TOPP.
THE MYSTERY OF A BUNGALOW.

Clifford (Mrs. W. K.). A FLASH OF SUMMER.

Cobb, Thomas. A CHANGE OF FACE.

Collingwood (Harry). THE DOCTOR OF THE 'JULIET.'

Cornford (L. Cope). SONS OF ADVERSITY.

Cotterell (Constance). THE VIRGIN AND THE SCALES.

Crane (Stephen). WOUNDS IN THE RAIN.

Denny (C. E.). THE ROMANCE OF UPFOLD MANOR.

Dickinson (Evelyn). THE SIN OF ANGELS.

Dickson (Harris). THE BLACK WOLF'S BREED.

Duncan (Sara J.). THE POOL IN THE DESERT.
A VOYAGE OF CONSOLATION. Illustrated.

Embree (C. F.). A HEART OF FLAME. Illustrated.

Fenn (G. Manville). AN ELECTRIC SPARK.
A DOUBLE KNOT.

Findlater (Jane H.). A DAUGHTER OF STRIFE.

Fitzstephen (G.). MORE KIN THAN KIND.

Fletcher (J. S.). DAVID MARCH. LUCIAN THE DREAMER.

Forrest (R. E.). THE SWORD OF AZRAEL.

Francis (M. E.). MISS ERIN.

Gallon (Tom). RICKERBY'S FOLLY.

Gerard (Dorothea). THINGS THAT HAVE HAPPENED.
THE CONQUEST OF LONDON.
THE SUPREME CRIME.

Gilchrist (R. Murray). WILLOWBRAKE.

Glanville (Ernest). THE DESPATCH RIDER.
THE KLOOF BRIDE.
THE INCA'S TREASURE.

Gordon (Julien). MRS. CLYDE.
WORLD'S PEOPLE.

Goss (C. F.). THE REDEMPTION OF DAVID CORSON.

Gray (E. M'Queen). MY STEWARDSHIP.

Hales (A. G.). JAIR THE APOSTATE.

Hamilton (Lord Ernest). MARY HAMILTON.

Harrison (Mrs. Burton). A PRINCESS OF THE HILLS. Illustrated.

Hooper (I.). THE SINGER OF MARLY.

Hough (Emerson). THE MISSISSIPPI BUBBLE.

'Iota' (Mrs. Caffyn). ANNE MAULEVERER.

Jepson (Edgar). THE KEEPERS OF THE PEOPLE.

Keary (C. F.). THE JOURNALIST.

Kelly (Florence Finch). WITH HOOPS OF STEEL.

Langbridge (V.) and Bourne (C. H.). THE VALLEY OF INHERITANCE.

Linden (Annie). A WOMAN OF SENTIMENT.

Lorimer (Norma). JOSIAH'S WIFE.

Lush (Charles K.). THE AUTOCRATS.

Macdonell (Anne). THE STORY OF TERESA.

Macgrath (Harold). THE PUPPET CROWN.

Mackie (Pauline Bradford). THE VOICE IN THE DESERT.

Marsh (Richard). THE SEEN AND THE UNSEEN.
GARNERED.
A METAMORPHOSIS.
MARVELS AND MYSTERIES.
BOTH SIDES OF THE VEIL.

Mayall (J. W.). THE CYNIC AND THE SYREN.

Meade (L. T.). RESURGAM.

Monkhouse (Allan). LOVE IN A LIFE.

Moore (Arthur). THE KNIGHT PUNCTILIOUS.

Nesbit, E. (Mrs. Bland). THE LITERARY SENSE.

Norris (W. E.). AN OCTAVE.
MATTHEW AUSTIN.
THE DESPOTIC LADY.

Oliphant (Mrs.). THE LADY'S WALK.
SIR ROBERT'S FORTUNE.
THE TWO MARY'S.

Pendered (M. L.). AN ENGLISHMAN.

Penny (Mrs. Frank). A MIXED MARAGE.

Phillpotts (Eden). THE STRIKING HOURS.
FANCY FREE.

Pryce (Richard). TIME AND THE WOMAN.

Randall (John). AUNT BETHIA'S BUTTON.

Raymond (Walter). FORTUNE'S DARLING.

Rayner (Olive Pratt). ROSALBA.

Rhys (Grace). THE DIVERTED VILLAGE.

Rickert (Edith). OUT OF THE CYPRESS SWAMP.

Roberton (M. H.). A GALLANT QUAKER.

Russell, (W. Clark). ABANDONED.

Saunders (Marshall). ROSE À CHARLITTE.

Sergeant (Adeline). ACCUSED AND ACCUSER.
BARBARA'S MONEY.
THE ENTHUSIAST.
A GREAT LADY.
THE LOVE THAT OVERCAME.
THE MASTER OF BEECHWOOD.
UNDER SUSPICION.
THE YELLOW DIAMOND.
THE MYSTERY OF THE MOAT.
THE PROGRESS OF RACHAEL.

Shannon (W. F.). JIM TWELVES.

Stephens (R. N.). AN ENEMY OF THE KING.

Strain (E. H.). ELMSLIE'S DRAG NET.

Stringer (Arthur). THE SILVER POPPY.

Stuart (Esmè). CHRISTALLA.
A WOMAN OF FORTY.

Sutherland (Duchess of). ONE HOUR AND THE NEXT.

Swan (Annie). LOVE GROWN COLD.

Swift (Benjamin). SORDON.
SIREN CITY.

Tanqueray (Mrs. B. M.). THE ROYAL QUAKER.

Thompson (Vance). SPINNERS OF LIFE.

Trafford-Taunton (Mrs. E. W.). SILENT DOMINION.

Upward (Allen). ATHELSTANE FORD.

Waineman (Paul). A HEROINE FROM FINLAND.
BY A FINNISH LAKE.

Watson (H. B. Marriott). THE SKIRTS OF HAPPY CHANCE.

'Zack.' TALES OF DUNSTABLE WEIR.

Books for Boys and Girls

Illustrated.   Crown 8vo.   3s. 6d.

THE GETTING WELL OF DOROTHY. By Mrs. W. K. Clifford. *Second Edition.*

ONLY A GUARD-ROOM DOG. By Edith E. Cuthell.

THE DOCTOR OF THE JULIET. By Harry Collingwood.

LITTLE PETER. By Lucas Malet. *Second Edition.*

MASTER ROCKAFELLAR'S VOYAGE. By W. Clark Russell. *Third Edition.*

THE SECRET OF MADAME DE MONLUC. By the Author of " Mdlle. Mori.'

SYD BELTON : Or, the Boy who would not go to Sea. By G. Manville Fenn.

THE RED GRANGE. By Mrs. Molesworth.

A GIRL OF THE PEOPLE. By L. T. Meade. *Second Edition.*

HEPSY GIPSY. By L. T. Meade. 2s. 6d.

THE HONOURABLE MISS. By L. T. Meade. *Second Edition.*

THERE WAS ONCE A PRINCE. By Mrs. M. E. Mann.

WHEN ARNOLD COMES HOME. By Mrs. M. E. Mann.

The Novels of Alexandre Dumas

Price 6d.   Double Volumes, 1s.

ACTÉ.

THE ADVENTURES OF CAPTAIN PAMPHILE.

AMAURY.

THE BIRD OF FATE.

THE BLACK TULIP.

THE CASTLE OF EPPSTEIN.

CATHERINE BLUM.

CECILE.

THE CHEVALIER D'HARMENTAL. Double volume.

CHICOT THE JESTER. Being the first part of The Lady of Monsoreau.

CONSCIENCE.

THE CONVICT'S SON.

THE CORSICAN BROTHERS ; and OTHO THE ARCHER.

CROP-EARED JACQUOT.

THE FENCING MASTER.

FERNANDE.

GABRIEL LAMBERT.

GEORGES.

THE GREAT MASSACRE. Being the first part of Queen Margot.

HENRI DE NAVARRE. Being the second part of Queen Margot.

HÉLÈNE DE CHAVERNY. Being the first part of the Regent's Daughter.

LOUISE DE LA VALLIÈRE. Being the first part of THE VICOMTE DE BRAGELONNE. Double Volume.

MAÎTRE ADAM.

THE MAN IN THE IRON MASK. Being the second part of THE VICOMTE DE BRAGELONNE. Double volume.

THE MOUTH OF HELL.

NANON. Double volume.

PAULINE ; PASCAL BRUNO ; and BONTEKOE.

PÈRE LA RUINE.

THE PRINCE OF THIEVES.

THE REMINISCENCES OF ANTONY.

ROBIN HOOD.

THE SNOWBALL and SULTANETTA.

SYLVANDIRE.

TALES OF THE SUPERNATURAL.

THE THREE MUSKETEERS. With a long Introduction by Andrew Lang. Double volume.

TWENTY YEARS AFTER. Double volume.

THE WILD DUCK SHOOTER.

THE WOLF-LEADER.

Methuen's Sixpenny Books

Albanesi (E. M.). LOVE AND LOUISA.

Austen (Jane). PRIDE AND PREJUDICE.

Bagot (Richard). A ROMAN MYSTERY.

Balfour (Andrew). BY STROKE OF SWORD.

Baring=Gould (S.). FURZE BLOOM.

CHEAP JACK ZITA.

KITTY ALONE.

URITH.

THE BROOM SQUIRE.

IN THE ROAR OF THE SEA.

NOÉMI.

A BOOK OF FAIRY TALES. Illustrated.

LITTLE TU'PENNY.

THE FROBISHERS.

WINEFRED.

Barr (Robert). JENNIE BAXTER, JOURNALIST.

IN THE MIDST OF ALARMS.

THE COUNTESS TEKLA.

THE MUTABLE MANY.

Benson (E. F.). DODO.

Brontë (Charlotte). SHIRLEY.

Brownell (C. L.). THE HEART OF JAPAN.

Burton (J. Bloundelle). ACROSS THE SALT SEAS.

Caffyn (Mrs)., ('Iota'). ANNE MAULE-VERER.

Capes (Bernard). THE LAKE OF WINE.

Clifford (Mrs. W. K.). A FLASH OF SUMMER.

MRS. KEITH'S CRIME.

Connell (F. Norreys). THE NIGGER KNIGHTS.

Corbett (Julian). A BUSINESS IN GREAT WATERS.

Croker (Mrs. B. M.). PEGGY OF THE BARTONS.

A STATE SECRET.

ANGEL.
JOHANNA.
Dante (Alighieri).   THE VISION OF DANTE (Cary).
Doyle (A. Conan).   ROUND THE RED LAMP.
Duncan (Sara Jeannette).   A VOYAGE OF CONSOLATION.
THOSE DELIGHTFUL AMERICANS.
Eliot (George).   THE MILL ON THE FLOSS.
Findlater (Jane H.).   THE GREEN GRAVES OF BALGOWRIE.
Gallon (Tom).   RICKERBY'S FOLLY.
Gaskell (Mrs.).   CRANFORD.
MARY BARTON.
NORTH AND SOUTH.
Gerard (Dorothea).   HOLY MATRIMONY.
THE CONQUEST OF LONDON.
MADE OF MONEY.
Gissing (George).   THE TOWN TRAVELLER.
THE CROWN OF LIFE.
Glanville (Ernest).   THE INCA'S TREASURE.
THE KLOOF BRIDE.
Gleig (Charles).   BUNTER'S CRUISE.
Grimm (The Brothers).   GRIMM'S FAIRY TALES. Illustrated.
Hope (Anthony).   A MAN OF MARK.
A CHANGE OF AIR.
THE CHRONICLES OF COUNT ANTONIO.
PHROSO.
THE DOLLY DIALOGUES.
Hornung (E. W.).   DEAD MEN TELL NO TALES.
Ingraham (J. H.).   THE THRONE OF DAVID.
Le Queux (W.).   THE HUNCHBACK OF WESTMINSTER.
Levett=Yeats (S. K.).   THE TRAITOR'S WAY.
Linton (E. Lynn).   THE TRUE HISTORY OF JOSHUA DAVIDSON.
Lyall (Edna).   DERRICK VAUGHAN.
Malet (Lucas).   THE CARISSIMA.
A COUNSEL OF PERFECTION.
Mann (Mrs. M. E.).   MRS. PETER HOWARD.
A LOST ESTATE.
THE CEDAR STAR.
ONE ANOTHER'S BURDENS.
Marchmont (A. W.).   MISER HOADLEY'S SECRET.
A MOMENT'S ERROR.
Marryat (Captain).   PETER SIMPLE.
JACOB FAITHFUL.
Marsh (Richard).   THE TWICKENHAM PEERAGE.
THE GODDESS.
THE JOSS.
A METAMORPHOSIS.

Mason (A. E. W.).   CLEMENTINA.
Mathers (Helen).   HONEY.
GRIFF OF GRIFFITHSCOURT.
SAM'S SWEETHEART.
Meade (Mrs. L. T.).   DRIFT.
Mitford (Bertram).   THE SIGN OF THE SPIDER.
Montresor (F. F.).   THE ALIEN.
Moore (Arthur).   THE GAY DECEIVERS.
Morrison (Arthur).   THE HOLE IN THE WALL.
Nesbit (E.).   THE RED HOUSE.
Norris (W. E.).   HIS GRACE.
GILES INGILBY.
THE CREDIT OF THE COUNTY.
LORD LEONARD.
MATTHEW AUSTIN.
CLARISSA FURIOSA.
Oliphant (Mrs.).   THE LADY'S WALK.
SIR ROBERT'S FORTUNE.
THE PRODIGALS.
Oppenheim (E. Phillips).   MASTER OF MEN.
Parker (Gilbert).   THE POMP OF THE LAVILETTES.
WHEN VALMOND CAME TO PONTIAC.
THE TRAIL OF THE SWORD.
Pemberton (Max).   THE FOOTSTEPS OF A THRONE.
I CROWN THEE KING.
Phillpotts (Eden).   THE HUMAN BOY.
CHILDREN OF THE MIST.
'Q.'   THE WHITE WOLF.
Ridge (W. Pett).   A SON OF THE STATE.
LOST PROPERTY.
GEORGE AND THE GENERAL.
Russell (W. Clark).   A MARRIAGE AT SEA.
ABANDONED.
MY DANISH SWEETHEART.
HIS ISLAND PRINCESS.
Sergeant (Adeline).   THE MASTER OF BEECHWOOD.
BARBARA'S MONEY.
THE YELLOW DIAMOND.
THE LOVE THAT OVERCAME.
Surtees (R. S.).   HANDLEY CROSS. Illustrated.
MR. SPONGE'S SPORTING TOUR. Illustrated.
ASK MAMMA. Illustrated.
Valentine (Major E. S.).   VELDT AND LAAGER.
Walford (Mrs. L. B.).   MR. SMITH.
COUSINS.
THE BABY'S GRANDMOTHER.
Wallace (General Lew).   BEN-HUR.
THE FAIR GOD.
Watson (H. B. Marriot).   THE ADVENTURERS.
Weekes (A. B.).   PRISONERS OF WAR.
Wells (H. G.).   THE STOLEN BACILLUS.
White (Percy).   A PASSIONATE PILGRIM.